Brothers Unite

Brothers Unite

An Account of the Uniting
of Eberhard Arnold and the Rhön Bruderhof
with the Hutterian Church

Based on the diary of his journey to
North America 1930-31
and
letters written between 1928 and 1935

Translated and edited by
the Hutterian Brethren

Introduced by
John A. Hostetler and Leonard Gross

PLOUGH PUBLISHING HOUSE
HUTTERIAN BRETHREN
Ulster Park, NY, USA
Robertsbridge, England

Translated from
Eberhard Arnold's Diary of his journey to America 1930-31
and letters 1928-35 related to the uniting of the
Rhön Bruderhof with the Hutterian Church

Library of Congress Cataloging-in-Publication Data.

Eberhard, Arnold, 1883-1935.
    [Selections. English. 1988]
    Brothers unite : an account of the uniting of Eberhard Arnold and
the Rhön Bruderhof with the Hutterian Church / translated and edited
by the Hutterian Brethren ; introduced by John A. Hostetler and
Leonard Gross.
    p.   cm.
    "Based on the diary of his journey to North America 1930-31 and
letters written between 1928 and 1935."
    Includes bibliographical references.
    ISBN 0-87486-023-7 (alk. paper)
    1. Rhön Bruderhof--History. 2. Eberhard. Arnold, 1883-1935
3. Hutterite Brethren--History.   I. Hutterian Brethren (Rifton.
N.Y.)   II. Title.
BX8129.B632R4642513 1988
289.7'3--dc19   88-23560
                                           CIP

Printed in USA

CONTENTS

In 1920 Eberhard and Emmy Arnold with their family and a few friends moved from Berlin to the little village of Sannerz in the province of Hesse, Germany. They were earnestly seeking the will of God for their lives and had turned their backs on the unjust life of the world.

Through much sacrifice and trial and by the grace of God, a life of Christian church community came into being. As men and women were drawn to the common life, it became necessary to establish a larger settlement for the growing community. In 1926 the Sparhof was purchased, a run-down farm in the Rhön hills northeast of Frankfurt. This became the Rhön Bruderhof.

Eberhard Arnold believed that love and unity were the fruits of a Christian life. Therefore he sought for brothers with whom he and his little group could unite. Through his studies in Anabaptist history he discovered the wonderful writings of the Hutterian Brethren. Then he was made aware of the Hutterian Brothers still living in Bruderhofs in North America. By 1928 he was writing to Elias Walter of the Stand Off Colony in Alberta of his determination to unite with them. In 1929, Eberhard Arnold sent a letter to all "Bruderhofs belonging to the church of God established by Jakob Hutter during the years 1533-1536" in which he asked that the Rhön Bruderhof be incorporated into the Hutterian Church. An English translation of these and other letters exchanged with the Brothers and with scholars of Anabaptism between 1928 and May 1930 make up the first chapter of this book.

In May 1930, Eberhard Arnold set out for North America to visit all the Bruderhofs and to seek this uniting. The journey took a year. This was a great sacrifice for the little community at the Rhön Bruderhof and for Eberhard Arnold personally. But the sacrifice was made gladly and the goal was achieved: incorporation into the Hutterian Church. This incorporation was carried out by the elders of the Dariusleut and Lehrerleut groups in Alberta, with the prior recommendation and agreement of the Schmiedeleut in Manitoba and South Dakota. Chapters two and three contain a translation of the

Diary of this journey and correspondence between May 1930 and May 1931.

On his return to the Rhön Bruderhof in Germany, Eberhard Arnold continued to fight for the building up of the Hutterian Church on two fronts: in Europe, where the coming into power of Adolf Hitler and the Nazis soon brought even greater poverty and persecution; and in openly sharing his concern for the future of the whole Hutterian Church and the weaknesses and dangers he saw, in letters to the elders. All this is vividly recorded in chapter four.

With Eberhard Arnold's untimely death in November 1935, the Bruderhofs in Europe lost their Word leader (elder). A time of confusion and division brought about by sin followed. The precious unity he had fought for was lost.

Through God's great mercy, this unity was established anew in January 1974 at Sturgeon Creek Bruderhof in Manitoba. Here Eberhard Arnold's son, Heini Arnold, as elder of the Bruderhofs in the eastern USA and England asked for forgiveness on their behalf. This was granted and the unity, for which so much had been sacrificed in 1930-1931, was restored. May we all protect it from every attack and strengthen the bond of unity between all Bruderhofs and brothers and sisters of the Hutterian Church.

July 1988   THE EDITORS
                                                        on behalf of the Hutterian Brethren

We wish to thank those Brothers who sent letters to be used in this book. The Mennonite Archives in Goshen, Indiana, kindly gave permission to include letters from their files.

Every attempt has been made in translating to preserve the original style of the letters and the Diary. Unique forms of expression and variations in the spelling of names have been retained.

INTRODUCTION
by John A. Hostetler

The publication of Eberhard Arnold's diary is a milestone not only for the Hutterian Brethren but for the various branches of Anabaptism. Twentieth century seekers of community life, renewal groups, and historians of Christianity will be astonished at yet another sourcebook coming from the Plough Publishing House.

The record shows that Arnold had prepared himself well for his mission in North America. His communal group in Germany had existed for almost ten years. His deep involvement with history, theology, and the Bible led him to contact Elias Walter, Robert Friedmann, John Horsch, Harold Bender, and others vitally interested in Anabaptist renewal. He had tried unsuccessfully to have the American Hutterites come to Europe to take over the major leadership responsibility of his group. On invitation from Friedmann he lectured in Vienna. Both Friedmann and Bender visited the new Bruderhof.

Arnold's spiritual vision was clear: "Our goal is not 'to be free' for the sake of freedom, but like the apostle Paul, to be bound and committed to a life active in love." In his personal zeal he openly challenged Robert Friedmann, a Jew, and his wife, a theosophist, with these words: "Forsake your middle-class life; leave behind your vain efforts in social democracy and your dabbling in the too many individualistic pursuits open to you in private life in a large city today; leave also your connection with a scholarly profession which does not practice what it allows to be published. Set out to join the Hutterian communities in America or our own small new beginning in Hesse." Friedmann's response together with other exchanges are contained in this volume.

What were Arnold's expectations in America? In his Sendbrief to the North American Hutterite leadership, Eberhard appealed to unity and mission. He asked for support in publishing the Hutterian writings and for help in "spreading God's Word and providing housing and hospitality for those already won and those newly awakened to Christ."

He stated: "We ask that you accept us in love and faith as a people who belong to you and stand at your door in order to be admitted into full unity and to come to our task and mission for the German-speaking lands." His small flock had, in his words, "a tormenting hunger" and "a burning thirst for the justice of God and his church."

Eberhard had three concrete requests: (1) that the Bruderhof in Germany be united with all American Bruderhofs as an expression of complete incorporation into the church of God, (2) that it be ministered to with the service of the Word, this to be done through Eberhard's ordination, and (3) that the Bruderhof in Germany be supported in both spiritual and temporal matters. Some months later and following his ordination, Eberhard wrote to his wife expressing his deep desire: "In place of a will that a rich man would make, I want to establish our community life on as deep, strong, and firm a foundation as possible, to ensure its continuance beyond my death."

In coming to North America, he faced personal stresses and the heavy weight of a struggling Bruderhof in Germany. In spite of an ailing and very painful left eye, he wrote a journal and conducted extensive correspondence with his wife and others in Germany for an entire year. It was not easy to leave behind a community deeply in debt, hosting an average of about fifteen visitors daily.

His reception among American colonies was deeply gratifying. "I am showered with love" he wrote to his wife Emmy. Every place he went "the meetings were wonderful, with their many hours of uninterrupted attentiveness and enthusiasm and thankfulness." But communities and persons were easily hurt if time was not taken to visit all. They wanted to know about his wife and children, about the new community and the discipline. He often read from Jakob Hutter's writings to gathered groups of young people. Extra benches were brought to the apartment rooms. Others stood outside for hours even after a long day's work. Sometimes they moved to the dining hall, but this had a disadvantage, for Eberhard observed that the women and girls would not take part in discussions in more formal settings. The leaders brought their old Hutterian books and writings and gave him many to take back to Germany. To "write in peace" and to find time to prepare parcels of books and Hutterite clothing for shipment to Germany was in his words "extremely strenuous for me." Although he found love and respect everywhere, Eberhard soon learned that "nobody can decide anything without word from the elders." "Decisions," he wrote to Emmy, "move very slowly here." Individual colonies could give alms, old books, head coverings, and clothing patterns, but questions of unification, ordination, and major financial assistance required "word from the elders." One colony had gone so far as to offer a location with 5,500 acres and immediate occupancy. Obtaining the unanimous consent of the Hutterian Church required visits to all the colonies, especially the elders of all three *Leut*, and this meant prolonging his visit far beyond his original plans.

The response of the older leaders to unification was not everywhere the same. One "dear old brother" in South Dakota left the decision to the brothers in Canada. He complained of being too old, too weighted down with burdens, and wished only to look after his end. Joseph Stahl of Lake Byron wrote: "Arnold is a second Jakob Hutter in all his efforts, especially against greed and personal money in the church." In a letter to Alberta he said: "The whole community was gathered in front of our house, old and young, big and small, until twelve every night. For myself I have to say that I no longer have any doubt but that we should unite with him and his little group because we need such a man very much. I cannot express the spirit and joy this man has in our forefathers and their writings. It puts us to shame." To this Arnold Vetter[1] responded, "I get quite scared when they set too high expectations of me." The Dariusleut elder wanted to know whether he was led to community life by mere knowledge, learning, and curiosity instead of by faith that brings forth surrender and love. Eberhard says he was astounded by the serious questions asked. Elias Walter, servant of the Word of the Stand Off Colony, historian, and Eberhard's active supporter, came to his defense repeatedly by interjecting, "Why, he's got all that better than we have." Christian Waldner emphasized the difficulty of the matter. He cited examples of outsiders who came into the brotherhood, and their children "caused trouble for us." He was doubtful about taking in members who had been baptized by immersion. There were others who cited incidents in the Great Chronicle for receiving outsiders. It was decided that a second visit was necessary to all of the 18 colonies in Alberta.

Eberhard was a keen observer of human nature. His journal contains observations on the personalities of men, women, and children. He did not overlook the economic activities. "Christian Waldner," he observed, "showed the well-known Hutterian sharp thinking, objectivity, clearmindedness, thoroughness, and caution, caution, and again caution. He is without a doubt a very capable elder and is highly regarded also by the Lehrerleut."

He described another elder as "a patriarchal peasant-prince; you

---

[1] A term of respect for an older brother, or one carrying a special responsibility in the church.

wait for him to speak to you, without being able to bring up anything yourself." Another was "sparing of words. But when he speaks, everyone hangs on his words, and what he says carries great weight. Repeatedly he proved himself ahead of me in knowledge but above all in spiritual clarity and certainty, so that I learn more from him than from all the others."

Emmy's absence was everywhere noted, but her void was made up for by her gracious letters to the wives of the elders. Eberhard had instructed her whom to thank and how to address them. Anna Wipf, his hostess, was to be addressed as "Anna Basel" and the nurse who helped to care for his eye was "Elizabeth Basel." The housemother in Wolf Creek was in Arnold's terms "childless, brave, energetic, blunt, often loud-voiced, and enjoys the trust and respect of everybody. She tires herself out daily and is constantly concerned about the well-being of the community. She has cooked and brought all my food and washed my clothes more often than I needed. She would complain loudly that I don't eat anything. Just imagine, dear good Emmy, at eight in the morning there appeared fish, cheese, sausage, honey, white bread, butter, coffee, porridge with cream, and a glass of Southern wine." At noon there was either two pigeons, or a broiler, or half a chicken, or a big fish, or lamb or mutton, or pork or ham, etc., with potatoes, dumplings of all kinds, noodles, or grits with dripping poured over it. Instead of gravy there was pure cream. There were often very good vegetable soups made with milk. Mid-afternoon there was strong coffee with cream, as well as bread and sausage, plus honey or fish. All of this attention with the knowledge of a very poor colony in Germany must have contributed to his pain.

In rare sentences Arnold speaks of the natural beauty which he saw. There were almost no newspapers, no fiction books, art, or anything consciously romantic. "But there is unmistakable joy in beauty—in a book or lettering, in woods and fields—a delight in simplicity, clarity, and a clean style in houses, rooms, clothes, and furniture."

Eberhard recognized some of the cultural "obstacles" to unification such as picture-taking. These he said "must not be overlooked." Eberhard sensed a deep reason for their rejection. It was a part of "their great, main struggle against individualism, the world church, and the idolizing of human beings."

There was vitality in the North American Hutterian colonies. Eberhard described them as "an amazing unity." The thirty-five Bruderhofs, he said, "stand virtually unshaken right to the present. The power of faith is very strong here, and everything is judged according to the Spirit—whether one is living in the Spirit, speaking and working in the Spirit, whether one is full of love, and whether one speaks the truth openly." Eberhard also saw what he described as weaknesses. The wealthy colonies were more inclined toward exclusiveness. They were less inclined to share with other colonies. The mechanization, or what he called "machine-ruled economy," has harmed the Bruderhofs both spiritually and temporally. This view was also shared by some of the elders but was not seen as an insurmountable problem by most.

In the past, private possession of property destroyed unity. Today, the devil, in Eberhard's view, is "using a more cunning way. The temptations come through collective property and its democratic majority, acting in the interest of the families 'owning' the hof." Some of the colonies are "too soft and indulgent" and permitting blood relatives to "stick together."

The accomplishments of the American trip did not come easy. There were personal and community stresses and challenges. There was the unbearable lengthening of the journey because of a variety of difficulties. Eberhard mentioned three: his eye infection, "the indescribable difficulties of asking for money," and the work on handwritten manuscripts. He would never again, he wrote to Emmy, undertake such a journey without having her along.

But it was the uniting that meant the most to him. He wrote: "We are now the first Bruderhof to belong at the same time to the Dariusleut, Schmiedeleut, and Lehrerleut." Spiritually and financially the Bruderhof in Germany would now be supported by all of the North American colonies. "This safeguarding of our Bruderhof's future," wrote Arnold, "could be cancelled only by our own unfaithfulness." The uniting, he pointed out "applies to our own five children, our children in the flesh and spirit. . . it applies to the dear children of the other parents and mothers in the community. It is truly a miracle of the Holy Spirit how the future of the Kingdom pulses in these children, who are truly ours."

Fifty-eight years have passed since the Eberhard Arnold journey to America and the initial uniting of the groups. In spite of division and separation during the years of 1955-1974 the spirit of uniting is working on. On January 7, 1974, through the leading of Heini Arnold, the eastern communities became part of the Hutterian Church again. Then on October 9, 1987, there was a very historic meeting in Milltown, Manitoba, where for the first time in history all four elders of the Hutterian Church met in one room: Johannes Wurz Vetter, Wilson

Siding, Alberta, Elder of the Dariusleut; Johannes Wipf Vetter, Rosetown, Saskatchewan, Elder of the Lehrerleut; Jacob Kleinsasser Vetter, Elder of the Schmiedeleut; and Johann Christoph Arnold Vetter, Elder of the Eastern Hutterian Communities.

Johannes Wurz Vetter asked Jake Kleinsasser Vetter at this meeting whether the eastern communities live according to the teachings of Peter Riedemann. When Jacob Kleinsasser Vetter assured Johannes Vetter, "they live more according to the teachings than western brothers and sisters," Johannes Vetter was completely satisfied.

What will the future hold for the entire Hutterian Church, including its various *Leut*? If the four elders can meet together frequently to discuss and resolve common solutions, as they now have begun, then Eberhard Arnold's call for a new awakening will not have been in vain.

The shaking of the nations and world events since 1930 have greatly altered the geographic destiny of the Bruderhof in Germany. The publication and the re-reading and re-living of the events of history can have very positive benefits. The young people who knew nothing of Eberhard Arnold will most certainly benefit from this knowledge of their own history. We pray that its publication will further the building of the true community life and the mission to the wider world.

Willow Grove, Pa, July 1988

RECLAIMING THE HUTTERIAN VISION
by Leonard Gross

The history of the Hutterian Brethren extends back in time some 460 years to A.D. 1528, to the land of Moravia in present-day Czechoslovakia.

The rich and variegated Hutterian story in turn may be divided into various chapters. The Moravian chapter lasted till the Thirty Years War of 1618-48. Here, people and groups from many lands came together, as many as 20,000, gathered within some one hundred Bruderhofs. Jakob Hutter in the early 1530s for example led many Tiroleans into the gathered community.

The Slovakian chapter ended with Maria Theresa's program of recatholicizing her empire, in the mid-eighteenth century. The Romanian chapter began in 1621, when a handful of Hutterites settled there, in Transylvania [*Siebenbürgen*].

Fortunately, some Carinthian Lutherans expelled from Austria in 1755 were soon accepted into the Hutterian community. Carinthian Lutherans who became Hutterites, namely, were a genuine saving factor for historical continuity of Hutterianism. Indeed, descendants of these same Lutherans make up the majority of the Hutterite population in Western Canada and Western United States today.

Later that same century the combined group of Hutterites emigrated to the Ukraine (today, part of the USSR), the beginning of yet another Hutterian chapter that lasted till the 1870s, when all Hutterites emigrated to North America.

The next chapter begins with a North American setting (1874 ff). It takes on a new and profound dimension in 1930 when in December of that year Eberhard Arnold was baptized and ordained as *Diener des Wortes* (spiritual leader) of the German-based Bruderhof he had helped to found in 1920. This was a genuine coming together of two peoples, with a Hutterian presence once again to be found on European soil. In 1939, then, as the war clouds grew darker and darker, Joseph Kleinsasser and David Hofer confirmed the 1930 actions, acknowledging that the Hutterian Brethren included both North American and European groups.

Indeed, the war clouds had already taken their toll by 1939: the German Bruderhof had been closed; its members, expelled; and some, imprisoned. Resettlement took place, first in Liechtenstein and England, then in Paraguay. And although some differences of opinion between the new groups of Hutterites (by now, living in South America) and the Western North-American Hutterites led to estrangement for a time, there was again a reuniting of the groups in 1974. This took place after the Bruderhof again relocated, moving from Paraguay to the United States and England.

The Schmiedeleut took the lead, this time, in the reuniting. Soon, regular contacts, east and west, were established. The Dariusleut and Lehrerleut also slowly but surely began to establish contacts with the Arnoldleut, as the Western Hutterites sometimes called the "Eastern" group, so that by the latter 1980s growing goodwill on all sides prevailed.

Just as the Hutterian movement was regularly strengthened with the influx of Catholic Tiroleans (1530s, ff), then of Lutheran Carinthians (1760s), and in Russia, of Mennonites (1800s), so in 1930, a new, yet well-established German-based Bruderhof also added its own richness and strength to the larger, ongoing movement called Hutterian.

With each addition, there were changes in Hutterian culture. The sixteenth century saw mission and outreach, persecution notwithstanding; the seventeenth century saw a pulling back, caused by the ravages of warfare and pestilence. The eighteenth century yielded its own form of outreach, where spirit and faith of Lutherans meshed with one specific history—that of the Hutterites. The nineteenth century brought in some Mennonites—and contacts, that perhaps changed the Hutterian structures, making each colony a bit more autonomous than had been the case in earlier Hutterian history. The twentieth century brought a group of Germans—but also, others from many lands, a sort of transcultural group—into the Hutterian fold, again, thanks to a historical awareness, leading to the discovery of the Hutterites. Here, indeed, is a twentieth-century parallel to the eighteenth-century Carinthian Lutherans!

As in the past, such a uniting of a new people with an old has already brought with it certain cultural changes. Although it is too soon to know all the effects of such change, it is already apparent that the newest group of Hutterites is also very much interested in maintaining the sixteenth- and seventeenth-century roots of

Hutterianism—to be more explicit, a recovery of the early Hutterian vision.

The pages that follow in this Hutterian chronicle of the 1920s and 30s speak to such concern: that all Hutterites be unified, spiritually, in the ultimate Spirit of the peace of Jesus Christ, the Lord of History. Eberhard Arnold comes across as a brother with strong views and ideas, steeped in Hutterian history and vision; he also demonstrates true *Gelassenheit* (surrender) and *Demut* (humility), as he genuinely opens himself up to the counsel of his sisters and brothers in North America, in the twelve months he spent among all three Hutterian groups: the Dariusleut, the Lehrerleut and the Schmiedeleut. He and the German-based Bruderhof were accepted with open arms. There was an authentic mutual respect—on all sides.

Eberhard Arnold's love and respect for each of the three *Leut* is seen on almost every page of his journal and correspondence. The response of Hutterites such as Elias Walter, Joseph Stahl and David Hofer was equally cordial and affirming. It is apparent that many Hutterites were longing for renewal, and for a rediscovery of the Hutterian vision in all its depth and meaning.

Eberhard Arnold, throughout his whole journal, is asking on behalf of all Hutterites, one question, essentially, that of the nature of the Hutterian vision, and what this means in its substance and vitality. To be sure it includes a radical *Nachfolge Jesu* (discipleship), realized within the *Gemeinde Christi* (the gathered church of the faithful), molded by the Gospel of Peace.

There was no question on Eberhard Arnold's part as to the content of the vision, at its center. This is clear. Rather, the question emerged: How, to claim this vision in the twentieth century? Some of the issues in particular:

—The question of witness and mission: although no movement is without a witness, can more be done, currently, in the light of the mission spirit during the first decades of Hutterian history?

—The question of unity: wherein lies the road to greater unity of spirit and truth? Should there again be one *Vorsteher* (overall elder), or at least a coming together of the elders of each of the Leut, on a regular basis, namely, the Schmiedeleut, the Lehrerleut, the Dariusleut, and the Arnoldleut?

—The question of equality: how can genuine mutuality be effected, to eliminate rich and poor Bruderhofs? How can private property be won-out-over? –a concern for all Christians. For the Hutterites, the knotty question of *Zehrgeld*, or spending money.

—The question of family relations: are there ways to transcend the family ties that have slowly developed, where everyone (almost) on some Bruderhofs is related to everyone else?

A careful reading of the content of this volume cannot help but instruct all Hutterites—and many others as well, including the Mennonites—on how God has led in the recent past. This crucial chapter of how a German-based Bruderhof became Hutterian is essential reading in this regard. Most of Eberhard Arnold's concerns are still current and relevant, as are also many insights of Emmy Arnold, Harold S. Bender, Robert Friedmann, Elias Walter, and countless others who are reflected in Eberhard Arnold's journal entries, and in the correspondence that chronicles so well this whole era.

May this publishing venture lead to a deepening of unity of spirit and life for all Hutterites—in North America, in Europe, and in Japan. And may the vision and wisdom found in these pages also find its way into the hands of all true seekers who look to the way of Jesus of Nazareth as the very foundation of truth and life.

Goshen, Indiana, July 1988

Discovering Brothers

Introductory Remarks

The letters of this chapter were all written between January 1928 and May 26, 1930, shortly before Eberhard Arnold's departure for North America.[1] Several are addressed to Elias Walter, servant of the Word of the Stand Off Bruderhof[2] in Alberta, and to other brothers of the Hutterian Church in America. In these letters, he expresses the intense longing of the Brotherhood at the Rhön Bruderhof to become part of the Hutterian Church, and the readiness to lay the whole future of the little community and its services into the hands of this Church.

Eberhard Arnold explains how the church community in Germany came into being and its origins. He tells how they were led, through the experience of communal living in discipleship of Jesus Christ to a form and Orders which were essentially the same as the *Ordnungen* of the early Hutterian communities. The Brotherhood of the Rhön Bruderhof unanimously agreed that Eberhard Arnold should travel to America to seek a uniting with the Hutterian Church. A Sendbrief, or letter from the whole church community in Germany, was sent to all Hutterian Bruderhofs expressing this longing to unite and appealing for spiritual and temporal help in the work of mission in Europe.

It was through his historical studies of Anabaptism and the old Hutterian writings that Eberhard Arnold first became aware of the existence of the Bruderhofs in America today. So there is frequent reference to the search for old manuscripts in the correspondence with Elias Walter of the Stand Off Bruderhof in Alberta, Robert Friedmann, the Jewish student of Anabaptism in Vienna, who later became a Mennonite, and John Horsch, author of *The Hutterian Brethren*. For Eberhard Vetter his interest in the oldest and earliest writings was not academic. They were a call to give up everything to follow Jesus Christ, which we need to hear today. They were a challenge and inspiration to him and the whole Brotherhood and he tried to win even the scholars to surrender their lives to a life of practical brotherhood. He saw *Aussendung* (mission) as essential to the life of any living church and pleaded with the Hutterites in America to support the little Rhön Bruderhof in Germany in this task. Above all it is the longing to become fully united with the Hutterian Church that speaks through these letters.

---

[1]All the letters throughout this book were written by him unless otherwise indicated.

[2]Bruderhof: "place of the brothers," community. The shortened form, hof, is sometimes used.

Bruderhof, Post Neuhof
Kreis Fulda, Germany
January 9, 1928

Very respected and dear John Horsch,

It is a joy to me that we are not unknown to each other. We know the confession and life which has been entrusted to each of us, you from my books and writings and I from yours.

We, the whole Bruderhof, thank you from our hearts that you so faithfully sent us the Family Calendars for 1928 and 1929, from which we have read frequently.

You can immerse yourself in a very living way into the spiritual life of our Bruderhof through my book about the early Christians after the death of the apostles, if you apply these recognitions of the truth to the twentieth century, as the early Hutterians did in regard to their day. We are in a different situation from our Hutterian brothers on the Bruderhofs in South Dakota and Canada, whom we esteem highly, in the following way: the twenty-eight believing members of our present household, all surrendered in the practical work, as well as about twenty-five children, whom we love very much, have all come out of modern society.

Eberhard then explained that the spiritual roots of the Rhön Bruderhof went back to many different sources, among others, the Christian revival movements in Germany in and outside the state church, the Baptists and the Salvation Army; the Quakers with their peace witness; the Youth Movement with its love of nature and interest in community; the workers, some politically-minded and seeking to establish workers' settlements, others wanting freedom from all restraint.

Recently, individuals who have not previously been members of any movement are coming to us from the country, and from worker and middle-class circles, simply through our witness to the gospel. In response to all these movements our life is very active, especially in the summer when we have very many guests coming to us.

For the past ten years we who have come from the modern spirit of our time, our friends and our background, have had to fight and still are fighting through to the real church life of the Hutterites. We can testify with deep thankfulness that time and again the Holy Spirit is active among us with penetrating power. You will understand from all this our strong conviction that the new beginning of the Baptizer movement of the Reformation may under no circumstances be limited to narrow circles. Rather, God himself wants to move the whole world in this direction. With hearts on fire, we ask you to believe this too, to expect, as we do, that God will intervene and act through his mighty Spirit.

Therefore, dear John Horsch, I would like so much to discuss with you the task of mission and evangelizing today. So far, I have not been able to find out anywhere that the American Hutterian Brothers of today carry out any effective mission comparable to what happened so powerfully in Moravia in the first two centuries of Hutterianism. But perhaps it does happen, only we don't know about it? Is Bertha W. Clark[1] to be understood as saying that, according to her information, the 3,000 big and little inhabitants of the Hutterian Bruderhofs all belong to only sixteen more-or-less old families? This would indicate that the great growth among the Hutterites in the fifty years of their community life in America would then be only the outcome of their natural increase through birth. Or can we conclude from the information about those Mennonites who have come to the Hutterian Church that we can, after all, look for quite a number of new names and families on the Hutterian Bruderhofs today? I was very glad for B. W. Clark's statement that there is moral purity in the Hutterian communities. In Mennonite circles in Germany the evil rumor is spread that illegitimate births are common among the girls of the Hutterian communities. How could such a rumor arise and get to Germany?

We would also like to hear more exactly about the difference between the Hutterian groups, the Lehrerleut, the Dariusleut, and the Schmiedeleut,[2] and about the grouping of what must now be twenty-nine Bruderhofs. Which is the fourth group? Not Huron, Lake Byron of the Dariusleut?

We thank you very much for referring us to your Mennonite Library in Scottdale, Pa. Every help with books will be important for us. What we miss most of all in the history of Hutterianism are the orders for the craftsmen and other very down-to-earth information about their manner of work. Among the modern writings and books only Wolkan's *Die Hutterer*, published by the Bibliographical Society of Vienna, contains anything about this point which is so vital for our own workers. We would also be very thankful if you could tell us about the School Order of the Brothers. In which German educational journal has it appeared, and in which bigger English work can we get further information about it?

Our school and children's community is quite a special joy to us. It is also that branch of our work which has received most official recognition, also in the highest places. For us it is a miracle of God

---

[1] Wrote "The Hutterian Communities," 1924.

[2] See Introduction to Chapter 2.

that the awakening spirit of the church is active with such unique power among our children that we adults often see ourselves led forward by them.

We welcome very much your article printed in the *Wahrheitsfreund*[1] in connection with our task of really spreading and representing the truth of the Hutterian Baptizer Movement of the Reformation, which has so much more in common with true Mennonitism than with any other group of believers. I will let you know in the next days which books, etc. we would still like you to send. In view of the very complicated task in Germany, I sincerely ask you to take up these suggestions of mine so openly that you see them only as a brotherly encouragement to revise these works to meet the present situation in Europe.

We are very interested in the *Wahrheitsfreund*. We would be very thankful if you could put us in touch by letter with the two editors who are of Hutterian descent. We would very much like to receive this periodical published in Chicago regularly. We would also be thankful for all of your own works you can send us. Unfortunately, because of the very hard beginning of our common life, it is not economically possible to acquire all the books we absolutely need. The library in our house dates from the time when we were still living without community of goods or community of work, in very favorable financial circumstances for the Germany of that time. But we are so strongly penetrated by the commission of Christ to the early church in Jerusalem that we could never again leave this commitment, even in the face of serious and oppressive need. I am sending you an article of mine going into all this, once published by Professor Dr. Siegmund Schultze,[2] whose efforts for peace you know well.

Two of us formerly worked in the German Student Christian Movement and in their *Furche* Publishing House. Apart from these two, who are trained publishers, we have a third brother who is a very efficient bookseller. Therefore it would be very desirable for our "Source Book" series (of which you know *The Early Christians after the Death of the Apostles*) and our publishing house to continue to expand. But we lack the financial means for this. Might it perhaps be possible for you of the Mennonite Publishing House in Scottdale to make an arrangement with us whereby our work could be spread among all German-speaking Europeans? This would especially include

---

[1]Literally "Friend of Truth," published by the Krimmer Mennonites in Chicago and edited by D. M. Hofer and J. W. Tschetter.

[2]Professor in Berlin, who already in 1920 was working on behalf of the oppressed workers.

my writings on the Baptizer movement and on our whole community life-witness as part of the series "Sources of Christian Witness through all the Centuries." We would be everlastingly thankful to you if you could find a way to help us substantially with the financial foundation of our Bruderhof from among the circles of your acquaintances. This would be a truly Christian deed for the future of our Bruderhof and its mission as God intends it. Surely there must be a small number among those American Mennonites who really believe, and among your acquaintances, who would be ready to give money, not for the maintenance of their standard of living, but because of their strong and active interest in the witness to the truth made to the whole world by a powerful, living Bruderhof arising in Europe again, like the influential and vital households of the Baptizers of the Reformation. We therefore ask you sincerely for help through your advice and deeds, so that as quickly as possible we can come onto a financially healthy foundation for our faithful and surrendered circle of creative workers. Just as the Mennonites did such a great service of love through practical financial devotion at the beginning of the seventeenth century, today also a new, unforgettable step of brotherly help could be dared.

Perhaps the first step that could be dared right away would be your financing a contract for the publishing work in Germany and Europe. This would include my literary work, research in archives, the "Source" series, and the bigger book I have already prepared about the peaceful, morally pure Baptizers-on-confession-of-faith of the Reformation century. I am enclosing an article for the *Wahrheitsfreund*, from which you can see that all income from my work and that of other brothers goes to the common tasks of our Bruderhof without any deduction or privileges. Perhaps this article could appear very soon in the *Wahrheitsfreund*, and so prepare the way for help from the Mennonites.

However things may turn out, we are thankful from our hearts for your brotherly interest in the development of our Bruderhof and for your wish that God may lead and bless us. We thank you.

Your Bruderhof members joined heart-to-heart with you
in the spirit of the old original Baptizer[1] movement
Eberhard Arnold

---

[1]'Baptizer' has been used wherever *Täufer* occurs in the original.

Rhön Bruderhof, Nov. 6, 1928

My dear Elias Walter,

I received yesterday your so loving, detailed, and heartfelt, brotherly letter of October 16. I thank you for it from my heart, and our entire Bruderhof thanks you for the great joy which this letter has brought to us. We are especially concerning ourselves with the very meaningful letters of Andreas Ehrenpreis, which we are having copied so that we can send your copy back to you. We are also very glad about the article by John Horsch and would like to correspond with him to see in which way this article could be adapted for the German public. Then we would like to print it in the *Wegwarte*[1] and also distribute it as a pamphlet. We also thank you especially for the descriptions of the other writings, notes, sermons, and the books and writings you sent us. Of course, your indexes are of special value to me.

I thank you warmly for the very encouraging words from Andreas Ehrenpreis about baptism by immersion. As in all his writings, Andreas Ehrenpreis has found the right emphasis also here. He is doubtless right that we should not let this question divide us and not attach any exaggerated value to it. We have written to you already that also on this point we are prepared for any agreement with you.

Also in the question of the millennium we are thankful from our hearts for any instruction through you and your old writings. In any case the chief thing remains that we really live it out in community here and now, live as the prophets proclaimed the kingdom of God. The word of the Apostle is decisive for the practical life. The kingdom of God is then justice and peace and joy in the Holy Spirit now.

We thank you especially for your loving, thorough answer to our letters of August 22, 1928, in which we declared with final, decisive determination our resolute will, which shall never be withdrawn, to be really united with you and your communities. We want to be completely incorporated for our spiritual as well as our material care. We are convinced that God in his indescribable grace will accept a decision born out of faith and the obedience of complete love, and that he will show you and us the way. We thank you from our hearts that with your present letter you have made a beginning in this. We cannot describe how deeply your letter has strengthened, encouraged, and gladdened us.

We were astonished that you are not the leader of the church and

---

[1]A small magazine, from 1924 on edited by Eberhard Arnold.

that you have no special head of the whole church. Is this most important fact among the first Hutterian communities—that a particular brother was in a unique way responsible for all—no longer the case among you? We take a wholehearted interest in all you have experienced in your sixty-six years and wish you for the future a long life of very vigorous work and joy.

I have seen from your writings that in 1914 you informed President Wilson that your young men could not take part in the military establishment, also not in noncombatant military service, without violating your principles. It is exactly the same with us. There is no man or youth among us who could serve, even indirectly, in any military establishment. We have the great joy of having, in addition to our four married men, five unmarried young men in the community. Among them only Kurt Zimmermann is still in his time of testing and asking for baptism. But he is already a genuine and dependable Hutterite, prepared for any sacrifice.

Even in clothing we are so similar to you that as long as we have lived together our women and girls have never worn hats, and we would never in any circumstances tolerate cutting the hair by our women and girls. Only our men must become more like yours in the way in which their hair and beards are cut. In any case, here in Germany and particularly in the cities, to our joy we attract very much attention by our simple, medieval costume.

In your two letters you mention Robert Friedmann, who is very well known to us. By a remarkable coincidence he has written a long letter to us just as you were writing yours, in which he invites me very urgently to give some important lectures in Vienna. I would be very thankful if you would intercede in the church in your prayer that my witness in Vienna might strike home. It is a very deep concern for me that just there on the soil of Austria the Hutterian movement of faith and way of living might begin anew. I will also visit your relatives in your old houses and proclaim to them the witness of the truth. It would be very important for me if Robert Friedmann could visit us at our Bruderhof. He once heard a lecture by me in Vienna and since then has had great joy, as he writes, in our "Bruderhof work." Unfortunately, so far both of us have lacked the money for such a journey, which he also would very much like to make.

Robert Friedmann also has a sincere respect and love for you. I hope that he comes out of his scholarly interest in our cause to obedience in deed and that he joins our community life.

Robert Friedmann has special joy in Peter Walpot's letter in the

Chronicle.[1] We read this out some time ago to the anger of some old Christians still living in private property who were present. We want to print it in the *Wegwarte*. We know well the letters of 1571 to Simon the Apothecary in Poland. We have unfortunately not yet been able to get a copy of Beck's history book,[2] which I know very well. We are trying to get it again, because we need it for our church meetings and for Sundays. We would be very thankful to you if you could let us have some more song books and could send us some more copies of Andreas Ehrenpreis. The members of our community borrow again and again from my library the only copy of this or that writing which we have received from you, and I am anxious for fear some may get damaged in spite of all care and caution.

We have felt very deeply your comments that it went well with the church as long as people came from the highlands and the lowlands, but as the children grew up, the church often experienced a setback. We had already seen this with the history of the Hutterites in the course of these four hundred years. We cannot say enough how endlessly thankful we are that, through the love of God and the working of Christ and his Holy Spirit, new life from God has risen up among our nearly thirty children, especially among the bigger ones. Their faithful willingness in daily life proves that they have a burning love for the life in community, a real discipleship in Jesus. How glad we were again to discover some time ago that three children of nine, ten, and nearly eleven years were reading the New Testament together in the evenings, quite without our knowledge and completely out of the urge of their little hearts. In our next letter we will send you two essays written independently without help from the teachers. Perhaps you could give these essays to the children in your church. Our children ask that they be accepted as a greeting from them to your children. The house for our children's community is now finished. The children will move in during the next days. On November 23 the government will send an inspector to examine everything.

We are very sad that you think it scarcely possible for leading brothers from your Bruderhofs to come to us, to be some years with us, and to take over the main responsibility for the development of our Bruderhof. Nevertheless, we have to express our innermost thanks

---

[1]*Geschicht-Buch der Hutterischen Brüder*, Prof. Dr. Rudolf Wolkan, ed., Vienna 1923. Translated as *The Chronicle of the Hutterian Brethren*, Vol. I, (Plough Publishing House, Rifton, NY, 1987) 413-415.

[2]*Die Geschichts-Bücher der Wiedertäufer in Oesterreich-Ungarn*, 1883.

that you, in trust in the wonderful help of God, speak your conviction that we, having been led thus far, should for the present continue with the work without the presence of you brothers.

We thank you very much that with such faithfulness you make us aware again and again that we should search in the old writings of the Hutterites, should read and think about them for our living and loving in true community. We are following this faithful advice out of our own deepest necessity. God has enlightened us in such a way that in these books, writings, letters, and songs of the old Hutterian communities we find the decisive, genuine truth.

A few days ago I had the opportunity to witness to this truth in a gathering of Baptist preachers. I will send you a small part of my talk. The preachers had to admit that in the light of the early Christian church in Jerusalem they could not make the objection that it was unbiblical or fanatical. I had the feeling from the discussion that they were frightened by the demands of Jesus and the apostles. But in addition I hope that through the witness I gave in Hersfeld in Hesse on October 25 some will come to the way. An old preacher said that if he were young he would leave everything to live with us. If he really wanted it, he could, through the grace of God, win a renewal of his youth among us. I ask that you remember in your church meetings that I have the opportunity this winter to proclaim the truth in our neighboring villages in the Rhön mountains of Hesse, also in Hanau, Hersfeld, Dresden, Halle-on-the-Saale, and, as said already, in Vienna. Ask God that he guide our church community so that we come to a right decision about which area we should give our first efforts to. We are convinced that Jesus sends us into the world as he himself was sent by the Father. We have the faith that men will arise and risk their lives for the church.

Unfortunately, we are hindered in carrying out this mission by our very oppressive economic situation. We thank you for your faithful sympathy through which we feel that you share with us this need that lies heavily on our hearts, just as you feel burdened by the situation of the church in Manitoba. For this reason we greet particularly our brothers in Manitoba and tell them that we feel especially united with them in their economic need. You are so right to make us aware that we must be very careful. The forefathers did not possess any land but cultivated rented land. We too were always of the opinion that possession of land by the church is not altogether desirable. We would gladly have remained on our rented land in Sannerz, where for six years we felt happy working rented ground. But we were clearly led in the direction of not retaining that rented land and even less of increasing it, and our present Bruderhof lands were shown us by God. In Germany there will scarcely be a region that offers us such cheap possibilities within the German borders for work and expansion, as on our mountain land. Here, if it is given to us as we believe it is, we can build up our life undisturbed in keeping with the Hutterian faith.

We hear now from you that all your Bruderhofs as a whole are not in a position to take over our hof so that it would belong to the entire Hutterian Church living in community today. We understand that with you each Bruderhof manages its affairs and therefore its property and responsibilities by itself. We ask you now to accept us into the union of your Bruderhofs in such a way that in keeping with your suggestion, we carry the responsibility for our Bruderhof life, its work, and commitments. Only we must ask you from our hearts to carry our great need of money with us, and at least to help us with money in good measure. You can scarcely imagine how unspeakably hard it is to build up community life and orderly, efficient, common work without money. We began this community work literally without a penny to our name. We trust God, who has often helped us already through the darkest need, to bring us also through this winter. Thanks to the harvest, if we exercise the utmost economy and simplicity, we will not starve. But our debts press heavily upon us, and it is to be feared that some to whom we owe money may deal harshly with us, bringing our community life into danger.

We ask you from our hearts to intercede for us, so that through your help it might be possible for us to pay off this winter at least 30,000 marks, that is, about 7,000 dollars. If that could be given through God's grace, our hands would be free to work effectively in spreading the gospel of the church in the German lands and gathering upright men into the common life.

We thank you warmly for your loving advice to write to David Hofer and Johann Entz. We are doing that now. Perhaps you will have the goodness to ask them, as from you, to help us. We ask you at your Stand Off Bruderhof to intercede for us before the face of God in your meetings which you have described so wonderfully to us.

[Eberhard Arnold]

At a meeting at the Rhön Bruderhof in November 1928 Eberhard Arnold spoke about the inner concerns of the Brotherhood:

. . . We searched through our present age and through past centuries as thoroughly as we could alongside our practical work. The unique fact of the Hutterian Brothers' existence then brought us to a halt. We got into contact with the American Hutterites in Canada and South Dakota and absorbed all the Hutterian writings we could obtain: books, letters, songs, and regulations for the craftsmen [*Ordnungen*]. Elias Walter particularly has helped us to get them. This all sets the direction and way clearly before us: the way of the awakening spirit of true personal faith and real love, of the spirit of freedom, yet with real personal responsibility, inwardly moved by the holiest 'Thou Must' and 'Thou Shalt.' This leads us again to define our direction more clearly through the Hutterian witness of truth.

The Hutterian Church and its communal brotherhoods had a special significance for us from the start. To anyone who understands everything we have brought to mind about the history of our common life, it will be evident that this had to be so. From the beginning we have concerned ourselves with these earliest Baptizers and been deeply interested in them, some of us as early as before the First World War. As time went on, the Evangelical and Fellowship Movements, both inside and outside the established church, lost power, and so did other movements we were in touch with, such as the German Christian students. The Youth Movement and the settlement move- ment, including current party politics and political pacifism, did have some elements that were genuine. But they contained too much that was sham and superficial and therefore grew weaker and weaker in their real effectiveness. All the more, we felt drawn to those most powerful times in the history of the Christ-Spirit. All the more, we felt urged toward the earliest beginnings of the earliest movements. The strongest areas were: early Christianity, Montanism and the Waldensians in their first enthusiasm, the early Baptizers with their radical communal life, and the earliest Quakers. (For the moment we are disregarding the Reformers of the sixteenth century.) The bond of loyalty in these movements depends on faith in the Holy Spirit, his unity in the church, his justice and peace in the coming kingdom. It is a bond that unites and gives full unanimity.

As a result of these experiences and the strengthening of our permanent circle, the tempo of work in our household has increased considerably. Practical work is the expression of love that arises out of faith. For us, just as it was for the Hutterites of old, practical work is the best way to be freed from self-will, self-importance, and the sickness of the individual soul and to give oneself up to the greatness of the task.

And yet all this—the daily work on our hof, in the children's community, in the publishing, and with the guests—is not enough.

We would not be satisfied with this way we are going unless mission were combined with these other tasks. The early Hutterian churches had an enormous power for mission. As early as four years after their actual founding by Jakob Hutter, a hostile observer reported that "their communistic households include 1,700 members." In contrast to this, the best we have been able to do after so many long years since 1920 is fifty members at the most, including children; we are quite ashamed about this. We feel clearly that each individual who passes through our house should be confronted with a decision. Each one must decide whether or not the moment has finally arrived to give up his self-life and his self-will (every aspect of it, including career and possessions) and therefore to join us unconditionally. Just at this moment we are in the midst of preparing to dedicate our children's house, and we also have a number of guests and co-workers among us. This is a suitable moment for us to think about the origin and direction of our way of life. We need to remind ourselves of our purpose in coming here, of what brought us to this life and has kept us here.

Our origins go back to the time when Christianity was living, when sin was judged as sin and salvation revealed as salvation. It is of decisive importance that we search inwardly and reflect on the true, original Christianity of those first living years. For those among us who were allowed to help found our own community work, this went together with the freedom that came through breaking away from the institutional church and with the secret of the mystical Body of Christ.

The principle of *life* is essential to a living church; Christianity has nothing dead about it. Only what was really alive could be acknowledged and lived out. It was this aliveness that gave rise to the rescue work affecting people's social and inner lives. The confusion of people was seen as arising from their material need as well as from their emotional distress and suffering. There were two contrasting types of movement, both of which had a stimulating effect on our own movement in its beginnings: the Salvation Army and the Quakers. The Salvation Army set an example by awakening people to repentance and faith so as to save their souls. In the Quaker movement there was work with children and the experience of fellowship—often with no words spoken—a fellowship of shared feeling on the basis of their faith and inner life. There was practical responsibility for righting public wrong, that is, social need. For the sake of this social need the Quakers also entered the sphere of personal salvation of souls.

The second source of our movement, of our direction, seems entirely different from the first. Yet it is basically related to it. The Free

German and Workers' Youth Movement met us at a time when it was vitally alive and was therefore still putting into action this life principle. Here were rich testimonies to faith in the future. So we realized that here too something of the old reality and of God's will was at work. Something was really happening. If the children refuse to speak, the stones will speak; if believers have no love, unbelievers will have to take on inner responsibility.

Therefore, a feeling for public responsibility developed out of all these movements because of their longing for future peace. They reached out beyond personal salvation of souls. They took part in politics. Uppermost here was the conviction that God's interest is not limited to the personal salvation of the individual soul. He is just as much interested in the fate of nations and in the removal of the curse of social injustice. These movements, together with the pacifism of brotherly life, stood up against military service and for the communism of brotherhood. They took a stand against property based on formal legal rights and for the unity of the church in the Christ-Spirit. Even in groups of the Youth Movement that seemed pagan in their direction, there lived a belief that all nature belongs together and that there is a religious mystery in nature; also the faith that all mankind belongs together and has a religious future. A dormant seed lay here: biblical faith in the unity of the church that belongs to the coming kingdom.

Rhön Bruderhof, probably 1928

Dear Joseph Waldner,

Through Elias Walter you have heard of the joy we have in your Bruderhofs of the Hutterian brothers in America. The fact that you are there and faithfully continue the way of Jakob Hutter has deeply strengthened us. Elias Walter has helped us very much through his letters and by sending us writings and books. We have repeatedly expressed our earnest request to him that he continue to teach us and support us in community, together with you other Hutterian brothers. For about ten years God has been convincing us more and more clearly and decidedly that Hutterianism, as the way of faith and community of goods, is our life, which we can never again abandon.

We reject bearing arms and military service, war taxes and oaths, public office, and taking part in political elections and parties, all private property and all private life, all evil occupations for earning a livelihood, all work for self, all self-will, and sin. We can only do this through the love that comes from the faith of the apostles and prophets in the Father through Christ and the Holy Spirit. This faith works in us through the Holy Spirit and through Holy Scripture.

Peter Riedemann's Confession, the Chronicle, Andreas Ehrenpreis, the Hutterian song book, and the other Hutterian writings are for us the guidelines of faith from which we never want to stray. Church discipline, including the biblical ban and judgment, baptism, the Lord's Supper, full community of goods and of work with mission to village and city are the consequences of this faith, for which we are determined to live and suffer.

Our communal set-up in Hesse is carried through more clearly according to the old Hutterian orders from year to year. We do not want to depart from these orders in any point. Our community in eating and working, in devotion, in education, in the school, and in every service we do for one another, as well as in our hospitality and taking in of poor children, is so necessary to us that we could no longer live differently. So we have built up our Bruderhof with its houses and work, also representing it to the world and its authorities in the Charter of our Corporation (Introduction and Paragraph 1).

All members and all who want to become members give all their possessions and their whole working strength to our Bruderhof, without self-interest or self-will.

We have six older people and twelve younger ones at the moment who have made this decision and proved themselves in it, and there are an additional twenty-two children. In summer we have sixty to seventy at our table, which includes our guests, who are co-workers struggling to find the truth. We live in the need of extreme poverty, similar to that of the beginning at the time of Jakob Hutter, the time of the expulsion from Moravia described at the end of the Chronicle, as conveyed in the begging letter to the Dutch Mennonites, and the time of your forefathers from Carinthia, the time in Walachia, and as you also experienced later in hardship and agony.

This poverty brings very strenuous work and great privation in food and in heating. Unfortunately the initial joy of some fellowmen who gave us loans and credit has recently changed to strict demands for repayment of these debts, so that our communal life is in danger. Also, in spite of everyone's obedient and devoted willingness to work, we cannot build up properly in face of this poverty. But the more than eight and a half years of communal life and work in Hesse have proved that God will lead us through and onwards, and give us faith and strength to work. We do need support to begin with for the basis of our existence. We are united in the faithful resolution to stay together and to hold firm, also in the greatest need. For the sake of our many children and of the shame that threatens the witness of the holy cause, we have the urgent request to you to relieve our need through immediate help. We ask you to take on our Bruderhof as a most humble daughter colony like an adopted child and set us up and equip us. We also want to fit in and be incorporated in every respect. We have asked Elias Walter to send us two leading brothers for the service of the Word and for the steward's service or for the service of temporal affairs. However, Elias Walter did not really think this possible.

Our work consists of agriculture on 100 acres, cabinet making, turning, work in the smithy, growing vegetables, upholstery (saddle-making), education and schooling of our children, and written and spoken spreading of the truth of Hutterian teachings. All this work needs $10,000 as a basis for a sound Hutterian establishment. We ask you from our hearts to send us help before it is too late, either as individual communities, or as Dariusleut, Schmiedeleut, or Lehrerleut, or in the communal agreement of all Hutterian Bruderhofs. We are well aware that this request is almost impossible to fulfill, and it is very hard for us to approach you with it, but for the sake of the holy work of God we have to do so. Therefore, in deep suffering we surrender to you and lay our most urgent need on your believing, loving hearts. Please carry with us what we have to do and suffer, and decide to send us the help without which we can see no way out of our need.

Eberhard Arnold

John Horsch   Joseph Kleinsasser
Scottdale, Pa.   Milltown Bruderhof, March 22, 1929

Worthy and dear Friend,

I have received your letter of March 14, and my answer is: if you still need my book (the history by Beck), you may keep it for a while and then send it to me afterwards.

I have also heard already through Elias Walter of Alberta about the people who have begun community of goods in Germany and have myself recently received a letter from Eberhard Arnold too. Whether they will be able to carry the matter through in warlike Germany is a question to me. Unfortunately those poor people are so much in debt that they are already in danger of losing their property (in part).

They are asking for financial help, but the Manitoba communities are mostly in a very needy state, firstly on account of the low price they sold their land in South Dakota for, and the very high cost of land in Manitoba, and secondly through a poor harvest and uncertainty in the farming industry in Canada. Therefore help from us here is out of the question. May the dear God give these poor people a way out and grant them strength to remain faithful.

Otherwise we are reasonably healthy, thanks be to God, and we wish you likewise everything good from the giver of all good things. May he lead you and us to the right recognition of the truth and grant us a blessed end.

Greetings, your friend,

Joseph Kleinsasser

This letter from Joseph Stahl of Lake Byron Bruderhof, South Dakota, is the only one we have in this collection from a brother in America to Eberhard Arnold before his journey.

Huron, South Dakota, March 24, 1929

My dear Arnold,

May God's love and peace and the power of the Holy Spirit be with you and us all. Amen.

I received your pleading, spirit-filled letter on March 20. Therefore I thank God our heavenly Father through his dear Son Jesus Christ for you and all the devout children of God with you. I rejoiced to hear and learn about your godly zeal and urgent love and longing to be included in the number of God's chosen. O that God would grant that not only you but many thousands more would set out on this way. And may the mountain of the Lord be exalted above all mountains and hills, for this is the only way to blessedness; yes, as our Savior says, it is narrow and small and there are few who walk on it. Because most people of this world, including the so-called Christians, do not want to surrender in such *Gelassenheit*,[1] although many already know and have heard of this way and also recognize it as the work of the Holy Spirit, they go sorrowfully away with the rich young man and will not come to the Supper of the Lord. Thus the Lord cursed them in his wrath, and they shall not taste of it.

But may our gracious heavenly Father give you and all of us strength

---

[1]Literally: a letting go, self-surrender.

and power to endure to the end, so that we may be recognized as true branches on the vine of Jesus Christ, as faithful servants and serving maids who can produce our talents with interest, and may then also partake of the friendly answer from his gracious mouth, "You have been faithful over a little; I will set you over much." This I wish for you and all of us through Jesus Christ. Amen.

Now dear Arnold, I hope you don't mind our not moving fast enough for your wish and longing to unite with us, nor proceeding without questioning and testing you. For it will not be unknown to you how the little flock did it with their servants of the Word in Jakob Hutter's time, as Offrus Grüssinger [Onophrius Griesinger] also warned Hans Ulrich, which you will see in the letter you have asked me to send you. But we do not expect that of you. Rather, it is a great joy to us that there, where our dear forefathers suffered so much for our faith, you have once more set the work in motion and are also seeking out all the old writings and intend to bring them out anew. May God give you grace for this. For our yearly meeting of all servants of the Word and of temporal affairs in 1927, I suggested that Elias Walter be sent over to collect such old writings. At that time we knew nothing about you. Now that you are there, it is not necessary. We will spare no pains in searching for these things so that nothing gets lost, for our Savior also commanded his disciples to save the "*Übrige Brocken*" (crumbs left over). It is not that we are so very far any more from each other spiritually, but only that now, right at the beginning, you are asking for a sum of money for your temporal needs. That will be very difficult to produce because many of our Bruderhofs are in great debt and need help on all sides. So I can only commend you to our Father in heaven, that he may help you spiritually and temporally.

I wrote to Elias Walter a while ago that the best would be to call a meeting of the servants of the Word and of temporal affairs to talk about you together. In that way I believe we would find a solution with you. Or maybe, it would be better if you yourself, or two of you, would come over here. We would tell you when to come.

Since old Elias Walter, the elder, died last year right after our meeting, it looks as though no one will continue his work or his duties. Elias Walter (his nephew) is said to have been seriously ill some weeks ago, so that all servants of the Word visited him; but now, I hear, he is getting better. May God be thanked!

You write that David R. Hofer in Raley has put many questions to you. It is as *Sirach* (Ecclesiasticus) says, a fool can ask more questions than ten wise men can answer. I grew up with him in the community. He has been a troublesome person in the church from youth on; therefore he also didn't remain constant.

After a few years this David R. Hofer, his father, and two brothers with their families left and entered a complaint against the church with the government, demanding their share.

I understood also from your letter which Elias Walter sent me that your thirteen-year-old son wants to be baptized. It is not the custom with us to baptize so young. Most of our children wait till they are eighteen or twenty. Our forefathers did not consider it good.

How is it with the schools over there in militaristic Germany? Don't they bother you? Here it is very bad, and in Canada even worse, since most communities do not have their own teachers for teaching English, and therefore are forced to use teachers from the outside. This means that for eight to ten months a year our children are under the influence of a warlike, worldly education, which cannot do any good; and we're very aware it is leading to corruption. May God be gracious to us!

Since Easter is at the door, we have also become of one mind to hold the Lord's Supper, in remembrance of our Lord and Savior Jesus Christ and his bitter suffering and death. May he make us ready to be worthy partakers at his table. This I wish from God. Amen.

Joseph Stahl

P.S. I am sending you the points of the Easter letter and the prayer at meals of our children. If a meeting takes place to talk about you, I will not be against helping you, for Moses said to Joshua who wanted to forbid them when two were prophesying, "Would to God they would all prophesy."

Paul and Peter Gross
Iberville, Manitoba, March 30, 1929

To respected Elias Walter,

The peace of the Lord, the love of God, and the community of the Holy Spirit be with you and us. Amen.

Much-loved Elias Vetter, I come to visit you with this writing. God be praised, we are all cheerful and well. We wish you the same from God the heavenly Father. We have also survived the cold winter again, and sowing time is close at hand. May God the heavenly Father give us his blessing again so that in the future we can receive and enjoy our daily bread.

I also want to tell you that dear old Babeka Basel Gross died on March 24, after suffering for a long time. I think she was bedridden for nearly four years, being lame (her feet). Otherwise her understanding was good until two days before her death. Then she lost her sight and her speech, lying almost as one dead for those two days except that she was still breathing. On March 26 we laid her to rest in the earth. Servant of the Word David Hofer gave the burial sermon and servant of the Word Zacharias read out the lines of the funeral song we sing, "O God, a blessed parting." Blessed are the dead who die in the Lord. . . .

Now Elias Vetter, I will report to you that a week ago I received a letter from the Hutterian Brothers, as they call themselves in Germany. I read it carefully and also sought advice as to what we should do from our servants of the Word, Joseph K., Zacharius Hof., and David H. at the burial.

So I told them I had already decided what we could do, and told them my suggestion. They did not say anything against it, so that means they are in agreement with it. I have considered with much care how we could help the brothers spiritually and also temporally. When we consider their burden of debts, it is, to put it briefly, not possible to help them, for we in Manitoba are in a similar situation and how then can we help in temporal things? For spiritual help we could send them two brothers which they have asked for, a servant of the Word and a steward. We cannot deny them that, but to draw $1,000 out of the bank and travel to Germany, I cannot manage that. But if there is no other way, it wouldn't be so bad if each of the ten Bruderhofs would contribute $100. Then they would be helped.

According to my knowledge there are two strong Lehrerleut Bruderhofs in the States and one strong Dariusleut Bruderhof, Wolf Creek, and there are twelve Bruderhofs in Alberta which are rich in temporal things and have no lack. They should open their hearts and minds and fulfill this request. They cannot excuse themselves through lack of means. They have been so greatly blessed among the Bruderhofs in Alberta, it would be possible for one Bruderhof to take on the whole sum, but this is unnecessary, as it can be divided among them all. That would be following the teaching of the Savior and the apostle Paul. If you, Elias Walter, have another suggestion let me know as soon as possible.

I want to write you something about the past. If old Schmied-Michel Vetter were still living, his whole spirit would be stirred up and he would use every means, way, and opportunity to seek out the Bruderhof in Germany and to get to know them with everything which belongs to community, both spiritual and temporal. But that's how it was . . . God knows if that will come again.

Who would have ever thought that in Germany, after the war which lasted five years, when all manner of godlessness was instituted by force, a people would still be found starting to live in community of goods, and in the full order of the Church! But with God all things are possible. Now what shall I still write about the sad and tormented world? My father, old Jakob Maendel, is still the same. Sometimes the message comes he is improving, then comes another: Maendel Vetter almost died last night. He is always in bed. He waits eagerly for his release.

I will close with many greetings to all, from us, your humble servants,

Paul and Peter Gross

A SMALL SENDBRIEF

sent by Eberhard Arnold in May of 1929 from the German Bruderhof, Neuhof, Kreis Fulda, Hessen-Nassau, to the Hutterian Brethren in South Dakota, USA, in Manitoba, Canada, and in Alberta, Canada. This letter was sent to the Bruderhofs there belonging to the church of God established by Jakob Hutter during the years 1533-1536 in the full community of Christ, in the discipline of the Holy Spirit, and with true order in mission and in work according to the Word of God. In accordance with God's will this church exists today and for all time and should be gathered out of the whole world in far-reaching power and complete unity.

The small church community of the Neuwerk Bruderhof in Germany wishes you the great and eternal joy of God which is revealed in his perfect unity of faith, love, work, and communal sharing of all property!

This church, which is just coming into being and is struggling for its life, wants to become a church of the Hutterian Brethren, completely united with you. May your and our lives be penetrated, directed, and determined by this mighty power of the Holy Spirit which stirs and awakens everything by the mighty presence of the living Christ and carries out his work.

In this joyful faith of holy love we send over the great ocean to you all the wishes and prayers that our beloved Jesus Christ made to his Father on our behalf. He still pleads for us in the same way today and will plead through all eternity. These prayers are written in the seventeenth chapter of the Gospel of John as his high priestly prayer. We believe that these prayers proclaim the holy will of God which is our greatest need today when unfaithfulness and unbelief spread so rapidly, when injustice grows always more cruel, and love turns to icy coldness. Today the hour has come anew in which Jesus Christet wants to glorify the name and character, the life and love, the judgment and grace of the Father by following the way of suffering and yielding himself to death. He wants to reveal them to the world, shining and full of light, for everyone to recognize the one true God who sent his Christ as the life of his church. The name of God is everywhere misunderstood. Jesus Christ has the will and the power to tell of this name far and wide, also today. He is given power over all men, that through him and through his church they may find true life. For this purpose he, who is himself the Word, revealed the truth by becoming man, by the way he lived on earth, by proclamation of the Word, and by his deeds. For this purpose he completed his work. He went through a shameful death and through wonderful resurrection into the glory of the Father. He sent his Spirit down to his church. He gathered, protected, and appointed to his service all those whom his Father had given to him out of the world. To this church of his disciples and followers we too should belong, since we have accepted with you the Word in order to obey it in the sincerity of faith and love. Consecrated to him and his calling, we must live accordingly because we believe that Christ has been sent and because we know that the spirit of this life, like all that is good, comes from God.

Jesus prayed to his Father expressly for you and for us who have come to faith through the apostolic word. Our Christ on high now prays for you and for us whom the Father gave to his Son as his possession. He prays that we may truly be kept in his name, you among yourselves together with us, and we among ourselves together with you.

He has to pray for us so urgently because we must remain here in this extremely dangerous world. The world continually draws our senses away from the love of Christ toward worries or wealth and into the greed of the satanic will to possess. Satan wants us also to perish in pride and coldness, in selfishness and hardness of heart. Even Jesus had to give up one of his faithfully protected disciples and lose him to the devil. This fallen man was the one who had looked after the money for the community of the disciples. Even today the

v.1-3

v.26
v.2

v.17

v.4
v.1
v.14-16
v.12

v.17

v.9-10
v.9-11

v.11

v.12

stewardship of church property brings with it chilling danger, and Jesus must continually plead to the Father that his grace may keep us in his love.

The other danger, no less threatening to our existence, is the tremendous power of hate in today's world. It is the cold contradiction of love in business competition, war, bloody uprising, and the persecution of the church, by which the evil one, the dark prince of our time, rules over the whole world today. He wants either to enslave us to this power so that we too obey it, or if we resist the spirit of the times on every front, he tries to persecute and destroy us with his hatred. One way or the other we are to cease existing as a holy, united, loving church. So we know well what the enemy of God has in mind. He will not tolerate the fact that we are still in this world without belonging to his world, to Satan's world. The evil spirit of the abyss wants either to keep us from unity and sacrificing love, so that we forget the teaching of Jesus and of our forefathers, or else he wants to destroy and blot out our existence. In each case evil wants to stop our being a united church practicing mutual help. Unless God himself protects and fills us with the same spirit of sacrifice as our forefathers, we will all be helplessly overpowered by one of these two dangers. But Jesus intercedes for us. He knows that the world will believe that he was sent only if it sees that in his church all are completely one in all things, perfectly *one* through the love of God, as Christ is perfectly one with the Father. Jesus says to the Father,

v.10   "Everything that is mine is thine, and that which is thine is mine." Just as the Father could never abandon the Son, nor the Son the Father—not even in death—so the mutual help in his church should make plain the perfect unity of all churches. For this reason we ask the Father for the unity and love of the Holy Spirit, so that by the light streaming out from the united church, everyone can recognize and grasp how the Father reveals himself as unity in the Son and in

v.20   the Spirit. Jesus Christ asks for this for you and for us, as for his church of the last days. Just this main point of the first church in Jerusalem and of the Hutterian Church of God—the community of goods of all with all—seems impossible and unreachable for countless churches, however different, easy or difficult, their circumstances may be. And yet from Jakob Hutter to Andreas Ehrenpreis and onward, the impossible proved to be possible. The early church under the leadership of Peter and James stood for this impossible possibility of faith and love. At the time of the early Christians, apostles like Paul were sent back and forth to gather money for the church living in community of goods in Jerusalem. The main task of the apostles sent out by the church to travel between the young, growing churches was to fan the holy fire of glowing love on the altar of faith and to let everything else burn up in it. In the Hutterian communities in Moravia the Holy Spirit prompted the same united leadership and the same apostolic mission from church to church and far into the world. In this way the mutual help of perfect love and unity was put into practice between the churches and between all who were brought to faith by this service. Today, too, Jesus wants to call men from among you and from among us. They, too, will be sent out to the brothers and into the world, just v.18-19 as he was sent out by the Father to mankind and worked among them. But for this, those who send and those who are sent must be truly ready for sacrifice, as Jesus was. Only through the power of his sacrifice on the cross can they do it, as our Hutterian forefathers showed powerfully and shakingly on their way of martyrdom with its unprecedented effect.

Dear Brothers, these thoughts of Jesus move us deeply as the thoughts God has in his heart for us and for our corrupt time. So we ask that you accept us in love and faith as a people who belong to you and who stand at your door in order to be admitted into full unity and to come to our task and mission for the German-speaking lands. God's will has been lit up brightly for us. The recognition of his will makes us ask your and our Elias Walter to advise us in our weak beginning and to guide us from far-off America.

For this reason we plead that, as an immediate necessity, at least one of us be allowed to travel to you and that we may receive responsible brothers appointed by you as our servants of the Word and of temporal affairs. First and foremost we must ask that all your servants of the Word and stewards, out of great love, decide unanimously how to help in accordance with God's will and guidance. This means temporal and spiritual help for us, and just as much for the other poor and weak Bruderhofs. Then they and we too can be established in the best Hutterian order for zealous, hardworking Bruderhof life in complete community. Finally, with our goal for the world in view, we must ask that all Bruderhofs able to contribute do their utmost for the printing and publishing of the Hutterian writings and that an equally strong effort is made to support mission. This mission must involve spreading God's word and providing housing and hospitality for those already won and those newly awakened to Christ, so that all zealous seekers for community may be gathered in.

We cannot and do not want to go such a way for ourselves alone;

we are too weak and insufficient for this. We are standing in the very first stages of purification and development. It is hardly ten years since we set out on the way which is leading us to the true church of God. But the reality of the church has been entrusted to you by the forefathers for 400 years now. It would be a serious sin if we did not turn to you. As a pleading, small, and weak band we stand before you as before God. We give ourselves to God first, and then to you. We want to be yours in the obedience of faith, love, and discipline. As we prayed to God, so we now ask of you: "Accept us! Instruct and equip us for service!" Just as we can do nothing without Christ, so we want to do nothing without you. Nothing, nothing at all without the church, apart from the church! For it is the church of our God, of our Christ, and of the Spirit, uniting and sanctifying us all. May God use our lowliness and smallness as the means to bring you to powerful action and firmest uniting—for your good and the good of the whole world! It is God's way to prove his all-prevailing greatness in the low and insignificant, to show his strength especially in weakness. Therefore, we will gladly remain the lowliest among you in every respect, if we may only remain in community, if we may only have part in the church and in the kingdom. Therefore, we want to love weakness, so that there is nothing but the strength of Christ to uphold us and give us grace to belong to the church of God.

2 Cor.8:5

Your Neuwerk Bruderhof of the Hutterian Brethren
as we ask to be allowed to call ourselves

P.S. Please read with your church communities right through the two chapters on mutual service that Paul wrote to the richly blessed and gifted church in Corinth (II Corinthians 8 and 9).

Rhön Bruderhof, June 6, 1929

My dear Robert Friedmann,

Please forgive us that we were unable to write to you sooner and thank you for your letter. This was due to the struggles with our difficult financial situation, the continual and strenuous work with our guests, as well as my other exacting activities. Your welcome visit is often recalled among us, and then you added to our joy by sending us the pictures, the small song book, and your detailed letter of the 9th. Thank you very much for them all. I keep the pictures of the old Bruderhofs in my office next to the picture of the Stand Off Bruderhof; I enjoy seeing them every day. As soon as we can reproduce them we will mail you good copies. We treasure this gift very much. The small song book is very important for me because it contains a different type of song from the large one. I would like to ask if I may keep it until I have received the copy Elias Walter is sending me for our Bruderhof in the near future.

Unfortunately I have not heard again from Lydia Müller.[1] In the meantime Christian Hege[2] confirmed my impression that a talk with her is really very necessary for the sake of the cause. Also I want to discuss the publication of the Hutterian writings with you in Vienna— to go into the question again very thoroughly and as soon as possible. Perhaps this will be sooner than we imagine. In any case I think it would be good to do this before my journey to America. Meanwhile both of us have had time to consider the opinions and convictions we expressed to each other.

In these days I am strongly reminded of you by the two-week visit of the very gifted scholar, Dr. Hermann Buddensieg. He works with Dr. Friedrich Muckle who is certainly known to you, and he has a very similar approach to yours. He goes so far as to say that the witness of our word and communal life is the only Christianity possible today; no other kind of Christianity has any authority at all when confronted by our testimony to the truth. The Hutterian writings I gave him make an extraordinarily strong impression on this man, who has an unusually deep approach to the history of culture. Nevertheless, he does not feel urged to venture with us upon a life based upon this same witness of faith.

I am enclosing for you and especially for your dear wife a corrected transcript of our inner meetings of faith held during that time. I spoke about prayer. My dear wife and I ask you both to read this together and consider it in a quiet hour. You will find there, in the witness of truth entrusted to me, an answer to many things touched upon in your kind letter.

Eberhard then responded further to Robert Friedmann's letter with the thoughts summarized below:

The Russian religious thinker Leo Tolstoy is far removed from Anabaptism. The first Quakers, at the time of their founder George Fox in England, were much closer to Anabaptism in spirit. In fact some scholars say their beliefs came from Germany and Switzerland through Holland to England. Modern Quakerism is unthinkable without the much more clearly

---

[1] Wrote *Der Kommunismus der mährischen Wiedertäufer* (Communism of the Moravian Anabaptists), Leipzig, 1927.

[2] German Mennonite historian.

founded truth of Anabaptism, even though, like other religious and educational movements today, it has been watered down into something "purely spiritual". People forget, however, that there is no such thing as the "purely spiritual." The creative spirit of God and Jesus Christ must take on form, must show itself by transforming reality.

Eberhard Arnold tells how he broke away from the traditions of his family and church. This cost a decision which was the starting point for his faith to grow. But such a decision has to be made again and again, through struggle and at times of crisis. It always leads to a practical life really in keeping with the decision. This decision must be made freely, for inner freedom is more important than food and shelter. But it is only true where our goal is not "to be free" for the sake of freedom, but like the apostle Paul, to be bound and committed to a life active in love.

Eberhard Arnold believes Robert Friedmann is still torn and divided because he has not fully committed himself. He reminds Friedmann, who is a Jew, that the Wandering Jew roams restlessly over the face of the earth looking for answers with his mind and reason. Yet he, too, is meant to find peace by doing God's will. The true Jew knows that anyone seeking first and foremost his own personal salvation cannot find real peace. Such a one has this in common with the Jewish prophets: both believe in God and that God reaches out in love to men. But whereas the one thinks only about his personal salvation, the man who lives in the spirit of the prophets is concerned that no matter what happens to him, the will of God becomes reality on this earth. Jesus understood very well that Nathanael and Nicodemus, true Jews as they were, sought nothing but the kingdom of God.

Eberhard Arnold continues in his own words:

Now it is a tremendous thing in the Hutterian Church that it allows faith to be expressed in deed, that here and now in the active community of church life the kingdom of God is shown as justice, peace, and joy in the Holy Spirit. Therefore you must put it down to the depth and certainty of my faith when I challenge you and your beloved wife today: forsake your middle-class life; leave behind your vain efforts in social democracy and your dabbling in the too many individualistic pursuits open to you in private life in a large city today; leave also your connection with a scholarly profession which does not practice what it allows to be published. Set out to join the Hutterian Bruderhof communities in America or our own small new beginning in Hesse. You will always be welcome with us, as soon as you put your intellect under obedience to the church. The attitude to the New Testament and to the holy prophecy of the Bible which you still find difficult is after all based on nothing but the eternal unity and unanimity of this church. What we find in the Holy Scriptures is the unchangeable unity of God's Spirit, the perfect agreement of all the testimonies of the Holy Spirit which cannot be contradicted. Let me restrict myself at the moment to this conclusion: the long time span of centuries does not separate us in any way from the early church in Jerusalem. As long as God in Christ and his spirit move and fill us, our experience in the present-day church cannot be any different from that of the early church in Jerusalem. Therefore the words which have come down to us are absolutely authoritative for us as words of truth. We in no way cling to the literal meaning of the letter, but are concerned with the unanimity of the Holy Spirit's testimonies. This unites us completely with the revelation of the Word in Christ's incarnation and in his first church.

How much I would like to write more to you, but unfortunately my tight schedule does not allow it.

To conclude, please accept for both you and your dear wife the assurances of our love from our whole Bruderhof. Our hearts and doors will always remain open for you, because we belong to you in the love of the church of God.

Your Bruderhof members

John Horsch   Rhön Bruderhof, June 9, 1929
Scottdale, Pa.

Dear John Horsch,

It is a comfort to me that you have heard more exactly from our beloved Elias Walter about the severe economic pressure which unfortunately has hindered me from replying punctually to your kind letter of Feb. 2, 1929. With your kindly understanding you will realize that my strength is exhausted to the extreme by the constant responsibility for the economy of our community of more than sixty people, which has been in existence now for a considerable time, by the very demanding task of ministering to and counseling our seeking and struggling guests, and by my studies in Anabaptist research. Now that you have once again given us such kind attention and love I will set about answering your letter today at last, with heartfelt thanks for your recent work, as for instance in the *Christian Monitor*[1] of April— May 1929. All this work is extraordinarily important for us. We are looking forward with special interest to the conclusion of your new work about Hutterianism. When it is finished, please have the kindness to send us a copy right away. With all my heart I also ask you to send us the copied-out Andreas Ehrenpreis book and other writings

---

[1]Monthly magazine published by Mennonite Publishing House, Scottdale, Pa.

which you have from Elias Walter—if possible by return mail. I
would be extremely thankful if you could send the two articles by
C. A. Fischer[1] to me across the ocean as soon as possible. The libraries
won't lend me such old books for use on the Bruderhof, and working
in library reading rooms is too expensive in our present situation.
Only with the greatest difficulty can we raise enough money for a
longer stay near a library.

You have rendered a great service to our cause by arranging for
the *Wahrheitsfreund* to print my little article. Could you please do
one more thing and arrange with David Hofer and Joseph Tschetter
to put twelve copies of this article at our disposal? This would be a
further service to our cause, and perhaps the editor could look on it
as a kind of payment. Do you think that the *Mennonite Review* would
also accept an article from me? I would of course offer an original
article which would naturally be different from the one in the
Wahrheitsfreund. In the meantime our witness has also found some
acceptance among the South-German Mennonites and in the Mennonite
papers which appear in Elbing. Indeed, I must say that contemporary
Mennonites, in spite of the softening of their witness, are nearer to
us than the Baptists. Only I believe that present-day Mennonites need
to experience a new awakening to the old and ever-new recognitions
of faith and attitude to life of the original Baptizers. What you wrote
to me on Feb. 2, 1929 is certainly true. We can hardly expect so
much joy among Mennonites today at the coming into being of our
Bruderhof for them to wish to contribute any help worth mentioning
to meet our need. But the almighty and all-powerful God can move
hearts much more strongly than we can anticipate. It was a great joy
for me to hear from you that several Hutterian Bruderhofs for the love
of Christ gave practical help to Mennonites newly come from Russia.
I would like very much to hear which Bruderhofs in particular did
this, because I have such a lively interest in the individual communities
that I wish to visualize more clearly the spiritual and practical life on
this or that Bruderhof. For instance, I would very much like to become
clearer about the elder service among Hutterites.[2] Is David Hofer,
Rockport, the elder for all the Lehrerleut communities which have
branched out from Rockport? Was the Elias Walter who died last
year, uncle of our Elias Walter, the elder for all the Darius Bruderhofs
which branched out from Wolf Creek? And does the service of such
an elder exist for the Schmiedeleut communities which branched out

---

[1]C. A. Fischer (1560-c.1610) wrote at least four books of slanderous attacks on the Hutterites.
[2]See Introduction to Chapter 2.

from Bon Homme? Our dear Hutterian brothers are always so very busy that one does not receive an answer, as one would wish, to all one's questions. I think that the service of elder with overall responsibility was as important for the entire Hutterian Church as the sending out of brothers on mission. However, it is a great joy to me that in the individual communities the moral stand taken by the Hutterites, the seriousness of their obedience, and the faithful perseverance in community of goods is still just as living today. Likewise it is evident that the foundation of the Hutterian faith is as valid as ever on all Bruderhofs. I am therefore looking forward very much to the journey to my beloved American Hutterites, although I am quite certain that not everything will have the original freshness and power of the beginning times after four hundred years of continuity, temporarily interrupted, and after more than fifty years of living in America. It is my conviction that the goodness and patience of our beloved High Priest Jesus Christ is vital here, he who knows and carries our weakness. Also vital is the faith that in every moment of history the Spirit of Jesus Christ can break in and break through, making us free and awakening us anew to holy fervour, so that the world-shaking historical hour of God's calling comes once again today, as it did once before.

You understand, therefore, beloved John Horsch, that nothing more can prevent or deter me from achieving a complete uniting with the Hutterian Brothers in America. After all, our convictions at our Bruderhof in Hesse are in every respect absolutely the same, that is, identical with the living, active convictions of early Hutterianism. And I am deeply convinced that still today this is the serious will and faith of the Hutterian Bruderhofs in America, no less than with us here.

I thank you from my heart for the information about where the School Orders are printed. The old Craftsman's Orders for which I have been searching have been preserved in the Austrian Archives. This was put together in great detail by Andreas Ehrenpreis, with numerous notes in his own hand. I think they must surely be in the hands of the American Hutterites also. I had hoped that you would have such a document in your possession and could send it to us, but I assume from your letter that this is not the case. This Craftsman's *Ordnung* is naturally of outstanding significance for our newly-established Hutterian life, particularly as we live so far away from the American Hutterian Brothers, whose practice in their community of goods and community of work must certainly have adjusted to their new conditions.

Unfortunately, my book on the Baptizers about which you so kindly

inquire has not yet been published. I have drawn up an index of
several hundred books and papers and intend to make a comprehensive
survey of the Baptizers of Reformation times from my standpoint—
namely, that Hutterianism in Moravia was the actual and complete
fulfillment of the Baptizer movement. Naturally this will cost much
work, so I cannot say anything definite about when it will appear.
It's quite possible, however, that before the main work appears I will
publish some papers which will clarify single aspects of the old
Baptizer movement. I must say frankly that I am not quite as satisfied
with the book by Dr. Ernst Correll as I had hoped. I would be very
glad if I could enter into correspondence with him. Nevertheless he
is much nearer the cause than a Dr. Lydia Müller whose basic attitude
I very much regret for the sake of Anabaptism and Hutterianism. Your
books, which you have sent us out of your sincere interest in our
life's work, are very important to us. Different groups in our small
community are continually occupied with working on them.

I am very thankful to you for referring us to such people as
Orie O. Miller[1] in Akron, Pa. Perhaps you may have time to write
and tell us something about him and others who sympathize with our
cause. Please greet him from us. But above all things I thank you
heartily for your loving gift of ten dollars and for your representing
our cause to David Hofer, Rockport, and David Hofer, Chicago
(*Wahrheitsfreund*). Even the smallest sum could mean a decisive help
of God to us in our daily difficulties. Also in this letter I could report
much, very much, about the endless difficulties which our extensive
hospitality and acceptance of poor children bring in the way of
economic need, care, and anxiety. But I do not want to burden your
heart too much with all this. Through God's grace, the faith is living
in all the Brotherhood members in our little community that at the
right time we shall receive at least as much help as we need to hold
us together—even if we have to endure the bitterest privation and
difficulties. And the very fact that for nine years we have been able
to carry through a life and work community for a slowly growing
circle without any financial means worth mentioning is in itself an
unheard-of miracle. God can continue to do this even if we often do
not see a way by which we can escape the threat to our communal
existence. With trust in the protecting power of Christ and his spirit,
I believe I may say that we will never forsake the way of communal
dedication to the service of the church, though we may have to go

---

[1]Member, later executive secretary, of the Mennonite Central Committee.

through the severest catastrophes, even destruction.

With the warmest thanks of our whole Brotherhood for your kindly interest in our task and situation, I remain in the sincerest love of Christ and God's Spirit, your thankful

Eberhard Arnold

Robert Friedmann
Neuberg in Steiermark, Austria
July 3, 1929

Dear Eberhard Arnold, dear members of the Bruderhof,

My greetings to you all! Thank you very much for your letter and greetings of June 6. Forgive me for not replying before; your kind letter required an immediate answer, but this was really not possible. I had neither the time nor the leisure for such serious business, and therefore I postponed answering until the long summer vacation, which began for us the day before yesterday. Now we are out here in the beautiful mountain area of Styria at the edge of a forest which leads up to a 6,000 ft. mountain. I will try in the quiet of the night to answer your letter as well as I can, and write about a few other things as well.

Your letter made a great impression on us, and I want to thank you for the truly brotherly attitude expressed in it. I took your letter very seriously, particularly your challenge to come to the Bruderhof. I really must say that basically I agree with it. If my way should not lead me there, I believe nevertheless that the way you have started to go is—I cannot say the only right one, but certainly one right way—indeed, a very significant one toward the goal: the kingdom of God. I feel as you do about this. If I still have not reached that point and decide differently, this has good and valid reasons. First of all there is my profession, which really satisfies me and does, after all, allow me a wide field of activity which I value not a little. Then I am already thirty-eight years of age, and any change is more difficult than it was in my young years, although, of course, I do not feel at all old yet. However, I am already somewhat less flexible than ten or fifteen years ago. Furthermore, I have to say that my wife, with whom, by the way, I am very much in harmony, feels somewhat differently from me just in these questions. She is a theosophist. She has learned a certain amount from me about Anabaptism and feels it as something foreign and unsuited to her. I understand and respect this all the more because I have the same reaction to theosophy, in spite of recognizing and appreciating the great value of this movement. Regarding living in a large city (which you mention), you are right, of course, that ultimately it is not a field of action for people like us, although it may sometimes appear so. For it must lead to too much distraction, superficiality, and illusion, even if, like Vienna, the large city is not a typical one. Yet the city has tasks for us. People there are pining for instruction, strengthening, guidance, and a meaning to life. Even the task of education is not just self-delusion.

In actual fact the "creed," the confession of faith, would not stand in my way. If I were living among you, the meaning of the biblical word, too, would become alive for me, and the spirituality which I carry to extremes would certainly be the least obstacle. By the way, I think perhaps you are unfair to me here. I do not particularly believe in a "pure" spirit but definitely follow Ragaz,[1] who speaks of a "holy materialism" because, after all, the Word became flesh. This is quite clear to me. Christianity makes sense to me even though my creed is still quite vague, like Tolstoy's. Because of my whole spiritual development this is only to be expected. On two occasions in my life I experienced moments of decision which made me what I consciously am today. But without such decisions nothing can happen, and *I* cannot bring them about at will. You know what it is to receive something—something that happens and one has to accept it and is humbled by it in spite of the "freedom" I have praised so much, and which you (apparently) misunderstood in my letter.

For I myself do not believe in an unlimited, anarchist freedom which one would not know what to do with, and I am in favor of the higher bondage accepted "in freedom." By means of this, the other, unrestricted freedom ceases to enslave one. This "freedom of fulfillment," of service, is what I had in mind—the freedom which makes all fear of death, all dread, all lack of freedom in life vanish. It is the freedom of the kingdom of God. In the last issue of *Neue Wege* (New Ways), Ragaz writes so well about "false independence" exactly in the sense I mean. And there is a task here for us *too*: through love to give other people such freedom, to give them trust, strength, awareness of a deeper security; to liberate them from chains (from which almost everyone suffers) and in this way make them able to live a true life. Only love can do this. For me this task means to carry out the work entrusted to me; it means fulfillment of the meaning of my life, as of every life. ... But enough of this!

---

[1]Swiss pastor and Religious Socialist.

Now about other matters. Yesterday (when I at last had complete quiet) I began to read the beautiful Jakob Böhme book, your present to me, inscribed in such a loving way when I was your guest. This is really a very wonderful book with a remarkable depth of wisdom and piety....

I received a very disagreeable impression regarding official church history from a small booklet which I worked through in Vienna. It is called, "Discussion of an Anabaptist with a Pietist," by Wolleb, Basel, 1722 (Mennonite library in Amsterdam). In the end the pietist went so far as to glorify making false statements, as long as it causes the Anabaptist to recant. This is a bad aspect of pietism, but understandable all the same if one bears in mind that for pietists the organized church had to be protected and it was the organized church that was attacked by Anabaptism, by the fighters for the kingdom of God. By the way, Bossert wrote to me that he believes it was just the Anabaptism in Württemberg which gradually changed over to pietism during or after the Thirty Years War. Perhaps Arndt[1] represents the connecting link. Strangely enough it was in Württemberg (Swabia), where the return from pietism to Anabaptism began: in Bad Boll. What you wrote me on this point, particularly about the contrast between pietism and prophetism, is very true and very profound. However, it is strange how these two movements could come to stand so close to one another.

Do you know that a very valuable Hutterian manuscript is to be found in Wolfenbüttel?[2] Liliencron described it in the reports of the Bavarian Academy of Sciences (1877). It contains hymns and some writings by Peter Walpot, particularly his three Articles. It also contains the letter of 1577 to the Swiss on the River Rhine and is about uniting. I am more and more of the opinion that the Great Article Book is the most important book of the Hutterites, alongside Peter Riedemann's *Confession of Faith*. As soon as I have finished my research on this book, I will publish it. Lydia Müller will have the whole work published by the Association for Religious History. Wiswedel has it at the moment; he has received in Schmalkalden all the one hundred folders of Beck's literary bequests from Brünn.

Please do not forget to obtain the beautiful book by Rufus Jones from the Quaker Publishing House: *The Spiritual Reformers of the 16th and 17th Centuries*. In it Hans Denck, Schwenckfeld, Bünderlin,

---

[1] Johann Arndt (1555-1621), German Lutheran, author of *True Christianity*.

[2] Copied out by Michael Hasel (Weber) who was captured when on mission for the Hutterian Church and died in prison at Hohenwittlingen, 1592.

Weigel, and especially Jakob Böhme are mentioned as the spiritual fathers of Quakerism. I point this out because on various occasions we discussed the relationship of Quakers and Anabaptists. To be sure, it is only concerned with the so-called "Spiritualists" (Troeltsch), and therefore with the actual opponents of Anabaptist biblicism in the narrower sense. The book, by the way, is good and valuable in itself. Actually historical facts by themselves can never prove whether this, that, or another conviction was held by George Fox. In any case I have to admit that for us today Quakerism is the type of movement which makes a somewhat watered-down impression when compared with strict Hutterianism. Nevertheless something great remains. Just two days before my departure I was invited to the Quakers because some "religious pacifists" were meeting there (the composition of the group was very important, it appeared to me), and my opinion of them was confirmed.

Actually I have much more to write to you, but this letter is getting longer and longer and, as a result, more confusing. So I will break off for now, as it is already 1:30 a.m. and time to stop. Just one thing more: we will be very glad to make preparations for your Vienna lecture or lectures in the autumn, as soon as we know when we can expect you. There will be many points of contact, many tasks for you....

Warm and loving greetings to you and to all your co-workers, brothers and sisters. I hope to hear from you again soon. My wife greets you most cordially too. I cannot greet you from my children, as they are still far too small for this. But they give us unspeakable joy in sunshine and love—you will be able to appreciate this best of all.

Your Robert Friedmann

Report of a meeting with the Brotherhood and novices at the Rhön Bruderhof, August 11, 1929.

On Sunday, August 11, 1929, at 9 a.m. and again at 5 p.m. the Brotherhood and novices (those new members who have been accepted for a time of testing) gathered to consider the meaning of our present times for the future of the Bruderhof. There were more than thirty persons together, all open to be shown the will of the church. And without exception everyone took part to get clear the following points:

1.   It is necessary to continually strengthen and deepen the basis of faith of our Hutterian Bruderhof. We need to gather ever anew in quiet hours to let the Holy Spirit speak to the church and bring about

the unity which shows itself as the strength to serve one another. We need to be led deeper and deeper into the Bible. During these hours reverence for the church, for the holy cause of the kingdom of God, should be awakened and strengthened in all, including guests and helpers. Our work in the spring and summer was strenuous—partly too much so—and now we see that we are at a turning point when again we have to win more time, strength, and vigor for the things of the spirit.

2. The fact that we have come nearer and nearer to Hutterianism and to our Hutterian brothers in America and that we, for our part, feel completely united with them, gives us a deep thankfulness for God's loving leading. For we owe it to the Hutterian writings and to the reality of the Hutterian Church founded in God that infinitely much has become clear to us, and that we have been helped forward. Therefore, we confirm again that Eberhard Arnold's journey should be undertaken as soon as at all possible, so that we may be accepted and taken in by the church communities in South Dakota, Manitoba, and Canada, and our task in Germany may receive their blessing.

3. The Orders of the Hutterian brothers, which our beloved Elias Walter Vetter sent us from America in three different books, arrived at the right moment, just as we were writing down the basis of our life in community, its structure and orders. Both belong inseparably together, since we recognize and affirm God's guidance in the fact that the orders of our communal life are in complete agreement with the old orders of the Hutterian brothers. The community, organically fused together in its order, as stated in the first section of our writing *Foundation and Orders*, should lead all members of the Brotherhood, all novices, and all sincere and resolute future members to find their true calling, giving their best and utmost in the daily work. So once again it becomes clear that the Hutterian services are as necessary with us as they were in each of the old Hutterian households in Moravia, and as they are on the Hutterian Bruderhofs today. We need a firm and concentrated leadership for the work. The Word leader, or servant of the Word, who oversees and is responsible for everything, should have at his side the housemother, the steward, and the work distributor. Each work department has its own responsible brothers who belong to the Brotherhood.

4. We are considering again how our poverty and debts nearly brought us to catastrophe in recent months. Only a miracle of God's grace enabled us to avoid it. We thank God and his church for the help we received. Some came from German and Swiss friends, from

the government, and from the work done on our Bruderhof, but most came through the Hutterian brothers in America. We thank God that we were able to prevent this catastrophe little by little. We thank God that it was not done all at once by the help of one large sum, but, because help has come through many little sums, we have learned something. It is clear to us that a catastrophe, though not quite so severe, still threatens us, and that we must still ask God and his church for support. Although the compulsory auction of the Werkhof,[1] set for August 9, 1929, was cancelled on July 25, we are now threatened with another compulsory auction through an order of payment from our main supplier of building materials. We owe him 8,000 marks for the children's house we built in 1928. At the same time we renew the decision that we reached together with Elias Walter: no new debts are to be made, and all we owe to people either unwilling or unable to prolong their credit, must be paid in full before we start any undertaking requiring new expenditure. This statement, however, does not prevent us from recognizing that the numerous visits we receive from guests and friends, and the growing number of novices and of requests for the novitiate, make it so absolutely necessary to extend and improve the buildings of our Bruderhof that we see in this the will of God. The capital must be raised, and a carefully considered proposal for a budget for all work departments must be drawn up.

5.   For the tasks involved in our work, it is clear that we must continue winning people who are fully dedicated to the cause. Our agriculture and market gardening, our income-bringing handicrafts, publishing house, office, and domestic work need the support of capable, reliable workers. When we draw guests and helpers into the work, it is of the greatest importance that they be led in real love and clarity until they reach the decision for church community, and so leave everything behind in order to devote their lives and all their strength to God's kingdom. Only if our working strength is increased by a good number of capable workers can we provide sufficient food for our large circle. In this connection we are particularly grateful that recently, after some very lean times, the above-mentioned help has improved our standard of food and general care. Unity, as mutual trust and confidence, must remain in full force in all work departments—as the frank word of direct admonition, both for the very smallest offenses, and in the sense of church discipline; and as mutual practical help in relieving one another in the work. It must be

---

[1]Part of the Rhön Bruderhof with workshops and farm buildings.

in the spirit of humility and tenderness, yet with firmness and certainty.

6.   At this moment, strengthening and extending our community goes together with the will of the church that a new people shall be called into being within the church through the marriages we have decided and affirmed. If God grants us the grace, a people will come into existence here, and continue into future generations, who will serve the church of God and the kingdom of God in obedience born of faith and leading to work. It is perfectly clear to us that this decision made before God creates the need for increased living space and opportunities for work, as stated in point 5. In great thankfulness for God's leading we declare that this decision on church marriages for our younger generation was affirmed with the holy earnestness and reverence that befits the church. This affirmation took place as we stood in a circle with flaming torches for the solemn reading of our *Foundation and Orders*.

7.   We are at a very important moment in our children's community also. The children in the top grades of our school have been sent by the Brotherhood to receive further trainings which will prepare them for life and work in the community. Hans Grimm and Hardy Arnold began this training one and a half years ago, Emy-Margret Arnold last year—the first three from our children's community. We have made it clear that the older children may remain on the Bruderhof only if they can honestly accept and witness to the foundation of faith and the ordered way of life of the church. It is vital to expect the same awakening of divine zeal and divine love in our middle and lower grades as we have experienced for years past in our present upper grades. In the coming months, and especially in the winter, the educational tasks of our common life should receive more attention than they have had up to now. Eberhard Arnold was asked to obtain as soon as possible a copy of the School Orders [*Schulordnungen*] of the Hutterian Brethren.

8.   The whole church emphasized anew that still this year we should act on the unanimous Brotherhood decision to send out on mission our Word leader, Eberhard Arnold, accompanied by another member of the Brotherhood if possible. So we have to face many decisions about next winter in order for us all to gain, by serving souls within the church, the strength and maturity to serve those outside.

We give thanks to God that his will for mission is confirmed again and again by the great number of our guests and helpers. In recent days, counting grownups and children, there have been ninety people on the Bruderhof. The number of novice requests is slowly growing.

The latest request comes from the Kunzelmanns, a family of five. This, together with the many visits from relatives and friends, is a sign from God that we are called and chosen to proclaim the truth, waken the world, and gather new people zealous in the faith. Vienna and Halle are to be the starting points for our mission of reawakening men to the gospel and gathering them through proclaiming the Word.

The following questions about our publishing work were also spoken about: the new issue of *Die Wegwarte*, especially devoted to Andreas Ehrenpreis's Sendbrief and the basis of our education; the publication of Hutterian writings—we are already reading them in our circle and they are a tremendous strength and inspiration (we shall always be grateful to Elias Walter for them); the collection of songs—and here the Hutterian songbooks are basic for the work; the writing of our ten-year-long history in connection with our *Foundation and Orders*; further work on the "Source Books of Christian Witness".....

Jakob Hofer   Rhön Bruderhof
Pincher Station   September 14, 1929
Alberta, Canada

Beloved Jakob Hofer,

Christian Waldner Vetter, now the faithful elder and father of our Darius Bruderhofs, wrote to us on July 2, 1929, when he decided upon and sent one hundred dollars for our need. In this letter he mentioned your name: "Herewith I send you, Eberhard Arnold, one hundred dollars from Jakob Hofer for those asking for help in Germany, with the hope of helping them in their greatest need."

If we understand rightly that you together with your Pincher Bruderhof have a share in these hundred dollars or gave them yourselves, please accept our most heartfelt thanks. God has helped us forward a good stretch through the alms of about twelve Hutterian Bruderhofs, so that we don't need to go as hungry as before. Still our need is great since we are hard pressed by about $7,000 of our worst debts, with the danger of our being driven from house and home this fall or at the beginning of winter. But we trust in God that he will continue to provide a way out of this serious need, so that we can find a way through and remain on the right path of true community.

If your dear community has done for us all you felt possible and right, as we believe, continue to help us through your prayers and perhaps also by encouraging other Bruderhofs, for instance those around Rockyford, to send us alms too. Or even your dear community might dare something once again? I am forced to make a repeated plea because I cannot leave our faithful, hardworking, dedicated brothers and sisters, our young people and children who are being awakened to faith and love, in their deep need and danger.

For the sake of our sixty big and small people, I take it upon myself joyfully to stand again and again at your doors as a beggar. I am encouraged to do so because Jesus our beloved Lord promises us that the poor are blessed and that he who begs, almost shamelessly, at the windows of his friend by night and before the strict judge has the promise of being heard.

Again and again we express only one wish: that you get to know us personally by meeting us face to face. I am ready to undertake joyfully the big journey over the ocean and across the wide American continent, all the more if the time has not yet come for two of your brothers to be sent to us for at least one year and possibly longer, one for the service of the Word and one for the service of temporal affairs. We heard that at the last preachers' meeting of the Dariusleut no unanimity could be reached on this matter, but instead God gave you joyful unanimity in deciding on the spirit-filled, blessed, and respected Christian Waldner as elder and father of our Darius communities. From our hearts we ask him and all of you to receive us, as a daughter community of Stand Off, into the circle of the Darius communities as soon as our gracious God gives you clarity and certainty that we are and will be a real Hutterian *Gemein*.[1] Right now we can get close to each other only by faithfully exchanging letters and writing frequently back and forth.

So we then ask of you also, beloved Jakob Hofer, in spite of the great amount of work you surely have to do, that you be so loving as to write to us frequently and quite in detail about how you are doing inwardly and outwardly at the Pincher Bruderhof, how many brothers and sisters and children you have, which old Hutterian writings you have on hand, and what counsels and prayers you have on your hearts for us. Surely you have already received several letters from us, and maybe my writing now may cause you to send us at last a loving letter from you and from your Bruderhof. We very much ask this of you. You can hardly imagine how endlessly glad our little flock is for each line and each word, even if very brief, from your American Bruderhofs.

---

[1] A church community in the order of the Hutterian Church.

The eagerness of our little flock for your love and for complete union with you, yes, for each believing and loving word from you, is like a tormenting hunger and a burning thirst for the justice of God and his church. Each day when the mailman brings the post, our most urgent and burning question is whether there is a letter from you. Please, please think of this and write soon.

Our little flock stands faithfully and firmly together. Not only the immediate circle of sixteen brotherhood members—now already proved for many years—but also the wider circle of nineteen beginners and young people growing up among us is on fire with the holy enthusiasm of God's love and with faith in Christ and his Holy Spirit. In spite of all the affliction and want we suffer, great joy and enthusiasm reign among us. And even when the brothers and sisters are ever so tired in the evening after a day of hard work, they are still there at the evening *Gebet*[1] and at the *Lehr*[1] in expectant watchfulness and enthusiastic eagerness, and they cannot hear enough about the faith and struggles, life and sufferings of the early Hutterian fighters. As often as a free moment permits them, they read the old Hutterian writings and history books, and best of all Peter Riedemann's *Confession of Faith*. This book has made the strongest impression on all of us, so that we confess to everything in it as the revealed truth of God and want to live by it entirely, as far as God gives us grace.

Our little flock is different from your long-proven Bruderhofs in that we have no one among us who is fifty years old or more except for a seventy-year-old guest, grandmother of one of our children, who is not yet united with us on the basis of true faith. There are only five of us between forty and fifty years old, six between thirty and forty, thirteen between twenty and thirty, and five between seventeen and twenty. Then there are also five young people of fifteen or sixteen, who are also founded in faith. As a result of the earnestness of our life of struggle, they have already clearly and joyfully decided to stand with God and his church. Even among our other younger children there is, to our great joy, a very strong and conscious life of faith and deep readiness for love and community. These children also come frequently together for prayer.

A further characteristic of our mission post, isolated in the midst of the large German-speaking areas of Europe, is our steady flow of guests, for whom we need your special prayers. For it is a great struggle and a heavy task both temporally and spiritually that in the

---

[1]*Gebet*, daily meeting for worship in the evening; *Lehr* is held on Sunday morning.

course of each summer several hundred people come to us to get to
know our faith and our community life. All too often these people
have very confused, dark ideas about God and his cause, so that it is
quite difficult to bring the witness of truth and the life of love home
to them in such a way that they are shaken up, moved, and put before
the decision to choose one of the two ways: the way to death or the
way to life. Nevertheless, we have the joy that some are deeply gripped
to feel and perceive what God wants. And even if many leave again
sadly because, like the rich young man, they will not give up their
own lives, possessions, civil or private professions, love for family
and home, and worldly outlook on life, nevertheless we know of many
others who, after their visit to our Bruderhof, struggle deeply within
themselves as to whether they should leave everything to join the true
community of the church of God.

For this reason we ask you from our hearts, beloved Jakob Hofer,
to stand at our side in all these struggles in faithful prayer and faithful
counsel and faithful help. The task is great and our strength is small.
Without Christ and his Holy Spirit, without God and his church we
can do nothing. So we are completely dependent on you, beloved
Hutterian brothers. We know well that we put a load on you. Nevertheless, we may give your faith and your love a little joy if we put
the great responsibility for this small Bruderhof in Germany on you,
asking you to carry it on your hearts and accept us, bless us, fit us
out, and send us out.

Your Bruderhof members in Germany!
Eberhard Arnold

Rhön Bruderhof
September 14 to October 9, 1929

Very dear John Horsch,

Your loving letter of August 16, 1929 has occupied me very much.
Above all, I must thank you for your great love and consideration
in sending us the Hutterian book from Elias Walter as well as
C. A. Fischer's attack on the Hutterites, to help us in deepening our
faith, and in our research and publishing work. Both books concern
us very much, and we are also looking for a reply to Fischer by the
brothers. We are very eager to see the conclusion of your article in
the *Mennonite Quarterly Review*. We would also be *very* thankful for
a copy of the Hutterian School Orders. We would copy it and return
it within a few weeks. Have you in Scottdale any more of the old,

good, original writings of the first Baptizers from the time 1525—
1545? Sometime later I will send you an article for the *Mennonite
Review* which will be put together differently from the one in the
Wahrheitsfreund, and I thank you for your understanding help.

I am very happy about your valuable conclusion as a historian that
Hutterianism in its best period is the purest expression of the original
Anabaptist idea. For me there is no question about it, not only because
of the inner experience of my heart, but also because of plain historical
facts.

Also I thank you from my heart for the trust you have shown me
in describing the close contact you and your dear wife had with the
deceased Elias Walter, father of the Dariusleut; you also tell about
your selfless work in your community settlement and your children's
work. This reminds us very much of the beginnings of our work in
Sannerz.[1] Last month I sent a ninety-page report to Elias Walter; in
this the witness of our history and the order of our community during
the last ten years are described in detail, based on exact historical
facts and on our own documents. You can see quite clearly from this
that orders which are in keeping with the spirit-led organism of the
Body of Christ must come into being, not only in times of weariness
and falling away, as when Andreas Ehrenpreis was elder, but also in
times of enthusiastic, spirit-filled advance, as at the time of Jakob
Hutter. We have experienced this here in a very small and humble
degree, and are experiencing it just now, after having received to our
great and deep joy three different little books, really old ones, with
Orders of the early Hutterites. The mystery of the Body of Christ is
entrusted not only to Paul, but in an especially deep and powerful
way to the life of full community.

If only you were not so far away, you and your dear wife, who in
the opinion of old Elias would make a good community sister, you
could soon come to visit us! Perhaps it will be possible one day?

It is understandable that you could find your way more enthusiastically in a new beginning of old Hutterianism as it is among
us, than in the faithful, obedient continuation of the old Bruderhofs.
For us, two things are wonderfully brought together in Hutterianism:
on the one hand, the gospel of personal conversion and rebirth through
the reconciling blood of Christ which makes each of us a child of
God; and on the other hand, the gospel applied to social relationships
which makes all life holy when we follow the early church and put
into practice the words of Jesus, the Sermon on the Mount, Acts 2-4,

---

[1]Where Eberhard Arnold's family and a few friends began community life in 1920.

and Jesus' mission task—Matthew 10 and 18, etc.

That is an infinite and undeserved grace for which we praise God. That and nothing else is needed by our age, which is under the curse and is crying out for God's kingdom. It is needed especially, but not only, by the working class.

This, and the enthusiasm of the Holy Spirit which overflows in joy and faithfulness to the community, explains our certainly slow but nevertheless evident growth. Up to now, we can count thirty inwardly renewed community members, and experience a wonderful awakening among the thirty children. This grace leads to the rousing, awakening effect which our Bruderhof has on its visitors, and we look forward to the same impact and so to rich fruits from the lectures and mission journey which will now take me to Vienna. But like all genuine life from God, this depends completely on the undeserved gift that, through Christ, God grants us his Holy Spirit again and again.

I have received several open-hearted letters, full of deep faith, from present-day Hutterites, and I now know that their servants of the Word believe in the biblical gospel, that they call upon the Holy Spirit, and value the old evangelical books of the first Hutterian era. An example is this splendid book of Baptism and Lord's Supper teachings copied out by M.M., Matthias Müller, which is in our hands. I therefore find absolutely no hindrance to seeking and believing in a complete uniting with the present-day Hutterites. This is in spite of the centuries-old tradition, which all too easily brings a gradual loss of the first zeal of faith, love, and personal experience of Christ. For to them is entrusted God's truth in its unique reality; and their calling on the Holy Spirit proves that the living breath of truth is not and cannot be extinguished.

I am very interested in your remarks on present-day Mennonitism, as represented by Correll, Miller, and Bender. I am having an exchange of ideas with them. Please give Harold S. Bender a most cordial invitation to visit us. The question of financial resources is certainly one of serious urgency for us, but it can never be the main thing; now, as always, the poorest guests are especially welcome among us. However, the financial help which we have received this year from twelve Hutterian Bruderhofs is more important to us than any other assistance, because it is for them, above all others, to support us and help us forward in all the concerns of our faith.

With the heartfelt plea that you may take my bold words as a living expression of my love for you, with sincere greetings, also to your dear wife, from our other Bruderhof members too,

                                                            Eberhard Arnold

Elias Walter, Stand Off Colony
Macleod, Alberta, Nov. 25, 1929

Friend Horsch,

In response to your letter, I want to say that I have not received the *Mennonite Quarterly Review* for this year, maybe because it was not paid for. About the corrections I can also say nothing. I received the *Blätter für Württembergische Kirchengeschichte* (Periodical for the Church History of Württemberg) parts one and two, 1929, from Herr Bossert; it must be a different one from the one you have.

C. A. Fischer's books, *Taubenkobel* and *54 Ursachen* (Dovecote and Fifty-four Causes) are now available bound in one volume only, not two. Fischer must have had it printed several times, but it deals always with the same content. It goes right against my conscience to give out money for these blasphemies. There are obviously barefaced lies in them.

Robert Friedmann has written me a long letter which I enclose and ask to have returned. Also Arnold writes letters, so fine and so long, that it would take a theologian to answer them. I have often wished I had such gifts. He is working on B. W. Clark, and it will be published shortly in German. The History Book also is under his supervision. It is indeed a shame that such people are so poor, else the researching would go better. It appears that the archives are not so closed any more, and much is being discovered. But it is regrettable that we Hutterian brothers do so little to bring to the light and to the public the teachings of our forefathers. This would be the easiest kind of mission. Although it is not to be expected that many people will in fact overcome themselves to live so. It might be, however, that there are many who admit that it is the actual will of God and a work of the Holy Spirit. Arnold speaks very well and deeply about these things.

It is already 20°F below zero; really horrible weather.

Greetings,

E. Walter

David Wipf   Rhön Bruderhof
Hutterian Church of Wolf Creek   December 31, 1929
South Dakota, USA

Beloved David Wipf,

Lately we have been thinking a lot about you especially and your Wolf Creek Bruderhof, because we had received news through Elias

Walter of your move to Alberta. We also heard again that Old Elm Spring is in the process of moving there. We would be very grateful to you if we could be informed in good time of such important things. We also hear through Elias Walter that in spite of the dryness you had the joy of harvesting good grain, watermelons, plums, and grapes.

But above all we are interested in the news that the two daughters of Dr. A. A. Wipf[1] were in Germany. We are very sorry they heard nothing about us and did not come to us.

If those traveling in Germany have visited the Mennonites, they must have heard about us at Erich Gotters in Danzig, at Dr. [of Theology] Händiges in Elbing, and above all among the Mennonites in southern Germany, for example, Dr. Neff and Christian Hege.

Much more important, of course, would be a visit from Dr. A. A. Wipf himself. He wanted to leave America already at the end of September and even had his ticket. For us it would be of great significance if he would visit us here, tell about you, and bring you news of how he found our Bruderhof and our communal life. If you can reach him, please write and tell him that we heartily invite him to visit us.

In the meantime we had the joy of receiving greetings from Zacharias Hofer and a few pictures of the Iberville Bruderhof through the Hamburg America Line Shipping Company. A representative from that line looked us up and took a few notes on how he found things. The Hamburg America Line told us they would send a letter to Zacharias Hofer with the impressions their representative received on his visit to our Bruderhof.

Please write to Zacharias Hofer asking for the letter, though I don't believe the Hamburg America Line will have a deep understanding for the community and I do not know the contents of their letter. Yet I hope their personal report will tell you a few things about us which we perhaps have not yet written to you.

In the meantime we had the great joy of receiving your December 7 and 9 letters and can look forward to your Christmas package in which you are sending us a suit and dress from your *Tracht*.[2] We thank you from our hearts for this deed of love and ask you to thank also Joshua Hofer, your wife Anna, and your Bruderhof.

For us the significance of our dress is just as important as it always has been to the Brothers. We stand out in our area in that we have

---

[1] Doctor of Freeman, S.D., who treated Eberhard Arnold's eye when he was at Wolf Creek.
[2] Hutterian style of clothing.

freed ourselves from the fashions of the times. Our clothing is in several respects similar to that of the oldest *Tracht* worn by the first brothers and sisters in Moravia. We are glad to be able to unite with you in this simple, modest clothing, as in all inner questions, for we are used to separating ourselves from the world in all things. A few of our brothers have already become used to a beard. I am sorry that I myself do not have much of a beard. We also want to adopt your way of combing our hair. In Moravia I had the joy of seeing your hair style with the parting in the middle and the longer hair.

Altogether my visit to Sabatisch and Velké Leváre (Gross Schützen) and to the libraries and archives there was important. I brought many important things with me, which I have reported about in more detail to Elias Walter. Most of all I enjoyed seeing the old houses, of which we have quite a few pictures. I believe that our communal life and the building up of our Bruderhof is most like the oldest Hutterian households. In respect to the economy, our situation is probably more to be compared with the beginning of the church of God in Moravia at the time of Jakob Hutter and Peter Riedemann than with your economic situation today in America. We are surely in a much more difficult situation than you because we have a constant increase of new people from outside. On the whole you have to provide only for the already firmly established Bruderhofs and for their extension as your families grow bigger.

The most difficult thing for us is that most of the people who come have very little or no money at all. But we have to take them in and include them in our communal life if they prove to be truly founded in faith, zealous and hardworking, and are truly submissive and surrendered.

At the moment our small, weak Bruderhof has to care for almost seventy people. Again in the last weeks four new people have asked to become full members and are prepared to submit to the church of God. These we are ready to accept for a time of testing, proving, and trial.

Because we lack living space and have no money to build, we have had to put off several older and younger people who are eagerly seeking the faith. We are really very sorry about this. These beloved people are really prepared to go the way of the church, and it hurts us when we cannot make it possible for them to come right away.

All these things I have to consider and talk over very carefully with you. I thank you from my heart for your and Joshua Hofer's readiness for me to travel first to South Dakota and Wolf Creek at the beginning of my journey in America. We thank you that you are satisfied and certain that then we will be able to deal with everything better than is possible by letter.

Elias Walter and Christian Waldner both wrote to me that I should come over to you as soon as it seems to me and to us all to be the right moment. We believe now that this moment should be chosen as soon as possible. We suggest February as the date for departure, and we have asked for the money for this journey. It is very painful to us, dear David Wipf, that because of our pressing financial state we have to write again and again about our money situation. I understand from your kind letters that your harvest is not a very good one and that both the Huron Bruderhof and the Bruderhofs around Rockyford have asked you for help. I understand also that because you have to carry out your great responsibilities toward your own communities, you cannot also think of helping our new beginning which is so far away. I can very much feel with you in this, and we all here would be very glad if you are able to give the help asked for by the Bruderhofs in Alberta near Calgary, and Huron. All the more, I can pour out my heart to you that for us it is a miracle that we got through the year 1929 without being driven from house and home.

After these wonderful experiences of God's help, also through the faithful services of your different communities, we should not be too anxious nor let ourselves get depressed. In spite of the prospects for January and February being good, as we look toward the new year of 1930, the demands of those to whom we owe money are very harsh and extremely dangerous for us.

We ask you, together with your dear Wolf Creek Community, to intercede for us, asking that God may lead us through the next months as he has done up to now through his indescribable grace. We thank you and all from our hearts that you have shown yourselves so faithfully concerned because the light of truth has been lit among us too. It is a great grace from God that our thirty-five to forty adult believers and those growing up are able to confess ever more deeply and joyfully to the true foundation of faith and that they seek the true church of God.

How much I will be able to tell you when I come to you, and how deeply I will take part in all that I will see and experience with you! I will then hear all that you will share with me about your planned purchase and move, about your sister and your two brothers in Canada, also about your brother Paul, who was teacher for nineteen years and servant of the Word for nine years, your father-in-law who was your elder, and of the faithful service your Josua Hofer is now performing among you with the help of your Peter Hofer.

We greet you with the wonderful impression we received through your Christmas teaching on Isaiah 9 and Isaiah 11. We found this old Hutterian teaching in a manuscript of 1652 at Herrnhut and we have copied it here. Johannes Waldner had sent it in 1804 to the *Brüder-Gemeinde* (Moravian Brethren). This teaching, like all old Hutterian teachings, has made the profoundest and deepest impression on our developing community. We really ask you to please send us again and again many of the old teachings and writings, also for the time when I will be with you in America.

As a heartfelt greeting our brothers, our steward Hans Zumpe, our work distributor Adolf Braun, our Arno Martin, and our storekeeper Alfred Gneiting send you a review of our small agricultural work here and its harvest.

Just when we were ready to send off this letter, your Christmas present arrived on December 30, so that we did not send the letter off on December 31 as planned. We rejoice from our hearts about the suit, the dress, and the apron. We are all very happy about them. Your feeling that the suit would fit me very well was right. Only the trousers were too short because I am nearly six feet tall. But we are used to wearing our trousers with long stockings coming up over them to the knees. So I was able to wear the suit on December 31 for the first time. We found it just like that on pictures of the oldest forefathers in Moravia. The dress also fits my wife Emmy very well. On New Year's Eve at the taking into the novitiate of our five newest members who had tested and proved themselves for about a year, both of us wore and introduced your clothing. All the members of our Brotherhood were very happy about it, and everyone is in full agreement to wear this. It is actually only a small change for us, but one we like very much. One can just add that the three weakest women among us found it easier to accept it for the men than for the women. One of them has only recently been admitted into the time of testing and will be fully accepted later. One of the others has not been admitted in spite of her wish that the church ask that the Holy Spirit come to her, although she very much wants to stay with us. This is because she has not yet found the true foundation of faith and true *Gelassenheit* and surrender. Hopefully she will come to that soon. Thus this dress will be a good means of discipline and education, especially for women and young girls. For this we are very glad, and we thank you from our hearts for this service to us from your loved ones.

Our housemother, my wife Emmy, has this request. Please could you also send head coverings like the ones you wear, if possible twenty right away. Also in this we want to be like you. On the

Bruderhof we have always been against hats, also already at our beginning in Sannerz. You can imagine that this has always made an impression on strangers and newcomers. If you can make us an additional joy, we would like to ask you to send used head coverings, because we had to pay 15.50 marks or almost four dollars duty on the new suit. We gladly paid this rather big sum for us, but it would be better in the future if we would not have to pay it, and we like to wear clothing that you have already worn. With this *Tracht* we will be reminded of you daily.

So we greet you in great anticipation of seeing you in Wolf Creek, as your faithful and thankfully united brothers and sisters of the Bruderhof,

Eberhard Arnold

Herr Professor Harold Bender   Rhön Bruderhof, April 17, 1930
Willenbacherhof
Post Oldheim, Württemberg

Highly regarded Harold S. Bender,

Your loving lines of April 7, 1930 were a very great joy to me and to all of us. We are greatly indebted to you, not only through our beloved John Horsch, and not only through your periodical *The Mennonite Quarterly Review*, but because we also have a great interest in the situation of all of Goshen College, where you represent the important task of teaching history and the biblical languages. We therefore thank you from our whole heart that you will show us the joy and honor of visiting us at our Bruderhof.

Since this year also we have a great number of new people and guests among us, I wanted to reply to you as soon as I could determine the best day to invite you. We ask you very much to give us the joy of visiting us on Saturday, April 26, to spend all of Sunday with us, and if possible also a weekday, so that you can get to know the work schedule of our communal life. I ask you, whenever your valuable time allows it, to let us know by return mail, if possible, if we may expect you on that day. During Easter week I have to take a short journey which will also take me to Christian Hege in Frankfurt on Main. Then as soon as at all possible, I should set out on my trip to America, which will detain me for about half a year at the Hutterian Bruderhofs there.

I see in your visit a leading of God which is very significant for us, as I hope that I and all the members here can learn much from you that will be important for my trip to America. We also believe and hope that, through your visit to our Bruderhof, you can take messages from us and represent us to the friends and brothers in America.

So that you may get a little feeling of the community before your visit, I am taking the liberty of putting at your disposal for the Easter week a manuscript which we have never yet let out of our hands or given away outside the Bruderhof. We guard it as the most intimate and confidential expression of our communal life. These are our *Ordnungen* and the basis for them (*Foundation and Orders*) which we ask you to accept in brotherly trust as our innermost confession, not meant for the general public.

At the moment we are seventy people, big and small, who have to be provided for in everything. We expect from this visit not only your interest in our middle and elementary school, which as an exception is approved by the government, but also your advice. Your suggestions would also be very valuable for the very thorough history lessons with abundant sources and writings that I also try to offer continually to the adult members of our Brotherhood, our novices, our helpers and guests, and our young people.

Finally I have to ask you to be prepared for extremely simple and poor conditions when you visit us, since our beginning is very similar to the most difficult beginnings in Hutterian history. To prepare you for the special situation of our Bruderhof, let me finally refer you to our article in the *Mennonitische Blätter*,[1] which I am enclosing here, although you must surely know it already.

In closing, we thank you for telling us of your wish to visit, and extend you a warm invitation. We want to express our great joy that we may expect you next week already. Also, in the name of our Bruderhof members, I ask you kindly to allow us to address you with the brotherly "Du" during your visit, as is our custom.

Closely bound to you in grateful respect,

> your Bruderhof members in Germany
> Eberhard Arnold

---

[1]German Mennonite periodical.

Rhön Bruderhof, May 19, 1930

Beloved John Horsch,

I feel ashamed that I have delayed so long in answering your very kind letter of January 21, 1930, and acknowledging the extraordinarily valuable package of your essays and books. On the one hand there was the shortage of money we know so well and on the other hand the very urgent work from which I have great difficulty in freeing myself.

Since I was hoping from one week to the next that my journey would be possible, and as I wanted to write only something positive, I could not give my answer until today. Please accept my apologies. I have asked the American Express Company to reserve me a place on the ship for next week or the week after. I will then follow your advice and go to the Alliance Hotel and get a minister's permit and then travel as quickly as possible to you. I am writing at the same time to the business manager of the Alliance Hotel, 260 West 44th St., New York, as I would like to be met at the ship. Perhaps you can also help to see that someone meets me. I can be recognized by the Hutterian *Tracht* and I am nearly six feet tall and not too thin. I will also ask my old acquaintance John Nevin Sayre of the Fellowship of Reconciliation, former editor of *World Tomorrow*, to meet me or have me met. But it isn't certain that my letter will reach him in New York.

It will be a great joy to be able to accept the hospitality you and your wife personally extend to me. My stay in your house will, if you permit it, take more than a few hours because I have very much to talk over with you and to ask your advice on. I am hoping for a deep innermost exchange with you, especially about publishing the most important of the Anabaptist writings. I also regard your counsel as very important to our uniting with the Hutterian brothers. Thank you very much also for drawing my attention to the New Baptizers or *Fröhlichians*[1] near Chicago, a group that has already attracted my notice. However, friendship and exchange with the Mennonites are just as important to me, and I thank you with all my heart for advising your dear son-in-law, Harold S. Bender, to visit us. His visit, which

---

[1] Apostolic Christian Church, founded by Samuel Fröhlich in Switzerland.

took place yesterday, brought tremendous joy to our whole Bruderhof, and we learned a lot from him. Harold himself will write to you in detail about his impressions. He has given me the task of writing a reply to Lydia Müller's book and also an article of around 10,000 words about our Bruderhof. These are for his *Quarterly Review*. Christian Hege has given me some work to do for the *Mennonitisches Lexikon*. I am very glad about this, but he needs a lot more help to see the encyclopedia through, as his book on Marbeck has run into considerable difficulties.

It is a great joy that Harold S. Bender has asked me while on this journey to give two lectures at his college in Goshen. I would prefer to do this on my way back because then Harold himself will be there. Harold also thinks it urgent that on my return journey we three have a thorough consultation about the necessity of publishing Anabaptist writings. I hope I will soon be able to speak with you personally about all this and much more, and I look forward to that very much. We have taken your article about the Hutterites, which is in English in the *Quarterly Review* and translated it back into German so that all our Bruderhof people can read it. We have two to four members working all the time, copying and comparing old Anabaptist books and manuscripts, since we believe that this is once more an hour in history when the complete truth of the Gospel and of the life corresponding to it should be revealed to all the world.

May God in his grace and through the presence of Christ, the strength of his Holy Spirit, and the powerful witness of his divine Word bless, empower, and confirm my journey so that we in Germany and Europe, and perhaps to some extent you in America too, may come to a deeper understanding of complete redemption and live more fully in real discipleship of Christ. It is also my innermost wish that my visit will strengthen, fortify, and awaken our American brothers a little. I am representing that the full truth God revealed to our brothers in the sixteenth century has come to us anew. Through the grace of our Savior Jesus Christ, the Word of God, and the strength of the Holy Spirit this truth brings us to faith and so fills us that we can never again turn from this way, as long as God's grace is with us.

As soon as I know on which ship I am traveling, I will let you know. The fresh joy we have had in your dear Harold gives me good hope that I will be able to share the deepest joy in Christ with you and your whole dear family.

In gratitude, yours faithfully,

Eberhard Arnold

Harold Bender   Rhön Bruderhof, May 20, 1930
Heidelberg

Dear Harold,

Your kindly visit has meant very much to us, and our friendship with you leads me to write you again expressing our heartfelt thanks.

From all our hearts we wish for you and your circle that God may constantly give you a new, living awakening through his Holy Spirit and his Word which alone is true, an awakening where everything begins anew quite fresh, becoming really new. Now is the hour when faith should come anew so that the great and mighty experience and event which came from God to the Brothers in the beginning may break through again.

We are completely in agreement with you, knowing we stand on the same basis of faith, that this event means that the full salvation of the crucified and arisen Christ must be revealed with all his words, teachings, and his completely sufficient example; it means that God's kingdom will come to us from his future world and his will really be done. We ask you from our hearts to pray earnestly for this indescribable grace for us, as we also shall never forget you.

We are deeply grateful that you have obviously been given the power and insight to realize that, in spite of our special way of expressing it, the only single thing of importance for us lies in representing the true and real gospel. That is of the greatest importance for us. The worst thing that could happen to us would be to be confused with those idealistic movements which, believing in the goodness of man and the false doctrine of the evolutionary development of human progress, try in vain to set up God's work or community. This is possible only in a true community of faith, so their attempts must end in utter ruin.

Our Bruderhof will be very glad if you and your dear wife come to see our common life once again this summer, but please let us know beforehand. I have just written to John Horsch, telling him how much we enjoyed your visit and of your suggestions for our joint meeting, which should take place on my return journey. I so much feel your trust in your invitation to spend two days at Goshen College and speak there, and I think it would fit in best on my return journey. For it would hardly be possible to come if you were not there. I look forward very much to meeting you again and seeing you on your home ground and in your sphere of work.

In the next days I hope to send you under the subheading, "A Book Review," an essay I have worked through about the old misunderstandings which Lydia Müller has unfortunately brought up again! I will have it translated into English here but ask you to change our school English into a more understandable form where necessary. Perhaps I will still be able to write the 10,000 word article on our Bruderhof before my departure; but unfortunately I cannot absolutely promise this. Otherwise, it must follow later.

You kindly offered to write me the exact route from New York to Scottdale, and if I understood rightly, to send recommendations and addresses of Mennonite friends who could give me lodging when I travel from Chicago to South Dakota. I will be most grateful if you can do this.

Finally, I want to ask you to send me the statement listing all the equipment you have given to the Mennonite emigrants to Paraguay.[1] If possible send it immediately. It would not only be a service to us, but it would also be important for my visit to the Hutterian Bruderhofs. Then I could tell them exactly what you have done for your fellow believers in this decisive hour when they were in need. All our brothers here see this deed, done in the spirit of Christ, as proof of a real, living faith in your Mennonite circles. This can be done only because God's grace is still living among you today.

So we greet you, bound in closest fellowship, with heartfelt love and in deep trust.

Your Eberhard Arnold

Harold Bender
Heidelberg, May 26, 1930

Dear Brother Eberhard Arnold and all
you dear friends at the Bruderhof,

I am still so deeply impressed and inwardly moved by what I experienced with you at the Bruderhof that it is not I who should accept thanks from you, but rather I who owe you a debt of great thanks. As my thanks, I can wish you nothing better than that God the Lord leads and guides you all as one, according to his will, so that in this world of dark powers you may be shining witnesses of his love and strength. This is what you have become for me. May God make me also alive in this spirit, although I do not live in the same lifestyle.

---

[1]The Mennonite Central Committee gave substantial help to Mennonite refugees from Russia in 1930.

I thank you especially, dear Eberhard, for your loving letter of May 20 and the love and community of faith it testified to, especially the community of prayer of which I am truly in need. I will always think of you all and will never forget you all, especially you as servant of the Word. I am looking forward so much to the moment when we can be together again in Goshen and can continue to think through the questions of life that are so important to us. I believe with certainty that God will use you among us as his instrument for our blessing and awakening, and in preparation I pray God for his grace. You will find things among us that are not according to the Lord's will, but just because of that we shall welcome your visit very much.

Concerning your journey, I suggest the following: on the way there, stop only in Scottdale with my father-in-law Horsch, and in Chicago with Hofer and Tschetter. On the way home you will certainly be able and want to visit different Mennonite churches, especially our Goshen College, where the semester begins on September 17. You will arrive in New York and want to go to John Sayre. Then in the morning you can easily go by the Pennsylvania Railroad from New York via Philadelphia to Greensburg, Pennsylvania without changing. There you will have to change trains. My father Horsch will be there to pick you up for a little side-trip to the iron city of Scottdale. If you leave New York early in the morning you will arrive in Scottdale (Greensburg) in the evening. You will have to send a telegram from New York with the time of your arrival. From Scottdale you can go in one day as far as Chicago, where Brother Hofer will meet you. Then in one more day you can travel to South Dakota. It would perhaps be better if you did go first to Elias Walter in Alberta. But my father Horsch can give you the best travel plans and information.

I am writing to my father Horsch about my impressions of the Bruderhof and also an article for our periodical, *Gospel Herald*.[1] I think it will be a considerable help in removing possible misunderstandings. It will be better if Father Horsch gives you the recommendations to our brothers because I don't yet know your exact plans. He can do it better than I. You should reserve at least two days, if not more, for your visit in Scottdale because they will certainly ask you to give a lecture or a sermon.

I have now heard that my wife will arrive in Germany at the end of July. You will surely meet her in Scottdale with her parents. If we

---

[1] An article by Harold Bender on his visit to the Rhön Bruderhof appeared in the *Christian Monitor* of January 1931. See Chapter 3, pp. 227-234.

have time we will still try to come to the Bruderhof, but we cannot say for sure yet. We thank you very much for inviting us.

I am enclosing a translation of the contract between our refugees and the company. On the last page you will find a list of the equipment. The list is changed somewhat, but it is complete on the whole. I ask you to treat this contract confidentially and not to publish it.

Could I also ask you for a copy of the booklet by Bertha Clark (in German)? If it is really all right I would have one more request, and that is that you would send me the big History Book for a few days. I need it for my work right now and cannot find a copy here. I would send it back soon. I want to remind you that Dr. Köhler very much wanted a copy of the Chronicle and since it is out of print here, I promised him mine. If you could bring to Goshen a copy either for me or for Professor Köhler, then we would each have one.

To you all: From my whole heart I wish you, as fellow pilgrims to our eternal home, God's richest blessing, and expect with you the coming kingdom. I commend you especially, beloved Eberhard, to God's grace for the long journey and important task ahead of you. Your visit can be of greatest significance, not only for your Bruderhof here, but also for the Hutterian Brothers there, and for us too.

Once more, warmest greetings to you all. Bound to you in Christian love, your brother,

Harold S. Bender

Enclosed, something for the little guest box.

A letter to the brothers in South Dakota, Manitoba, and Alberta from Eberhard Arnold, written at the German Bruderhof,[1] Post Neuhof, Kreis Fulda, Hessen-Nassau, and mailed from New York [corrected to Scottdale], on June 14, 1930, to announce his arrival in America to visit all colonies. A copy of this letter was sent off to each Bruderhof.

Beloved brothers,

I told you in February that I would start my journey to you on March 14 if everybody were well and everything went as we hoped. Unfortunately, sad and unexpected circumstances prevented this. First of all, with the crowding in of eager newcomers wanting to come to faith and to full community, our financial situation was very difficult. In spite of our need of land, in spite of our shortage of fodder and of

---

[1]Shortly before his departure for America.

food for ourselves, we had to sell nearly 20 acres of meadowland with grass, hay, and pasture for about $2,000. My presence was necessary for this. Since I did not receive enough money for the return trip, which is an official requirement for entering upon American soil, I had to raise it from the sale of this land and advances from other sources, although the money could hardly be spared. This cost much trouble, care, and time.

Furthermore, my eye trouble also kept me from departing. In 1920 when I was chopping wood in Sannerz during the early time of our community life, a splinter of wood flew into my left eye. This caused me to lose my sight in that eye. Ever since then this eye has been susceptible to infection, and this spring it was especially bad. Even now it has not quite recovered. But since I promised to be with you this summer, and the full uniting with you must not be put off any longer, and since it is urgent that we discuss the editing of the *Klein-Geschichtsbuch*[1] (Small History Book) we did after all dare to undertake the journey by unanimous decision of our Bruderhof. To make the journey cheaper, I am using the North German Lloyd ocean liner, Karlsruhe, which takes ten days for the crossing, whereas the fastest steamships take only five days. I will send this letter off in New York, where the steamer will arrive on June 9. So this letter will be your news that I have arrived safely on American soil.

I will go first to Scottdale in Pennsylvania to see the Mennonite, John Horsch, who wants to help me on my journey via Chicago. I will arrive at your Bon Homme Bruderhof in Tabor, South Dakota, first and visit you at the South Dakota Bruderhofs. From there I will travel to you dear Schmiedeleut in Manitoba, where I will probably arrive first at your Rosengart [Blumengard] Bruderhof at Plum Coulee, visit all the church communities in Manitoba, and then go to our Elias Walter at our Stand Off Bruderhof. I may stop off at Lethbridge on the way to see Johann Wurz and Darius Walter. Starting with Elias Walter and Christian Waldner at Raley, I then want to visit all the Alberta communities. Finally, I ask with all my heart for a conference of all preachers, so that our uniting will take place in the right order and with the right blessing of the church.

If there is anything you still want to write about my visit to your communities, I ask you to send me word during June via Michael Waldner, Bon Homme, Tabor, South Dakota, or to David Wipf and

---

[1]Zieglschmid, A. J. F. Ed. *Das Klein-Geschichtsbuch der Hutterischen Brüder*. Philadelphia, Pa: The Carl Schurz Memorial Foundation, Inc., 1947. English edition in preparation as Volume II of *The Chronicle of the Hutterian Brethren* by the Hutterian Brethren. Rifton, NY: Plough Publishing House.

Joshua Hofer at Wolf Creek Community, Hutchinson County, P.O. Menno, S.D. From our hearts we ask all of you to understand the indescribable grace of the merciful God, of our beloved Savior Jesus Christ, and of the Holy Spirit, by which God has brought us in these evil times to the true foundation of faith and the true order of God's church through the old writings of your forefathers. We experience much of holy zeal, of the joy God gives when we suffer for the sake of true surrender and community, and of enthusiasm for the service of God's word and for mission. We feel every day that all this is possible only through the grace of God and Jesus Christ and through the power of the Holy Spirit. Because of my eye trouble, I have not been able to answer individually your very loving letters, in which you welcomed me and sent me fifty dollars toward my journey. Please accept this letter as an expression of our joy and thanks for the great love in your many letters, which did us no end of good.

All our brothers and sisters accompany me in their daily prayers as I travel to you. They expect from God through you the confirmation of my task, without which our church life cannot continue. Take this into your hearts: we who are united with you in true faith and love and life can no longer endure the unbearable burden of standing alone without your blessing and confirmation. For the sake of our witness to the Hutterian faith, we have been completely abandoned by those in Germany who call themselves Christians and brothers, and we are therefore thoroughly isolated. Those who seek us out at our Bruderhof are almost all people who are troubled in their consciences and have been awakened to new zeal for true faith and life. We now number over seventy grown-ups and children for whom we have to care; and there are twenty to thirty more for whom we have to provide space and work, because they can no longer endure living outside our faith or outside full community.

So I do not come to you for myself but for this little flock of almost one hundred souls. For them I ask your faith, your love, and your trust. Further, I feel it as a task from God to ask you that our Bruderhof be allowed to copy in full all of the nearly one hundred books handwritten by your forefathers which were stolen in earlier times from the brothers and are to be found in libraries and archives in Germany and Austria. We believe it is God's will that after we have completed this task, we emigrate to you. While this copying is being done, the mission to our eagerly seeking guests and friends in the German-speaking lands will most likely come to a certain conclusion.

These two tasks will perhaps take a few years. But it belongs to the clear and definite basis of our faith, which we confess to just as you do, that the flock of Christ longs to and must come together. Christ's flock should not be allowed to remain scattered over all the earth. We should ask God that this gathering of his people be combined with taking the Word into all lands in the same real and powerful way, with the same joy in suffering and readiness for sacrifice, as in the early church communities.

So on this visit of mine, we lay our pleading hearts in your hands for blessing. For the sake of the Savior, we ask you in great love that you also learn to love us as your new brothers and sisters, not only a little but with all your hearts.

Completely yours in unity of faith and in the expectation of everlasting salvation, for the sake of Christ and at the cost of his precious blood,

Your Bruderhof members in Germany

Journey to the Brothers

Introductory Remarks

At last the moment came when Eberhard Arnold could set out on his journey to North America to seek in the name of the church community in Germany complete uniting with the Hutterian Church, and the confirmation of his service of the Word for the Rhön Bruderhof and for mission in Europe. On the eve of his departure he baptized nine brothers and sisters.

Eberhard Arnold left Bremerhaven for New York on the Karlsruhe on May 30, 1930. After his arrival in New York, he traveled to Scottdale, Pennsylvania, where he was the guest of his good friend John Horsch. He also went to Chicago before visiting all the existing Bruderhofs, beginning with Bon Homme, South Dakota.

Eberhard Arnold kept a diary of his travels and experiences which forms the main part of this chapter. He also wrote letters home to his wife Emmy Arnold (affectionately called *Amselchen* or *Emmchen* by him), to his daughters Emy-Margret (Emy-Ma) and Monika, and to the Brotherhood at the Rhön Bruderhof. These letters have also been included.

At the time of Eberhard Arnold's journey in 1930-31, there were three groups within the Hutterian Church as there still are today.

The Schmiedeleut, named after Schmied Michel, a smith by trade, who established the first Bruderhof in America at Bon Homme in South Dakota in 1874, had, apart from this one hof, all moved to Manitoba, Canada. Their elder was Joseph Kleinsasser of Milltown Bruderhof, assisted by David Hofer, James Valley.

David Hofer, the old elder of the Lehrerleut (teacher-group), lived at Rockport, the one remaining Lehrer Bruderhof in South Dakota. All the others had moved to Alberta, and his Bruderhof was soon to follow. Johannes Kleinsasser of Milford, Alberta served as elder there, and succeeded David Hofer in 1932.

The Dariusleut, named after Darius Walter, were also all in Alberta apart from the Wolf Creek and Lake Byron Bruderhofs in South Dakota. Christian Waldner of West Raley was their elder.

At Wolf Creek, and later in Alberta, Eberhard Arnold had to undergo extensive treatment for his left eye, which had become almost blind right at the beginning of the communal life, through an accident while chopping wood. He traveled to Manitoba in August of 1930, visiting all 10 Schmiedeleut Bruderhofs there, and winning the support of the Elder Joseph Kleinsasser, Milltown, his helper David Hofer, James Valley, and all the servants of the Word, as expressed in the letter of September 14, 1930.[1]

---

[1]See p.135.

He then traveled on to Alberta, visiting all 20 hofs. There, on December 9 and 18, the longed for goal was achieved. Eberhard Arnold was accepted through baptism into the Hutterian Church and confirmed in his service on behalf of the Bruderhof in Germany. This incorporation was carried out by the elders of the Dariusleut and Lehrerleut, with the full approval of the Schmiedeleut. Eberhard could write home jubilantly "We are now the first Bruderhof belonging at the same time to the Dariusleut, Schmiedeleut, and Lehrerleut."

It had weighed heavily upon Eberhard Arnold that the Hutterian Church was divided into these three groups from the time of their coming to America. He pleaded for the appointment of one elder, or after his return to Germany, for the three elders Joseph Kleinsasser, Christian Waldner, and Johannes Kleinsasser, to meet frequently and to seek unity in all important questions.

Now that he had been accepted into the Hutterian Church, Eberhard Vetter visited each Bruderhof in America once more, seeking financial help for his struggling community in Germany.

In May 1931 he returned home after an absence of almost a year.

In this diary and these letters, we can learn of his hopes and insights, of the strengths and weaknesses he saw in the Hutterian Church, and can sense something of what it cost him that 'brothers could unite.'

Maps of Eberhard Arnold's journey and a timetable of his travels are included at the end of the book.

Telegram,
June 5, 1930, 4:30 p.m. Bremen

Eberhard left on the Karlsruhe (May 30). Officer himself saw him through. Anneliese.

On the Karlsruhe, near Ireland
June 1 and 2, 1930

My eye gives me a lot of pain when I write. Friday and Saturday it was impossible. Only today, Sunday, after strict bed rest in the cabin, is there a little relief. The steward, Herr Novinszy, musician and composer, provides me with plenty of food in bed. I am enclosing the menu card. In Bremen, Anneliese, Eva, and Magdalene Dietrich read to me from my comments on the Habertshof.[1] Here I can't read a single line. You must invite Eva Dietrich to the Bruderhof for a year. She does not want to stay with H. any longer. My trunk did not arrive at Bremerhaven. Find out right away, please, whether it

---

[1] A community of the Free German Movement begun in 1919 near Sannerz. The comments deal with the relationship between the Habertshof and the Bruderhof.

went on the Bremen on Saturday. Then it will catch up with me. Otherwise I will be stuck in New York. I gave the papers to the North German Lloyd. Unfortunately I can't write any more. My eye must get better by the time I get to New York. I am carrying out the treatment regularly and believe in Christ, who wants to make the inner light clear to light up the body, and the outer eye healthy for his way. We have to hold on to the kingdom.

Telegram from Brooklyn, N.Y.,
June 12, 1930

Happily landed. Thinking of you and yours, Eberhard.

Chicago, June 18, 1930

At last my eye is so much better that yesterday I had only a little pain and today practically none at all. My experience in New York and Scottdale was that the love of the very faithful, very punctual, and very serious Mennonites left me with no time and even less strength for writing. My eye forced me to take to my bed to recover at every pause, however short. So today I am squeezing in an expensive hotel day, which I am spending in my room without going out at all. I am having all my meals in my room, which has a desk, a couch, and bathroom, though I ordered "the simplest room without any luxuries." So now I can think and write in all peace and quiet to you, to the children, and to the whole faithful Bruderhof, and at the same time take care of my eye. A friendly fellow traveler told me about this Hotel Atlantic, formerly the Kaiserhof, where they speak German. The constant traveling back and forth in New York to get the Clergy Permit was very strenuous.

It was a bit better in Scottdale, but with an American heat that made one drip with sweat. Because of my eye, I would rather continue to write with a black pen. I am after all your "dear black-haired husband." My hair has grown a bit longer, but only to my temples and in front over my ears, parted in the middle. The sprouting Old Yankee beard below is white. By the way, the blue Bavarian jacket sticks out more here in America than the Hutterian hook-and-eye jacket, which fits well, for which I want to thank Hanna Paulmann once more. The stockings and sandals too, make the Americans laugh at me behind my back, which is fine with me.

The American way of life doesn't impress me at all. I don't like it. The big cities appear more horrible than in Germany. But even the small town of Scottdale (5,000 inhabitants) is deplorably lacking in good taste, also in their sixteen different churches belonging to fifteen different confessions. In the Episcopal Methodist Church—an enormous, idolatrous steeple house—I saw an advertisement for "recreation" through sports, modern outdoor clothing, and nature. The Methodists here are, on the whole, liberal unbelievers, very many Baptist preachers also.

The old Mennonites are quite touching, the men dressed like their forefathers with jacket and vest buttoned up all the way, very manly figures, strong, worthy, simple and straightforward. The women look like deaconesses, with long, plain pastel or black dresses, with white gauze bonnets or sturdy black sun bonnets. But they have taken to singing modern English revivalist songs rather than the old Anabaptist songs. The German language has almost died out. Their meetings last many hours and are astonishingly lively, even with all the quiet Mennonite seriousness. Sunday School begins at 9 o'clock and is quite different from what we know. There are six classes or groups, in one the grown-up women and girls, in another the young men, and in still another quite old men. They have lively exchanges on Bible topics through questions and answers. In true American fashion, they can stretch out their arms and legs as much as they like, even letting out a loud unstifled yawn. In the midst of it all, small children cry, also during the sermon which follows. This causes the very old, former missionary to the Indians to shout even louder and to roll out his amazingly loud English "R's." The singing is heartfelt as they devoutly stand or sit. I could understand some of the missionary's sermon, as I had an English book in front of me. Evenings it is the same: first the youth meeting, in which however, just as many old as young take part, but at which only the young ones read, boys as well as girls. The Bible is read in very long passages from the Old and New Testament. Then I was given the last hour—exactly sixty minutes. As my message to the Mennonites, I took our special theme, the experience of Pentecost at Jerusalem with all its consequences. I emphasized strongly the gospel of Christ, and then went on to speak about complete love and community, in which everything belongs to God and to the church of the Spirit. When I was asked, I told about my background, especially a great deal about you and Halle, Leipzig, and Berlin. I witnessed to the Sermon on the Mount, and tried to awaken the religious-social conscience. Afterwards, John Horsch told

me that the brothers do not understand such difficult words as "social"!!
We then agreed that with our Hutterites too, I could only illustrate
this point through the prophets, the rich man and poor Lazarus, the
story of the good Samaritan, and so on.

Finally I told about Sannerz and the Bruderhof, especially about
the children's community, emphasizing strongly that it is not my task
to witness to the Bruderhof itself, but that the Bruderhof has to witness
to Jerusalem and the outpouring of the Holy Spirit with all its
consequences. I closed with Emy-Margret's very stirring song. As I
called out, "And after him run all who can," I ran quickly back to
my place among the benches, so that a joyful laughter closed the talk.
This impressed some very strongly, also the old Indian missionary,
who understands German well.

John Horsch's translation was passable, but not very good. I
clearly gathered this through the few English words I know. His wife,
who has been to Germany, said the same. John Horsch thinks that
communication with the Hutterites will be easier. He thinks I will
have no difficulty with their Tirolean-Bavarian dialect, but that for
them, my abstract, too carefully thought out German will be difficult.
So perhaps I will return home a simple farmer, also in my speech.

John Horsch told many loving and good things about the two
visits of leading Hutterites to Scottdale during World War I. Because
of their refusal to do military service, several brothers traveled to
Washington with a petition to President Wilson and the government.
This petition is known to us and was written with John Horsch's help.
Those who went were: Elias Walter I, former elder of the Darius
group; our Elias Walter II, who already then had much influence;
Joseph Kleinsasser, the dear brother from the Schmiedeleut; old Johann
Entz, since deceased; and old David Hofer from Rockport, Alexandria,
who interests us very much. About him, John Horsch told us that,
when there was the best of brotherly harmony among all the others,
David Hofer had always stubbornly held to his own especially sharp
conclusions. So the others had given way to him each time, except
in the question of emigration to Canada, about which he had stormed
mightily. He is an especially forceful personality and very difficult
to influence. Already then the two Elias Walters succeeded in
bringing about the emigration to Canada, recommended because of the
militarization of the United States, against his strong and vehement
opposition. David Hofer fought passionately against this and said he
wondered how they would defend themselves on the Day of Judgment,
because in Canada Hutterian children had to be under the influence

of the English state schools for ten months of the year. In the USA this was not the case to the same extent.

Who will be proved right in the history of the future? In any case, it became clear to me that the motive behind David Hofer's obstinacy comes from the best intentions. Certainly some Hutterites think, as I heard from John Horsch, that in the cool and over-careful attitude to us, the concern for the dollar plays a large role. David Hofer, Rockport, reckons that the setting-up of a Bruderhof such as we would need would cost $250,000, which is over a million marks. Well, that's enough to frighten anyone. I hope I shall succeed in finding the right balance. The main thing at the moment is the witness and the unity in the Spirit. The rest must take care of itself. We shall certainly need more than a little patience.

I have not yet been with Hofer and Tschetter of the *Wahrheitsfreund*, or with B. W. Clark or Tolles, and have not yet received the Clergy Permit for "West of Chicago." Therefore I cannot yet say whether I shall travel to Michael Waldner at Bon Homme on Friday or Saturday. I think it will be Friday. For the journey to Chicago, John Horsch obtained a very comfortable place in a sleeping compartment for five dollars, which he contributed from his own pocket. I think everything will continue to go well under God's protection, especially since my eye is very much better. John Horsch plans to prepare a good reception with the Hutterites. He wants to write to David Hofer, Rockport; Joseph Kleinsasser, Milltown; and Christian Waldner, West Raley, about the facts mentioned by Harold Bender. He will send copies to Elias Walter. Harold Bender wrote a really fine letter telling of the strong impression our Bruderhof had made on him. He calls us genuine Baptizers in the Hutterian sense, writes about our poverty and communal sharing, about our rejection of the liberal progressive direction, and our thorough knowledge of the Bible, which is, however, very far from pietism. He says that he finds a real conviction among us. While there are too many words with the Mennonites, with us words and deeds go together. This has moved him very much, without his coming to a final opinion. In any case, he thought I should speak to the Mennonites at Scottdale, which has already taken place. So much about Harold S. Bender, who still has many questions. John Horsch will write all this to the Hutterites.

Elizabeth Horsch is modest and well educated. Little two-year-old Mary Horsch is delicate. Little Walter is a model boy. He was afraid of me. I enjoy them because they remind me of our beloved children. Mö's and Heini's letters made me very happy. Heini writes so lovingly about you, tells me you try very hard not to cry, my dear one, and that you only think of me and wait for my letters.

I meant to send you a telegram on leaving Bremerhaven. Unfortunately I was prevented by the unsuccessful search for Hugga's suitcase, so nicely packed, which took my time right up to the moment of departure. Luckily the suitcase went to New York ahead of me on the Bremen. I enjoyed very much how lovingly you packed everything. Best of all were the carefully chosen and loving words written into the diary by you and Mö, which I read and showed to the Horschs. I shall begin to write in the diary only when I am with the Hutterites. Compared to what I shall experience with them, the journey so far is unimportant. I am writing this letter with a copy so that nothing gets lost.

I took the only opportunity to send you a letter at the beginning of the journey from Ireland, which owing to my painful and still-closed eye, was only short and badly written, and then from New York, where we didn't arrive until June 12, I mailed a pile of cards, etc. So today's letter is the first detailed report, because of the weakness of my eye. Since the last day in Scottdale, where through John Horsch, the doctor and pharmacist gave me a new supply of "atropine," it is now at last better. I also wrote you for Eva Dietrich's sake; you should relieve her need by inviting her to come to us at once.

Because of my lack of English, I have sought in vain for pictures to send you of the sea and the American landscape. Up till now the rivers are the most beautiful with their gigantic dams, reminding us, though in much greater proportions, of the Harz, but not of the Alps. Because of the expense of staying in a hotel, the friends waiting in Chicago, and my work on the Habertshof commentary, I must come to a close now, but I must still tell you of my great joy in your reports.

The question of leadership which was raised amused me in a quiet way without disturbing me. Oh! It is such a heavy and tormenting burden to have to be a Word leader or something similar. Whoever craves it desperately does not yet know what tragedy and need this all-too-holy obligation brings upon us weak men. Happy and blest are those on whom this has not been laid, if—yes, indeed, only if—they do not long for it with the secret covetousness of unpurified desire. Those who have to go forward to such advanced outposts, as I do on this journey, must bear more suffering than those dedicated to apparently simpler service.

The baptism was significant for the victory of the Spirit over all other spirits, also the physically tormenting spirits! May God give you this victory in richest measure! I thank Georg especially for his fine words, Hans for the faithful bearing of his responsibility, Trudi and Rose, and finally in the same way Roland and Irm for supporting you so well with getting everything clear. Eva von Thiele-Winkler will also have given you some help and encouragement. I am happy with these thoughts of hers and with Blumhardt's *Tag des Menschen* (Day of Mankind). I am also glad about the many different visitors on the hof, especially about the arrival of little Hans Hellwig, and Hans, the Brother of the Common Life.[1] I also enjoyed Hardy's poem, *Das Opfer* (The Sacrifice), which I discovered in my New Testament.

Tabor, South Dakota, June 20, 1930

I have just come into the best hands of the Hutterian Schmiedeleut. Michel Waldner, an old brother with almost completely white hair and beard fetched me with his son Paul. Now you can be quite at peace about me. Please correct the date on all the post cards I wrote this noon to June 20 instead of June 30.

I have just heard that Elias Walter has had a stroke. May God help him up. It is a great grace that I am allowed to be here. Greet the whole Bruderhof.

Tabor, June 24, 1930

While at the Tabor railway station with dear old Michel Waldner, I am sending you in great haste this short greeting today as I leave Bon Homme to go to Wolf Creek. I am well escorted from one Bruderhof to another. I am sending you and Hans, the steward, $300: $100 saved for you from my journey, and $200 given by the faithful Schmiedeleut of Bon Homme for your present needs and obligations, wherever you find it most important. You know my worries and concerns. The cupboard should not be sold, nor the chest and dresser. But from over here I do not want to say what is most important. You know better, and I hope later to be able to send something to you again.

The brothers and sisters of Bon Homme are very, very loving to me and to all of you. You must thank them with the words of Peter Riedemann and Jakob Hutter. The spirit and truth of today's Hutterianism, also here and now, surpass by far our expectations. An intimate relationship with God is living here, as also the belief in the Holy Spirit and in the redemption of Christ. There is here the deepest and strongest awareness that we need the constant coming of the Holy Spirit to stimulate and speak to us in the church. The faithfulness

---

[1]Christian Brotherhood, founded in 1905 in Switzerland, dedicated to a life of service.

to one another, to Michel Vetter the Word leader, to the servants and the steward, seems to me perfect, as they keep a firm discipline in conversation, speaking openly to one another and not about one another. Joy and happiness are expressed constantly in the humor of deep contentment, and in still deeper sayings from the Scriptures, from Proverbs, and from experiences. The simplicity of the life is still kept fairly well. For instance, cars are not bought for any hof because that is not wanted.

Not only the older brothers—best of all Michel Vetter himself—but also many of the young people and men and women have a deep joy and complete understanding for the flaring up of the fire of first love and the beginnings of community with its special characteristics. They say, "An older mother brings forth weaker children." So they always want to hear the most exact particulars about our faith and our community, our work, how we dress, and everything else. So I have had to tell them a great deal, and we have understood each other very well and have come very close in the spirit of unity. Therefore all here are certain that the uniting will come about through the grace of God.

The prayer, the sermon, and the songs are wonderfully clear and objective, also the community decisions in which I have taken part twice. Once I was also able to thank them for the $200 they gave us. Nevertheless, it is difficult for us to understand the wealth of their property and economy.

I have written much to you and to you all, and will send it as soon as there is time to look through it again. Likewise, Else will receive a list of writings from Bon Homme and other places. I had few quiet moments in Bon Homme, as every moment a whole group came into my room. Once I was driven around the whole property, and also hunted a wolf which has stolen a great deal here. But I must close with faithful greetings to all our family and to the whole beloved Bruderhof.

Wolf Creek, July 2, 1930
(Written down by Elisabeth E. Hofer)[1]

First of all a very warm greeting to you, my beloved Emma[2] and to our dear children and our whole Bruderhof. You, my dear, will be curious to know where I am now. I came to the Wolf Creek brothers

---

[1]Daughter of Joshua and Elisabeth Hofer, servant of the Word at Wolf Creek.
[2]Emmy Arnold, Eberhard's wife.

on June 28. Michel Vetter from Bon Homme brought me here. Dear Emma, it gave me great joy to come to these Bruderhofs. They were all so very friendly to me. If God the heavenly Father gives me life, I shall also visit the Lehrerleut brothers and Joseph Stahl.

Here I have already told them a lot about you, my dear ones. Dear Emma, Monika, and Heinrich, I received all your letters and read them with joy. I also read them to the women. They said that you are an educated woman, dear Emma, also your children and the whole Bruderhof. Do not worry about me. God the Lord is with me and strengthens me. The brothers were all so very joyful to see me. On Sunday June 29 in church we had the teaching on the second chapter of the Acts of the Apostles and were very well admonished by hearing about Ananias and his wife.

Dear Emma, I wanted to write more, but my eye hurts me, so I must close my little letter. A hundred thousand greetings to you, my dear faithful Emma, with our dear faithful children. Greet the whole Bruderhof from your faithful Eberhard Arnold.

I remain your faithful Eberhard until death,
Your Eberhard, who is not allowed to write yet

From me, Katharina C. Hofer
Wolf Creek Bruderhof
to Emma M. Arnold [Emy-Margret]   July 3, 1930

To you my dear friend Emma,

I want to tell you all that your respected father arrived here safely. He has a bad eye. Dr. Wipf of Freeman hopes, with God's help, to help him, and we rejoice in spirit that he is visiting us. Last Sunday he had many visitors. My dear father is starting a new home for us with fourteen brothers and sisters and also some help from other Bruderhofs. That is in Canada. My mother's work is the care of the younger school children, and my Anna Basel is busy in the kitchen. I want to tell you that the weather is good. It is going fairly well with the poultry. We have 900 goslings, 600 ducks, 3,000 hens, 700 sheep. Our dear God has blessed us in everything. We wish we were as blessed in spiritual things as we are in temporal. I am cooking this week. I hope your father's eye will get better. My mother puts ointment in his eye three times a day. Otherwise we are all quite well. Write to me how things are in Germany. I am very curious to hear something. I will close my letter now and greet you all with your mother many thousand times, also all the brothers and sisters. Greet the sisters as well; they should also write to me. Also greet the school mother and all, without leaving anyone out, because I don't know them by name, from Katharina Hofer. I am Servant Josua's daughter of Wolf Creek.

Wolf Creek, July 7, 1930

(Written down by fifteen-year-old Elisabeth Hofer without dictation and without correction.)

To my much-loved Emma and to our dear children and to the whole Bruderhof. The peace and the grace of God be with us and you all. Amen. Now my dear ones, how are you getting on in Germany? Dear Emma, I received your loving letter and was very glad to hear something from you all. I also spoke with David Vetter about the aprons, and he said they wear black and also dark blue. I will enclose a piece of the cloth. You will also all be curious about my eye. Dr. Wipf from Freeman has been here today and he says it is already getting on nicely. During next week, with God's help, I will travel to Rockport to David Hofer. Our David Vetter[1] travels to Canada tomorrow.

I like it very much here with the brothers. They take care of me so well. I have already driven out to the fields to see the wheat. Everything looks so beautiful out here in America. The brothers have already cut rye. The wheat is also ripe.

Dear Emma, tell our steward, Hans, I also received his letter. I read it and understood how hard it is for him. God himself will give him strength from above to lead our Bruderhof. Joseph Stahl of Bindell[2] is also here in Wolf Creek. On July 6 at church he took John Chapter 4, a very nice teaching about the harvest in spiritual things and in temporal. Dear Emma, together with the children, it is just like home for me here. I have my own room in which I sleep. The people here like it so much when I tell about you, my dear ones; they also wash my clothes. On Sunday we had many guests here. I tell them the truth about community. But it says in the text, "Do not cast your pearls before swine," and that is how it is with these people. Elisabeth Basel puts ointment in my eye three times a day. She is Servant Joshua's wife. Anna Basel is head cook. She is the steward's

---

[1]David Wipf, steward of Wolf Creek.
[2]Lake Byron.

wife. The weather is so very warm that the children have to go swimming. I already know some of the brothers here, too. In the evenings they come and listen as I talk about you all. The sisters have already made me trousers. When my eye is quite better, I shall go to see everything. I must come to an end now, otherwise my letter will be too long. My dear faithful Emma, I greet you and all our dear children and the whole Bruderhof. The sisters also greet everyone, and the girls greet our girls.

I remain your faithful Eberhard Arnold until death. Amen.

Wolf Creek, July 15, 1930

Today at last you are getting another little letter from my hand. Dr. A. A. Wipf, Freeman, practicing doctor and eye specialist, who has treated me all these weeks, has not yet allowed reading and writing but thinks I can try it after the next injection on Thursday, July 17. But the eye only hurts a little and rarely. And the red veins are only as visible as they were in the first days after the first illness on our Bruderhof when it was already improving. This time the attack was the most painful and the worst. It began when, after sending off the little letter from the railway station in Tabor, I arrived at the Lehrerleut Bruderhof, Rockport, with the very loving Michel Waldner from Bon Homme on June 26, 1930. On Friday I was very well taken care of by Maria, the midwife from Rockport who is deeply founded in her faith. As midwife she has overseen already one hundred births in Lehrerleut families, with only one case of a baby's death. On Thursday evening I still had to tell much, until the pain became too severe. I am reporting in the diary my deep impressions of the old people at Rockport Bruderhof. I shall be writing it this week. On Saturday morning, I had turned down the offer of medical treatment in Rockport, which was urged upon me. Then a car was ordered especially for me, and the Servants Michel Waldner, Bon Homme, and Peter Hofer, Rockport, drove me through the deserted colonies, Old Elm Spring and Milford, to our Wolf Creek Colony. Unfortunately I could not see very much on this trip. Here I gave in and let them send me to bed at once, and since then I have been almost three weeks in bed except for short intervals. Dr. Wipf drove out the fourteen miles from Freeman every third day to see me. As I have to wait with Dr. Wipf for the last injection to take effect, I shall travel to Rockport on July 23 for the very decisive talk with the elderly David Vetter, on which a great deal depends. I shall remain in Rockport until after July 26, and will probably travel on Monday, July 28 to Lake Byron, to our very faithful Joseph Stahl, who already visited me here. I will travel to Manitoba around the turn of the month. So a great deal of time has gone by on account of my sickness. But I believe these three weeks are not wasted. From my bed, from my large single room, I experienced the everyday life of the members in a special way and could take my time to find an inner attitude to everything which presses in on me. The Hutterian religious faith is real and genuine. It is deeply rooted in the hearts of all. They do not wish to live, nor can they, in any other way than in community. The practical self-forgetfulness in the service of the community is much stronger than it is with us. The seriousness of the divine witness of the truth is strong, also in the simplest members. The calling to God is deeply moving. How moved I was when I was invited to sleep in the room of the old Michel Waldner couple and found the old man in his white nightwear praying in the dark room by the ancient chest with the wonderful dignity, reverence, and earnestness of the Hutterian attitude in prayer: on his knees, his whole body from knees to head erect in a straight line, his hands before his face raised up to God. The brothers have no doubt that this is the apostolic and early Baptizer position: "Raise the tired hands, strengthen the feeble knees."

A sister told me about a Baptist who wanted to pray with them. How shocked she was when he suddenly flopped down off his chair and disappeared under the table as if he'd had an epileptic fit. She must have been sitting opposite him. His face was hidden in his hands. Then she said, "You want to pray like that! Your own good sense must tell you how unworthy that is, and that this is not the upright way to come before God." And another evangelist, D. M. Hofer, Chicago, when visited in his home by David Wipf of Wolf Creek, tried to pull him down at the side of his chair to pray. The huge heavyweight David Wipf (he weighed all of three hundred pounds) stood in his Hutterian clothes, straight as a post before this elegant evangelistic gentleman from Chicago. "Leave me alone, David. You live godlessly in property for yourself. According to the word of Christ you are a hypocrite. How can you want to pray with me and force me down?" And he went away. Yes, outsiders are told the truth bluntly. We have a false conception of the lack of mission among the brothers. Firstly, they are visited by unbelievably large numbers of people in spite of their extremely isolated location. Often there are fifty cars in one day. And then they speak to the people very clearly and specifically. But I myself, in many personal exchanges with such guests, have become convinced that none of them have questions or are seekers. They come only because of the worldwide renown which the Hutterites have. For instance, I made it clear to a professor whom I met in Bon Homme and again in Wolf Creek, who unfortunately intends to write yet another book about the Hutterites, how many books he would first have to read. "Oh, no," he said, "all that is not necessary." The brothers fight tooth and nail against such insolence and recognize clearly that these people only want to make money and become famous at their expense. As soon as they are convinced that a man is not seeking the true godly life, they turn away from him and say, "He loves his own too much. He doesn't want to. We are not going to give our holy things to such dogs. We will not cast our pearls before swine." There is a wonderful commentary here on this text. The same David Wipf, Wolf Creek, was called one day before a high government official and asked, "Why do you allow your young people to marry so early and so quickly at twenty-one years of age?" "I will tell you something," David answered quite at ease, firm in character, and broad of stature. "We do it in this way because we are against prostitution and because among us no one should be looked down on." After he had answered other questions in the same short, clear manner, the government official takes him to his big Parliament gathering, where, as David said, "the women sit in their short skirts without even being ashamed of themselves." There he says, "This man has given me such good answers that you all ought to hear him." Whereupon David, who is steward and not a servant, made a clear and open confession of his faith. Therefore my diary will have much more to tell about this (so called) "lack of mission."

But—America has missed the judgment of the World War, of revolution, financial collapse, and our movements of recent times. The social conscience is lacking. The feeling for the kingdom of God and its justice is missing. One preaches to deaf ears. Mammon rules unchallenged over the irreligious and the religious-minded, too, whose zeal for conversion and sentimentalism about the Savior is seen by our Hutterian brothers only as false prophecy. They also tell them this: "The false prophets, which is what the churches and sects in fact are, take the truth away from the people because they preach falsely about it, and cry peace, peace, where there is no unity." At the same time our brothers are aware that they fall far short of true mission because it takes so much of their strength just to keep alive their three thousand plus some hundreds. They complain, "The mother that bore us has grown old; she no longer brings forth the kind of children she used to." So they expect more from us than we have. For the power of faith is very strong here, and everything is judged according to the Spirit—whether one is living in the Spirit, speaking and working in the Spirit, whether one is full of love, and whether one speaks the truth openly. To sum up: it is life, true, godly life witnessing to the new birth, so that the unity is amazing.

With this I will close for today as my eye is pricking a little again. To sum up, I will say only what has come to me through the experience of present-day Hutterianism. The "old, familiar" things become filled with a new, unexpected reality and certainty for me, above all regarding repentance, faith, love, surrender, community, forgiveness, redemption, and giving of self in total dedication. Today's Hutterianism consists of an upright peasant people well aware of the cause it represents and with complete reserve toward all people who do not seek it. But they are full of love and ready to serve all those who understand this cause, want it, believe in it, and love it. I have experienced this brotherhood of faith in the fullest measure. (They like to call me "our brother in the faith," which means they recognize we stand on the same foundation of faith, but at the same time indicates that the practical union has still to come.) Even Peter Hofer, Rockport, the co-worker of old David Hofer the Elder—he is considered especially reserved—took a car and came the twenty-two miles to pay me a very warm visit during my sickness. The old elder is too ailing. He recently said, "If Arnold really comes from Germany and wants what the forefathers had, he will be very dissatisfied with us just because of our great possessions in land and money." He is very grieved about the development in Alberta and is also against the printing of books because through it, copying by hand, which is so personal and beautiful and has such a powerful effect, will fall into disuse. He is a watchman on the walls of Zion, one of the strongest characters of present-day Hutterianism. I am especially eager to meet him. By the time you receive this letter I shall just be leaving him.

Because of my eye I had to choose one of two things for this letter. Either to go into your so loving and important letters which deeply gladden me, or to write these impressions of my visit here. I believe you would want to hear the latter most of all.

Wolf Creek Bruderhof, July 18, 1930

Yesterday I was waiting for Dr. A. A. Wipf. It was already 5:30 in the evening when Anna Basel, the wife of the steward, David Wipf, who is at present responsible for the hof, came to me obviously alarmed. She is my hostess, sees to my food very well, is housemother and head cook. "There is a telegram for you," she said. "Who should bring it to you?" I think at once of you and ask quickly, "From over there, from Germany?" She says "Yes," with an anxious look on her face and I say, "I will fetch it myself," and start off. She calls out, "He's fetching it himself." However I was not afraid, but felt at once that you were worried about my eye sickness. But she thought you had died, because she knows our great love for one another. But now I had your cabled message, the important word of our united Bruderhof in my hand! I can well imagine and have been constantly worried that the letter in a strange handwriting using strange words, would make you more anxious than if I had waited to write myself. But from the start it looked as if this attack on the eye would last for quite some time, and there was no Tata, our dear Else, there to write in my stead, because I was unable to. So I thought to send you at least these two weak signs of life. But just think: Thursday evening after the result of the third injection, I had the intention of sending a telegram to arrive before the two letters written by little Elizabeth. Now I sat there very troubled and downcast knowing your faithful concern for me. Then right away the steward's helper, Joseph, came and said, "Don't lose heart so quickly! We'll take you to Freeman." In five minutes a car was there, and by about 6:15 I had covered the 14 miles to Freeman.

Continued on p.82. See: Here the Diary proper begins.

EBERHARD ARNOLD'S DIARY

While With the Brothers in America

TO MY FAITHFUL EMMY

Introductory Remarks About the Children
For My Mö[1]
and

First Book

Begun in July, 1930
at the Wolf Creek Bruderhof

The Spirit leads us
Through storm and darkness.
Let us pray fervently
That He remain with us eternally.

We want to let ourselves be led
Always by Him.
Though the road be arduous,
We remain true to Jesus.

We want no lying and deceit;
We have felt the love of God.
We have had enough of worldly things,
For God leads us ever onward.

For her dear Papa from Mö. May 30, 1930

---

[1]Monika, Eberhard and Emmy's youngest daughter.

For my beloved little Mö
first some introductory remarks about the children
before starting the diary.

You, my beloved little Mö, are the very dearest little girl I know.
You have given me so much joy and have also written such fine words
for me in this diary that the first words I put into this little red book
are to tell you about the Hutterian children. I am very fond of the
children here. On the first evening that my wretched eye was a little
better here at the Wolf Creek Bruderhof, I sat down on an outside
stair landing where some children were. It is a bit like our kitchen
stoop at home. Presently they came, one after the other, more and
more, until about thirty little girls had gathered. Some little boys came
too. But they laughed so much and teased the girls that I soon sent
them away. Gradually the children began to sing. Little Rebecca,
about six years old, started the song *"Weil ich Jesu Schäflein bin"*
("Jesus' little lambs we are") at least five times before they managed
to sing it. The other songs went better. Ask Tata for the small black
book, or see if our Mama has it, and read the songs the children here
sang for me. You in the Sun Troop[1] will like especially this song—a
real little sun song: *"Die liebe Sonne an dem Himmel / Kommet wieder
zu uns her"* (The pleasant sun in heaven high returns anew to bring
us light). They sang it with great joy, as well as *"Jesu Du allein /
Sollst mein Führer sein"* (Jesus, none but thee shall my leader be).
They went on to sing for me two lively songs out of the life of our
beloved Jesus Christ: *"Gott grüss Euch Singer alle"* (God greet you,
singers all), telling of Jesus out on the sea, and *"Es kam ein Fräulein
mit dem Krug / zum heiligen Jakobs-Brunnen"* (There came a woman
with a jar to Jacob's holy well), a song they especially like. Another
song they love very much is *"Ich bin ein Hirt spricht Gottes Sohn /
Die grosse Lieb die treibt mich an"* (I am a shepherd, saith God's
Son, and great love urgeth me). It describes Jesus' love for the one
lost sheep that strayed from the flock and fell among wolves. Another
song they sing with great vigor is against getting lost through following
one's own way: *"Der Herr sitzt in sein Himmelsthron"* (The Lord sits
on his heav'nly throne) up to *"Es ist alles zu späte"* (Now it is all
too late). The little children sang all these songs to me with great
enthusiasm. I was quite alone with them. The others, the grown-ups,
did not want to disturb us.

---

[1]Group of Bruderhof children who met on their own in the spirit of Jesus.

The children like to come to me and gaze at me for a long, long time. Mariale, eight years old, and her sister Rebecca, seven years, are with me most of all. In my room, using my colored pencils, they have colored something for you, which I am enclosing. The best enclosure of all also comes mainly from eight-year-old Mariale. It consists of twenty children's games, children's dances, and rhymes, all of very old German origin, probably going back before Reformation times. Quite possibly one or the other of these has long since been lost to scholars and is now being rediscovered here. In our German homeland this or that little song or dance may still be found here or there. Once I am better known here, I am going to have the children do all the circle games [*Reigen*] they know, and I will write them down for you. In general, the Hutterians and their children are very reserved about these old, traditional things and hide them carefully, exactly as you read in old stories about folk customs now lost.

They all *gleichen*, that is, like me very much already. In their old language *gleichen* means "to like," "to feel akin to," "to enjoy seeing," etc. Little Mariale is the one that tells me the most. She lives opposite me with her sister Susanna, who is married to Michel, the community's mechanic. Just the other day she had her first baby, weighing twelve pounds. And just think, Mölein, the little eight-year-old girl may—and has to—do for the little baby everything the young mother cannot yet do herself. And she does it very gladly.

You would be amazed to see how the little girls' hair is braided. To prevent hair falling over their faces or being cut off, even the very small girls have a fine, thin braid plaited around their forehead, making a firm frame around it from the part, which is in the middle, to the ears.

At the age of fifteen the girls, here called *Dierndl*, get their school-leaving certificate, as Elisabeth, Mariale's fifteen-year-old sister, did on June 8, 1930. They go at once into the communal work in kitchen, garden, fields, and milking (four cows per girl), etc. That also includes separating the milk collected every morning and evening in a huge barrel, which rolls on two big wheels. The school children have just eight months of school a year. However, the other four months are not simply holidays for playing, but are used to teach the children to work—the boys as well!

Oh yes—the boys. That's simply marvelous here! Best of them all is Joseph—he, too, a brother of Mariale. Although not yet twelve years old, for three years now he has looked after the six hundred sheep (with just as many lambs), always on horseback and assisted only by one dog. He has done it so reliably that Darius, the old brother responsible for the sheep, could feel free to go to Canada to set up the new hof there, leaving the sheep so completely in the care of the twelve-year-old boy that the steward had to check only from time to time. He always found everything in good order.

This little Joseph always stands up for his brother Joshua, who is more than a year older but quite lazy and childish and full of high spirits. It is wheat harvest time, and the other day Joshua, thirteen years old, was to have got up at half past three in the morning for stooking the wheat sheaves. But he slept in! Oh, that was bad. For he had been wakened. His mother called the steward's helper and said he or the work distributor should punish Joshua. But little Joseph, getting someone else to take his place with the sheep, did the work for his brother. And the steward and work distributor just laughed.

Joshua is a rascal. He is much attached to me, for he is grateful for the answer I gave when I was asked what I thought of him. I said, "He is not a bad lad; he is just childish." They all said, "Yes, that's it." And no one was angry with him anymore, even though he had kicked the enormous, purebred St. Bernard that always lies before my door. In the evening Joshua, the thirteen-year-old, called me and went with me to the river, the James River, where the boys and children go swimming. In spite of the heat I could only put my feet in the water, because my eye was not yet as well as it is now. Joshua showed me the stars, that is, the Great Bear or Big Wagon, and asked

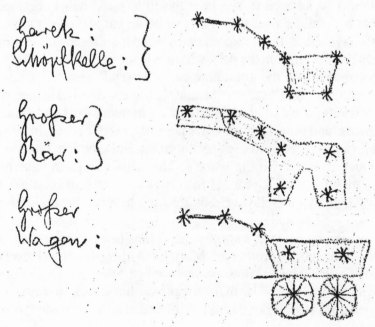

me if I felt homesick. "Oh yes," I said, "I am homesick the whole time." But I was happy that you see the same stars I see, although at a different hour. Joshua told me that they call the Great Bear the Big Dipper—*Garetz* in their language. And indeed, the constellation looks to us like whatever we expect it to.

While we were gazing at the sky, I asked Joshua, "Wouldn't you like to come with me to Germany?" "No," he said, "I'm too afraid of drowning in the big sea." Then we talked about calling on the Savior Jesus Christ and that we need a lot of strength to do always what is right, to be neither lazy nor superficial and to live to give joy to those whom we love, for they look upon us as the stars do at night. And we have to pray for that strength. Since then Joshua comes to my door more often than I can open it to him, as I have to take such great care of my eye. But now all that hurt me in my eye has got better.

So chubby Joshua with his laughing face and his trusting, merry eyes is the cause of much worry. Once he even earned money for himself by catching fish and selling them. For that he got such a terrible thrashing from his father, Joshua, who is the servant, that old David, the steward, did not think it at all good. But the boy himself told me, beaming, that his father had done right, for it had been very bad of him to earn money for himself.

The cowboys are a great joy to me—Jan, aged thirteen, and David, aged eleven. The two of them herd the cows from the back of a nimble, dark brown horse, with the help of a dog that obeys their every word, as they demonstrated with great pride. On arriving with their many cows at a big wiremesh gate in a fence, the younger one hops down, swings the gate open, and—hup!—he is back in the saddle. Riding round the cattle, they drive them through the gate; then the smaller one—hup!—is down again, shuts the gate, and with one bound—hup!—he rejoins his team-mate on the horse's back. Through it all they are beaming with joy and harmony; indeed, quarreling and strife are practically unknown here.

Now, dear Mölein, beloved Monika Elisabeth, this little "letter" is perhaps enough for an introduction to the diary. Even as it is, it has become the longest letter you have received in your life so far. It gladdens my heart to think how happy it will make you. As regards the learning of songs, the children's Sunday School, and the way the very littlest ones, the babies, are looked after—all that I want to tell in the main part of the diary, which I will send to dear, good Mama. If she stays with you, she will read it to the whole circle, including you, Mölein, just as it is written.

I am so infinitely happy at the thought that our dear, dear Emmy Mama, who will be my best companion, my greatest help and joy especially here, is ready to leave, with the unanimous agreement of all. But it is not yet the right moment for it here. And for you too, it is better if she, the best of mothers, can remain with you a little longer. But even now it greatly cheers and comforts me to know that the Brothers can invite her to come just as soon as they all see it that way. Many have already told me, "But your wife must come here too! You have said she is a good wife, the best of wives." She is indeed that, and it comforts me to know that you all and particularly you, Mölein, are helping your dear Mama to bear the long separation. So give her a hearty kiss from

> your Papa, who loves you very much

Here the Diary proper begins:
First Book: Summer 1930
Begun July 18, 1930 at the Wolf Creek Bruderhof, SD.

The cablegram went off to you this morning, my beloved. First, with the help of Dr. Wipf, I had to fetch the operator from his house to his office last night. It was too late for him to send it that same evening. But it will surely have got through all right. To my surprise, we found that his list of cable receiving stations included "Fulda, Germany," whereas your cablegram was sent from Frankfurt on Main.

As it was, I came with my doctor directly from a most thorough eye examination and third injection. By the way, Dr. Wipf wrote the text of the cable for me, as they were not used to my style of handwriting. He actually considered the eye treatment finished and wanted to let me go without a fourth injection. But because of the relapses I have had I asked him for a final preventative injection on Monday, and he agreed. Dr. Wipf is a very conscientious and experienced doctor of sixty-two, to whom the best-known eye specialists of this country have often referred very difficult cases. From the very start he looked upon the disease as serious and set about treating it with energy and persistence. But now he definitely thinks I will have no further relapses. He was completely satisfied with the condition of the iris and pupil, and even to laymen such as we are, it looks really good. You of course know what the healed eye looks like. The whole area around the iris is now pure white. Farther away faint pink veins are still to be seen, but Dr. Wipf thinks

they will completely disappear this time. In spite of my continuing
to use atropine in the left eye twice daily, the right eye functions
easily and smoothly, quite unhampered. Oh, it was a painful illness,
and for a whole fortnight I used even the right eye for only a few
moments. All the more do I thank God's loving-kindness for restoring
my health, and I pray that I may truly put it to his service.

You must write and thank Anna Wipf, my hostess here, and
Elisabeth Hofer, my nurse, to be addressed as "Anna Basel" and
"Elisabeth Basel" respectively. Anna Basel, the housemother, childless, brave, energetic, blunt, and often loud-voiced, enjoys the
trust and respect of everybody. She tires herself out daily and is
constantly concerned about the well-being of the community. She has
cooked and brought me all my food and washed my clothes more
often than I needed. She would complain loudly that I don't eat
anything, according to her way of thinking. ("He's eaten nothing
again!") But finally she came to see that for me it was indeed a lot.
Just imagine, dear, good Emmy: at eight in the morning there appeared
fish, cheese, sausage, honey, white bread, butter, coffee, porridge
with cream, and a glass of Southern wine. I have seen to it that now
I get "only" porridge with milk, coffee, bread, butter, and cheese. At
eleven o'clock, that is, an hour before the sun is at its highest, the
midday meal is served—either two pigeons, or a broiler, or half a
chicken, or a big fish, or lamb or mutton, or pork or ham, etc., with
potatoes, dumplings of all kinds, noodles, or grits. Instead of gravy
there is pure cream with dripping poured over it, often very good
vegetable soups made with milk, which I will describe in another
place, and finally mulberries or coffee or (twice a week) three cupfuls
of vanilla ice cream with frozen whipped cream, and so on. It is clear
that I can eat but little of these masses of extremely fat foods and that
I must select carefully. At about 3:30 in the afternoon I am served—
ever since my liking for it was discovered—strong coffee with cream,
as well as bread and sausage, plus honey or fish. Usually I take "only"
butter and honey. At this snack-time Joseph, David Wipf's deputy,
likes to turn up. He shouts for me to come out, "Eberhard Vetter,
let's have a chat and some coffee!" He gets such strong coffee only
with me, and he is just as fond of it as he is of frequent and nourishing
meals. Then Anna Basel rushes up panting, "Oh dear, Eberhard Vetter
said, 'Little water and much coffee,' and along comes Joseph Vetter
again and drinks it all up and leaves the poor man nothing! So tomorrow
I am just going to use more water. Ah well, go and drink it, Joseph,
I might as well make some more." In the evening yet another hefty

meal. Along with all that, I drink quite a lot of milk with the many medicines I have to swallow, and this does me good. In spite of the heat here in America, I feel in general very well.

Elisabeth Basel, the wife of Joshua Hofer, the servant, and mother of twelve children (as is common among the Hutterites), is the proved and tested nurse and midwife here. She has looked after me in the very best way and, following carefully Dr. Wipf's directions, has treated and provided me with everything I need.

Johannes Vetter, who takes care of the poultry and calves, is a widower who mourns deeply for his wife. Three times a day he supplies me with a pailful of ice and reads me wonderful things from the old teachings of the brothers—today, for example, a very important commentary on the Sermon on the Mount, including the following important passage:

Concerning Matt. 7:18

The reason is this: Since he perceives what the spirit of God writes into his heart, though he may not understand the letter written with pen and ink, he does understand the power of God's spirit, imprinted in his heart by the finger of God. The natural letter kills, but the Spirit gives life. Is it not so that he who has enough dollars has enough pennies too? The main thing is love.

It will interest our Adolf that the Hutterites regard all Baptists, etc. as people of the written letter, who lack the Spirit. They hide behind the printed letters of the Bible, which they misunderstand and misinterpret; they constantly prattle about it (which is greatly disliked by the Hutterites) and, not having the Spirit, they reject the meaning of the Word. Yesterday, once again two Baptists turned up here, a young preacher and an elderly peddler of religious books. The latter went on and on preaching with no reverence for the work of the Holy Spirit here, while the brothers and sisters (gathered informally outside one of the many house entrances) kept an icy silence. At the end the young preacher said, "Yes, you see, we are really close to one another in our faith. The differences are quite small." With a friendly smile and a good word he wanted to make up for the disturbance caused by his older colleague. However, from men and women he received the vigorous reply, "You are quite wrong. The difference is like day and night, for you do not do the will of God. We have nothing in common with you." The older man had actually used all kinds of passages from Paul to defend wealth. However, I want to leave it for the next letter to give a general picture of faith and life at the hofs here.

The first thing to do is to make clear the pros and cons of the situation for us and for your coming over, beloved Emmy. You see, everything moves very slowly here. Nobody can say anything about me, you, or our Bruderhof until I have spent some days with the Elder, David Hofer, in Rockport. They all love me very much and say they will miss me when I travel on, but nobody can decide anything without the word of the elders. Thus I am not permitted to preach or pray in church but am always made to sit next to the servant, except in Rockport, where they did not dare to do even that without "David Vetter." Hence, the individual Bruderhof can indeed "give alms" but cannot finance any large-scale relief for our Bruderhof until the elders have spoken. They all keep saying, "If only your wife were here!" But to your inquiry about your journey, they answered at once that they have to wait for David Vetter and the other elders—Joseph Kleinsasser and David Hofer, Manitoba and Christian Waldner and Elias Walter, Alberta—to give the invitation.

Now I have lost some time (particularly as regards writing the diary and copying manuscripts) but not all that much, for David Hofer, Rockport, was in Canada until the second week in July and afterwards was not well, and right now a most venerable old brother of seventy-five, Jakob Hofer—a wonderful patriarch—is on his death bed. So we must be patient. But if God gives grace, I hope I can send you the invitation and traveling expenses about July 26, as the very best birthday present for myself. That would be just glorious! It would be so wonderful for me that I cannot yet grasp it. And the money must be earmarked specifically for that purpose. Today I am sending you eighty German marks for journey preparations, above all for your teeth. Please use this money entirely for yourself.

Let us bravely face the fact that you cannot be with me for too long a stretch, away from the children. What a comfort it was for me that you, the best of all mothers, could be with Hardy in his hard struggles, which moved me very much. We cannot both be away from our children at the same time for too long. I see now quite clearly that, at the very earliest, I might come home a few days before Christmas. The task is too enormous, and the old brothers are slow. It is all the more wonderful how everything has been blessed until now. My illness, too, served our purpose, as indeed all things must work together for good. What matters now is to win the elders. Elias Walter's advice to travel via South Dakota and Manitoba was right. I shall stay in Manitoba for a shorter time and will see to it that most of the servants are called together. The program looks about like this: South Dakota till the beginning of August; Manitoba and Elias Walter till September 15; and Manitoba again probably just a fortnight. You could arrive at Elias Walter's place around September 10 and would then experience exactly half the journey with me. Actually, I am afraid that three and a half months is about all you could stand away from the children. And the journey must not be shortened by even one day if the lofty goal is to be attained: dynamic spiritual as well as practical economic unity with the Hutterites here. So, however much it flies in the face of my own longing and joy, there are two reasons why I advise against a too-early departure for you. First, because of the elders here, whom I must first win over for your journey; secondly, because of the length of our absence from home, which in my own case is not to be shortened. All the more glorious will be the reward when the time comes for you to travel from Halifax directly to Elias Walter's. That will be one of the best days of his life for your

Eberhard
who loves you with all his heart always and everywhere

Wolf Creek Bruderhof, S. Dak.
Monday, July 21, 1930

Today, the last day I am spending at the Wolf Creek Bruderhof on my way out, I want to try and describe the general impression I have gained at the Bon Homme and Wolf Creek hofs and also during just one day at the Rockport Bruderhof.

In Germany we had understood very well that the individual hofs still live in community and that their forefathers' foundation of faith stands even today. But with almost suffocating anxiety we asked ourselves if the living and life-giving spirit of 1525, 1528, 1533, of 1765 and 1770, of 1857 and 1874 might still be preserved on the American Bruderhofs—the spirit that is the Holy Spirit of God and of our coming ruler, Jesus Christ. With great joy I can declare that our expectations have been far surpassed. It is a miracle of God that after so many generations the fellowship of church communities stands in fresh bloom, showing a living faith and innermost certainty about the way. This is possible only through the Holy Spirit himself. All are deeply convinced of that; they testify again and again that only the spirit, the good spirit, the Holy Spirit, can give us life and community and keep us in it.

It is therefore a crass untruth for Krimmer Mennonites,[1] such as

---

[1] A small Mennonite Church from the Crimea, Russia, publishers of the *Wahrheitsfreund*.

Joseph Tschetter, to assert that the Hutterites neither know nor desire the Holy Spirit and rebirth. The opposite is the truth. They testify clearly that without conversion and rebirth there is no life. The old teachings, too, demand both but regard rebirth as more than conversion. The Hutterites are convinced that the evangelistic conversion and rebirth of those that merely profess Christ with their lips is nothing, since it does not bring forth the fruits that alone enable us to recognize the new life.

It is indeed my deep impression that what maintains the communities and their order is not moral legalism or slavish tradition. That is not at all the case here. Rather, the amazingly dedicated obedience to the community on the part of old and young alike is to be explained by the spirit of faith and discipline, which from within urges the heart to act communally and warns it against all that is of self. Just yesterday, on Sunday, we heard again, in the *Lehr* and *Gebet* based on John 14, that only the presence and indwelling of Christ and his Holy Spirit can form and preserve a church. All here are deeply convinced of this and constantly pray for it. It is not force or habit that makes them attend the *Lehr* and *Gebet*; on the contrary, they miss it deeply when, as now, with the move to Canada in progress, many an evening no servant is available for the *Gebet*. Here at the Wolf Creek Bruderhof Michel or Joseph Waldner drive many miles from Bon Homme Sunday after Sunday to hold the *Lehr* and *Gebet*. I have a deep and warm friendship with both of them, as with Joseph Stahl of the Lake Byron Bruderhof. We share our thoughts in love, and I can speak out quite openly all that burns in my heart.

They have a fine Sunday afternoon custom here. At Sunday School, which is held then, each of the young people and children tells what spoke most strongly to him in the morning *Lehr*. It is then explained anew by the brother who has this responsibility. Here at Wolf Creek that is at present the duty of the same Johannes Stahl who, during my illness, read to me from the old writings, and he does it in a very fine, free, and deep way. At the end, they read aloud from the New Testament, one after the other, right down to the smallest who can read. The old expositions of Scripture and "teachings" (sermons or interpretations of the Bible with practical applications to everyday life in community) are the chief spiritual nourishment in the Hutterian community life of today. These "teachings" are most remarkable. We absolutely must investigate them all thoroughly. Some two hundred in number, they are the sources for Johannes Waldner's account of the time of decline. Most of them come from the time between 1650 and 1700. They still represent through and through the faith and life of the early Hutterites, but with stirring laments about the decline and decay setting in then.

The difference between our Bruderhof and American Hutterianism consists largely in this: We seek to find our spiritual food and foundation in the first and second Hutterian periods, of 1525-1533 up to 1578, with their joyful going to the attack, whereas in the American communities it is the late period that serves that purpose. What Michel Waldner, Bon Homme, and in a similar way Elias Walter have expressed is probably correct: These teachings from the time of Andreas Ehrenpreis to the approaching decline fit the present situation in our communities best. But here the question must be asked: Along with the faithful attention given to these teachings, should not epistles and confessions of faith from the first and second Hutterian periods be laid on the church's heart every week also, so that their more vigorous fire may cause the glowing embers to flare up once again? May God grant us in Germany that we, with the aid of the brothers in America, can make those epistles and confessions of faith accessible to the communities, so that they can be read everywhere. At present the communities all have the teachings between 1600/1650 and 1700, but only here and there possess also epistles, confessions of faith, and article books from the earlier times.

The main reason for this striking fact is the habit, brought along from Russia, of making these teachings the basis of all meetings where the servant proclaims the Word. At every Sunday morning *Lehr* (about two hours) and at each daily evening *Gebet* (about three quarters of an hour) a longer or shorter part of these teachings is read out, and the brother taking the meeting has the freedom and opportunity to interrupt his reading at any time and "speak from the Spirit." It is said in praise of Johann Entz, Old Elm Spring, who died of stones in the bladder, that he could speak "from the Spirit" for two hours, without reading in between. But as a rule, they say, he did not consider it right to do so.

Sunday here is as follows: the servant comes for me and inspects my suit to see that everything is right. Children are sent out to summon people to the *Lehr*. I have to put my black hat next to the servant's and sit next to him. Then quickly, one after another, all come in, dressed in their black Sunday best. No one needs to be admonished or reminded. Every community member not detained by some exceptional duty arrives punctually and of his own accord. To begin with, many verses are sung. Twice Michel Vetter, Bon Homme, had them sing for me the moving song, "Oh, where am I to turn now, poor little brother that I am?" It is on pages 675-679 of the large hymn book, *Die Lieder der Hutterischen Brüder* (Songs of the Hutterian Brethren). On one occasion, Michel Waldner announced it even more appropriately, "Oh, where am I to turn now, stupid little brother that I am?" The song is read out line by line, and the people join in lustily. The song may last from a quarter to half an hour. It is followed by a *Vorrede* (preface), that is, the reading of an old sermon with no fixed Bible text, interspersed with comments by the brother reading. Every community has a real treasury of such prefaces in old or more recent hand-written copies. Next comes a freely spoken prayer, offered kneeling and with uplifted hands. Only then, that is, three quarters or a whole hour into the meeting, comes the actual *Lehr* (teaching), based on a brief Bible text. Then more singing (usually further verses from the hymn sung at the beginning) and finally a freely spoken word of blessing with an indirect prayer, "Now, beloved brothers and sisters, let us ask God, the heavenly Father, that he in the name of Jesus Christ. . . ." During this indirect prayer they remain seated but raise their hands to God. While the Bible text is read out, however, they stand but do not raise their hands.

If anyone thinks this regularly used form paralyzes participation in the meeting, he is mistaken. The people love this dignified form and are heart and soul in it. Somebody told me with an expression of dismay that the Baptists and Krimmer Mennonites preach "even with their hands. But we want our servants to preach with their mouth only. We want to hear the Word and the truth but not see a person waving their arms around."

On leaving the meeting room, one hears on all sides, "But that was a fine teaching!" or "That was a sharp teaching!" and this or that detail of the text or commentary is discussed. All enjoy such pungent expressions as *Madensack* (bag of maggots) and the like. After that particular *Madensack* teaching we talked so animatedly and with such merry laughter about where eating stops and gluttony begins that in the end Joseph, the loudest of all, said, "We are laughing too much and too noisily, and that's not good either."

More important, however, than these echoes of the teachings is the question: What is the difference between the sixteenth and the seventeenth century, between the Hutterianism of Reformation times and that of the Thirty Years War and its aftermath, hence between the first Hutterian writings and the later teachings? It is the old story: With Jakob Hutter, Peter Riedemann, Peter Walpot and still further down the line, every deed and word was brimful of the work of the

Holy Spirit to the honor of God. Man, called to be the image of God, was to receive the Holy Spirit and the Church in faith through the incarnation of the Word, so that in this way God's rulership would be revealed in the united work of complete love. The kingdom of God, taking shape in a church community united in faith and word—a community of work and possessions, a community of the table and of education—was to reveal the righteousness of God and point to his approaching and everlasting reign. The kingdom of God and its righteousness was the object of early Hutterian faith, life, and work. God was to be revealed to all the zealous, the questioners, and seekers. At the same time it was clear there had to be rebirth, baptism, surrender, forgiveness of sins, certainty of salvation through the Redeemer Jesus Christ, eternal blessedness, and the other personal experiences. Without all these a man has no share in what is objective. But the reality of the kingdom of God is and remains the one thing that matters in it all. The shift that set in stealthily and almost unnoticed clearly came about through the influence of Luther and Johann Arndt and later of Pietism on the Hutterian heritage.

Present-day scholarship regards Johann Arndt as the child, hence Pietism as the grandchild of the Baptizer movement of Reformation times. In the same way it sees Jean de Labadie's[1] community of goods as a child and Pietism, once again, as a grandchild of Anabaptism. But grandchildren, though resembling the grandparents, are far from being like them. "Only to be blessed!" The eternal blessedness of the individual comes more strongly to the fore than is good for the clarity of the holy cause, which alone can be the object and content of blessedness. Hutterianism, even that of later generations, cannot fall prey to such a personal religion with its exaggerated one-sidedness and unashamed self-love as long as it really and truly lives in community and remains on the forefathers' objective basis of faith. But it cannot be denied that the later Hutterianism, that of the 17th century "teachings" as well as the Carinthians, who had been awakened by Luther and Arndt, were both affected by this shifting at least of accent and emphasis. That explains why things are as they are.

In the face of this situation it is necessary, with the same careful certainty, to place the emphasis once more on God himself, on his kingdom and his justice as revealed in his church and his future coming, on his revealing himself as the spirit, the creative spirit of complete unity. This shifting back to the original emphasis should lead to mission!

---

[1]1610-1674, former Jesuit, established a community in Holland.

However, we in Germany must not deceive ourselves. Here with the brothers, community is so totally supreme that the salvation of the individual member (also as regards eternal life) is seen solely in terms of obedient yielding and surrender to the community, of joyfully and unconditionally placing the community above the individual. Hence, the oldest writings have not actually been pushed out by the later teachings, but they have been given a different place. Remarkably enough, the more personal "teachings" form part of the objective general worship service, whereas the factual confessions of faith, epistles, article books, and chronicles find their use when it comes to baptisms, to the copying of writings, and to reading in families, all of which are of a more personal nature. The connecting link is the hymn books, which belong to both worlds.

I experience daily how firmly even the present-day Hutterites in America hold to their more objective forefathers and their witness. Yesterday and today I read to the people here from Loserth's[1] introduction and other old writings. They were *very* moved. Old and young crowded around me, sitting or standing, and quite generally it has to be said that I meet with extreme interest from everybody here, regardless of age. When I stopped reading, the enthusiastic exclamation from the circle of listeners, "That was like being in heaven or paradise!" was characteristic.

Today, on July 21, I too felt such joy and enthusiasm. Today the beloved and respected steward, David Wipf, returned home from the new Wolf Creek settlement in Canada, where three new houses are being built and a well drilled. He brought along two wonderful, ancient little mission and article books. They measure only $4'' \times 2\frac{3}{4}''$, are almost $1\frac{1}{2}''$ thick and deal with baptism, the Lord's Supper, community, governmental authority, divorce, going to war and to law. They also have the confession of faith, put into song, and conclude with a discourse. Further, they include what seems to be Peter Riedemann's oldest "Account" from his prison in Gmünden in Upper Austria, as well as the confession of faith of the schoolmaster Hieronymus Käls, Michel Behm, and Hans Oberecker in Vienna from the year 1536; Anthonius Erdforder's epistle to the Falkenstein prisoners, written from Steinabrunn in 1539; the song composed by the same Anthonius Erdforder, who died around 1542, "*Wohl auf, wohl auf von hinnen*" (From hence now let us journey, 12 stanzas); the song, "*Richt mich nicht in dein Grimme*" (Judge me not in thine

---

[1](1846-1936) Austrian historian, made valuable discoveries of Anabaptist sources and wrote on the Anabaptists in the Tirol and Moravia.

anger, 25 stanzas) by Wolf Sailer (servant of the Word 1547, died 1550) and finally, here incomplete, the ancient Goliath song. All three can be found in *Die Lieder der Hutterischen Brüder*. Both these precious little books doubtless belong to the oldest period, one of them certainly from before the time of Peter Walpot's eldership, the other belonging at the latest to his period. Some leaves inserted later contain important missionary letters of around 1782/83, as well as a short account of the voyage to America in 1874. Now our beloved David Wipf Vetter, presently responsible for Wolf Creek, has surprised me with this great and important present, giving me both these little books, which he had received directly from the first Elder, Darius Walter[1] to take with me and keep for my service in God's church. And when I begged him to write something in them, he said he was too unworthy to write his name into such a book. Thereupon we gave each other the kiss of brotherhood twice.

July 21, 1930

That was the first of such valuable gifts from among the old treasures of faith which I have received on this journey, even two little books at once! I look forward to the moment when I can show you these wonderful little books and read them to you. I hope from the bottom of my heart that this can happen at Elias Walter's in September. How endlessly happy I shall be then! You can be joyful that my eye is so well again. It was and certainly is your prayers to our good and merciful God, and the prayers of our whole Brotherhood, which have brought about healing. I am now missing your most recent letters very sorely. Already a week ago I sent to Manitoba for them, but they still have not arrived yet today and I must travel on. But whatever comes here will be sent on to me, you can depend on it. The farewell evening (July 21) was very moving. I read out some parts of Loserth's introduction, during which one harvest wagon after another rolled into the hof till 10 o'clock. Many said they would accompany me with their thoughts, and David Wipf, the brother responsible in Wolf Creek, told me that in these days he had told Elias Walter in Stand Off much good about me and that I truly was a brother. Now I go to Rockport. You, my beloved Emmy, with our whole Brotherhood will be with me in your thoughts.

---

[1] 1835-1903, appointed servant of the Word 1858 in Russia, later first elder of the Dariusleut in America.

Rockport Bruderhof, South Dak.
July 26, 1930

Now on my birthday I am so far away from you that we cannot hasten quickly to one another. And the task which I have to fulfill here is so great that it cannot be completed if we shorten the time. You know that it is not my nature to be slow in regard to a duty once recognized, and especially in face of a pressing need. But certainly my impulsive actions have not always been for the best.

I had not thought that I would feel homesickness and longing so strongly on this day; for I never attached the importance to my birthday that our beloved, fine boy did. But it was always a day of reflection for me. I have also told about it here, as there was no fear that they would make a big thing of it—and they don't either. For here everything personal is always seen and approached in relation to the great cause of eternity and of community life. But they gave me two Hutterian shirts, and they were even our color of blue.

Today at last I will answer your questions about clothing. All are completely in agreement with your suggestions. However everything, also in this matter, is left for the brothers who are elders to decide. But I am not nearly so far yet with David Hofer for him to listen to me on such questions. He is a kind of patriarchal peasant-prince; you wait for him to speak to you, without being able to bring up anything yourself. They are completely in agreement with our women and girls wearing our blue. The whole dress should be sewn in one piece and certainly quite long. It should not touch the ground, nor the top of the foot, but should reach to the ankle; the sleeves should be quite long, certainly at least to below the elbows; not too open at the neck, but also not too tight round the throat. In summer women and men always go without stockings in low shoes similar to sandals. Shorts above the knees and going barefoot, as our men and boys do, would surely not be tolerated, but they would accept "stockings over the trousers," as they put it here. Except on Sundays and for *Gebet*, you see the men only in shirts and trousers.

South Dakota, July 30, 1930

Unfortunately I was unable to continue writing, although there was still much I had on my heart. Quite generally, my impressions and experiences here are so strong and rich, beloved Emmy, that what I would like best is to just write and write to you all day long, so that you could then tell it to all at home. So, too, the short week I have just now spent at the Rockport Bruderhof was a great and deep experience, which stirred me to the depths. But before I attempt to give an orderly account of at least the main things, I want to tell in advance the result of this patient, quiet, tough, and nevertheless so exciting struggle. Then you, beloved Emmy and all you faithful ones at home, will not have to wait until the end of this long report as anxiously as I had to wait for the conclusion of these days—the longest I have lived through here.

In the two last days, July 28 and 29, I received at long last better news from David Hofer Vetter, the strictest elder among the present-day brothers. It was brought to me by the following brothers and sisters, who stand up loyally for me and you and all of us: Johannes Hofer, teacher till now at Buck Ranch (Elm Spring); Jerg Wipf, work distributor [*Weinzedl* or *Weinzierl*] at Rockport, S. Dak., now retired but still doing lighter work; Maria Hofer (midwife and nurse, who has been tending my eye, widow of one of the war martyrs of 1917-18, now remarried, granddaughter of the founder of Old Elm Spring, "Jakob *Lehrer*" Wipf), and others. David Vetter himself had still not said anything of importance with regard to our request, but at last spoke to me twice warmly and lovingly, telling of the beginning in America during the seventies and of his worries, fears, and unhappiness about the present condition of the Bruderhofs, in particular of the Dariusleut and Schmiedeleut. He spoke also of his wife's illness, and showed me wonderful old books in which his heart, grown almost equally old, lives and moves. In the course of his long life he has copied out 160 old teachings and many other manuscripts.

But then something happened similar to what I, too, would often do in Sannerz and on the Bruderhof, with guests and new people who had been waiting just as I had to wait here. When I had finally decided to leave and was about to depart along with some pigeons destined for Chicago—which, as I remarked to David Vetter, was perhaps symbolic—I was suddenly told to my amazement, "David Vetter wants to go with you to town." That was something quite unexpected after his previous attitude, which had been cool and forbidding, indeed, as cold as ice to begin with. On the way he said again and again, "I give you one piece of advice, Eberhard: stay in Germany as long as you can keep the school in the hands of the church." I told him that now I would surely be asked everywhere about his attitude to our Bruderhof, but I did not want to give the wrong answer, and would he please tell me what I should say. So at the last moment, while we were still sitting in the wagon (similar to ours) at the Alexandria railway station, he gave me the reply I had already heard from those faithful brothers and sisters, but which, of course, I could not mention to him: "Tell especially Joseph Vetter in Manitoba, Christel Vetter in Alberta, and Johannes Vetter in Alberta that I am too old, too weighed down with burdens, and looking toward my own end. Also, I am too alone here in South Dakota to arrive at a joint decision with all of you. But you can tell all of them that I am in agreement and satisfied with any decision that the brothers in Canada will come to with you, Eberhard, and for your people. Do not take it amiss that I have not taken up your cause better. But I could not do it, for I have already too much burdening me, and the others in Canada are too far away from me."

I had forgotten to mention the second servant at Rockport, Peter Hofer, aged forty-two. As he told me, he had represented very strongly to David Vetter that our cause should be seriously and vigorously taken up. In his opinion, what I have just reported is the best and utmost I could have got out of David Vetter at this first visit.

Things really did look bad the first days and even on July 26. I had had a wonderful ride along the James River in a two-horse wagon driven by a faithful brother from Wolf Creek. When he took me to David Vetter, the latter scarcely looked at me and just shook hands with me fleetingly and at once turned sharply to the man from Wolf Creek who remained very quiet and good-willing. He asked him, "Is it true that both your servants are up in Canada?" (The two, Joshua and Peter are overseeing the building of the new Wolf Creek Hof in Alberta. Without any paid labor, but with the help of twenty-five Hutterian men from many Dariusleut hofs, they have within just a few days—five, I heard—put up another large house, the third one.) The Wolf Creek brother answered meekly, "Yes." "Don't you people know," continued the old elder, "that it will take you many months to rebuild spiritually what you now neglect for a few weeks for the sake of the temporal? You place the temporal above the spiritual, and you will find out where that will take you." He went on to say that it was only an excuse, saying the servants were both needed up there to hold the twenty-five workers together. He declared further that the *Gebet* (the big meeting held every evening) was the one and only thing they could not do without. The good brother from Wolf Creek said nothing but took leave of me without delay and each of us shook the other warmly by the hand.

So then I sat on a bench outside the house without my faithful companion from Wolf Creek, next to the deeply dissatisfied, venerable old man, whose fine but sad countenance is framed by a billowing mass of white hair. But we were not alone. It was the evening just before *Gebet* and, as is always the case at every Bruderhof, a crowd of brothers and sisters stood around us. When we had driven into the hof, with its very spacious layout, they had greeted me with great love and almost with enthusiasm.

I went at once to the attack: "Beloved, honorable David Vetter, how I have waited for the moment when I would see you face to face and could lay on your heart the request of our brothers and sisters in Germany: Test us and accept us into complete union! We neither can nor want to live any longer outside the great church of God, and that means not without you brothers and sisters either."

"How can I do that?" was the reply. "I have let you know through Peter Vetter (Peter Stahl, Lake Byron) what you should do. If you really know the Scriptures and our forefathers and live according to them, you don't need me as well."

"Yes," I said, "that is true. But it would be a sin for us and would not have God's blessing if we wanted to remain on our own now that we have heard about you brothers and know that we share the same foundation of faith (Peter Riedemann, Jakob Hutter) and live in community according to the same order, even though in weakness."

His answer amazed me: "You are quite mistaken. The Lord has his people all over this vast earth, even where we do not know it—as long as they recognize the truth and live according to it. After Paul had been called by the Lord, he worked alone for years, without Jerusalem, without seeking contact with the other apostles."

"But in the end," I replied, "he did come to Jerusalem (Acts 15) and sought union, just like us. So did the Carinthians in 1763."

He answered with great earnestness: "Paul only did it after fourteen years. And instead of turning to our forefathers, you should turn to the apostles and prophets, as our Hutterian forerunners did themselves."

I said, "Yes, that is true. But we have now waited ten years. Must we really wait another four? And we have found out that no one has understood and lived the cause of the apostles and prophets as did the Hutterian church of the early days. And we now hope the same from you."

Once more, his answer amazed me: "There you are again mistaken. We here are on the brink of decline. What are you looking for with us? You want to unite. Unite with whom? We are no longer united ourselves. Here is Dakota, there Manitoba, there Alberta. Here we are Lehrerleut, there Schmiedeleut, and there Dariusleut. Where is their bishop? Who takes any notice of the elders? If you want to unite, you must try to unite thirty-three times with thirty-three different churches. And the Lord alone knows who is still faithful in these churches. I don't want to wish for it—but only a time of great persecution could purify us, reduce our number, and unite us. If God has given you true zeal, faith, and spirit there in Austria, you had better stay there and make do without us. Here we are being corrupted by the English school and through economic matters taking control. True churches ought not to run into debt the way they do in Manitoba. That puts them completely under the rule of the devil in matters of finance, and the spiritual has to give way.

"And how can I say anything about your people over there, Eberhard? How can I unite with you? Anybody can come along and tell wonderful tales. First of all, two brothers from here would have to go to your place in Austria and inspect and test everything before a uniting can even be thought of. Otherwise a very great misfortune might come upon us through you."

"Yes," I said quietly and firmly, though probably waxing a bit pale, "that is surely the right thing. For two years we have been pleading with you to send two brothers to us. And now I ask you: Come to us yourself and help us, David Vetter, or send two of your brothers to us!"

"So that is what you wrote," he replied, "but what I don't like at all about you, Eberhard, nor about Elias Vetter, is that you both use a typewriter. I have read but very few of your letters, for I don't like typewriters. What's happened to our beautiful old copying? By copying things one writes them straight into one's heart—much more than by just listening to them. But typewriters—I don't like them!"

That is how it went and how it remained the following days, only that he said less and less, mostly just, "About you folks I can't say anything at all." That is how the days went up to the turning point I told about in the beginning. Thus the unfriendly pessimism of the seventy-five-year-old elder has deep spiritual reasons. What adds to it on the human level is that his equally old wife has been somewhat mentally disturbed ever since she was past the age for bearing children, though she has not wavered in her faith. That is why he said to me: "You have to remember that I have been suffering in my own flesh for over twenty years. My family situation, with my wife's illness, so depresses me that I cannot take anything more upon myself. I am asking God to let me depart with her before the move to Alberta. The school over there will ruin us anyway."

In the meantime I have become close friends with the other brothers and sisters in Rockport, so that they all wish for union with us. Above all, I have been looking through their wonderful books and have also copied a very small part of them. I am sending over the fruit of that laborious work, committing it to Else's faithful care. From this you can see how well my eye is. Tell Hans and everybody that Hans should especially read out the epistle by Jakob Hutter, just as soon as it is copied, that being my birthday letter to our Bruderhof.

Unfortunately, I haven't got anywhere with your and my and our wish and hope that you, beloved Emmy, might come to me and the Bruderhofs here, even though I brought up this request very urgently. As regards money, all I have been given is ten dollars for the continuation of my journey (the other hofs did the same), so I am sorry I can enclose no more than ten marks for you today. I still have to go briefly to Scotland and Bon Homme, since Michel Waldner has asked me very lovingly and helpfully to consider with him the outcome of what we came to in Rockport for the Schmiedeleut. He is determined to bring about my appointment and our uniting as quickly as possible. Michel Vetter commands a lot of respect everywhere, also among the Dariusleut and Lehrerleut.

On Sunday I shall be with our good friend Joseph Stahl in Lake Byron. Then north to Manitoba, at long last. I look forward with great longing to finding letters from all of you there, especially from you, beloved Emmy. Unfortunately I must close for today. Before I can send off what I have copied—twenty-eight pages of titles of old writings, with a description of their contents; thirty-three pages of the church chronicle of Wischinka, Raditschewa and so on; and especially the Jakob Hutter epistle of fifty-three pages—it will still take me many hours of work to go through it all and check it. For this purpose and for writing this letter in my diary I have had to find a hotel in Mitchell—also in order to nurse my eye. Everything will go off together, including a teaching on Pentecost, and will reach you in good condition, I hope.

Lake Byron, August 5, 1930

. . . I was also glad to receive the pictures which are very dear to me, and likewise the excellent report of Emy-Ma's joy, interest, and liveliness, even in the eyes of Maria Keller,[1] who is so very strict.

---

[1] Principal of 'Soziale Frauenschule' where Emy-Ma trained as kindergarten teacher.

In 1930 Eberhard Arnold copied out by hand the whole of Jacob Hutter's first letter from the Tirol to the Church in Moravia, while at Rockport Bruderhof, SD. This is the first page of his copy.

Josef Stahl has given me her father's[1] most important book, *Die Reformation*. . . . I am sending it to you as soon as I have finished reading it in the train, as it is suited to you "Arnoldleut."

I also received the letters from faithful Mö, Tata, and Trudi, so that I could again imagine myself completely in your experience. In addition to the postcard from you from the railway train at Frankfurt, in which you and Hans expressed your shock, I had received your last news of June 15, 18, and 19 with the recognitions and greetings from Erich Mohr, Georg, and Lene Schulz. At the same time, Tata wrote about the financial statement, and Hans had read to all the Sendbrief and my letter to the Brothers on my arrival in America. I read these letters again and again, especially yours, in which, in your great love, you bring everything so close to me. With Lene, Mö, and Georg I rejoice over the greatness and extent of the mission work; I rejoice with Tata over the decisive hour of the Spirit; with Erich Mohr over the work-week; with Trudi over the blackberry picking, and in the Kampfmeyers' feeling for the powers of decision. Above all I rejoice in Mö's work with the children and in the courageous support of all our children for you and me; in the many visits, and not least, that my telegram relieved you of your worry about me and made you so glad. I was so deeply moved by your telegram that I trembled in every limb. My great joy at your coming and the nearness of spirit of all of you was mixed with anxiety that little Elizabeth's letters, had shocked you all too much. This really was the case, although for such a child the letters were so lovingly meant. I myself did not know exactly what she had written because during my illness, when Elizabeth and Kathrina Hofer read the letters to me, I did not yet quite understand the hutterisch dialect. I had thought it would be a relief to you all to hear that my eye was coming along "nicely" (according to them), but I still had the question whether one could honestly say that. (Actually it looked dreadfully ugly.) At this both mother and daughter cried out at the same time, "But Dr. Wipf said so."

Ah, beloved Emmy, the great thought that behind the united Brotherhood there stands God's infinitely good will, according to which you should come to me is a real comfort to me. But our most faithful Josef Stahl fears it will take a long time before the Brothers, in their slowness, can reach clarity about it. I hope that the very warmly disposed Schmiedeleut will perhaps see to it; their elder, Josef Kleinsasser, stands very strongly behind Elias Walter in support of

---

[1]Ludwig Keller, one of the first historians to write positively about the peaceful Anabaptists.

us. Elias Vetter recently sent out the almost too enthusiastic reports from South Dakota about my visit to all the brothers. To my shame much is said in it about my honesty, humility, spirit-filled clarity, and firm foundation of faith. Josef Stahl was a little embarrassed that it was sent around like that. But our faithful Elias will try everything possible to hasten a decision in our favor. So he sent word to me that I should remain with David Hofer, Rockport, until his answer becomes quite clear, so that it doesn't have to be all "studied" again later to find out what he had meant. Well, I think what I reported thoroughly to you last time is the best and clearest I can say about this melancholy but deeply spiritual old man. Above all, the brothers in Alberta will then have full authority and agreement beforehand for everything they may do. Michel Waldner expressed the same, but even more positively. He thinks that if Joseph Kleinsasser Vetter, Milltown, would give a written statement (Joseph Stahl's suggestion), the Dariusleut would have the task: 1) to incorporate us and 2) to appoint me. They say I have done my utmost to achieve in advance the agreement of the other two groups. So now I face the second stage of my journey in Manitoba with the best of prospects, very, very different, much, much better than before the first stretch in South Dakota, where I was still very uncertain how it would turn out. I am deeply moved and inwardly stirred through all these things, and also through the reports from you and all the others.

Only how is it with this holding back about various matters? I refrain from writing my opinion from such a distance. It would look too sharp. Rather I trust completely all you Brotherhood members, especially you, Hans, Tata, and Trudi, that you will not overlook or leave unchallenged anything that might destroy the church community. I hope you have received my big work about the Habertshof[1] and have read it out. It could have shown up very clearly just these points which now seem to arise among us too. But if the decision for your journey came from the spirit of unity, then clearly these evil things which were revealed must have been put right. Because some of the letters went ahead of me, I do not quite have a picture of the order in which everything happened. Hans, as my representative, should have sent me a report to Stand Off in connection with all this—or be sending it off as soon as possible. Unfortunately, your birthday parcel is still sitting there. I will have it sent to Manitoba now. Your fine, loving letters make me so very happy about the children, the

---

[1]See note Chapter 2, p.62.

hay harvest, and the calf from the best cow. Are Josef and Albert
still away? What is Paul doing? Did he also receive the Paul Hofer
card I sent to all of you? Is Milly still with you? How did you celebrate
Sannerz 1920?[1] I thought and still think much about it, how above
all, God has given you unlimited strength and clarity again and again.
And it will be given to you also now for the Brothers of the Common
Life. How fine and meaningful it must have been when you told about
our engagement and uniting for Christ and the richness of our
experience on our way to the goal. You should write that down,
complete with details for me and the children. I was glad about the
witness that Hugga and Trudi made at the summer solstice. I was
astonished and surprised that Erich [Mohr] won over not only A. Paquet
and F. Siegmund-Schulze but also Martin Buber[2] and the German
Quakers for the work week. That is sensational! How did Pappert
come to offer his cottage? And can I get more definite information
about reasonable offers from our neighbours while I am at Stand Off?
Now you can see how many thoughts are aroused in me by two out
of your eleven letters, which have only partly reached me till now.
Then there is Tata's letter where she calls you a genuine Hutterian
woman, which you truly are; where she tells about the important and
encouraging visit of the Kampfmeyers and also about Grunewald
(Pentecostal Baptist Movement) and Lades; about my library; about
Emy-Ma's coming home soon and her task—to take your place as
soon as you leave, and how happy she is that you yourself will
introduce her to it! Yes, our Bruderhof is unbelievably rich in inner
and outer experiences. Today we still cannot grasp fully the grace
that is given us in all this. May we all make the most of this unheard-of
opportunity to live a true life.

I heard from Elias Walter that your birthday parcel arrived partly
opened and that he was glad to see from it how thankful all are towards
me. First give them all my heartfelt thanks for their love.
Unfortunately, I cannot write often, or to many, because on the
Bruderhofs the days and evenings are very fully occupied; and anyway
the letters to you, dear mother and housemother, are intended also
for the others, in so far as you read them out. I have written one
hundred and fifty pages in the diary for you, and besides that, about
twenty-five more. Also today's letter will be a long one as I am
traveling to Manitoba and will slip in one or two days at a hotel again
to complete it. Otherwise I cannot manage it with my weakened

---

[1]See P.S. to letter from Else von Hollander, June 30, 1930, p.200.

[2]Jewish writer and philosopher, well-known already in pre-Nazi Germany.

strength. And now the question of the confirmation of our service is drawing nearer. And how deeply and strongly the Hutterites understand that!

Lake Byron, Wednesday, August 6, 1930

In my last hours in South Dakota, before traveling on to the brothers in Canada, I want to put in here the text of an important church action I came across here. It is what I have to request on behalf of our Bruderhof in Germany. If God's undeserved grace grants it, the Brothers will proceed with me according to old Hutterian tradition, and if not with me, then with someone else from among us as follows:

Dear brothers, God heard our prayer and showed us that from among the brothers our brother _____ pleases Him for His service. This we accepted with thanksgiving and made known to the Church, appointing our brother _____ on trial, according to the praiseworthy Christian custom of our forefathers.

Now he has served together with us for some time and has stood the test, so that we and all the elders are well satisfied with him and know of no further obstacle. If the Church gives him the same united testimony, the service of the Word should be entrusted to him without reservation.

So I ask you, Brother_____ , to come forward and stand before the Church.

First, I ask you, my brother, how do you stand? Are you willing to be obedient and allow yourself to be used, inside or outside of the country, as needed, whether or not the time suits you, however God the Almighty may lead?

Second, I ask you, are you willing to use brotherly admonition with true courage and zeal, thereby to teach and work in the Church of God, so that through you the Church may continue to be built up and adorned in the Lord?

Third, I ask you, my brother, do you agree with and accept the twelve articles of our holy Christian faith, and do you further acknowledge the Hutterian Confession of Faith, and are you determined to live accordingly, to the best of your ability, until your death?

Fourth, I ask you, my brother, are you willing, as long as you live, to remain steadfast in all these points to which you have committed yourself before God and the Church, until the Lord takes you from us through temporal death?

Now, my beloved brother, since we have all heard your

confession, answer, and agreement, let us conclude this action in the name of the Lord, go on our knees, and call upon Him for you in prayer.

After the prayer the brother remains on his knees, and the elder asks (while still standing at the table):

Now I ask you once more, my brother, is your attitude still the same as you declared publicly before God and the Church?

Answer: Yes.

Then the elder goes up to him with two or three others and asks:

Are you determined to remain faithful unto death to God and his Church in this service, to be an obedient witness of the truth, since we will be the first to be condemned to death by fire or the sword for the sake of God's word:

Answer: Yes, with God's help. (Amen!—Eberhard Vetter)

Then the elder says:

My brother, since we have given you our trust, we lay our hands upon you as a testimony in the name of the Lord Jesus Christ and in the strength of God that the service of the Word is entrusted and laid upon you and that you are given full authority to carry out this service, together with us, for the salvation and betterment of men, and to do the work of the Lord, teaching, admonishing, excluding, and reaccepting, according to the Gospel and the Word of God.

> I wish you herewith the blessing of the Most High God. May He clothe you with power from on high. May His Grace and the gift of His Holy Spirit lead you and be with you. This I wish you from the Almighty God through Jesus Christ, for ever and ever. Amen.

(Copied in December 1792 from an old sheet, itself a copy made at Alwinz, Transylvania, by Mertel Roth . . . who was a teacher . . . from Sabatisch . . . sent to Alwinz)

My beloved Emmy, you who on our path of life together have suffered and fought through with me everything good and bad, will feel with me that such an ordination fills me with apprehension; and that I understand very well the slow thoroughness of the Brothers, especially of the elders. I am thinking not only of the twelve Articles of Faith (the apostolic Confession of Faith in the Hutterian sense) but in the same way of Peter Riedemann's very important Confession; and in addition, I think of the discipline and order for keeping the Church pure and for the unity and uniting of the Brotherhood, as you have now experienced it anew. Thus I feel my weakness and sinfulness so much that I would rather see someone else from our circle in this position. But I dare not shirk it, for certainly the all-powerful God in his mercy will accompany me to the goal just because it is so hard for me. You, beloved Emmy, will certainly read the words of the appointment as often as I do. And what reverence does the origin of this appointment demand!

This extremely important document is shown to be of very early origin by the reference to condemnation to death by fire or the sword and the reference to mission. The last instance of a brother and sister being sentenced to death was in 1618, and mission as practiced in the beginning came to an end with Andreas Ehrenpreis (1662), and even before—from 1622 on—it had changed and weakened. I copied this writing from a reliable copy Joseph Stahl had in Lake Byron.

In a most self-sacrificing way Joseph Stahl has given me for our Bruderhof a number of very old manuscripts, all of which I will send to you in the next days, to be put into Else's care. They are the following extremely important and meaningful writings (mainly "teachings," a baptism formulary, and an old poem):

1. An old book on baptism, written before 1700 (probably around 1660), similar to the Matthias Müller book we have, but with "only" 73 leaves (each leaf having two pages).
2. A significant Pentecost preface (i.e. an address not based on a Bible text, used to introduce a worship meeting) about the working of the Spirit, in a valuable copy of 1783 (probably by Johannes Waldner).
3. Another "teaching" on Pentecost (commentary on a Bible text) about the fruit of the Holy Spirit (Galatians 5), a very old manuscript, certainly written before 1700 (17 leaves).
4. Yet another "teaching" on Pentecost (Acts 2; 38 leaves), copied in 1790, probably by Johannes Waldner.
5. An interpretation of Matthew 8 (20 large leaves), copied in 1780 in Wischinka from an old teaching.
6. A remarkable dialogue between Jesus and the soul (together, with other things, 6 leaves). With its mystical character it will be a rare joy to you, beloved Emmy. You must read it to Georg and Moni. It probably derives from some mystical circle. In my copy it is stuck on to a handwritten collection (incompletely preserved) of old songs, dated 1873 (36 leaves). The 6 leaves with the mystical conversation, however, were written in Wischinka between 1780 and 1800, most likely also by the diligent and reliable Johannes Waldner.
7. Finally, Joseph Stahl made me a present of a more recent good

copy of a teaching on the first chapter of the Sermon on the Mount, and of another on Romans 8, because both of these are of special significance for what we experienced at home in Berlin, Sannerz, and on the Bruderhof.

In addition, he gave me important books on the Bohemian, Waldensian, and other Baptizer brethren; to these I will return later. You see, dear Emmy, Joseph Stahl is our genuine friend, one of the best. His excellent library of ancient books has given him a deep and broad insight into the history of the Baptizers, the Brothers, and also the older mystics. He has, for example, a very old book by Tauler![1] Quite generally at every Bruderhof I have been to, I have found many books concerned with the history of God's kingdom apart from Hutterianism. However, these writings always come only from such circles within that history as were of a deeply spiritual character, were called to a thoroughgoing discipleship of Christ and to community or to a deep faith in redemption, or bore enthusiastic witness to the Spirit. Because of my eyes, which have been fully restored to health now for more than three weeks, I unfortunately did not find time during my present stay in South Dakota to make a list and description of this important collection, but have to leave it for the journey back. What I will do right now is send you dear ones some of these books—also for Georg to bind. They will give you an idea of the breadth and depth of the present-day Hutterites' insight into all those who stand close to the reality of God.

However, before returning to the description of the present inner and outer situation of American Hutterianism, I must tell you, dear *Amselchen*, my little blackbird, of my last days at the Lake Byron Bruderhof, which is so specially close to us, so that you always have the most up-to-date news of how I am getting on and can pass it on to all our faithful ones over there. Of all the communities, Lake Byron was most like home to me, to the extent that all there seriously considered whether our seventy-two people in Germany should not unite with the seventy-two of Lake Byron to form one Bruderhof!

In particular Joseph's very fine wife Katharina Stahl (closely related to the Walters) possesses deep insight and fights for a life lived earnestly and with Hutterian decisiveness in the Holy Spirit. She would so like to see you here and share her thoughts with you; she is also the one most in favor of our community in Germany moving together with Lake Byron, for she expects it to bring about a deep

---

[1] 1300-1361 German mystic.

renewal and revival among her own people. Here, as in all the hofs, the unmarried girls between fifteen and nineteen help the "housemother" (mostly the wife of the steward) in her own small household. With their active support and showing great love and devotion herself, Katharina Basel has provided me most generously with everything for my own personal well-being. Please write a short, loving letter to her, too.

Also others here told me how they would miss me if I had to leave for "up north," that is, for Manitoba and Alberta; what they would like best is to have you folks there, indeed all of us, with them for good. Joseph Stahl himself and the most capable among the brothers had another practical suggestion. With the help of the American brothers we should first build up our Bruderhof and gather and take in all the "genuinely zealous"; we should also compare all Hutterian manuscripts in Europe with theirs and copy out those not found on the Bruderhofs here or only as imperfect copies. We ought to print as many of these writings as possible (at least three hundred copies each) on our own hand press—a wonderful task for the near future. For that purpose we should buy, with the brothers' help, good-quality "old" typefaces and anything else needed. What a delight for Else and Hans and all the brothers and sisters in the office! We should gradually make our daily life more like theirs, while they on their part would (as also suggested by Michel Waldner, Bon Homme, So. Dak.) provide us with money for cattle, machines, and more land. Then, after perhaps five years we should, to begin with, rent Joseph Stahl's Lake Byron Hof, making it possible for his people to rent a place in Alberta. They would give us the buildings, ten horses, and a corresponding amount of cattle and machinery (as would the other brothers in South Dakota). Once we had made sufficient headway on such a rental basis—possibly some ten years later—we should then buy land in Alberta.

I don't know whether things will turn out like that, or if they are meant to. However, I rejoice from my heart with our whole Bruderhof that, on the last and smallest Bruderhof in South Dakota, a love that wants to become deed is giving such firm shape to the proposals that others have brought forward. In fact, outwardly too, the Lake Byron Bruderhof is situated a bit similarly to our beloved Rhön Bruderhof, for which I long every day. It is located on a hill—to be sure, only a low and gently rising one—that the wind can sweep over, whereas Wolf Creek and Bon Homme are situated too deep down in a valley or hollow. This is not good in the oppressive heat of an American summer.

From their first beginning in 1874, all Bruderhofs in South Dakota have done a fine job planting trees. Dense, giant trees make the communities appear like oases in the wide, almost treeless agricultural prairie. They all say that a hof without trees is no good. It makes me think again of having a wood on at least part of our *Küppel*.[1] I think particularly of fruit trees. All here want to know if we have any.

The trees at the Lake Byron Bruderhof present a very fine view, especially toward the James River. There are just three dwelling houses here, making only a little over twenty large rooms, so that many children sleep in one room. But many attic rooms could be added under the steep roofs with little expense. As at every Bruderhof, the schoolhouse has one large schoolroom, and that is where I have been sleeping all by myself, with plenty of glorious, fresh air—a great boon in this heat. Well over one hundred could be seated in that room. The dining room is only a little larger than ours at home, but the adjacent kitchen is quite a bit larger. We could expect to "inherit" the fine equipment it has, as well as a lot more, such as an ice house, huge washing machines, and a milk separator (cream and skim milk). But now enough of this dream, which only a very definite divine leading could make a reality.

The land actually owned by the hof comes to "only" 1,200 acres. Earlier on, Christian Waldner and his people (now at West Raley, Alberta) lived here. From him, Joseph Stahl's group, only half as big, took over just half the area of the original Lake Byron Hof (that is, "only" 1,200 acres) but later rented that much more land in addition. Lake Byron, now almost free of debt, is one of the smallest hofs. Even so it has, along with the necessary livestock and good machines, a hundred horses of the best Belgian heavy breed. They are all home-bred and can often be sold. Again this year two of the horses fell victim to the tropical heat in July (two also in Wolf Creek, three in Rockport). It seems a miracle that no one died of sunstroke during the heavy harvesting work, but in all these years that has happened only once, in Manitoba.

Katharina Stahl said to me we should not let our women do such heavy outdoor work as they have to do here because they have so much land. Several of the women also told me we should make our dresses lighter in weight; theirs make working in the heat a misery. Katharina, Joseph's wife, showed me with pride the brightly colored clothes she still has from the time in Russia and wears only on Sundays. Bertha Clark had admired them also. These old-style skirts have many

---

[1] A small hill immediately behind the Rhön Bruderhof.

more gathers than the present ones. You can take the longest strides in them and jump over the widest stream.

While you at home suffered for nine or more days from constant rain (which, I hope, did not cause too much damage), we here had been praying daily for a heavy downpour, in particular because the maize crop (here called "corn," which is apt to be misleading) was seriously threatened by a complete drought of more than four weeks. Now at long last a thunderstorm has brought Lake Byron a short but heavy rain. At Wolf Creek, on the other hand, 600 acres of corn are said to be just about shriveled up. Rockport, too, with 1,200 acres in small grain (which is yielding an excellent harvest at all communities here) has 600 acres of corn still out, while the reverse is true at Bon Homme: 1,200 acres of corn and "only" 500 acres of small grain. Corn likes the heat, which hovered between 80°F and 110°F here over a period of four weeks and more.

In a hard winter the temperature often sinks to -10°F, sometimes even lower than -20°F, that is, 52° below freezing point. But the climate does not hinder the work of the brothers and sisters. It is on a huge scale, but thanks to good order and the hard-working devotion on the part of all with almost no exception, they cope with it calmly and unhurriedly. Because of my eye and the very important copying and correspondence work (the present "letter," too, requires a whole day) I unfortunately could give but little attention to economic matters. However, having now taken leave of South Dakota for the present, I would ask you to read once more what Bertha W. Clark says about the Bruderhofs there. At this point I just want to supplement her account by a report about the economy of the Bon Homme Hof.

The Bon Homme Bruderhof on the Missouri River, to which I returned for a joyous reunion just before coming to Lake Byron, has 168 souls—about as many as Wolf Creek and Rockport, which have over 170 inhabitants, big and small. Lake Byron has only 72. Of these 168 in Bon Homme, 82 are children under fifteen, while the 86 grown-ups consist of 43 men and boys and exactly the same number of women and girls, here always called *Weiber* and *Dierndl*. Of all those over fifteen, some are over sixty-five and three over seventy. They, too, still take some part in the work—voluntarily, as is true of everything that is done. An old man of about seventy-three in Wolf Creek, Johann Stahl, still helps with stooking the sheaves every summer. I was out there and saw the fine work of both men and women.

Bon Homme has four large dwelling houses. The upstairs, too, is used in part for accommodation—lovely, old rooms wherever you go. For "several" years now floors and walls have been painted with oil paint—the walls mostly a beautiful uniform blue. Twenty to thirty years ago everything was plain white; the floors were left unpainted and strewn with white sand. These four houses, plus the building for the dining room and kitchen and the one housing the *Kleinschule*[1] and the children's dining room, are nicely arranged around a large, rectangular courtyard. One side of the yard is left open and faces a little wood they have planted. If further accommodation is needed, that side could be used for a fifth and sixth dwelling house. At the northern side of the hof stand wonderful, huge poplars or cottonwoods, which cast a broad shade—in other words, not the tall, slender poplars we know from Sannerz—those used for lining avenues since the days of the Emperor Napoleon. To the south the land falls away toward the Missouri River, with a fine view of the woods and hills on the opposite bank.

The very large mill stands down by the river; there, too, are the "old" orchard and the vegetable garden, which together cover five acres. The women often have to enlist the help of the men for their work in the garden. (In Lake Byron the weeds often get the upper hand in the garden due to shortage of manpower, as the women cannot manage it by themselves.) In Bon Homme the garden is in top-notch condition. A "new" orchard is located toward the east, near the stables and workshops. The trees have been bearing fruit for several years already. The hogbarns are situated farther down toward the river. Here I helped with the inoculation of the pigs, an almost machine-like mass operation.

The large schoolhouse, whose hall is also used for *Lehr* and *Gebet*, has a quiet, undisturbed location to the northeast by the wood. It is still the children's task to summon people to the meetings—"*Zur Lehr, zur Lehr!*"

A large area to the east of the hof, which was built in 1874, is occupied by various workshop buildings, all set at a good distance from each other because of the danger of fire. There is a house for the smithy and carpentry with a special motor shed; a cobbler's and broom-maker's shop with a cellar for wine and gasoline, an ice house, a laundry, dairy with a motor of its own, a bath house, and also a tannery.

There is an excellent stable for the 80 horses, with 35 foals at present. The yearly average is about 20 foals. The magnificent stallion cost $1,200 (same price as for the one at Rockport). Of the 600 head

---

[1]Kindergarten for children about 2½ years to 5 years.

of cattle (and 175 calves) only about 40 cows are being milked and kept in the cowstall. The milking is done by the women in turn, with ten women milking four cows each for a fortnight. The milk yield is enormous. Once when I was at Wolf Creek and the men were all out threshing, I took the two-wheeled cart with the huge container full of milk over to the separator with the help of a woman. Calves are not slaughtered as they sell well. Animals to be butchered come only from among the remaining 560 head of beef cattle, which are kept out in the open (!) and are eventually shipped to Chicago for sale. The hides go to the tannery, the leather to the cobbler and saddler. The cobbler, a fine old man, has made to my measure a pair of very nice Hutterian shoes. They fit my bare feet without socks, which is the usual summer wear here.

There are 600 pigs. When they have a slaughtering day at Bon Homme, they always butcher 20 at a time. Thanks to the ice house, the pork kept over from the winter (cured somewhat like ham) can be eaten even in summer. There are 800 sheep and 600 lambs. These are slaughtered mainly in the summer. (Yesterday Joseph Stahl himself slaughtered here.) Apart from chicken and other poultry, the home-killed mutton and lamb is the finest meat I have tasted here.

In Lake Byron yesterday they killed two hens to provide me with a whole carton of chicken for my train journey to Manitoba. Bon Homme has 1,200 hens, 150 geese, and 60 ducks. Its 20 beehives were shown to me by the bee-keeper, a brother in poor health who has a deep understanding for the genuine community among his beloved bees. He quoted to me a number of "good words" about bees and ants from old Hutterian teachings.

Because of the large number of livestock, Bon Homme has 20 acres in potatoes. If field-grown vegetables are included, the garden land comes to 12 acres. I have already told of the 1,200 acres in corn and 500 acres in small grain. All in all, the hof has 4,500 acres, comprising woodland, pasture, meadows for hay, and grazing land for sheep. There is also some bottom land overgrown with willow. Every year a piece of this land is reclaimed with a huge tractor and gigantic plow.

The three big tractors resemble dragons of a mythical age. In addition, there are still two "smaller" ones for plowing. Some have 60 hp, others 40 hp, and one "only" 20 hp. For threshing Bon Homme still makes use of a steam engine, while Rockport and Wolf Creek have motor-driven threshing machines of the most modern type, one costing $4,250, the other $4,500. In the Canada album you see a picture of the gigantic thresher here, which by means of a turbine hurls the straw through a sort of steamship funnel high up onto a big heap. All the hofs have the same type of threshing machine; its work capacity is so big that from eight to twelve teams have to cart sheaves to it all day long. Besides the two tractor-drawn plows there are still twelve horse-drawn plows, each pulled by four horses. The plowman rides on the plow. Similarly, there are six harrows, each drawn by four horses, and the same goes for the four seed drills, each twelve feet wide. The binders, also drawn by four horses, are especially splendid. They cut the grain and gather it into bundles which they bind with strong twine, tying and cutting it as required. The binder then drops the finished sheaves on the ground right where they have been cut; all that remains to be done is to set them up into stooks. However, since the fields are so huge, the stooking still means much work for many, many hands. All eight binders work together on one enormous field covered with grain as far as the eye can see.

The six mowers that cut the grass for hay are similar to ours; the three horserakes are familiar, too, but less so the one stacker (which piles the hay up into stacks) and the four hay sweeps. Only Adolf—and even he might shudder at the thought of these many, far too many machines—will be able to explain to you the four corn planters and the one Lister planter, which in one operation makes furrows and drops the seed into them. He would enjoy the twelve cultivators and the threshing drum for beans with a special, small, 20 hp motor. The two tractors pulling the plows are 40 and 30 hp, the motor for the mill 25 hp. The motor for the smithy and carpentry shop provides sufficient power for several machines at once, among them two saws. There is also a small feed mill with its own little motor. In addition there is the big Missouri River ferry with a large, engine-driven paddle-wheel and the swift motor boat with its aluminum propeller. I liked the boat even better than the ferry, but in either case it was lovely to be out on the river.

This not quite complete account of the work and the machinery at Bon Homme may be enough for today. Adolf would be horror-stricken if he could experience with us how these massed machines threaten to enslave the brothers and sisters. I spoke out very earnestly and frankly everywhere, but especially right at the end at Lake Byron, about how this machine-ruled economy dominates the community life. It increasingly determines the amount of work and the size of the fields, swallows unbelievable amounts of money and labor and thus the undoubtedly very great advantage of saving human labor comes to nothing. Today, those in the communities, provided as they are with such splendid machines, are more consumed by their work and kept away from better occupations than they were when they still plowed with oxen here in America and hauled their crops to the distant city. David Hofer, Rockport, too, laments deeply that the excessive influence of the economy closely connected with the use of machines, is a serious danger. It is a powerful threat to the spiritual life of American Hutterianism, even though this is still rich. Even now it has become rare for brothers not in the service of the Word to copy out the wonderful old writings. When those now forty years old were young, this was still a common practice.

I am listened to all the more thankfully when we sit together outside in the evening air. At Lake Byron I sometimes had to talk to people until midnight. Some of the descendants of Hutterites, now baptized members of the Krimmer and Hutterian Mennonites—about five hundred of them in each group—come to the hofs almost daily, just to listen to me. I tell them the truth sharply and from my heart. Knowing my weakness, though, I am afraid Joseph Stahl expects too much of me when he thinks that the Bruderhofs will receive from me awakening, new life, renewal, and spiritual change, which all brothers and sisters, really all here, consider necessary. But also your prayers, beloved Emmy, and those of all of us go in the same direction. May God's own indescribable grace completely renew and equip me for that!

So, during the night from August 8 to 9, I traveled with this long letter and all my valuable old books over the border into Canada, arriving in Plum-Coulee. I am sending off from here this letter which has grown so long, before I travel out to Blumengard Bruderhof. So now, you Emmy and all the others with you, have the fresh news that I am now in Canada.

Completed on August 9 in Plum-Coulee, Manitoba, Canada.

Winnipeg, August 1930

In a teaching that Johann D. Hofer gave me at the Blumengard Bruderhof I read just now, "O Lord, thou dost make me weak and dost make me strong and once more mighty." So it is. God himself has to make me weak so that his strength and might can come over me. And that strength shall from first to last prove itself in battle against myself. Against nobody may I be as firm and sharp as against myself. So the strength of God will purify my thoughts and the stirrings of my will. Then the deeds, too, will be pure, for that is what we are called to. When we ourselves let the pure love of God, which is what that strength is, rule in ourselves, we can also bring that love to others.

I pray to God that in that spirit, in the victory over myself, I may be allowed to say to the Hutterites in America that it is love to the brothers and to our fellowmen that drives and urges us in Germany, and that we feel the burden of their lot as our own. May the Hutterites come to see that it is on behalf of *all* men that we live in community— that these others, too, may find the community that is God himself. But of course, for that to be given, first and foremost, love to God and love to Jesus must fill our hearts—among us over there as well as here. Then we can and must keep his word.

Here everybody strives for his blessedness. But when we attain that blessedness, what will it be? Nothing else but joy in God and his kingdom, in Christ and his community, in the Spirit and his unity. God wants us to have no other joy than the joy springing from love to him, to the brothers, and to our fellowmen, that they may all be in God. But then we can no longer seek our own enjoyment; even as a community we cannot pursue the collective self-interest of our own Bruderhof. Just as we have given up and crucified our *individual* self-enjoyment, so love will lead us also to surrender our *communal* advantages. God's love poured out into our hearts through the Holy Spirit—this is blessedness. This alone will be our blessedness up in heaven too. Only, we shall then see our beloved Savior and Healer Jesus Christ as he is. We shall be like him or likened unto him. His heart of love and unity and purity will be our heart. So it shall be more and more even now through the power of the indwelling Father, Son, and Spirit!

Winnipeg, August 1930

Today I can write to you only a shorter letter than the last ones which were too long; also I won't write in the diary, because I can find hardly any time to copy out manuscripts. You can see from the packages I've sent off all together that I have a very responsible and meaningful work to do in this area for us, and for the present-day world. Added to this, since the Schmiedeleut live so closely together in their houses, there is even less quiet left to me here than in South Dakota. The love of the Schmiedeleut to me and to all of us is—if possible—still greater than that of the first Bruderhofs. They are constantly around me, and always want to hear more and talk things over. I have been in Blumengard, in James Valley, and in Milltown

Bruderhofs. This is true not only of our loving "president" of the Schmiedeleut Corporation (corresponding to our German E.V.) David Hofer, James Valley, but also of the elder of the brothers in Manitoba, Joseph Kleinsasser, Milltown, a deep, very loving, very realistic brother, always to the point, and the most outstanding, deepest man and Christian I have met so far. These devote to me every minute that they can possibly spare. But the other servants of the Word also use every minute to see and speak with me: Johann Hofer, Blumengard, a real Tirolean with a huge black beard and manly bearing; Peter Hofer, James Valley, and Joseph Kleinsasser Jr., Milltown, the two modern servants, who try to present the old writings and teachings in High German, and who have acquired an astonishingly high standard of education for our time, while still remaining on the old foundation of faith. Both of them are trained state-certified school teachers. Then there are Joseph Waldner, Huron, who knows all about the old handwritten material, and Joseph Waldner, Bon Homme, Manitoba, who with his overwhelming beard and mass of hair and his powerful figure puts me in mind of the old Russians. The two Joseph Waldners missed work days (of threshing!) and a Sunday (which is very seldom done) and came over from their Bruderhofs to visit me before I could come to them.

Joseph Vetter from Bon Homme, the one who looks like a Russian, is the first Hutterite we have met who is almost always talking, and for that reason has sometimes to be corrected by the others. At the Sunday *Gebet*, as he interceded for the young people, the tears streamed down his face so that he could not continue speaking until he had controlled himself. Two of his sons are "outside." One of them, Michel, I met at Joseph Tschetter's in Chicago. Nevertheless, both of them write to him that it is nowhere so good as on the Bruderhof. The two servants who speak High German look to me in a different way from those of the old way of speaking and thinking. Peter Hofer, James Valley, and Joseph Kleinsasser Jr.(who support the two experienced leaders) expect perhaps too much from us. Peter says again and again that American Hutterianism must become awake, alive, and united through me. They see in us their only hope for it. And Joseph, the younger Kleinsasser, certainly over-emphasizes the importance that my visit and our "new zeal" has had for them; he says they think a great deal about it and have become very stimulated because of it. But for me such a man and personality as Joseph Kleinsasser, the elder of the Schmiedeleut, means far more. He will not so easily say such a thing. He is sparing of words. But when he speaks, everyone hangs on his words, and what he says carries great weight. Repeatedly he proved himself ahead of me in knowledge but above all in spiritual clarity and certainty, so that I learn more from him than from all the others. I will describe this more clearly in my diary. Today you should picture him in your mind's eye: a small figure with a very loving face and a patriarchal character. While very many of us are gathered around him, and we others are talking very freely back and forth, he, in response to our thoughts and statements, opens the Bible, the Hutterian Chronicle, books of church history and even of German culture; suddenly he speaks and reads to us. Everyone is quiet, and his words convince us all. He was able to express what we had struggled with in our conversation in just the way we were seeking to express it. He could and should be the bishop and elder of all the Bruderhofs. In everything where we go more to the roots and are more Hutterian, he very clearly acknowledges that our beginning is right, rather than his own people. But he is very much against any forcing, any trying to act in one's own strength. He is a man of faith and of the Spirit, who depends completely on God. I am sending you the songs, with the wonderful conversation with Jesus. They all ask me to sing, and I always say you must come and sing everything to them.

Winnipeg, August 25, 1930

According to the message I received today at the Hapag office, the Hamburg America Line expects you in Halifax, on or about September 12. So I do not know if this letter will reach you at home, or whether, to my boundless joy, I may expect you here in Winnipeg so that I can take you with me to Macleod, Stand Off. I wrote to Elias Walter that he should send me all the letters and parcels which have arrived there for me. But you know how slow the brothers here are. A month is like a day, like "a thousand years in the eyes of the Lord." So I have received neither confirmation nor cancellation of this message about your sailing. I am waiting now for the package of letters from Elias Walter. I certainly cannot leave here yet, so I'll probably have to wait on tenterhooks till your arrival in Winnipeg. I myself did not have the courage to invite you or encourage you to travel, as I was not given the task to ask you to come and also not the money. "Regarding our temporal needs," we have still received very little for our Bruderhof. But in the spiritual matters of incorporation in the church and appointment to the service and for mission, everything has gone well—and that, beyond all our expectations.

The ten Manitoba Bruderhofs have debts totaling $700,000, that is over 2,800,000 marks, almost 3,000,000 marks, but certainly the value of their property is more than double this sum. So they cannot give us much money, as we knew. I am completely of "one heart and one soul" with the Manitoba brothers and with Michel Vetter, Bon Homme, S. Dak.—that is with all Schmiedeleut Bruderhofs —that we become incorporated and that I am appointed. On Sunday, September 11 there is to be a meeting of all the Bruderhofs with "Kleinsasser Vetter" (Joseph, Milltown), when a decision is to be made and I should be given a letter of acceptance to take along. David Hofer, James Valley, and Joseph Waldner, Huron, two of the most important brothers, represent that we are sufficiently proved and tested through the fact of our existence over a number of years, and because of the inner attitude of our "Orders and Foundations" about which they are enthusiastic. Therefore, only the questions and answers befitting the order of the church are still to be exchanged with me. So please gather together in a special way on September 11. I enclose two letters from Elias and Michel which will confirm this report.

Then in the second half of September and the first half of October, the same thing will take place in Alberta, and we expect it will be with the final acceptance and sending out, when everything that is necessary will be given us in greater measure than it has been till now. Your presence, most beloved Emmy, would be of the utmost importance. Only then can the question of financial means be settled. Many think we should buy 250 more acres and receive money to build as well. It would be a great grace—and just as great a responsibility— if I could bring this money with me. Unfortunately I cannot write much today, as I get interrupted through visits also here in Winnipeg, and on the Bruderhof I cannot find quiet for writing at all. Here I talk, with free discussion, to a little crowd of folk mostly till twelve midnight, sometimes till one o'clock, at least till ten or eleven. I get from these gatherings the strongest impressions of the faith, love, and decisiveness of the brothers and sisters, who all take part, and the sisters especially want to know everything in detail about you, and all, and about the children. In Joseph Kleinsasser, the elder of the Schmiedeleut, I experience the deepest strengthening and clarity, as I have already written to you.

I must now hasten to a close, for Herr Gottfried Schwarz from Darmstadt is coming very soon. He is newly married and often visits

the Bruderhofs as an agent for agricultural machinery. Margeri and
Thekla are in England. Maendel Vetter, whom I have seen with the
geese at Rosedale, said to the agent of Hapag, honestly but not exactly
politely, "One can drive out the Devil with a broom, but not you
agents!" He doesn't know photographs have been taken, just as
Christian Waldner does not know of the pictures from West Raley
which I am enclosing for you. "Christel Vetter" turned his back on
them when he noticed the Hapag people taking photographs. You will
find him several times on the pictures (with glasses and a fine profile).

Winnipeg, September 3, 1930

(Letter enclosed in a parcel for Emmy)

It would be nicest of all for us if I could travel home as quickly as
possible. But it would not be a real homecoming if I did not bring
back everything I was sent here for. So all I can do today is to give
you a little joy and undoubtedly a lot of fun by sending you the things
from the Hutterites. You would do best to make the strong woolen
yarn into winter sweaters (dyed). Who's going to wear such enormous
stockings? They are certainly warm. You should take great care of
the head coverings and sunbonnets as they are personal gifts and hold
special memories. On very many of them are the names of old sisters,
servants' wives, one of them even from Russia. How I would enjoy
seeing these sunbonnets on you, Emy-Ma, Tata, Trudi, Hugga, Rosel,
Gretel, Kaethe and all the other dear, faithful sisters! Soon Mölein
too will move with the necessary dignity to wear one. You will have
the honey on your breakfast table—on our table if only I could be
with you. Packing the things has cost more time and effort than if
your skillful hands had done it.

Winnipeg, September 4, 1930

I can't describe to you the deep joy that takes hold of me when I
immerse myself again and again in your letters which have so much
depth. Tell all the others too, especially all the children, how happy
it makes me to receive the very many letters they write so faithfully.
If only I could answer everything in them! I'm not referring to the
inevitable difficulties, for if possible I would like to avoid going into
them by letter. In the first place, I cannot deal with them promptly
and justly at this vast distance. In the second place, it is obvious that

God is lending you help and strength to overcome them so well. What stands out for me is your clear insight and undivided will. And I am so glad about Hans, who is called to his service by God. The brothers here have requested that now he carries such great responsibility he grow a beard. However, one of the sisters (the wife of Joseph Stahl, Lake Byron) immediately added, "But he must ask your daughter first, and she won't let him." You will have a good laugh over it when you ask Hans and Emy-Ma! Emy-Ma! I think about her again and again, and about her exam which I am sure she passed successfully. I think of her coming home and being introduced to her task among you. Everyone here is very sad that our young people cannot marry because of our lack of accommodation. In their opinion, all brothers of twenty-one to twenty-three and all sisters over nineteen must want to be married. And the church must provide for them to do so. Unfortunately Manitoba, with debts of $700,000 (an unbelievable sum—nearly 3,000,000 marks) is unable to give much money, although the debts are covered by twice or three times that amount in capital assets—or even more. Out of ten Bruderhofs at least eight of them each brought $250,000—$300,000 in cash (each one!), a total of roughly two and a half million dollars with them from South Dakota. In addition, our good Michel Vetter in Bon Homme, South Dakota, has sent about $150,000 in seven years for the support of the youngest branch Bruderhof, Bon Homme in Canada. However, the Schmiedeleut plan to give us considerable help in another form. They want to give us a motor and threshing machine, and five tons of wheat flour, a hundred pounds of honey, and other food supplies for the winter. I am negotiating with the German consul here, and you must obtain duty-free import by an assurance to the district magistrate [*Landrat*] and the president that we will not use the food for trading purposes.

I will tell you about the Bruderhofs, which I have come to love so much, only after the decisive meeting has taken place. But I will explain the photos[1] for you and all the others. I am sending them to you because you should have the first look. Perhaps you should give one copy of each to Else to put away for my album (the photos from Raley, too) because the children don't get into her things as much as they do into yours. The numbers are on the back. People come first, then buildings, and then other things. I hope you have a magnifying glass, as I do. From No. 1 you can see with what lively interest the

---

[1]See Illustrations section.

brothers and sisters everywhere gather around whenever I am talking or telling them something. The old man to the far left is a wonderful person and very kind to me. In contrast to Germany, the old people are much more sparkling with life than the young. The younger members begin only at baptism on the long road toward the same depth of faith. The delightful baby on the right is absolutely true to life. I love the Hutterian children with their unspoiled naturalness. You can see from the dress that the skirts are not so long as I thought. But according to the other Bruderhofs, Manitoba has allowed its nearness to the big cities to have a bad influence on dress and furniture—although this evil is rejected in every annual meeting and in such a thoroughgoing way, that for this whole year no material may be bought and no garment cut out in any of the ten Bruderhofs. And everyone is obedient.

On photo No. 2 and No. 3 you can see the "fancy clothes" they are fighting against. The older grown-up girl who is talking and pointing with her finger and the child with a hand to her forehead are both "too dressed up." The woman with her hand on her chin and the two other children are wearing proper, traditional Hutterian costume. But the "lighter" clothing is allowed because there is no wish to force people who are not in agreement. No. 4 shows a group of women and children eagerly watching: *Luftschiff* (Airplane!) No. 5 shows a group of children with every variety of expression: some amazed, some happy, some shy, and some uncomfortable because the Hamburg America man is taking photos again, and he actually isn't supposed to. These children are much younger than you can guess from their clothing. No. 6 and No. 7 give the best view of one side of a Hutterian Bruderhof. It is difficult to take a picture of the whole Bruderhof, since the buildings are well spread out over level land. In the background on No. 8 is a typical schoolhouse, built with plenty of windows on the side where the most light is. Front right is a dwelling house. No. 9 is of the Bruderhof nearest the big city and shows a dwelling house that is no longer built in true Hutterian style (because of the front gable). No. 10 gives an idea of the size of the dining room. You can see it in the foreground with two windows in the gable, three windows at the front, and two at the back. Here (but not in South Dakota) they have living rooms upstairs just as we do.

Nos. 11 and 12 give some idea of the vast scale of Bruderhof agriculture. No. 11 is a stable. No. 13 has captured the sheaf-loading machine at work. It picks up the sheaves from the ground (without any hand labor) and lifts them, as you see, into the wagon moving alongside. No. 14 and No. 15 show one of the many tractors and its wheel. Finally, No. 16 is a photo of someone watching the sheaves of grain being loaded onto the threshing machine. Threshing the harvest from these thousands of acres takes until far into the night, and so I have to visit the brothers out on the fields. In Iberville, Peter Gross stopped the machines and I had to read out your letters to them and give a special talk to the young people. On No. 17, a picture of the threshing machine at work, you can see one such lad coming to us full of smiles. The cheerfulness of the Hutterites would astound anyone who has believed the myth of the sour-tempered saints. In Manitoba I find confirmed all my best impressions from South Dakota. But there is some grounds for the fears that decline threatens—fears especially represented by the exceedingly old David Vetter, Rockport. The young people are the problem, in Manitoba more than in South Dakota. But the abundant love and gratitude with which I am welcomed here is proof of their will, longing, faith, and pulsing life. I am often extremely embarrassed when people say to me here on several hofs that I ought to be the elder for all the Bruderhofs in order to draw them together in the manner and strength of the early Hutterites and to lead them in the task of mission. I know only too well that someone different from me is required for this task.

But today I will not speak so much about Manitoba. I will rather go into your letters, which, like all the other letters from our brothers and sisters, have made a tremendous impression on the people here. They simply cannot hear and marvel enough. They all say, "You ask for mission, but your community with its guests is mission." There is a great deal in this remark which we may only understand later, when our flood of guests is perhaps a thing of the past. Hutterian mission is different from evangelization by sermons and talks because it seeks out and speaks to the "zealous"—and only those—in every place. It challenges and gathers them and calls them to their true home. Modern evangelists gather in everyone, absolutely everyone possible. They then sift out from their mass meetings the small handful who are finally converted, and hold prayer and study meetings with them. The Hutterites say that we find, seek, and welcome the zealous from near and far, and call to God and the church community those who are ready. Wider mission would be beyond our strength. And yet many ask me if I also go on mission journeys to the cities. David Hofer, Rockport, said, "If the church is on the right path, there will be mission; if not there will be none." In his view, the church in America today is not on the right path and is all too imperfect and endangered, so that one can have questions about mission. The brothers have a really deep-seated horror of "irresponsible" evangelists, who have not been sent and who preach a false and sweet Savior without demanding any break with private property, worldly power, and the spirit of the times. In all seriousness they are all false prophets who cry, "Peace, peace," where there is no peace.

But I want to go further into your letters, and have picked out your last letter of August 9. Your article for Bender's newspaper is magnificent. I read it out together with Grunewald's to the amazement of everyone in Iberville. This is the Bruderhof where the late Paul Gross often told about us and spoke on our behalf. (His widow sent some of the things in the parcels.) As soon as the tremendous demands on my time permit, I will look it through a third time and then send it on. The question raised by the guests at the end of August would receive this answer from the Hutterites here, "You question us about mission? But are you ready to listen here and now to us and our message, 'Leave everything' etc.?" That is how the people at Maxwell admonished our "Herr Schwarz" from Darmstadt, especially a very outspoken old Vetter (a grandfather or great-grandfather), who added, "Your God is the daler (*Thaler*, dollar) and you cheat whenever you can . . ." When "Herr Schwarz" "made excuses" he was told, "You love the daler too much," and the conversation was at an end. For what is holy should not be thrown to dogs and swine.

Oh, I long so much for you to be here. But those in Manitoba cannot give any help, and I must stay here another week. In our situation it would not be advisable for you to travel until we are certain we have the money. Hapag is completely ready to take on the whole business of transporting us (the entire community). But when will that be? All the brothers think unanimously that we must remain in Europe as long as there continue to be zealous people, and as long as the school laws and the authorities are not against us. It is so loving and faithful how everyone on our Bruderhof, especially the children, courageously free you to come to me—yes, really courageously. Especially when I read your wonderful letters I am so moved that I have to pull myself together in order that my emotions don't overwhelm me. The goal I am working for here is almost too great for me—it is certainly beyond my strength. So we must grit our teeth and not turn aside but go slowly and steadily forward until we reach the goal. This is the way of present-day Hutterites. This, unfortunately, most unfortunately, will mean staying six months in America.

My eye is in splendid condition, as you have undoubtedly seen

from my work and letters. How thankful I am! For it was not really
going fine, in spite of Elizabeth Hofer writing, "But Dr. Wipf said it
is doing fine." I don't like to think of the anxiety this illness caused
and am so glad that, for six weeks and more, Dr. Wipf's treatment
has led to a steady improvement. Your prayers! I hope to return home
in better health than I've ever been. Then all your worries about the
wet harvest, about the milk and the new cows should be taken away
for a long time to come. I am so glad for all you write about the
vegetables harvested from field and garden, but especially for what
you tell me about the children. This time I have made a special effort
and let the Bruderhofs here take second place while I worked for
several whole days sorting, packing, and writing, to send off parcels
VIII to XII. Probably I'm not very good at it and you would certainly
have done it quicker and in a more practical way. But in any case
you could not very well have packed the parcel that is for you. This
little parcel (like the "little books" to Else, and the consignment for
Hans and the publishing house, Nos. VIII to XI and XII) contains
presents from the sisters here, gifts without great money value, put
together with great love for you and all the others. The only secret
that I will give away is that parcel No. XII to the publishing house
has a jacket meant for Hans. Only if he and Emy-Ma don't want it,
it can be passed on to whichever boy would value it most. But the
greatest gift I am sending you is in No. X of this consignment of
parcels. These precious fragments gathered from the earliest years of
the Hutterian church are meant for your quiet hours and for you to
read out from.

Winnipeg, September 8, 1930

I have at last discovered a quiet spot where I can write undisturbed
to tell you of all my experiences here. Please apologize for me to all
our loving, faithful Brotherhood members and novices, and especially
to our children, for not writing to them. It has simply not been possible
because my time is completely taken up with the eager interest of
these marvelous Hutterites who are so closely and firmly bound to
me and to us in the love given through the holy spirit of community.
If the brothers in Manitoba had not given me so much courage and
confidence through their great and joyful love, and finally through
their united and historic decision, I would not know how to bear the
long separation from you, from our children, and from all our brothers
and sisters, who are gathered to share a common life with us. My

letters to you, dear Emmy, are to bring my heart's feelings close to you and to all of you.

Winnipeg, September 8, 1930

How am I to put down my impressions of the church communities in Manitoba? The strongest is the great, holy love I have experienced at all hofs. It so overwhelms me that I often feel crushed to the ground. Deepest and closest is the friendship I have formed with David Hofer in James Valley. He is considered the most intelligent and gifted leader and speaker, but has struck me as the most interested, concerned, and loving friend. He has already sent three letters to Alberta, in which he represents our cause in a very thoroughgoing way.

My next strongest impression is the deeply-believing and devout character of present-day Hutterian life. I must say I have never felt so far removed and distant from the world in a city as I do here. In spite of all their weaknesses, I find in the faith-centered life of the Bruderhofs here a greater tranquillity and detachment from the world than at our Bruderhof at home. Perhaps we have gone too far in the way we react against a striving for eternal blessedness. At any rate there are many words of Jesus that say clearly that a good life will be rewarded in the sense he means it. These words are rejected by worldly-wise theologians who always know better. But we must not want to be better and wiser than Jesus was—and is. Perhaps we lack the simple thinking, the childlike spirit that expects evil to be avenged and good to be rewarded—the idea of hell and heaven. But as I understand the words of Jesus, Joseph Kleinsasser (Milltown), the elder, goes too far in declaring: "The millennium is of no importance to us. The one thing that matters is that we lead a devout life and attain eternal blessedness." I suppose though, what he means is the way the idea of the millenium is presented by the Plymouth Brethren and other evangelistic groups who set their hopes on the millenium. We also have found this unpleasant ever since Sannerz and our religious-socialist beginnings. They put off all justice on earth to some future millenium and in the meantime plod along—as far as social and economic problems are concerned—in the same unchanged injustice as the whole wide world.

When meeting with statements like the one by Joseph Kleinsasser, we must never forget that Hutterites of both the early time and of today understand piety as surrender to God and the Holy Spirit. That is, to them it means to overcome the individualistic, self-centered life, to give up property, and to attain to a life in complete community, which, measured by the social demands of a communal society and economy, surpasses the very boldest expectations. In this sense it is rightly said here: "Believe in God in such a way that you live out here and now the justice of the kingdom of God. In the church of God the devil is bound 'for a thousand years.' " This is Hutterian piety. It means that on their Bruderhofs and, if God grants it, in their mission, the earth and everything on it belongs to the Lord, hence to his church.

However, we religious-socialist Europeans will reply to that, as I did to Joseph Kleinsasser: that is correct, but the idea of the millennium means that God created and intended the earth to be ruled by him and that at least once, if only for a "short time," it must be completely his. What belongs to that thought is that we on our Bruderhofs live "here and now" in the strength, the spirit, and the order of the world to come.

It is true, though, that in the time after Hans Hut, indeed, already with Jakob Hutter—I underlined it when copying his first epistle to his church—the expectation of the Lord's approaching return is seen in close connection with his final judgment over the ungodly and the granting of heavenly blessedness to the devout. The idea of reward and punishment plays a big part in this. That is also the way the millennium is explained in the two Hutterian commentaries on Revelation that Johannes Vetter read to me in Wolf Creek. (I am about to send home the giant copies of those commentaries—on loan only.) Even so modern a Hutterite as Elias Walter's son-in-law Joseph Waldner, teacher at the Roseisle Bruderhof, wrote in his essay on the martyrdom of the early, first Hutterians: "Now their souls are under the altar and cry out, 'Lord, how long before thou wilt judge and avenge our blood on those that dwell upon the earth?' "

And yet Lydia Müller is completely wrong in asserting that our Hutterites are motivated by fear of hell and by hope for the reward of blessedness, without the love that springs from faith. The opposite is the case. All their teachings testify only to that faith which is active in love, and insist that only love born of the Holy Spirit makes community life possible. And it was not just in the early times that, powered by a Spirit-born enthusiasm lasting a hundred years, this love was strong enough to be the determining characteristic of the Hutterites; on the contrary, it is the same today.

Regina, Saskatchewan, September 19, 1930

Beloved Emmy,

The great events in Manitoba and the equally important work of copying out manuscripts and mailing the parcels unfortunately prevented my writing any more in Manitoba. In spite of changing from the first hotel to a second and from there to a third, I was again and again tracked down and torn away from the work of writing and mailing—by Hutterites, who are so dear to me; by Gottfried Schwarz, not quite so welcome; and by people from the Hamburg America Line and other Germans in Winnipeg, for the most part very unwelcome. I therefore entrusted to Gottfried Schwarz the mailing of the last four parcels, all packed very firmly and containing extremely precious writings, and went on my way. Right now, en route to Alberta, I don't want to pack any further parcels (even though I am still carrying around far too many books, writings, etc.). Today is Sunday, and at this quiet place I am at last finding the longed for peace for a more detailed report of my time in Manitoba and a further account of my general impression of present-day Hutterianism. Even though the beloved and venerable Joseph Kleinsasser tried to let me have undisturbed quiet in Milltown, it proved impossible. Brothers and sisters constantly dropped in on me with presents, nursery rhymes, or questions. I enjoyed it heartily, but it prevented my writing. In addition, various brothers, especially the two, Joseph Waldner and David Hofer, came from miles around (three, four, and even seven miles) to "see Eberhard Vetter (or Arnold Vetter) again and hear him tell us some more." Such love and gratitude cannot be rejected. As soon as I show my face on the hof for even a moment, I hear my name called from every direction by children and women, "Arnold Vetter! Arnold Vetter! Arnold Vetter! Arnold Vetter!" To my great delight I have to tell the women again and again about you and the children, about the dress and work of our women and girls, about your own and the others' singing, and about Hans and Emy-Margret. They want to know if the steward is really so young and really still unmarried, if the children really wrote their letters to me quite freely "from the spirit," and if Else really hand-lettered the epistles. How is it that our mothers entrust their young children so soon into the education of the church, what about our church discipline and "punishment," and so on.

But what interrupted my writing most is something quite different. I already wrote to Else that you, beloved letter-finding *Amselchen*, are right also on this point (as in so many other things), namely that the Hutterian community knows no "private" correspondence. The letters that I received from you and others via Blumengard and in part Stand Off had been opened. Some days ago we were together with Joseph Kleinsasser, the elder, and he was reading to us (as he often does) the wonderful letter Hieronymus Käls wrote to the children of the church (about 1538) and other splendid, equally old epistles. We noticed that Joseph Kleinsasser Jr. was missing. (Joseph, intelligent, delicate, and refined, and his wife Sanna, energetic, strong, and zealous in faith, were my hosts at Milltown and looked after me with great love). Well, when I came to my room dead-tired at about midnight (as is mostly the case here), I found the lamp burning and Joseph and his wife bent over my letters and books. For hours, glowing with eagerness, they had been reading to each other out of my diary!

This had its consequences in the following days, when David Hofer of James Valley came to Milltown once again. I had to produce the diary and read out what I had written about the kingdom of God and "only to be blessed," about the millennium and the shift of emphasis through pietism, about objectivism and subjectivism and about the elder, Joseph Kleinsasser. The talk went deep between the two elders and me. The others present listened quietly, and David Hofer told Joseph Kleinsasser Jr. that he (David) would not have dared to read my diary. There was indeed no secrecy between us, he said, but all the same not everything gets written down in such a way as to be understood by anybody without explanation. When asked if I could forgive Joseph Kleinsasser Jr., I of course said a joyful "Yes." In regard to the subject matter itself, I was seen to be right in the sense that our life and word must reveal God's glory throughout the world. Our mission, with its concern for the lot of the "poor" and with its struggle against all injustice has to make known everywhere the kingdom of God and its justice. But, they said, the world as a whole would not acknowledge it, not even at the return of Jesus, which to the stiff-necked and to those in high places could bring nothing but judgment. Joseph Kleinsasser, the elder, gave as the reason for his opinion that he largely found Revelation too hard to understand. He said, though, that there was no question of a division between us in our basis of faith. I met him halfway by emphasizing the difference between our spiritual understanding and the literal understanding of those sects which think they can calculate the exact date of the millennium. At the end of those difficult hours, I said that I found it hard to translate what I had written from our religious-socialist language and my own all too High German—into theirs. But David Hofer, James Valley, replied, "So what, if it makes us love you even more than before and makes us see that what you have to represent you represent to whomever you meet—even to Joseph Kleinsasser, the elder!"

So this *Handel* (affair) ended happily shortly before that important date, September 14 (not September 11). Meanwhile I had the great and deep joy of receiving your telegram, to which I replied on September 15 with news of the decision of September 14, 1930. I thank you, beloved Emmy, and all of you, also in the name of the great cause, for your loyal support and for informing me about the postponement of your journey, Emmy. That decision, though very sad for me, could not be otherwise seeing how matters have stood up till now, and it has lifted me out of my agitated uncertainty. Before long now, Elias Walter is to make the decision, together with Christian Waldner. He wrote such a loving letter, telling me to expect nothing but good out there. Even the second elder of the Lehrerleut, Johannes Kleinsasser (Milford, Alta.) wrote in a similar vein; he is very happy about the good testimony preceding me from South Dakota and Manitoba.

Because it is so amusing, I want to tell about yet another incident, this one concerning the picture that Hardy took of the two of us on the station platform at Fulda. The junior Kleinsassers found this, too, among my things while I was absent. "So now we know what Emmy looks like" they said, highly pleased. But since having one's picture taken is severely frowned upon, the daughter-in-law had to dig the photo out from where she had hidden it deep in her trunk and give it back to me. I am glad to have it back, but the photo I like even more is the one in your passport, because it brings out your character better.

If I remember rightly, I already wrote of the trouble that Tekniepe of Hapag caused me with his photography. Something else I have told here is about the many books and pictures we have, but the misgivings against those have not been very strong. After all, our study of history has led us step by step to a truth that is deeper and closer to reality. Nevertheless, the obstacles that present-day Hutterianism puts in the way of our cultural work and task should not be overlooked. Up to now it seems to me that instrumental music, for example, is absolutely rejected and fought against. Their hostility to portraits and pictures and their objection to instruments cannot be explained simply by reference to Bible texts such as, "You shall not make for yourself any image or likeness." This command could be interpreted and understood differently as it is followed by, "Do not *worship* them nor *serve* them"—especially when one bears in mind the Hutterites' opposition to a literal biblicism. There is a deeper reason for that rejection: their main and great struggle against individualism, the world church, and the idolizing of human beings. When it comes to the portraying of a person, a craze for having one's picture taken as often and as attractively as possible—that anti-communal emphasis of self—this idolization of men turns into downright, silly vanity and makes love and affection become carnal and superficial. All this is so totally against the Hutterites' remarkable inner dignity and sense of community that they properly detest having their own pictures taken. The humor, definitely not unconscious, of that real old Hutterite I marked for you on the group picture was simply marvelous: "Arnold Vetter, I have to admonish you. No one has ever yet got me on a picture, and now that I am seventy-five, you have to come and bring with you that crafty shipping man, and he takes my photo—and from behind at that!" Actually, it wasn't quite that bad, it was more from the side, but that made it worse inasmuch as it brought out unmistakably his rare profile.

Those are small but definitely not unimportant incidents, and I am telling them rather graphically and in such detail because they are characteristic. They mean more than might be thought by one not familiar with the kind of humor that has some depth to it. In writing this way I also provide a contrasting background for the great event to follow now—the uniting.

There are differences between the origin of our modern culture and classical education (samples of which, in Latin and Greek, I often have to read out) and the quite unique Hutterian culture, which is very deep but difficult for strangers to understand (not for me). You should know that those differences have not remained hidden, nor could they. It can be sensed that we come from the world and religion of the twentieth and, still worse, of the nineteenth century, so different from the fighting church of the sixteenth century with its readiness for martyrdom, and also from the conservative-minded church of the eighteenth to twentieth centuries, so careful to preserve true communal piety. The brothers and sisters here admire and marvel at the leaping fire of the first enthusiasm given to us. They admit freely and frankly that we show greater zeal and that, in this respect, we have something to say and give to the Hutterians in America—something that can lead to a renewal and revival of a cause that is growing old but still remains very much alive. This is often emphasized so much that I have to dampen their exaggerated expectations, especially where they concern me, very weak human being that I am. But they also perceive the smoky fuel in the fire of what we hope is a truly-growing first love among us, and they are well aware of their own rich experience and the testing they have endured. In this they are far ahead of us. So there is a unanimous, deep conviction that by God's will the two belong together. This is what led to the wonderful talks and decisive resolution of September 14, 1930, which I now want to report in as much detail as my memories of those extremely rich hours will yield.

The weather was cool and damp when Joseph Kleinsasser, the Elder, David Hofer, Peter Hofer, and I traveled about twelve miles in a horse carriage from James Valley, where Joseph Kleinsasser had held a very earnest *Lehr*, to Rosedale, where the other servants of the Word were already gathered. We were first served refreshments— tomato salad and two kinds of melons—by the married daughters of David Hofer, James Valley. Next, there was the welcome and a preliminary discussion at Zacharias Hofer's, where also a letter of blessing was read out from Schmied Michel's oldest daughter, who lives at Huron.

At about 4:30 in the afternoon we went to *Gebet*. All twelve servants of the Word sat in front with me, facing the crowded schoolroom of the Rosedale Bruderhof. At the request of the Elder, Joseph Kleinsasser, the *Gebet* and the *Lehr* preceding it were held in a clear, vigorous yet inward way by the young preacher Joseph Glanzer from Huron. In the morning, in James Valley, the Elder, Joseph Kleinsasser, had spoken very deeply about the word that "certainty of salvation comes only by doing, through deed." Before that, I had spent the morning by myself in the wood, reading the seven letters to the seven churches lettered out by Else. After *Gebet*—it was then past five o'clock—I was asked to leave with all the others. Only the twelve servants of the Word (remarkably enough, exactly twelve in number) remained behind to speak about my request.

In the meantime I visited with Joseph Maendel, grandson of old Maendel Vetter, who unfortunately was away for a medical examination. "Young" Maendel, a black-bearded Tirolean type, and his wife (still his first—not a second wife!) are the parents of fourteen children of every size, down to the smallest, who to my amazement was still being nursed by his mother at the age of one and a half. This sometimes goes on here even up to the fifth year, and quite generally the way that mothers sacrifice themselves for their numerous children is unheard of. To be sure, I was asked, too, whether in the weeks after birth our young mothers are, like theirs, provided with fourteen chickens, twenty pigeons, thirty bottles of beer and so on, and are free from communal work for six or seven weeks. That explains why the mothers of so many children—as in this case of fourteen—are extremely healthy and strong. What a lesson for "modern" Europe!

Joseph Maendel, Rosedale, is acknowledged to be the most capable steward in Manitoba, so that the Rosedale Bruderhof is completely free of debt and this year is selling nine hundred pigs, something no other hof manages. To be sure, Zacharias Hofer complained that Joseph spends money just as liberally as he brings it in. Joseph takes a deep interest in our cause. On my way back he will have several hundred dollars for me to take home. With a beaming face he showed me your letter of thanks, my dear, good Emmy.

At 5:30 the servants of the Word had supper with me in the large dining room, a very good one as always. I was made to sit between the two elders. The conversation was lively and intense without, however, touching on the event of the day. Right after supper I was invited to come with the servants of the Word to the dining room of the bigger children. This room is especially dear to me with its Tirolean wood paneling on the walls and ceiling (with a simple oil finish). We sat on benches without backs along the long sides and one narrow side of the two tables standing there, that is, at a right angle, I again by the two elders on the long side. Kerosene lamps provided light.

Joseph Kleinsasser conducted the meeting, with David Hofer breaking in a number of times, the others very little. The elder first presented our request by saying that I wished to take a letter with me to Alberta from the brothers in Manitoba, in which they would express what they felt about our desire for a uniting. Accordingly, he said, after *Gebet* the assembled servants had agreed that in order to come to clarity on this question, they were under obligation to test and question me jointly so that they could then decide on the basis of my answers.

The first part of the proceedings that followed (which went according to our very highest expectations) was taken up with a consideration of those incidents in the Chronicle that resemble or approximate our own important and unique request. So far, Elias Walter had regarded the acceptance of Daniel Zwicker[1] by Andreas Ehrenpreis and his co-workers as the event closest to what we ask for, since it right away called for mission. Joseph Kleinsasser and his brothers see the uniting with Lorenz Huef and with Farwendel[2] (by the Rhine River) as more

---

[1]Chronicle 764-765.
[2]Chronicle 331-339, 388-391.

similar, since Daniel Zwicker, in his ample correspondence with Andreas Ehrenpreis, had continually contradicted the community, whereas we have actually lived in community for ten years and for at least two and three-quarter years have declared our readiness and agreement regarding all important points. Apart from the elders themselves, several brothers emphasized this point, especially Joseph Waldner, Huron, Joseph M. Waldner, Bon Homme, and Peter Hofer, James Valley. Farwendel's fervent entreaty and his acceptance while in prison (hence "outside," just as all of you are "outside") which was read out at my request, made a very deep impression. You must please read about both in Andreas Ehrenpreis's printed epistle.

Many of those present were deeply moved and said it would be wrong to refuse our request. They had me read out from my diary the conclusion that David Hofer (the Lehrerleut Elder at Rockport, SD) had come to with respect to us. Joseph Kleinsasser, though not finding it correct, considered it more than sufficient for the decision to be made now.

On another occasion, the union with and the confirmation of the Carinthians in 1763 had been used as a comparison, and all of us felt grateful that the present-day communities are still holding faithfully to community, while at that time Hänsel Kleinsasser had hands laid upon him by an almost completely extinguished church. But what shook me most deeply was to hear our uniting compared with the union that Jakob Hutter, also on behalf of his absent brothers and sisters in Tirol, effected in 1530 with the church then coming into being in Moravia. The readings from the Chronicle were an event I shall never forget. (In Milltown, Man., Joseph Kleinsasser with other servants had read to me about the later life of Daniel Zwicker from Joseph von Beck's "Latin" history book.) When reading about Farwendel's acceptance and the later joining of his whole group, Joseph Kleinsasser commented, "That is indeed very similar."

As we passed to the second part of these important proceedings, it was said about our baptisms that the earlier baptisms by immersion should be recognized wherever the water baptism included confessing one's faith, giving oneself into the death and resurrection of Christ, and pleading for the Holy Spirit. There was also the important question whether my service of the Word had been given to me with apostolic power and validity by our communal church at home, to which I said "Yes," calling to mind the hour of outreach we experienced on New Year's Eve. It was asked, too, if this fact should simply be acknowledged at the uniting; or if I should be newly appointed to the service of the Word, that is, on trial, without the laying on of hands; or if I should be confirmed in the service with the elders' laying on of hands. This threefold question was not decided separately at this meeting but was left to Alberta.

Thus we came to the second part of the meeting, to the questions and answers the Hutterians use at baptisms, appointments, and confirmations in the service. Joseph Kleinsasser, the elder, sitting next to me, read the questions out slowly, word by word. I looked him in the eye and answered them all with "Yes," without any reservations. In several cases I backed up my "Yes" with more detail and, where important, I also spoke in the name of our Bruderhof, recounting our own confessions at home. Please, all of you over there, read and discuss these questions. You will find them in the baptism books, in one of my letters (from Lake Byron), and among the numerous handwritten books just now mailed by Gottfried Schwarz (dated September 15).

It was a deeply moving hour, for which I cannot give enough thanks to Joseph Kleinsasser and the other brothers, but above all to our God, who truly is love and has sent his call to us in Christ and his spirit. And I also thank you, beloved Emmy, Hans, and all of you for making possible this big journey and my long absence which are so important for laying a foundation for us.

Meanwhile, I had also read out Elias Walter's important new letter, at the request of Joseph Kleinsasser, who knew it. Here Elias Walter writes that the success of this first part of my journey has given him great joy and has taken a load of anxiety off of him and that nothing now stands in the way of our wishes being fulfilled in Alberta.

I then submitted once more our three distinct requests:
1. That our Bruderhof in Germany be united with all American Bruderhofs, as an expression of its complete incorporation into the church of God.
2. That this Bruderhof in Germany be provided with the service of the Word, this to be done through me.
3. That our mission outpost be supported by providing for our Bruderhof in both spiritual and temporal matters.

It was said regarding the third point that the spiritual care was already covered by the second; all the same, it would be good for two brothers to make a journey to us. I was also asked very pointedly if we would be ready to move to America if the church were to think it right. I replied with a very definite "Yes," but referred to our European task both with books and the gathering of the "zealous." In general it was thought that the time had not yet come for us to emigrate. There is as yet no definite clarity about that.

Now, before I was to go out once more so that each one of the brothers present could express himself freely concerning each of the three proposals, Samuel Hofer, the representative of the weakest Bruderhof, Barickman, asked me whether I on my part felt satisfied with them or if I was not finding them weaker and worse than ourselves, hence if it was worth our while to desire union with them. Gazing at him steadily, I replied, "We desire union with you because none of us has yet been proved and tested to the very end, whereas many of you have." Joseph Kleinsasser agreed with that, and I told of a young brother in Milltown who had said to me twice, "The beginning is good, and the middle must continue equally good, but both are nothing if we don't carry on in the same way to the end." With this we came to the end of the second part.

The third part of the meeting was the shortest; it just consisted of informing me of the decision. I was brought in a second time—as before, by Joseph Kleinsasser Jr.—and welcomed with joyous faces. Once more I sat down next to Joseph Kleinsasser Sr., and he announced, "We have unanimously decided to agree with your request. We are all for the uniting." Deeply moved, I replied, "This is a great grace from God. We ask him for power to live on our Bruderhof completely on the basis of faith and by the strength and order of the Hutterian Brethren. We want to do this ever better and more faithfully. I thank you also in the name of the church of God and of our Brotherhood in Germany." This expression of thanks was waved aside inasmuch as several remarked, "But it was only right and could not be otherwise, for you are more zealous and in some respects closer to the early forefathers than we are." "But," I replied, "it takes much grace to recognize and do what is right. We are very weak and ask for your continual, faithful prayers for us. It is a joy for us that you are there, that you really live in community and plead for the Holy Spirit, and are infinitely far ahead of us in experience and in proving yourselves. After ten years of life together we know very concretely what this means and that only God himself could bring it about."

Then I asked the question, so important to us, about what they had decided about the second and third proposals. I received the clear and definite reply: "That is all included in our decision. We have unanimously answered your three questions with 'Yes.'" Joseph Kleinsasser, the elder, who gave me this answer, had been given the task of writing a letter to the brothers in Alberta, on behalf of the Schmiedeleut, for me to take along. Although it does not mention the three requests, the granting of them is included and implied in this important letter I am to take with me: 1) Union and incorporation, 2) my service of the Word, and 3) temporal and spiritual support for us.

My beloved Emmy and all of you, Joseph Kleinsasser's letter, seen together with Elias Walter's above-mentioned anxiety, joy, and confident readiness, makes it clear to you (especially bearing in mind the Lehrerleut in Alberta) why I had to stay so long in South Dakota and Manitoba. As the letter is short and of such importance for us, I insert here a copy that exactly reproduces its wording and spelling:

1. Envelope: Milltown Hutterian Brethren
P.O. Benard, Manitoba
To the Hutterian Brethren in Alberta, Canada

2. Text of the letter (one large page):
Milltown Hutterian Brethren
P.O. Benard, Man.
September 14, 1930

To the brothers and servants of the Word
of the churches in Alberta, Canada:

The grace of God, the love of Jesus Christ, and the fellowship of the Holy Spirit be with you and us all. Amen.

Dear brothers, we brothers and servants of the Word of the churches in Manitoba, Canada, let you know herewith that Eberhard Arnold from Germany has spent a considerable time with us here in Manitoba. During that time we have had many and various godly and blessed talks and discussions with him and found, as far as we could ascertain and learn by inquiry, that he agrees completely with the Hutterian Brethren on matters of faith. We therefore see no obstacle to the union he desires and seeks with us, the Hutterian Brethren in general. For this reason we gladly grant him our consent and agreement to this union and wish that the merciful God and heavenly Father will bless it in his love and unutterable grace. Indeed, may he himself lead and guide it all according to his will and pleasure, to the glory of his name and for the good of his people.

With warm greetings I sign myself, on behalf of all servants of the Word in Manitoba,

your lowly brother and fellow helper,
Joseph Kleinsasser

With the copy of that extremely important letter I have come to page 200 and the end of this diary from Mö. The next and main decision, beloved Emmy—the one in Alberta—will be recorded, if God wills it, in your diary, which looks even nicer and I hope will have an even better and more joyful content. The above copy is quite exact, including punctuation, spelling mistakes, and the underlining of the word "union". I rejoice thinking of the moment when you will all read it in the Brotherhood. But may all honor and worship for this undeserved grace be given to God, the Almighty, the perfectly good and loving, now and forevermore. Let this be our concern.

Now, my dear, good *Amselchen*, before I conclude and mail the longest and most important letter I have written to you from America and which I want you to read out in the Brotherhood, I must still give a brief account of the wonderful close of that meaningful 14th of September. We were still together in the Rosedale children's dining room, which has become so dear to me, and were all in a mood of great elation and thankfulness. At about nine o'clock it was suggested that I should read to the servants of the Word Jakob Hutter's first epistle to the church in Moravia, dated 1535/36, and Zacharias Hofer, the dear old Rosedale servant, had the wish that all the Rosedale people who wanted to should listen. Within a few minutes the smaller dining room proved too small, so we went over to the big dining room, which immediately filled with all the Rosedale brothers and sisters, some 170. Again I sat with the servants at the table across the upper end. Joseph Kleinsasser gave a brief introduction. It was the first proper church meeting I was allowed to hold in Manitoba, which means, the first one in America, and it began with one of the most important Hutterian writings known to me, one of those I sent to you from Rockport, S.D. I read with deep inner feeling, rapidly and with a strong stress on the most important passages, without adding anything. I really warmed up doing it, as could not be otherwise, so that dear black-haired Joseph Hofer, Maxwell, exclaimed, "My, what fire and life he has!" What I read made the strongest impression on the large gathering, and the servants of the Word went on discussing it with me for a while in the others' presence. We were deeply moved by Jakob Hutter's love to his people, his sober-minded and yet so daring courage in the face of death, the apostolic power of truth given him, his prophetic gift, and the strong consciousness that his mission would endure. I longed very much to have you here, dear Emmy—and of course it had been our great wish that you might be here for this.

Regina, Saskatchewan, September 19, 1930

How happy you would have been at the intent way everyone listened—all eyes and whole heartedly—to the whole of your splendid, flowing letter, which took almost an hour to read.

As the description of this one day and all its little incidents took up so much of this long letter, I must now put off the account of my Manitoba visits until I can write on the train and send it to confirm my arrival at Macleod. Then I will tell you how I visited nearly all the Manitoba Bruderhofs one after the other and the general impression I received. To summarize, I can only say that the present-day Hutterites, too, are so completely unique in their almost perfect brotherly communal life; in their high level of achievement, which amazes their neighbors; in their absolute dependability, admired by everyone in Winnipeg, including people in the highest positions; in their trust and faith in Christ and their love of the Holy Spirit which solely and alone is the main thing for them; and in their manliness, honesty, faithfulness, ability to see things in their true light, simplicity, and fearless humility. We in Europe have never met anything approaching it anywhere—not even among the Brothers of the Common Life. All our expectations of faith coming from the Christian Fellowship Movement, as well as the time of the youth movement and the religious-social movement, have the possibility of fulfillment here, even though certain signs of weakness are unmistakable, as in everything human. The fears of David Hofer, Rockport, are almost nonsense.

Medicine Hat, Alberta, Canada,
September 23, 1930

You will see how difficult it was to write in Manitoba, from the way I used the days in traveling from there to Alberta. Here I will give to you, and through you to our dear, faithful brothers and sisters, an insight into the more personal experiences and circumstances, something of which I already began telling in the previous letter. From much of it you will sense that it now becomes more and more difficult for me to remain away from home for such a very long time still. My homesickness gets continually stronger, and the decision to be made soon whether you should still come and fetch me will mean very much to me! Now I am on my way to Elias Walter, our best friend in America, and hope to find the quickest advancement of our

cause on the basis of what has already been reached. Because the pull
from home is far stronger, I am not in the least influenced by the fact
that many faithful, loving Hutterites, also in Manitoba, want to hold
on to me for a long time—almost with loving force. I must fulfill
my task, even if it is often extremely strenuous to hold out, as the
necessary quiet is very hard to achieve.

After the quiet hours in Regina, Saskatchewan, where I was able
to write undisturbed, I met two very dear brothers from Bon Homme,
Man., in the train to Alberta. We recognized each other at once—the
clothing was enough. I read to them my account of the 14th of
September, and they were very glad about it and hoped very much
we would all move to America quite soon. One of them, Michel
Kleinsasser, a witness brother (*Zeugbruder* or *Gerichtsbruder*, roughly
equivalent to a member of the managing board in our Society, regarding
spiritual tasks in particular) wanted very much to know about the
single people among us. He found it wrong that fear of debt kept us
from building a house for the couples waiting to be married. He
pointed out that Darius Walter, founder of the Dariusleut, and David
Hofer, the successor of "Schmied Michel" Waldner, founder of the
Schmiedeleut, had both said, "When people want to get married, one
must hurry as with a dead body." That means a wedding within one
day or at most six or seven days, against which there is no law in
America.

While the two brothers are sitting at another table in the same hotel
room, I will report first some less weighty details of my journey
through Manitoba, for lighter reading and reading aloud, in contrast
to my account of the 14th of September. Then I want to go back to
relating the essential general impression I have gained. For, as they
say here, you will surely be *neugierig* (curious) to hear how things
went with me at the various Bruderhofs.

With the exception of Blumengard and Roseisle, each hof lies about
three to eight miles from the next. Between the eight hofs there I
mostly traveled in one of the Bruderhof wagons. They are generally
for two horses, at times for just one, and are similar to ours but have
better springs. I rarely used trains and even more rarely the Hapag
(or Schwarz) car.

The prairie scenery shows patches of scrub, almost no woods, huge
grain fields, large herds of cattle and smaller ones of horses, as well
as gigantic heaps of straw which they hardly use, often lining the
whole horizon. As the selling price for straw is bad, they are simply
burned, in quantities of 100-150 tons (!). You see amazing machines,

capable of doing an immense amount of work (for example, excavating roadside ditches 4 yards deep and 7 yards wide) with a single scoop and dump of the huge machine, operated by just one or two men. All the same, the scenery is very monotonous and extremely bare; it strikes one as disagreeably industrialized and controlled factory-style by big corporations. Although the Hutterian Bruderhofs, as communities, go along completely with this capitalistic direction, there is a contrast. The privately owned farms, scattered at intervals of one to three miles, give a very isolated and self-centered impression. On the other hand, every Bruderhof, with its communal buildings—a solid, imposing complex viewed from a distance—with its copse, woodland, river, and garden—strikes one as an oasis of communal life amidst a desert of individualism. The impression that here a power is at work that makes for community is strongest when the hof is seen from several hundred yards away. The larger hofs comprise, if the barns for chickens and ducks are included, from thirty to sixty buildings. From a distance they look somewhat like our Rhön Bruderhof, as seen from Gundhelm, or "Major" Roth's farm estate from the Herolz Road, only much bigger, more imposing, and closely clustered.

Whenever I approach a Bruderhof, usually with a servant of the Word driving the horses, all who are at home quickly flock together, and their joyful welcome and hospitality soon make us feel as much at home as we felt at the hof we have just come from. Often the servant who has taken me to this nearby Bruderhof will stay and spend the night there and thus help to start the conversation at the right point and enliven it. These discussions, which at times go on past midnight, were most lively and vigorous in Milltown, James Valley, and Huron, and feeblest in Bon Homme and Rosedale.

First I was at the Blumengard Bruderhof. It is the third hof that the old steward, father of David Hofer, James Valley, and of Johann D. Hofer, Blumengard, has helped build up. He is a fine, serious, inward Christian, who can tell quite a bit about the Inspirationists of Amana.[1] Not only here but at many hofs, one can hear the older people speak with respect and sympathy of the Amana people and also of the Rappists.[2] Here and there I am also shown some of their books. It is deeply regretted that the Rappists (who rejected marriage on principle)

---

[1] German pietist group, migrated to U.S. in the mid-19th century and established a community in Iowa.

[2] German Separatists, settled at Old Economy, Pennsylvania.

came to a complete end with the death of the last old members. The Hutterites also feel sad that the Rockists of Amana, our Wetterau neighbors of the eighteenth century, are becoming noticeably more worldly with the waning of their inspiration (about which strange things are told). They are increasingly losing their traditional costume and letting property come in more and more. But their unclear basis of faith is seen to be the ultimate cause of their decline. Joseph Kleinsasser, the Elder, goes so far in his frankness that he said to me as we drove to Rosedale on September 14, "When the apostle Paul wrote that he wished all might be like him (that is, unmarried), it was against God's will and purpose." All the same, the Brothers love the two communal ventures just mentioned, whereas they do not think highly of the Doukhobors.[1]

Of the other "Christian" groups only those are acknowledged whose Christian words prove themselves in deed, such as the Salvation Army which is well-known on the hofs. So are the Mennonites, Baptists, millennial sects, Pentecostals, Lutherans, and others—all of which are completely rejected. They recognize the weakness of biblical content in the Salvation Army but also the strength of its insistent earnestness.

The Brothers speak to the people outside a good deal more than we thought. Michel Kleinsasser, who with his brother-in-law is on his way to earn money for the community, has just told me how on one occasion he had said to a Mennonite, "Come to us where you can live in community!" When the other answered that this was not necessary, Michel had pointed to the first Christians in Jerusalem. In reply to the Mennonite's numerous counter-arguments from the New Testament, he had kept repeating, "But you don't have any Bible passage to set against what the first—the really first—Christians did and had to do." Thus taking a job outside is always linked with a bit of outreach. The hofs in debt try to help themselves by sending their ablest men outside by twos or twenties in the autumn and winter to take on harvesting or smithy work or the like. All money earned is at once sent home to the steward. In that way Michel, my present companion, once earned $140 in a fortnight. For himself, his wife, or his children he is given 15-25 cents, as is generally the case with every trip, large or small.

These 15-25 cents for expenses are very controversial, even though they have been the practice for many years and in all three Hutterian groups. One senses that at this point a tiny entrance gate for the little

---

[1]Russian sect, rejecting all outer authority.

devils of private property is left open. These pennies go beyond what is needed for food and drink on the journey and are meant for bringing something home. Experience shows that in spiritually weaker colonies and others not only candies for the children have been bought, but also gold-rimmed cups and other tasteless knicknacks, to be kept on the living room shelf as "property." This and the alteration in dress (visible on the photo showing the girl from Barickman with raised forefinger) are signs of the decay of which David Hofer, Rockport, speaks so much. But it must not be overlooked that these indeed quite-unimportant trifles come to the fore particularly at Bruderhofs where the unity, otherwise so unassailably strong at all places, is showing serious cracks. Of the fourteen hofs I have now come to know quite well, only two really suffer from a lack of unity: Barickman and Bon Homme, both in Manitoba.

It is said here and there that also the two neighboring Bruderhofs, Maxwell and even Iberville, have been to some extent infected by the influence of the city. I myself noticed nothing of it and believe— just to summarize—that the deeply-rooted strength of Hutterian community is such that even the slightest straying from the way or becoming superficial (as in cups, furniture, or clothes) is seen as a threatening sign of a falling away. But the Bruderhofs as a whole are far removed from such a decline; in fact, even the weakest hof does not depart from the common basis in any more obvious manner.

It is clear, though, that just such little visible things cause the more prosperous Lehrerleut to stop and ask if it is right to help such a sickly Bruderhof with money, knowing that it is likely to be used in a wrong way. Precisely Bon Homme and Barickman—leaving out the more innocent Roseisle—are the communities most deeply in debt! On the other hand, such an attitude on the part of the Lehrerleut cannot lead to unanimity between the three groups. Indeed, at the yearly meeting of the Manitoba Schmiedeleut it was seriously considered whether to refuse the Lehrerleut the fellowship of the Lord's Supper because their hofs, wealthy as they are, give no help to the poor ones—an attitude totally uncommunal and un-Hutterian. It is being said quite openly that there is no true community between Manitoba and the Lehrerleut, even though the two groups profess the same basis of faith. Here lies the deepest harm to present-day Hutterianism: the all too great independence and self-sufficiency of the three individual groups, the individual Bruderhofs, and individual families. In regard to the families, so far this independent attitude shows up only in the small beginnings mentioned above. As I see it, Barickman and certainly Bon Homme could be helped if there were one strong elder over all Bruderhofs, who, putting love into deed, would administer glowing church discipline and help in the strength of the Spirit. Only so could the original Hutterian mission and also the educational work with children and young people be powerfully revived. At present, of ten Manitoba Bruderhofs five are without a *Kleinschule*—a situation unheard of in Hutterian history.

So it is not hard to understand that the communities in Manitoba are looked upon with concern, distress, and pity by the other Bruderhofs—because of their indebtedness and because behind it, deeper reasons are seen for God's permitting it. Therefore it cannot be shrugged off as empty talk (as some here tend to do) when David Hofer, Rockport, told me, "I pity those in Manitoba with all my heart." All the same I have to say: If the Manitoba hofs really show present-day Hutterianism at its lowest level, then the general level is amazingly high. I was shown great love also by Samuel Hofer (Barickman) and Joseph M. Waldner (Bon Homme) even though it pained me that their two hofs were the only ones among the fourteen communities I have been to that did not call together a larger meeting to consider our cause, in spite of the fact that I visited Barickman three times. The only meeting I had there was a small and brief one with the women, in the courtyard out in the open, without Samuel Hofer. He gave me not only books, like the "Latin" history book by Joseph von Beck, which is so important to me, but also an especially fine jacket (of not quite the prescribed length), a preacher's coat for the proclamation of the Word, and other things. I had to try on all these clothes and let myself be looked at from all sides!

Samuel Hofer gave me his trust to the extent that he twice (in Barickman and in Winnipeg, where he looked for me and visited me in the hotel) had a deep-going talk with me on the question whether, in a difference of opinion, it is the servant of the Word or the majority of the church members that should have the decisive voice. In reply I gave the following twofold advice: In our community we would go on counseling together and also asking God for the inner voice and complete guidance of his Holy Spirit until we found unanimity (just as the Manitoba decision of September 14 was unanimous). However, if the servant of the Word, deeply certain of representing the will of God when the majority have strayed from it, still cannot convince them and lead them to unanimity, he has to admit his weakness in the service and ask for the help of the elders (in this case Joseph Kleinsasser, Milltown, and David Hofer, James Valley), so that these may decide what is right. Thus, a case of extreme need requires a strongly authorized elder with the courage to intervene.

I don't know if Samuel understood me. He is certainly intelligent, being one of the servants of the Word that had been a teacher (with a proper state training). But through all his reading and listening to non-Hutterian opinions he has somewhat lost his sense of direction. For this reason I do not regard him as one of the modern Hutterites (the teachers and ex-teachers), but see him simply as a servant weakened by the influence of the city—indeed, as the only such servant.

Joseph M. Waldner, the big, emotion-tossed child of Bon Homme, Man., showed me even warmer love. He, too, gave me fine writings and books and was the one to come to Milltown most often to see me and talk with me. He also took me on an expensive, long car ride to David Glanzer's Roseisle Bruderhof. (This, by the way, was only the second time a Manitoba hof rented a car for me; typically, it was Barickman that provided me with the other such car trip—a symbolic "coincidence!") On the way, Joseph told me very openly of some well-intentioned but tremendously foolish things he had done, for which he had apologized and promised improvement before the gathered church. He again showed himself swayed by overpowering emotions, much more than is usual among the generally manly Hutterites.

In Roseisle I found a Bruderhof of such outstanding scenic beauty that it quite overwhelmed me, and I felt a great longing for home— woods like those around Sannerz and the Rhön Bruderhof, with valleys and ravines as at the *wilde Tisch*.[1]

Economically, too, quiet David Glanzer (whose hof has never undergone real privation) has it so good that he told me twice, "All will be well if only we remain devout to the end." His wheat is free of blight, whereas several other communities, including Milltown, have lost half of a promising crop. At Roseisle, Sanna, Elias Walter's daughter and her husband, Joseph Waldner—former teacher and present work distributor—hosted me just as splendidly as the other places had done, and with a special love radiating from Elias Walter himself, so far away. I consider Joseph Waldner, Elias Walter's son-in-law, one of the modern Hutterites, who, strongly inclined toward

---

[1]Large flat rock near the Rhön Bruderhof.

High German and other cultural ideals by their teacher's training, nevertheless want to hold firmly to Hutterianism.

The three hofs where the church of the Holy Spirit is present most powerfully lie together in the middle between the northern and southern communities: They are Milltown, James Valley, and Huron.

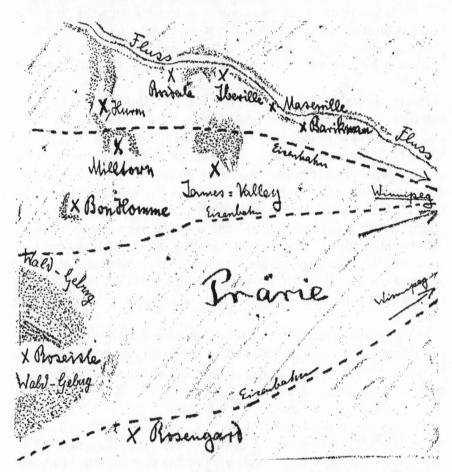

This will help you to get a picture of how the communities are located.

In James Valley, I had my most intimate talks with the second elder of the Manitoba brothers, David Hofer. Along with Elias Walter and Joseph Stahl, he belongs to the close circle of our best friends. Economically, he is the best Hutterian "honey man," getting an income of almost $4,000 a year from eighty hives. As a preacher he speaks very forcefully and urgently. As a scholar he is one of those who know best the "teachings" and their differences. As an elder he is a helper who carefully watches and weighs up matters. As a friend of his fellow men he likes open, courageous admonition; as a Christian he is plain and simple, and conscious of his smallness. We are going to have a lot of correspondence with him, for he is a truly loving and reliable friend.

While in James Valley, I shared a room (a very quiet one) with Jakob Hofer, the father of Peter Vetter. With him, a very serious-minded old man, I spent the one day when the atropine gave me trouble. For over two months now my eye has been so well that I no longer take atropine, though I always keep it at hand. This time the cure is a lasting one. How thankful I am to God, who is so good— thankful, too, for the prayers from all of you, for the nursing care of the loving folk at Wolf Creek, and for the evidently correct treatment by Dr. Andreas Wipf!

I enjoy a very special relationship with the two younger servants: Peter Hofer, James Valley—the one who had *sich losgekreizigt*[1]—and Joseph Kleinsasser Jr., Milltown. Both have drifted too far away from the old Tirolean dialect of the Hutterites into the New High German, but do stand absolutely on the right foundation. Both have put too much trust in me and my possibilities. I think that these two brothers, both ex-teachers and gifted above average, will have much to contribute to the future of the holy cause if they hold out faithfully. I want to be a true friend to them.

I feel the greatest respect for the Elder Joseph Kleinsasser, Milltown. With the loving tenderness of his heart, as well as in his outer appearance he resembles Michel Waldner Vetter, Bon Homme, SD, who is so very dear to me, but he surpasses him in his knowledge of the early and very early history, in keenness of thought, and clarity of vision. He is a rare man of faith and kindness. I am grateful to him for spending long evenings making clear to me many a historical and factual question concerning Hutterianism. As a personality he will remain a true example to me.

Huron is only three miles away from Milltown, so Joseph Waldner (with a long, narrow, gray beard) frequently came over from there, and I on my part spent two nights at his place. He is one of the best, clearest, and most inward brothers in Manitoba. He has carefully read our church orders, historical writings, and letters, and taken up our cause most loyally. The following old people live at his Huron Bruderhof: Fritz Waldner (cabinet maker); Jakob Waldner (smith);

---

[1]"Managed to avoid something unpleasant."

Rahel Basel, the oldest daughter of Schmied Michel; also Sarah Basel, the old widow of Peter Janzen, the historian. (The Mennonites took an old Zurich Bible away from her.) So I had some good talks there; the room was crowded with people, and there was lively interest. I was also liberally supplied with old writings; Sarah Basel, for example, gave me an old article book. I also had a look at Peter Janzen's handwritten Small History Book with his own additions, and in Milltown I was even shown the very old original, written by Johannes Waldner himself.

When I saw that original, it was in the hands of old Sepp Waldner Vetter, who is nearly eighty, white-haired, and unfortunately almost deaf. In Milltown I also met the old poultry man, Zacharias Hofer. In Roseisle I got to know Paul Glanzer, father of both the second servant at Huron, Joseph Glanzer, and of the Roseisle servant, David Glanzer. In Blumengard my host was old David Hofer, the exact and hardworking steward and father of both David Hofer, James Valley, and Johann D. Hofer, Blumengard.

But of all the older ones the one that impressed me most was old Maendel Vetter—Jakob Maendel, over seventy-five, about whom I have told a number of times. He is full of life, and they all call him a "true communitarian." I wish I could recall all the golden words of his spicy humor. The old father of the second servant there, Johannes Hofer, a blacksmith, lives also at the same hof, Rosedale.

Zacharias Hofer, the first servant of the Word at Rosedale, is quite old too, actually the oldest of all the servants, though not so long in the service of the Word and in a leading position as Joseph Kleinsasser Vetter, who far surpasses good, faithful Zacharias Vetter in spiritual gifts. For the readings on September 14, dear Zacharias had to bring out his own books of copied writings in which he had entered the questions asked at baptisms, appointments, and confirmations in the service. Wherever he had not understood the old terms, he had simply left a gap in the copy. As a result, David Hofer (James Valley) admonished him strongly before the great servants' meeting about his bad copying of such important matters. The leadership of the Rosedale Bruderhof is more in the hands of the extremely capable steward, Joseph Maendel, grandson of Maendel Vetter. Joseph's father—that is, Jakob's (Maendel Vetter's) son—with a billowing gray beard, is Rosedale's clever teacher and beekeeper. He greatly enlivened our talks there. Rosedale is also the place where I was given the big box with wool and clothing.

Neighboring Iberville is still in good shape both in temporal and spiritual matters from the time of Paul Gross, especially as Jakob Hofer, Peter Gross's father-in-law, an older man with almost white hair, is a capable steward. All the same, he has his eye a bit too much on business and on the one Iberville Hof and ought to let his son-in-law Peter Gross have more of a say. Anna Basel does so; she is the deep-thinking widow of Paul Gross, who stood up so faithfully for us before he died of stones in the bladder. And Peter Vetter's own father, Andreas Gross, even though advanced in age, does let his son have the needed elbowroom. As things were at Iberville, I could speak with hardly anyone but the old steward, Jakob Hofer—with the exception of a talk I gave to the threshers out in the open air. However, many other folk were listening, and the work distributor (without a beard) would repeatedly and vigorously point to things that were not right, even while representing these himself.

At the Maxwell Bruderhof as well (only about three miles away from Iberville), the one that impressed me the most was Johann Hofer, the very old, gruff, and honest beekeeper, who always talks of his temptations and makes a vigorous stand for Christ and community. He is the father of the two preachers, Joseph Hofer, Maxwell, and Samuel Hofer, Barickman. Joseph Hofer, with his black beard and simple loyalty, very much resembles Johann D. Hofer, Blumengard, but is more joyful. He is assisted in his service at Maxwell by young, slender, fair-haired Jerg Waldner, whose father, Jerg Vetter, as well as Johann Wipf, the noisy one, and Michel Hofer, the cobbler, belong to the circle of the elderly.

Joseph Hofer's cheerfulness, also when tackling the worldly-mindedness of his sister-in-law Grete in Barickman, together with Joseph Waldner (Huron) Vetter's outstanding optimism contrast with the pessimism of Samuel Hofer, Barickman. There at Barickman even the aged Michel Tschetter and his Hester Basel, both snow-white and with trembling hands, are emotionally concerned with themselves. Strange how this one Bruderhof combines everything: city influences, corruption of dress and style, use of cars, debts, disunity, human emotionalism. One wonders what will become of it.

But such exceptions as Barickman only serve to underline my overall impression of present-day Hutterianism, to which I will now return, on the strength of what I experienced with the Manitoba brothers.

The clear, biblical ground of truth—faith in God, in Christ and the Holy Spirit as shown by Peter Riedemann and the other oldest writings—is and remains the basis. Purity in relationships one to another and the resultant trust, truthfulness, and simplicity of conduct have been generally upheld. Everywhere, active love, showing itself in mutual help and in free-willing, almost frictionless obedience in the work, is the stamp of Bruderhof life. In spite of the invasion of some little foxes—gold-rimmed cups, 15 cents, candy, ownership of books, and so on—community of goods without private property remains the banner around which the brothers and sisters remain gathered. Joseph Kleinsasser Vetter even declared that statements like "this old book is mine" or "these cups belong to my daughter" are not only inaccurate but downright wrong. Absolute community of goods without private property remains firmly established, as is love in mutual relationships, in spite of speech that is plain and frequently rude. Even so, there is often too much concern not to hurt the other. The leading old men in Manitoba told me—in particular after the Rosedale meeting—I should bring a hammer back with me from Alberta and, having been recognized as a servant of the Word, should gain the Manitoba servants' consent and before their eyes break and smash the gold-rimmed cups and other unfitting things. But why don't they do it themselves?

All the same, in spite of this clearly noticeable softness, apparently stemming from consideration for family relationships, the confessed faith is still firmly held to. Elias Walter raised the question concerning how many would fall away today if all our Bruderhof people were to be beaten every day until they were half dead, and yet not killed—the way it was done at the time of the Jesuits. In fact, during the war (1917/18), out of fifty Hutterites that were called up, not a single one weakened in spite of kicks, beatings, and threats. I have learned much from Andreas Hofer of Rosedale, Man., about that firm stand during the war, and also through the diary from Blumengard, which I either enclose or will send soon. Adolf, together with Walter, Fritz, Kurt, and others concerned about refusal to bear arms, should go through it, write out parts, and send it back to me here.

The old teachings are used faithfully in the communities. The printed Hutterian books are being read, but the oldest handwritten books are no longer read or copied a great deal—epistles least of all, article books and collections somewhat more. All this you will have gathered from my letters and also that everywhere some, and at several places a great many non-Hutterian old books can be found; further, that almost no newspapers are seen and no fiction, art, or anything consciously romantic is to be found. They don't produce any of that because it is alive in them. But there is an unmistakable joy in beauty—

in a book or lettering, in woods and fields—a delight in simplicity, clarity, and a clean style in houses, rooms, clothes, and furniture.

That all this is hindered by the mass of machines and by having too much land, is clearly seen by some. But to change the course things have taken in America would demand the heaviest sacrifices. And one can only hope that the present-day Bruderhofs as a whole may be ready for such unaccustomed sacrifices, bearing in mind how bravely they stood the test and were willing to suffer during the war.

It is the same with the mission task, which none can doubt or question. The call of Jesus for mission is deeply anchored in their consciences. But they doubt if the present world is ready to hear and receive it. All around them they see the Americans, shallow-minded and indifferent to God—people whom they have tried so long and so fruitlessly to bring to the truth—so that they feel reminded of the word, "When the Son of man comes, will he find faith on earth?" But Elias Walter rightly replies to these misgivings, "Even when thousands come to faith and to community, it is still as nothing compared to the thousands of millions living on earth." The last family to stand the test came to the church three (or five?) years ago at Big Bend near Woolford, Alberta. There had been vigorous mission work among the property-owning descendants of Hutterian families speaking the same Tirolean dialect; Schmied Michel in particular was very active in this. In the first period after 1874, many of the property-owners from Huttertal, Hutterdorf, and Johannesruh did join the community; then there was a time when few joined, and finally almost no one came any more. Living in private property had hardened their hearts, and the daily sight of Hutterians living in community left them unrepentant. Not only that, but of those whom Schmied Michel brought over from Russia at great expense, the majority were poorly tested, causing him to suffer greatly as a consequence.

This may help you a bit to understand the extremely delicate reserve with which they have met our pleadings. But everywhere now they are beginning to rejoice all the more in our Bruderhof, in its hospitality and sphere of influence as a Hutterian mission station. They regard it as a real miracle of God, something one cannot marvel at enough. Now if God's good, gracious, and strong spirit overcomes the natural self-assertion of the individual hofs and unites them, so that they are ready to take action and make sacrifices for the outreach and gathering that Jesus both demands and grants, we can experience great things.

Cardston, October 2, 1930

In the meantime I have traveled on to Macleod, where Elias Walter picked me up at five in the morning on September 24. That meant that I could no longer finish and mail this long diary letter. I am very happy to have at long last reached the main destination of my journey. My reception and everything I meet here is fulfilling our high expectations. I feel a warm love for Elias Walter, the venerable champion who has guided our path. So great is his loving readiness that he at once had Joseph Kleinsasser's letter typed and sent to the twelve nearest communities in Alberta. He also said straight away we should waste no more time now, go on Saturday (that is, tomorrow) to Christian Waldner and get him to arrange for an early meeting of all servants of the Word in Alberta (Dariusleut *and* Lehrerleut!) and then have me immediately go out and proclaim the Word at the various Bruderhofs in Alberta. We also got down to work right away and tried to get an oversight of all existing writings. I shall have work for many days to come in Elias Walter's fine, valuable collection of writings. This is going to be my home and chief base for visiting all the other hofs in Alberta.

Unfortunately, I cannot give you any hope of your being called over here during this present journey, and I really suffer from it. They say it is hoped you will soon come over in order to remain here permanently with all our brothers and sisters. Elias Walter has so many debts through the founding, against his will, of the large and expensive Michael Tschetter Bruderhof, that he cannot give us any money now. Also Christian Waldner recently bought so much land "so that the young brothers have plenty of work," that he also does not have much to give. Besides, the seventy-six-year-old elder with all his concerns is almost as slow-moving, anxious, dubious, and unbending, as unyielding in his seriousness and dignity as David Hofer, Rockport, so that I have only come forward a little quicker with him than I did with David Vetter.

The fact that such quite old men have the leadership has the advantage that it assures to a high degree the holding on to what is old and proven, to genuine and original Hutterianism. This advantage compensates for the disadvantage of less flexibility and receptivity, which is to be felt in such old men in spite of all their alertness and aliveness of faith, and which results in a marked hindrance and delay for my task. On the other hand Elias Walter is, for his sixty-eight years, youthfully active and daring.

I have been received with great love and kindness and feel sorry for Elisabeth Basel with her leg trouble and other ailments. Elisabeth Walter appears much older and more spent than her husband, our faithful, active Elias Walter. Because of her constant leg pains (probably due to eating too much meat) she no longer takes part in communal meals, and her only work—though it goes on right through the day—is taking care of her four (?) smallest grandchildren, who are not yet old enough for the *Kleinschule* (Kindergarten). But even that is more than she can cope with, so that good Elias Walter himself, now assisted by me as the dear children have come to trust me, has to take his grandchildren on his knee, put them on the pot, pacify, and occupy them. This has seriously interfered with the great mental work the two of us are doing. This last year in particular, Elisabeth's exceptional stoutness—rare even here—and her pains have hampered her altogether too much and made her feel depressed. Especially at night, she sighs and groans a good deal, so that her faithful Elias does not get much rest. She looks after me very well, with the help of her capable daughters, as do all those who care for me. I sleep by myself next to Elias Walter's apartment—a rare exception here—since usually guests that are to be honored share the bedroom of the elder and his wife. In Blumengard I slept in one double bed with the very old father of David Hofer, James Valley, and of Johann D. Hofer, Blumengard.

Elias Walter, a self-taught layman, is a true scholar. He appreciates my own studies so much that he tries in every possible way to provide me with the necessary quiet. His absolute readiness to work for our cause in Germany and his unending pressure to get the American hofs to support it better deserve admiration. All the more does it sadden him that this effort is greatly held up by Michael Tschetter's starting a new place. Elias Walter declares openly and firmly in front of everybody, "Eberhard, we need you just as much as you need us."

His cousin (their mothers were sisters) David from the East Cardston Bruderhof, with his kindly, deep-seeing eyes, interrupted me again just a little while ago by fetching me out of my hotel room. He has told me just now that, even before my arrival in America, he had said to Elias Vetter, "God has called and gathered Eberhard Vetter and his zealous folk in Germany to discipline (or 'punish') us." As he explained to me, he means discipline in a threefold sense: 1) admonition, as the lowest grade of church discipline, 2) putting to shame, and 3) establishing guilt. Through us, the American Bruderhofs are to recognize to what extent they have weakened and are no longer truly going forward on the right way.

David Vetter (East Cardston) keeps telling me how greatly the miracle of our being gathered into community amazes him and that he wants to do all he can for us. With his white beard and hair, and his infinitely kind and deeply joyous and loving eyes, he looks so unforgettably endearing that I have never yet seen a man that so completely expresses goodness. Only with Michel Waldner (Bon Homme, SD) and Joseph Kleinsasser, the Manitoba elder, did I see something similar, but their features are different. To be sure, Joseph M. Waldner (Bon Homme, Man.) with his all too emotional good-heartedness, and Joseph Hofer (Maxwell) and Johann D. Hofer (Blumengard), who are younger and less mature, also have very kind eyes—eyes shining with kindness. Other significant Hutterites have a look that reflects mainly a thoughtful, carefully considered realism— something that actually holds true for most Hutterites. But what streams out to me from the eyes of our best friends—Elias Walter, as well as Joseph Stahl, Lake Byron, and David Hofer, James Valley— is even more: a quite personal relationship, the love of friends that know me well and have joy in me. Actually this also applies to old Maendel Vetter, Rosedale. I found a decidedly hard look only with David Hofer (Rockport) and at times—but by no means always—with Christian Waldner (West Raley), our Dariusleut elder.

There are surprisingly many instances of manly beauty here. Elias Walter stands out by a very special beauty and dignity characterized by manly seriousness and deep spirituality, even though at sixty-eight his hair is not yet completely white. It was really touching that, for my sake, he got up at three-thirty in the morning to pick me up in Macleod while it was still dark; also that he took me across the barren Indian Reservation to Christian Vetter, in a car owned and driven by his Mennonite schoolteacher. The old Hutterites know what leadership means much better than any of the Youth Movement folk of the Hans Blüher–Marie Buchholz direction.[1] Our Mennonite driver was forty years old and inwardly not really one of us. Still he obeyed every direction given by old Elias Vetter to the letter, driving us this way and that over the almost trackless Indian prairie land and he repeatedly got stuck in the mud. This actually led to some small clashes with Indians.

You must tell Heini, Hardy, Hans-Hermann, Richard the Reckless, and our other boys that the Indians' riding style is more marvelous than anything I have ever seen. It is the complete opposite of the way

---

[1]Leading figures in the German Youth Movement before and after World War I.

the Prussian military or the German farmers ride; quite different, too, from the international riding style one sees in circuses and at races. Here I have seen for the first time what is meant by a horse and rider being one. Once when we could get no farther with our car on the Indian Reservation, an Indian came galloping up from an almost invisible distance, approaching in a wide arc, as if not aiming for us at all, until suddenly he was right in front of us, staring at us silently from his now motionless horse, as though demanding an explanation. Elias Walter had expected this and told the Mennonite teacher, who was quite scared, to keep quiet. Elias needed only to say a few sentences and he had won over the Indian, for the Indians often receive generous help from his and other hofs. Another time we were being watched by an Indian and his wife on horseback. A third time a very wild-looking man with four big dogs came riding up to us. And there was a time when an Indian on a magnificent, fiery white horse rode for half an hour directly by our side, no matter how slow or fast we might drive. The whole time he never looked at his horse or the road, but always only at us, as he changed from an easy trot to a full gallop without the least bit rising or bouncing in the saddle. Once when an old Indian and his wife were being given many sacks of potatoes at the Bruderhof, I said to him in English that I love the Indians. Thereupon he, actually a son of the greatest chief in that area, responded with a wide grin, showing magnificent teeth, yet with none of our noisy laughter. (The Hutterites likewise are not supposed to laugh very loudly.)

The Hutterites and the Indians get along so well that, for example, the Indians have learned from them a good deal about hunting wolves with dogs. (In one winter a single Bruderhof here has accounted for fifty wolves.) The government warns against getting involved with the Indians, but the Hutterites have no need to heed this. All the same, just a few years ago there was a threat from the Indians (who have actually lost much of their former strength) who said that their chief had ordered them to attack farms and a town with no regard for lives and property unless a certain piece of land was returned to them, whereupon they did get it back. Here, around Cardston, Raley, and Stand Off, there are only about twelve hundred pure blooded Indians but a good many of mixed blood.

Quite apart from the romanticism attached to the original inhabitants (who unfortunately are rather dirty and lazy), the scenery and climate here are much nicer than in South Dakota and Manitoba. But instead of telling you of my daily views of the glorious Rocky Mountains, which are so much like the Alps, I enclose some picture cards for you.

As I now return to Elias Walter after this little interruption, I must first of all tell of his happiness at the beautifully done Michel Hasel Book and Else's lovely hand-lettering. He has read it twice already and wants everybody to look at it. He showed it around at West Raley and, reading out with great delight our lengthy dedication, he declared, "No one can take that from me." Jacob Walter, the son of the West Raley steward, Heinrich Walter, picked us up with a team of horses from the Indian Reservation that lies between Stand Off and West Raley. Jacob is still single and vigorously upholds community; with him at the reins, we rode last Saturday (at the end of September) into the West Raley Bruderhof with its beautiful, spacious layout. Viewed from the nearby or the more distant heights, which I passed over at two different places, this large colony, almost like a medium-sized village, looks nearly as beautiful as the Stand Off Bruderhof on its swiftly-flowing river when seen from the glorious rocky and wooded heights around it—a view that delighted me so much. Stand Off, with its several thousand acres, lies as if on an island between two rivers flowing down from the Rocky Mountains, one of them forming the boundary of the Indian Reservation. (The Indians drink only river water, never water from a well.) I hope I can get a picture taken of each of the two hofs, showing an overall view, but alas, this will scarcely be permitted.

At any rate, I am sending you today three photos (taken at my request) of one of the oldest books of "teachings" as a small companion-piece to the Michel Hasel Book. They are pictures of Bible texts printed for the Hutterites before 1610. We badly need these because of the typefaces (for our future print shop) and the old Zurich texts. These three pictures are for you, beloved *Amselchen*, to remind you continually of the wonderful books I am working with here. With the next and very important book mailing, Else will get identical photos of that book, bound in 1610, for her and my archives. As a supplement to my own reports I send you today a letter written in 1873, which gives the Russo-German Mennonites' and Hutterites' first impressions of Canada. As that report will scarcely be obtainable again, Else should paste it up for the archives and store it carefully.

So unfortunately I have not yet managed half of what I wanted to write. And any minute David Vetter of East Cardston Bruderhof will fetch me and take me there. So to my distress I must close this letter. And my heart is still so full. Today is October 2nd, the day when in 1899 I had the first fully conscious experience and encounter with our

Redeemer and Savior Jesus Christ. Also you, young as you were, had the deepest impressions of him, our beloved Jesus, and surrendered yourself completely to him. I am confident that the uniting with the Hutterites will bring to you and me and all of us and above all to our own family the complete fulfillment of our longing in faith for so many years. . . . For this reason also, I wish to hold on faithfully through this long-drawn-out journey, with my mind constantly set on the longed for and expected reward. Then if God wills and we live, I shall return home before the Christmas festival you love so much with such joy and help that we can then undertake a wonderful new beginning of tenfold blessing with our beloved Bruderhof.

Lethbridge, October 8, 1930

The time is now beginning which you have prophesied: the time when I would no longer be able to bear the long separation from you, from our children, our home, our dear faithful Bruderhof members, our completely different and unique way of life. But it is necessary to remain firm and hold out. Also here the Hutterites are very loving, attentive, interested, and have very warm and awakened hearts for our cause. And yet it is harder than I can say that still—until today—I can speak only seldom of the pressing need of our financial situation, a need which is unknown here. All are of the opinion, which is held with the well-known unyielding firmness of the Hutterites, that first spiritual matters must be settled, and only then the temporal. Therefore I am provided here and there with only five or ten dollars which I need for traveling and postage expenses. At West Raley Bruderhof I spoke repeatedly about the $400 journey expenses which Christian Vetter has promised to refund, and I told here, as everywhere, of our selling meadows and of our scarcity of food and milk. They assured me again that I would receive it after the main articles had been put in order. And how much I would have liked to send it to you and all! Please never think that I forget the economic task for a moment, or put it on one side. But I cannot write much about this here on the Bruderhofs or in my letters which are included in the pages of this diary since the attitude of the Hutterites to what I write in confidence is very similar to your own, along with their whole character and attitude. Whenever I can, without hurting our cause, I speak of the $25,000 which I would like to bring home at Christmas. Then they would ask in their Hutterite innocence and with earnest eyes, "So much at once?" I am looking forward to your letter on economic matters; Hans should please write me such a letter immediately. At the moment of economic decision which is at last drawing near, I will then be able to proceed with better support. . . . How much I would like to answer your very loving letters, whose news I can hardly wait to hear. But it is more urgent for you and all to have this letter even if it insufficiently reports the events.

Today, October 8, 1930, I find myself at last at the stage where I travel from one Alberta Bruderhof to another. So far I have been to five hofs: Stand Off, West Raley, East Cardston, Big Bend, and Old Elm Spring. Thanks to God's undeserved grace, everything is going well also here, although the brothers' unhurried pace is not always to my or Elias Walter's liking. We have specially warm friends in David Hofer, East Cardston, and Johann P. Entz, called Hannes Vetter, Big Bend. Christian Jr., too, has shown me much love. Like Jakob Wipf, the second servant of Big Bend, he did not want to leave my side day or night. Peter Kleinsasser, the second servant of the Word at Old Elm Spring, is not of such vital importance to us as Andreas Gross, Old Elm Spring, although he is a little older. (Andreas Vetter's name is not Kleinsasser as we were calling him by mistake.)

Like Christian Waldner (West Raley), the Elder, Andreas Gross was at first very cautious, reserved, and questioning. He had earlier written to E. W. that there is so much swindling going on in the world today that one would first have to find out if everything is as we had written. So he made careful inquiries, probably through Pastor Haendiges[1] or our old acquaintance, the fair-haired sub-editor and "pastor" in that coastal town. He should not be mentioned by name. How fortunate—indeed, what a leading from above—that he is no longer linked with the present-day Neuwerk! He has replied that he knows us well from earlier times and has produced a really splendid letter of recommendation written by Professor Unruh, the most important Mennonite leader in Germany and Russia. In that letter Unruh stands up for us most warmly, stating that we are the only communal settlement in Germany that has endured, in spite of very great poverty, that our circle of co-workers is very serious-minded, and that we are genuine Hutterites through and through. He also writes that my father, a Lutheran pastor, had disowned me for embracing the Hutterian faith and life but had become reconciled to me before his death, and so on.

It looks as if the Lehrerleut—and quite certainly the Dariusleut—will decide unanimously for a uniting, for our service of the Word,

---

[1]Chairman of Union of German Mennonite Congregations.

and for support. Only, it will unfortunately be just as time-consuming as my journey has been all along. Not until I have achieved my main object may I undertake an all-out attack on the *economic* aspect of the task. All this is a hard test of patience for me, as well as for you, my *Amselchen*, and all of us. But if the final outcome is good, it will make up for all the sufferings of our long separation. The goal I have set myself is high, and I hope to reach it completely.

The decisive visit was that with our Elder, Christian Waldner, in West Raley, one of the richest hofs. Elias Walter got very impatient when, after receiving the letter,[1] which might well be regarded as decisive, Christian Waldner emphasized anew the difficulty of the matter and wanted to start all over again. The children we had taken in whose parents have not decided for community, and whether our baptisms would stand, having been carried out in another form, were very disturbing problems for him. There was also the question whether many might not have come to us through the purely outward pressure of poverty and unemployment. Finally there was the principal question whether we had been led to community life and to the Hutterites by mere knowledge, learning, and curiosity (we would call it a theoretical or intellectual interest), instead of by faith that brings forth surrender and love. Thus I was once again thoroughly questioned and examined. Some questions—long since answered in my many letters—really astounded me, for example if we know Peter Riedemann's *Confession of Faith* and believe in it. Elias Walter, unable to restrain himself, repeatedly broke in with, "Why, he's got all that better than we have!"

What greatly interested me during that examination on Peter Riedemann's *Confession of Faith* was the way Christian Waldner, the Elder, stressed that while other religions speak of three persons in the Godhead, the Hutterites confess there is but one and the same power in the Father (Creator), the Son (Jesus Christ, Word, and Revelation), and the Holy Spirit of the Church.

You must all read Ulrich Stadler's important comments on his quite similar questions. They correspond so completely to the way the Spirit led us at Sannerz, that along with Jakob Hutter and Peter Riedemann I should like to see Ulrich Stadler—one of the first and earliest epistle writers among the Hutterites—as the special leader of us "Arnold Leut" (as they already call you here, I am sorry to say). Then we would have to be styled, somewhat complicatedly, Hutter-Riedemann-Walpot-Stadler-Hans Hut-Leut! That would certainly be better, but it would be still better if all human names were dropped and we were

---

[1] Of recommendation, from the Schmiedeleut, p.135.

called—well, what? That is where human speech fails. Or we return
to the basic ideas of the truth: sonship of God, mankind's calling, the
kingdom of God, the church, brotherhood, love, faith, hope, work,
and community. However, all too many have already taken these
names to themselves; besides, like "God's righteousness" and "social
justice," they sound too bold. The fact that we already call ourselves
a Hutterian Bruderhof and are regarded as such in Germany has made
a great impression here, in particular on the Lehrerleut.

As for the rest, our Elder Christian Waldner, displayed the
well-known Hutterian sharp thinking, objectivity, clearmindedness,
thoroughness, and caution, caution, and once more caution. He is
without doubt a very capable elder and is highly regarded by all the
Lehrerleut too. The discussion he held with me—pretty well alone,
though in the presence of many others—lasted five and a half hours.
But when he afterward asked Elias Walter as the oldest one present
(aside from himself) to hold the *Gebet*, he received the almost rude
reply, "What am I to hold *Gebet* for now? We hear the Word of God
just as well here with Eberhard Arnold. Let's stay here and get on
with it!" However, the elder had spoken, and we went to *Gebet*, but
it was taken by Hannes Vetter, Johann P. Entz, Big Bend, Woolford,
of the Lehrerleut.

So, also at the West Raley Bruderhof, all I could do was to resort
to my tried and tested method: Instead of relying on persuasion and
pressure, I simply stay there until unanimity is reached or at least
promised. That is what happened here too. To begin with, we agreed
on the necessity of my making a round trip through the Alberta
communities *before* the conclusive main decision, even though Elias
Walter objected and found that too small a step. It is a repetition of
my Manitoba round trip—equally happy and even more successful,
I hope. But there are eighteen stops in Alberta and only ten in Manitoba.
Elias Walter had so longed for me to go from hof to hof teaching,
arousing, and stimulating in the full power and authority of the mission
task, but the present arrangement will not allow that. As the program
now stands, by the time the confirmation and union take place it will
be just about time for me to travel home. Through the grace of God,
through my persistence in investigating the old writings, and also
because by a wonderful providence sharp church action had to be
taken against the very hateful people around David R. Hofer,[1] I came
very close to Christian Waldner as the days went on. So much so that

---

[1] Left the Hutterian Church with some of his family and others and formed his own group.

at my departure he wished me the very best success for our undertaking; he also has good confidence for the great meeting of the Dariusleut and Lehrerleut, which he will probably preside over.

He states correctly that Joseph Kleinsasser's letter does not express the completed union but rather a unanimous decision that the Manitoba Schmiedeleut (and, of course, Michel Vetter, Bon Homme, SD) are in complete agreement with such a union—a distinction that to us may seem very small but is nevertheless very essential for the authority to be granted. Christian Vetter shook his head doubtfully as he drew my attention to it and asked: If the hofs in Alberta would do no more than declare their *consent* to the proposed union and appointment— which is what the Schmiedeleut *are* in fact doing—would the Schmiedeleut be ready to actually carry it out? "They would most certainly do so," I replied. Then he smiled and said with marked friendliness, "But we are not going to do that—we are not going to shove you off onto the Schmiedeleut." And at the great meeting in West Raley, in which also some Lehrerleut servants took part, Elias Walter, our loyal friend, went so far as to declare very forcefully, "Now that the Schmiedeleut have tested and acknowledged Eberhard (as he—and only he—often calls me, without the "Vetter"), there is nothing left for us to test. I at any rate will do no more testing." In this respect as in some others, Christian Vetter is more like the Lehrerleut than his own Dariusleut. Like almost all the leading men, including Hannes Vetter (Big Bend), he was a teacher for many years, with a proper state diploma.

After leaving the hospitable Raley hof, which, due to Christian Jr. and in the end also the elder himself, has come to put great trust in me, I went to the St. Maria Bruderhof, as David Vetter had first called his East Cardston Hof. Its location is as beautiful as that of the Stand Off Bruderhof or even more so. In glorious autumn sunshine, hidden in the wood along the Mary River, I worked away at the old books and writings but was always fetched out quite soon with loud cries of "Eberhard Vetter! Eberhard Vetter!" either by old David Vetter himself or by a crowd of children sent out for me. As at West Raley, Big Bend, and Old Elm Spring, here too the discussions went on well into the night. The crowd was so big that the large room (a bit bigger than our Brotherhood room) could not contain it, in spite of extra benches brought in. More brothers and sisters, *stood* outside the open door and the open window eagerly listening and asking questions— *stood* there for hours, and that after a long workday! Once, here too—actually at Hannes Vetter's suggestion!—the thought came up of moving to the large dining room, but as my confirmation in the service of the Word was still lacking, it was left. This, however, does have the big advantage that in "the house" (as they here call the living and sleeping quarters of the individual family), the women and girls take a lively part in the talks, something they do not do in the solemnity of the *Esstube* (dining room).

Especially at Andreas Vetter's Old Elm Spring Bruderhof, but actually everywhere, they questioned me particularly about you, beloved *Amselchen*, about our women's dress (down to the smallest details), about their work, and about our children. It makes me ever so happy when I can tell a lot about you, dear *Amselchen*. "Is she really fat, your Emma?" According to age-old ideas of health, fatness is here considered the one true qualification for feminine beauty. When they get hold of your photo—something I try to prevent because of the ban on photos—they all cry out, "Just look how lovely Emma is!" Then they admire me twice as much as before. In a man, too, size and stature are valued, as is any gift in God's nature and creation. In these matters the folk here are so very simple as only children are among us.

It amazes them to hear about the education of our children: the baby house, kindergarten, and school with its three groups—above all that the children are all day long in the care of the school sisters (teachers) and of a teacher of practical work. Also that from early on they are instructed in hand work and crafts, and that they are taught wholly in the spirit of the church, without outside influences—even when learning English. I also tell them about our communal sewing room and laundry and above all that our babies are breast-fed only at regular intervals and not at all at night. "Here they suckle whenever they want to," they say.

Again and again I hear, "None but the Holy Spirit could have shown you all our orders of true community, when you had never even seen a Bruderhof." They mean that quite seriously, even when it comes to little things such as the benches without backrests and the chests [*Truhen*] in our dining room, or the long skirts of our women and girls, in contrast to the fashion of the day, and so forth. On the day before I left, even Christian, the Elder, said to me, "It is really so that the Holy Spirit has led you to us." And in the *Lehr*, too, the Holy Spirit comes to the fore as nowhere else.

I am particularly impressed by Hannes Vetter of the Big Bend Bruderhof. He is intelligent and clear-sighted, cultured and well-read, deeply believing and loving, has a sense of humor and is a friend of men. (The highest praise to be bestowed on a Hutterite is that the brothers speak of him as a "friend of men.") At the same time Hannes Vetter is very firmly and deeply Hutterian. His judgment leads to clear views: "David Hofer (Rockport) and other rich Lehrer hofs are too reluctant to give. With them the individual hof and its interests come too much to the fore." The Hutterites call David Hofer "Dauf" Vetter, which, though it sounds like the German word *doof*, is not at all meant to imply that he is in any sense stupid. In fact, he is very intelligent, deep-thinking, perceptive, and capable in practical matters. But in Hannes Vetter's opinion David Vetter's excuse that his dislike of typewriters kept him from reading my letters would not stand before God and the church. He thinks, too, that David Vetter's holding on to Rockport's wealth has resulted in his word as elder no longer having the weight it should have among the Lehrerleut in Alberta. According to Hannes Vetter, the richer a Bruderhof gets, the more it is in danger of withdrawing from those who are in varying degrees poorer. The magnificent and truly amazing machine economy, he thinks, has harmed the Bruderhofs both spiritually and temporally. It has done harm spiritually because it claims and uses up man's mental and spiritual interests and denies him the use of his muscles and the sweat of toil. And it causes temporal harm through the resultant enormous increase in the land required (in Alberta often up to 7,000 acres for one Bruderhof), through debts and interest payments on the expensive equipment and fuel needed (one hof spends annually $4,000 and more just on gasoline, diesel oil, and kerosene), but especially because the machines replace so much manpower that no community can grow to more than 170 souls without causing or allowing idleness.

Hannes Vetter is equally right in considering it a principal mistake among the Dariusleut that they frequently form new Bruderhofs on the basis of close blood ties. That is the case, for example, with Darius Walter and his sons, who broke away from Joseph Stahl, Lake Byron, and whose life at the Felger Farm, without a service of the Word and the orders relating to it, Hannes Vetter does not recognize as Hutterian. Another example is the recent exodus of the Tschetter group from Elias Walter's hof, and also that of the Joseph Hofer group from the St. Maria, East Cardston, Bruderhof. The Lehrerleut, on the other hand, bring together quite different families from different hofs to form a new Bruderhof. The Lehrerleut have the right attitude, says Hannes Vetter: the leaders must lead, and the people must follow. Among the Dariusleut the people will often push so hard and so long for such things as a new branch community that the leaders finally give in. As a result, he says, family bonds carry more weight there than among the Lehrerleut, and the leaders are faced with cases like the one where a young man from the David R. Hofer group simply carried off a girl plus furniture and other things from Michael Tschetter's hof so he could marry her. Christian Waldner does indeed show caution, strength of will, and decisiveness; Elias Walter has a deep insight into genuine Hutterianism, and the Christianity of the Dariusleut is marked by warmheartedness and depth of faith. Nevertheless, they are, in Hannes Vetter's view, too soft in the way they handle matters such as separation, avoidance [*Meidung*], the dress, and the like. And the state of things among the Schmiedeleut in Manitoba, he thinks, has suffered greatly from the influence of the city that is too close, especially as regards clothing and the use of money. His people, the Lehrerleut, would be glad to have the Schmiedeleut Elder, Kleinsasser Vetter, and other older brothers from Manitoba among them, and such a visit would be a great blessing, but they are not keen on being visited by younger brothers from Manitoba. Both Hannes Vetter and I regard a more frequent getting together of all servants from all three groups as the only remedy for all the ills listed. By the nature of things, that would have to lead to the election of one common elder with strong authority.

Hannes Vetter is a tall, gaunt man of about sixty-seven, with a somewhat Russian appearance and a kind, intelligent face. After Johannes Kleinsasser he is the third elder of the Lehrerleut. He showed me the great love of driving me to Andreas Vetter in Old Elm Spring. More than that, he went on all by himself in his two-horse carriage to New Elm Spring and the Rockport Bruderhof and there (as I got to know right away) spent hours trying to win hearts for my task, for union with us and support for us. When I gratefully called him our guide and escort to the Lehrerleut, he replied in characteristic Hutterian fashion, "You may yet find a better one." Among our men with firm convictions in Germany one would scarcely find such a matter-of-course awareness of how small one is and how easily replaced, along with such a deep consciousness of standing for the truth.

Also the second servant of Big Bend, Jakob Wipf, gives a strong impression, and so does the steward, Peter Entz, who has charge of the extremely valuable *Dröscher* book (written by a hewer and thresher in the 1500s). Both are widowers and speak of their deceased wives with the same deep sorrow, the same gratitude, love, and respect as does Johannes Vetter in Wolf Creek, SD—the one who read me the commentary on Revelation. If one might say so, family love among the Hutterites is too strong rather than too weak—precisely the opposite of what is generally assumed outside. In Rockport, SD, the servant of the Word, Peter Hofer, told me Hutterian mothers would be reluctant to let their children intermarry with our young people, for though now acknowledging our faith and life to be right, they do not know our ancestry and bloodline. Here in Alberta, on the other hand, a kind and loving servant of the Word brought to me his beaming grown-up son and asked me if I would give him a girl from our Bruderhof to be his wife.

Thus I conclude the first volume of these diary notes, confident that our Bruderhofs will merge completely, that we will be helped and strengthened by the American hofs in every respect and that we, too, may be of some benefit to them.

Lethbridge, October 23, 1930

You will be worried by now. And in fact it was again my eye. But one treatment by the Lethbridge eye doctor, this time with only one injection, has cured me. But it cost one week and thirty-five dollars. I will now travel again more slowly through the Bruderhofs. When I go too fast, especially when I have to share a bed with Andreas Vetter of Old Elm Spring, it immediately puts a strain on my eye. We must accept that this journey will cost so much time. My longing for you and for our Bruderhof becomes ever stronger. At the same time I am showered with love—too much followed after. I get quite scared when they set too "high" expectations in me. I believe that the abundance of old writings which we are being given is very promising of help in other respects which will also surprise us.

October-November: The packages I to IV are sent as answer to the very loving and beautifully written inscription from both of you in the second much nicer diary. This is the beginning of the second and last diary of the journey in America which—if God wills—will report the solving of all the difficulties of our beginning. My eye is better again, so that I hope to write in it the report about the really fine, deep, strong, serious-minded Lehrerleut. And—I can send it home— in the blue carbon-copy. Because it is not good for my eyes to travel on an open wagon when there is a keen wind, I shall be driven today in a closed car by the servant of the Word and steward of Buck Ranch, Milford, to visit Johann Wurz at Richards Bruderhof near Wilson.[1] I am again sending money today . . . .

---

[1] Wilson Siding Bruderhof.

I was again unable to finish the letter and could not send it off with money. The brothers stormed my quiet room until I had permission from the doctor to travel in a closed car. As soon as that was granted I could not wait another minute. For immediately there were three cars from three different Bruderhofs at the door. The Elder, Johannes Kleinsasser, had to be given preference together with his steward Paul Wipf and drove me to the Wilson, Richards, Bruderhof. The others with their punctual act of love, had to withdraw sadly. Johannes Kleinsasser remained one day at the Wilson Bruderhof, and on the day after his departure and that of the three visitors from Rockport, Elias and Elisabeth Walter came, since they had not spoken with me for so long, and stayed two days. You can well imagine that with such enthusiasm I do not have a minute of quiet, since the brothers and sisters of the Bruderhofs come in crowds to me. This is not a complaint; we thank God alone from all our hearts that, as Johannes Wurz said, God has aroused such "excitement" (we would say "awakening"), through my visit from which very many, though not all, expect renewal, unification and mission amongst the Hutterites. I do not like to write this in the diary as it could be wrongly interpreted and misunderstood. But when I make a visit, or go into another house for the sake of getting an old writing, then the whole group who have been listening to me till then follow me across the hof. And if I have been in one house and said good night and shaken hands with everyone there, and then go across to the Word leader's house, within five minutes they are all gathered there again, filling two rooms. And the more sharply I speak or read, the happier and more thankful they all are. And so it is almost without exception on all of the twenty-six Bruderhofs I have visited so far, so that the evenings are always very late, and in the morning at six o'clock, again I hear, "Arnold Vetter! Are you getting up?" Perhaps that is not suitable for reading out loud. But I have to write it down once, so that you understand that I cannot get to doing any writing on the Bruderhofs and have to go to town also for this reason. That's why I am completing this letter in a hotel, having been accompanied here by four brothers from Wilson, Rockyford and Felger Farm with their reluctant agreement, and I had to give instructions not to be disturbed for two hours. I was therefore unable to send off parcels XVI and XVII and other parcels. However, the worst thing is that the date of my departure is brought into question through this high pressure and especially through the urgent requests and representations of our most faithful Elias Walter. Please do not do anything to hinder this. Every fiber in me is urging me homewards. But the goal of this costly and strenuous journey must not be endangered by our impatience and longing. It must be fully and completely achieved and the prospects for this grow daily. We are sending money today in another way, and more will soon follow. The main large sum will however come with my return. Believe and continue to pray. God will hear everything.

Lethbridge, November 12, 1930

Everything draws me to you and the children and to all our dear faithful ones. But it is difficult here to get away. The Bruderhofs are so close and so big that I do not have a moment of peace to write, to work, or send off a parcel without the help or disturbance of two or three who certainly want to be there. That is extremely strenuous for me. Also they all want to talk over everything. There is a good prospect that we can "set up" our hof. Already we are talking quite freely about 300 acres and a dwelling house together with provision for printing and other handwork; a first payment of between $25,000 and $30,000 is thought of. But it has not yet been achieved. If I remain in good health it will need one more month in Alberta and then perhaps three older brothers will travel home together with me. I will try to arrange that they come to us a quarter of a year after me so that we can make preparations. Oh, it is such a great thing I have dared! Now I must also accomplish it or rather hold out until the Creator of all things has also accomplished it.

Lethbridge, November 1930

These head coverings are a gift from the Elm Spring brothers and sisters to all the women and girls of our Bruderhof who belong to the church. They are given in order that you may all wear them the whole day, and that through this unity of dress you may make it known that you love and belong to the brothers and sisters. The covering of the head is a matter of order for Hutterian women and girls, a sign of their belonging to the Brotherhood. Even more it is a matter of faith, because for them it belongs to God-willed womanliness, chastity, and protection from evil glances. All were so joyful when one after the other brought these head coverings, nearly all of them used. Greet all our women, girls, and children.[1]

Eberhard

---

[1]With this greeting, written by Eberhard and typed by Else von Hollander, every sister at the Rhön Bruderhof received two beautifully embroidered head coverings for Christmas 1930.

Crows Nest in the Rocky Mountains
of British Columbia, November 1930

I can hardly bear it anymore to be separated from you for so long,
also from our own children and our family, and not least, being so
far from our beloved circle, our old and new faithful fellow fighters,
indeed from the whole unique spirit and life of our Bruderhof. I
experience much love here, also among the Lehrerleut, whose elder,
Johannes Kleinsasser, accompanies me throughout the day and
overwhelms me with proof of his trust and his readiness to help, in
a way none of our best friends could surpass. Also on nearly all
Bruderhofs the meetings were wonderful, with their many hours of
uninterrupted attentiveness and enthusiasm and thankfulness. I could
not find one half-day of quiet for writing because I was so keenly
sought after and questioned, whether it was in Lethbridge, Macleod,
Cardston, Calgary, or even in smaller places. In town there are
constantly some of the 1,500 Hutterites who live on the eighteen
Alberta hofs. And all community members—not only our own—are
easily hurt when "such a guest from so far away and one living in
true community" has not time for an important inner and brotherly
talk! So, as at the time of our engagement, which I must repeatedly
tell about, I have escaped to the mountains to write you at least a
short letter. It should be at least a little longer than the one sent with
the head coverings a week ago. But all this love and attention cannot
for a moment drive away my homesickness for you and you all. Even
the wonderful writings which I work at daily and read out to others
do not help in this. And when I read your precious and priceless letter
and also for the second time Emy-Ma's fine, loving letter from
Dresden, I sobbed like a child; that was in Wolf Creek, Alberta and
in Buck Ranch, Milford. Should I be ashamed? I am not too old to
be childish. In Wolf Creek I even put on the fur coat belonging to
our dear Elias Walter and said, "I want to go home." But I must
overcome that. When I spoke about this to the very friendly
Johann M. Wurz of the Richardsleut, Wilson Bruderhof, who is very
close to me, he said, "But you are not a child anymore." I said to
him, "I would gladly be one." Without faithfulness there is no
homesickness; without homesickness there is no faithfulness. There
cannot be love on this earth without pain. He then gave me his hand
and said it would be exactly the same for him. But I must be brave
and reach the goal, towards which Hans's letter and especially yours
of October 29 are a big help. Wherever I read it to others they called
out, "How can your wife write such a letter! Our women could not

write such a good and wise letter." It is the same again and again with Emy-Ma's letter: "You must have a good school!" And then they called to the young people, "Could you write a letter with so much spirit in it?" No, they said, they couldn't. The aging community here does not give the same fire to the young people as our lively young beginning was able to do. In spite of this the same Johann Wurz said he knew he could depend much more joyfully on the young people (meaning those between twenty-five and thirty-five) than on the gray-haired ones. But the very oldest are the deepest and most lively. I will however tell all this later in my diary when my round trip finds at last a point of rest at Stand Off and West Raley. Before that I have to visit five more Bruderhofs. Please continue to pray that through the grace of God this may succeed. Be assured that I shall travel round as quickly as my poor health and the demands of the task allow. Please encourage me to accomplish everything without weakening until it is all fulfilled. For whatever is broken off now cannot be made up for later. For this reason I can set no fixed date for my return, but be certain, I shall be home the very first day the task allows it. I will write an open letter to our Brotherhood, after I have written to Hans today about money, smoking, music, and pictures, and my, your, and his journey. Unfortunately the last letters I received have given me concern for our Bruderhof members for the first time; but tomorrow I shall receive more recent news when I am with Elias Walter. I was already saddened by the loss of Hanna Paulmann and still more Paul and the three children, although Hanna was not very open and the Jannash boys not very well able to face life, and I didn't like the work week from the beginning, already not the planning by Erich Mohr, so that I could not write anything to him in spite of his request. And now this need for spiritual help and such long night sessions as on October 27! I implore all Brotherhood members with all their strength to remain in faith, love, objectivity, trust and of one voice, since the least breakdown must weaken my task and its fulfillment from within. The firmer all at home stand together, the more certain and sure I can be here—and come home with great new strength. This is the first time that I have had to write like this[1] since the end of May. I rejoice all the more in the fact that I could feel the strength of a true holding together of those at home for such a long time. I rejoice that the baby house—as a symbol—has twice been given new life, first from Siegrid and then from Irmgard who has now received a second Ulrich Stadler;

---

[1]See pp.168–170.

I am glad that Emy-Ma, Sophie, and Liesel have passed their exams; that the young people have stood firmly against the attractions from outside; that Emy-Ma has such a fine work; that all are working faithfully everywhere and that again and again the spirit of God has given you all a pure atmosphere.

So also today then I embrace all you faithful ones with the arms of my heart, and I beg you, if you wish, to give each one of them the kiss of the spirit of unity from me.

In answer to Hans's question: there is nothing to be done about shipping flour from Manitoba. But we will receive cash instead of it.

Rhön Bruderhof   Rocky Mountains, British Columbia
Germany   November 26, 1930

My most beloved brothers and sisters,

   . . . And here I come to what my letter is actually about. How happy, how glad and joyful I am about the clear guidance through the Holy Spirit which you have been given during all these months, and indeed again and again through the tools appointed by God and his church. And with what faithfulness you have stood to the Brothers and the communities called Hutterian, because Jakob Hutter founded them with such glowing, burning fire of love and with equally glowing and fiery discipline. In the same way you have stood to their deeply tested orders, almost without the slightest interruption, which would have been all too understandable humanly. I can limit myself to a few brief sentences of reminder in this second, objective part. For you have been crowned by the Spirit himself, far better than the old priests and rulers!

   And now you have a veritable treasure of writings that radiate the Spirit, already more than 150 handwritten books, "little books," pamphlets, and leaflets, among them more than fifty old and very old pieces; only very few of the American Bruderhofs have such a precious treasure of old handwritings. So great is the love of the Brothers to us that they will surely not let us down on the economic side. However, with their persistent thoroughness all this will take time, much time. So with a heavy heart I must again ask you for leave of absence, even with my poor health and bad eye, which varies but has never again been as bad as it was at home in the spring, during the journey, and in June in Wolf Creek. Be assured that I shall come home as fast as possible, as soon as my task of finding unity and support for the service and for the economic basis of our Bruderhof has been solved to a certain degree.

Now since I feel all the time how strong or how diverted and weakened the flow of strength is that comes to me from your unity in truth, in prayer, in the breaking of bread, and in community, I ask you in deep and heartfelt trust: Do not urge me to return too soon, for this might put into question the whole success of these great sacrifices.

Trust in your leading, that it will guide you through everything in unity through God's spirit. Be openhearted, open and ready for one another! Have joy in one another! You have much cause for this! Together with your openness and alertness to the Spirit, preserve your fine feeling for purity and unity in the Spirit. But become free and remain free from personal touchiness, from worry about being treated differently from others, also in your tasks, duties, and services! For there is really no cause for this!

Rejoice in your spiritual unity and in your real standing together, even in your diversity, without trying to make equal, align, level and paralyze—and thus to dissolve and extinguish—all special qualities. Community lives only in living interchange! Therefore be glad that you are all different and never get irritated about it!

But with all this diversity of typical, characteristic, and varied gifts and talents, there are things that can never be allowed—selfishness and pettiness, talking behind others' backs, envy and jealousy, fear and worry, and worse things. Like self-seeking and self-will, these enemies of life are not gifts of the Spirit, but sheer loss and damage. There is no one who has received so few gifts that he has to make a good-for-nothing of himself through his concern with these dangerous trivialities! Such poison and nothingness is beneath us! Please, yes, I plead with you, persevere for yet a short while all together, in full unity and divine love and joy. Don't waste a single night on things, questions, and discussions which would be unnecessary if we stood together more faithfully, more firmly, more trustingly, and more gratefully. In other words, make such nights unnecessary by not letting anything come to pass that would make them necessary.

Please, yes, I earnestly ask you: Carry your great and holy responsibility steadfastly, like a burning light in your hands. For the sake of this warming, radiating light, do not let yourselves be pushed or shaken or even knocked over! Then the fullness of your burning candles will send its light over to me as in a Christmas vision and will strengthen me and bring me back with everything you need. You know that the incarnation of the Creator and his word of love, and Jesus' word and work in the outpouring of his spirit, is the strength in which you can do everything.

My dear, good Emmychen has always reported everything in such a way that I have been able to sense in all the happenings and struggles your victorious faith and the power of unity.

Therefore, let no strange, dark, unclear, or apathetic spirit enter among you or rule over you, not even through your guests, relatives, visitors, or old and new friends, and please least of all, through a work camp in any way similar to the last one. Since 1922, 1925, and now 1930, the time for such concessions to the foolishness, vanity, and insolence of people who are enemies of redemption should once and for all be past for us.

Let nothing, not the slightest thing, come among you that offends Jesus Christ, his world redemption, his smallness and humbleness and redemption in the manger and on the cross, his following on his way to men and to God, his obedience to the words of his Sermon on the Mount, his now truly outpoured spirit of full unity and purity and active reality.

The Lord is the Spirit. Only in the spirit of unity shall we see the Christ of purity. Only thus shall we come to faith in the all-powerful Creator, God of all worlds and suns and earths, who in Christ and in the outpoured spirit of his church has become our Father, to whom we belong and whom we trust to provide us with everything we need.

Your Eberhard,

who wishes for himself and for all of you, yes, for us all, and for his longed for safe return home, this grace of Christ, this power of the Spirit, this love of the Father, as all three work indivisibly together, your Eberhard who loves you all immensely in this threefold manifestation of this same power.

Stand Off Bruderhof with Elias Walter
December 1, 1930

I do not know when I shall be able to send you the next longer letter since, as in these last weeks, I am going to be very much occupied in the next fourteen days with Elias Walter who with his great love will be accompanying me to the communities furthest north. Also my eye is not bad but at the same time not quite right. Whenever possible I try to ride in a closed car because of the frequent keen winds. I feel completely at home with Elias Walter. Once again he has made me so rich with old writings and papers, which he has given me, and which I will be sending to Else as soon as I have a longed for day of quiet both for my eye and for my work with the old writings, hopefully in Calgary next week.

Lethbridge, Canada

For Christmas and your birthday

I would never, never have thought that I should have to write to you from so far away for your birthday and Christmas! But the view becomes clearer and I already distinctly see that this severe self-denial is leading towards the goal. You will see from the following pages of this diary that my persistent endurance, yes, also even my eye infection are being used by God, who guides *everything*. He is so leading the brothers in America that they open up without reserve their all too cautious hearts to the cause entrusted to us in Germany, in the same way as our faithful Eckhart, Elias Walter, has done already for years.

So it is that today I can write to you for your dear Christmas birthday for the first time as a "brother"—a real Hutterian brother. They all say now that you and I need have no more care or anxiety of our making it—yes everyone—Elias Walter's steward, Johannes Tschetter, Jacob the steward of the richest Bruderhof, Rockport, and in the same manner Johann Wurz and his and our very dear steward Darius Walter of Richards Wilson Bruderhof. They say now that as I am accepted as a brother it means that they will care for us in a brotherly way. And that the time of their giving alms to us is now past. Now, they tell me, it is a matter of setting us up and sending us out; one member must and will care for the other. If I had not been so short of money, I would have sent you a telegram long ago. But I will give you news by Christmas, although this letter will be going with the Europa[1] on December 16 and should reach you for Christmas. But there is no guarantee of this, also not with the Christmas packet which I sent you. But now I will write about the last few days.

God the truthful, just, and faithful One has brought about my acceptance into the Church of God here among the Hutterian Brethren. This is at the same time an acknowledgment that you over there have truly proved yourselves in a life of full community. And, in spite of previous misgivings, in the end the incorporation did take place at the Stand Off Bruderhof of our Elias Walter, who is so outstandingly

---

[1]Fast transatlantic mail ship.

faithful and loving. The confirmation of my service of the Word is likewise to be carried out at our beloved Elias Walter's Bruderhof. It will at the same time mean a confirmation of your loyalty, which God has placed like a seal on my service (as several of the leaders put it).

It would perhaps never have come to this; perhaps the incorporation and being charged with mission and all that goes with it would have been delayed several more months if my eye trouble had not so touched the hearts of all. My left eye, blinded already during the first year in Sannerz in the service of the community, where "even parsons learn to work," has thus been accepted by God's unspeakable loving-kindness as a sacrifice pleasing to him, for the purpose of setting our Bruderhof on its feet both inwardly and outwardly. In Manitoba I had almost forgotten the very severe inflammation of that left eye, which in Wolf Creek had kept me in bed for nearly four weeks and prevented reading and writing. But the very sharp winds and storms of the blustery Alberta weather called forth more and more frequent signals that the eye was again crying for proper attention. At first, things went very well as I set out to travel from hof to hof, as told in the other diary. While going from Stand Off to West Raley, from there to East Cardston and on to Big Bend and Old Elm Spring, the eye hardly made itself felt. But it did get bad while I was at Old Elm Spring with Andreas Vetter, who is as reserved as he is kind and loving—in fact, one night his love urged him to make me a gift of ten teachings. I slept in one bed with him—something that unfortunately has been for me a nervous strain I could not get used to from childhood on—and before long I became aware of the stealthy approach of the eye pains I know only too well. Because the nightly rest was so brief at Old Elm Spring and the days so long and so loaded with most responsible tasks, the pains presently increased. I at once broke off my trip around the Bruderhofs and wrote to you at length from Lethbridge, where I sought help from Dr. Woodcrook, a doctor who speaks a little German, having trained for a while at the Vienna eye clinic. Since then I have been to see him several times—in fact, that's what I am doing now. So the eye improved.

I then traveled on to the second elder of the much respected Lehrerleut, our very loving Johannes Kleinsasser, who in many ways sets such an example. He has become one of our best and most dependable friends and has proved himself as one of us in a difficult situation. He stands very close to us in the one wonderful spirit—the spirit of God, the spirit of Sannerz and of the Bruderhof—that has guided us so gloriously. Whom should I meet at his Milford Bruderhof but the two beloved, loyal witness brothers I got to know at Rockport, SD, whose hearts are so moved for our cause: Johannes Hofer, the profoundly well-educated teacher who gave us a large book of epistles, and Jakob Hofer, whose hair is already turning white, the best-known blacksmith and all-round craftsman of the Bruderhofs. They are the sons of the old miller at Rockport, SD—the one who struggled with death a number of times and had charge of the large epistle book and of one of the two existing originals of the Chronicle. The days at Milford were extremely precious ones; I had large and inwardly moved meetings with all the folk there, and they were full of lively questions about all of you and about the faith and life of our Bruderhof.

Then Johannes Vetter, the best of friends, accompanied me via the new and third Rockport, which will be called Hutterville, to the second Rockport in Alberta, to Joseph Vetter, son of the founder Jakob *Lehrer* Wipf of 1878.

Johannes Vetter, starting with $100 himself, wanted all the places to contribute some money to relieve your present situation. As a result, you were sent $575, even though my eye treatment meant that many a dollar had to go to the doctor, the pharmacy, and the hotel. But Dr. Woodcrook's help kept me going as far as Rockport III (Hutterville) and Rockport II. At the rich Rockport II, however, a not unexpected inner difficulty arose over a letter David Hofer (James Valley), the second elder of the Manitoba Schmiedeleut, had written to Elias Walter. David Vetter is our most loyal friend and fights for us side by side with Elias; he even had the thought, and brought it up for decision, to send a whole railway carload of wheat flour to Germany for us if it could go customs-free. Now in his letter to Elias Walter he said that in the richer communities it would do me more harm than good to plead for the complete union of all hofs under one elder, like a new Andreas Ehrenpreis, for that would mean a merging of the Manitoba hofs, even the poorest ones, with the very wealthiest hofs in Alberta. Well, our outspoken Elias Walter sent every Bruderhof an exact copy of this letter, in which dear David Vetter speaks—with warmest enthusiasm and pretty certainly overdoing it a bit—of my and your life in full commmunity. Thereupon Joseph Wipf, Rockport, Alberta, declared he would never agree to such a union of all Bruderhofs, as the Schmiedeleut are too easy-going and the Dariusleut too soft. In the following pages you will hear of the further, and not yet concluded, development of this Lehrerleut position, which is of great strategic importance. There was none of that hardness in Joseph Vetter's attitude toward me personally or our Bruderhof, and the evenings I spent with him were very worthwhile. One afternoon, I spent more than an hour addressing a vigorous appeal to the men of Rockport out on the huge wheat fields in the threshers' caravan (just like the gipsy wagon we had in mind).

Joseph Vetter very lovingly drove me to the adjoining Bruderhof to the west, New Elm Spring, presently engaged in building up a daughter hof, Crystal Spring. Johannes Entz the son of Hannes Vetter, Big Bend, at once returned home from the new hof to see me and speak with me. He is the second, Peter Entz the first servant of the Word at New Elm Spring. My stay there was just as pleasant as at the other Lehrerleut hofs.

From all the Lehrerleut I get the impression of a very earnest, deeply founded, and firmly rooted stand for community and Hutterianism; they live harmoniously and in their clothing and style are purer and less subject to outside influences than the Schmiedeleut and Dariusleut. But that basically wrong feeling for the economic and financial independence of the individual hofs, with every hof claiming the right to do with its money as it pleases—a right not in keeping with the church of God—is perhaps even stronger among them than among the Dariusleut and Schmiedeleut. I put up a most passionate fight against this cursed collective egoism. Communistic collectives and communities of from ten to twenty or maybe thirty and more families pursuing a collective interest should be left to Bolshevism and its violent compulsion, to be misused for the benefit of its satanic power center. We, however, are called to the church of God, the church of Christ, which is the church of the holy, uniting spirit, in which therefore everything belongs to all who are filled and ruled by the same spirit of complete community. So I speak frankly of the threatening danger of property intruding once again—for the third time in Hutterian history.

The first time, community of goods collapsed through an inner weakening of true community, due to giving in to little property rights, and under the terrific pressure of a hundred years of warfare (the Turkish wars from 1592 on and the Thirty Years War). Nevertheless, as long as the orders governing the common life were faithfully upheld by a thorough overseer of all Bruderhofs such as Andreas Ehrenpreis, the stormy ardor of the early martyr enthusiasm continued from 1528/1533 until 1699, that is, for one hundred and seventy years. The second time that Hutterian communal life took shape in a church community united by the Spirit was of shorter duration, for it failed to measure up to the divinely inspired enthusiasm of the earlier period.

It lasted from 1763 to 1819, that is, "only" fifty-six years. But during the intervals—1700-1763 and 1819-1853—truth kept working underground with a strength I was made aware of only here through the old writings and through the recollections of the wonderful old men among the Hutterites.

Thus, four community beginnings in Russia gradually pressed forward to the present stage of Hutterian consolidation and expansion in America. Over many years the Russian government was approached time and again for permission to live in community, but the first practical attempt, made at Kolonisch in 1853, succeeded only for two and a half years. Of the three following attempts—1859, 1860, and 1866—the first two, by Schmied Michel (1859) and Darius Walter (1860) in Scheromet and Huttertal, were successful. On the other hand, the community attempt of the Lehrerleut in Johannesruh, while indeed preserving a good spirit, lasted only from 1866 to 1868, as they could not keep up the communal life they had begun with such energy in a big village consisting of widely spaced, individually owned farmsteads. But after uniting with the church when visited by Schmied Michel on his mission trip to Russia, they drew together all the more firmly in 1878 in America, at which time the two other communities, Bon Homme and Wolf Creek, already had four years of struggle and consolidation behind them. Hence the Lehrerleut started to live in community eighteen years later than the Dariusleut and Schmiedeleut, which perhaps accounts for their more vigorous and vital energy. With the other two big groups the present period of solid community living has already lasted seventy years, that is, fourteen years longer than the earlier and in some ways doubtless better period in Transylvania (Kreuz), Walachia, Vishenka, and Raditschewa.

The full "communism of production and consumption" of every individual hof comprising from forty to one hundred and seventy-five souls as well as the absolute unity of faith of all thirty-five Bruderhofs stand virtually unshaken right to the present—one could almost say, its purity is quite untouched. How then can the Elder David Hofer (Rockport, SD) speak of decay? He complains about the school being no longer Hutterian, the economy dominating the hofs, the growing worldliness and diminishing uniformity of the life style, and the lessening influence of the elders. But he is also said to have once remarked, many years ago, that he did not want to die until he had seen and experienced the merging of all three groups into one spiritual and temporal community of work under one common elder.

Here is the weak point of present-day Hutterianism. Even way back in Russia, the two hofs Scheromet, later Bon Homme, and Huttertal, later Wolf Creek, under their chosen elders Schmied Michel and Darius Walter tried in vain to come to a unified leadership. Those were earnest attempts, as was a later one around 1880 at a big joint meeting of Bon Homme, Wolf Creek, and Old Elm Spring at the Wolf Creek Bruderhof. There is no denying that they came to grief through lack of self-surrender on the part of the individual collectives, through the self-assertion of the individual Bruderhofs and later of their three groups, that is, through separation, which is *sin*. Thus Joseph Kleinsasser (Milltown), the Manitoba elder, is right with his honest admission, "Just as we can only half speak German, we are only half Hutterian."

The first one hundred and seventy years were the period of true Hutterianism, the great original and strongest period and, along with that of the Acts of the Apostles, the only fully determinative one. During that time it was never in doubt that the individual hof, the individual *Haushabe* (household) is *not* the church. Rather, the church is the whole, unanimous body of all witnesses, glorified especially through martyrdom, and members of Christ's organism living in community here and now. And that body is the church of God solely through the guiding and determining power of the Holy Spirit. He guides, determines, and brings about unanimity through the gifts and services he bestows, those of apostles, shepherds, teachers, and deacons or stewards. Very essentially, he works through the helmsmen, leaders, overseers or bishops, who, carried by the unanimous trust of the whole church and the faithful obedience of everybody, lead the church to unanimity. They speak out what all believe and think and yet cannot say or do without the leaders' guidance.

That is how Elias Walter and I and some others see original Hutterianism. What I therefore have to point out continually to present American Hutterianism, now seventy years old, is this: In the time before 1700 the devil deceived the Hutterians of the great *first* communal period, grown weary after Andreas Ehrenpreis's time, by means of his cursed private property. Before 1819 he managed to seduce the Hutterians of the second communal period, torn apart as they were by the quarrel between Johannes Waldner and Jakob Walter. Today the devil is using a much more cunning way to take you in. Instead of tempting you with *individual* property, he is getting you through *collective* property and its democratic majority, acting in the interest of the families "owning" the hof. Only one thing can help you: families claiming to "own" a hof must completely and forever give up any rights of ownership to the whole body as to the church of God, under one spirit-filled elder. A number of serious-minded brothers are expecting that God will one day give me the task of thus revolutionizing the life of the communities and leading it back to genuine, truly communal Hutterianism. But as I believe and hope, I am only called to *testify* to the need for such a change; I am not in a position to become the right man for a task involving so hard a struggle.

Just on this point hinge all questions concerning American Hutterianism, and you must grasp it in its whole seriousness and decisive significance—also, among other things, to gain an understanding why my quest on behalf of our cause is taking so long. Here is the all-important point where I came up against the first hard resistance to, and blunt rejection of, the letter sent by David Hofer, James Valley, at the Rockport Bruderhof, the wealthiest hof!

All the same, the journey from Rockport via New Elm Spring back to Old Elm Spring which is closest to the railroad, only about 2½ miles away, hence specially suited for arrival and departure by train, was wonderfully instructive, as it was an unbroken journey on Bruderhof land, all the way from Buck Ranch, Milford, via Hutterville, Rockport, and New Elm Spring to Old Elm Spring. Please consider and imagine: Just five Bruderhofs form here a little state within the state—an area 2-3 miles wide and about 14 miles long, without any intervening outside property. You over there could compare that with the area of Neuhof, Schlüchtern, and Steinau, right before your eyes. Now these are wealthy Lehrer hofs, but if you multiply that land area by six or at least by five, you will get a fair idea of the *overall* Hutterian strength in terms of land. As you will hear, we are to share such a hof of 5,500 acres with just four old-Hutterian families, as soon as we can move here.

The impression of that communal principality was overwhelming. Unfortunately, though, the icy north wind was even more over-whelming. Once more I went to Lethbridge with my ailing eye, then, having recovered after a few days, on to the Lehrer hofs Miami and Elm Spring (Warner), which are located east of Johannes Kleinsasser's Buck Ranch (Milford) Bruderhof. At both places, as everywhere among the Lehrerleut, I was received most lovingly and found an audience deeply interested in the witness entrusted to us and in everything I tell about you all and especially about you, my *Amselchen*.

At the Miami[1] Bruderhof, the richest hof along with, or just after,

[1]Then known as Miama.

the two (or now three) Rockports, live the two venerable brothers of
the Elder David Hofer (Rockport, SD). One of them, Peter "Old
Vetter," is an old man of moving beauty, almost eighty and blind.
As he wants to "do something" right to the end, his service to the
community consists in rocking babies to sleep in their age-old Hutterian
cradles. Thus the oldest life returns to the very beginning. This "Old
Vetter's" memory is wonderful and amazing. He tells most vividly
all he heard in his childhood and youth about Raditschewa from the
folk who were then as old as he is now. Above all he has such a live
knowledge of the Bible and the old Hutterian writings that he can
quote ever so much most accurately and knows where it is to be found
in the books. His memories, combined with what the old men of his
Johannesruh childhood could remember, go back about one hundred
and thirty years, and I learned a great deal from him. His brother
Joseph, whose hair is not yet quite white, is still the steward of that
important hof, while the "Old Vetter," who is also the father-in-law
of the first servant, Jerg Vetter, and the father of the second servant,
Peter Vetter, exerts a decisive influence from out of his deep inner
stillness. Though blind and advanced in years, he is still vigorous and
takes a keen interest in economic matters. Having in mind the
upcoming generations of grandchildren and great-grandchildren who
must be provided with an equally big hof unburdened by debt (which
means a lot considering that one married couple often has ten to twelve
children), he regards even the richest hofs not as rich and is quite
against making large donations. He also strongly opposes the uniting
of all Bruderhofs under one elder and thinks it could never be brought
about. He sees each individual hof, living as it does without property
in complete community, as a church of God.

Sorry to say, at this second very wealthy Bruderhof, I experienced,
along with that objective resistance, also the one and only personal
unpleasantness I met with among the brothers on this whole long
journey. I was sitting in a hotel room, applying hot dressings to my
hurting eye, and somebody took it badly that I kept him waiting for
a while before letting him in and that I had called out to him, "The
doctor will not let me have visitors as I have to attend to my eye."
Another brought up something similar, and one of the Manitoba
brothers I had met on the train between Regina and Macleod supported
both, finding it "proud" of me that I had not immediately recognized
him in the train—he was sitting to the left, where my blind eye is!
A man from Stand Off, who had several times already given our Elias
Walter trouble and happened to be in Miami at the time, helped spread

the gossip like wildfire through all the hofs, so that I had to face the task of winning back the trust I had only just gained. But in a case like that the centuries-old, firm Hutterian discipline proved itself. The servants of the Word stood by me solidly and clearly. Especially Josua Hofer, Wolf Creek, Johannes Kleinsasser, Milford, Johann Wurz, Richards-Wilson, as well as Jerg Vetter of Miami itself and, of course, right out in front our Elias Walter, Stand Off, fought a sharp and determined battle for the restoration of trust. Johann Wurz, also one of our very best friends, wanted all involved placed into the "great unpeace," which is equivalent to exclusion. Since I put in a good word for them, a simple apology and withdrawal of the accusation in the presence of the servants was thought sufficient. Johannes Kleinsasser, with real dedication and self-forgetfulness, spent several days on this foolish business. It also took much of *my* time and energy. When away from home and among strangers, trust teeters on a knife edge in the most delicate balance. Let us bear that in mind for the love we show our guests at home, and among each other we want to meet backbiting with sharpest church discipline. Here I spoke out against severer punishment only because I myself was the victim and granted complete forgiveness, which does not go together with agreeing to such punishment. The others wanted to proceed completely according to my wishes, as long as they accorded with what the spirit of the church demanded.

So that matter has been well and truly dealt with; it has drawn everybody's attention and pity to my eye and speeded up my incorporation as a brother. The most responsible servants, including the serious, old Christian Waldner Vetter, were now concerned to place me as quickly as possible under their brotherly protection, so that all weak members, such as are found everywhere, know about it and behave accordingly.

About the Elm Spring (Warner) Bruderhof, which has just recently moved here from South Dakota, I can only report what is true everywhere: a very lively interest in what I report and witness to. Michel Entz, like the two servants at New Elm Spring, Peter and Johannes Entz, is "still young," about forty, and it is true: Here the younger men are not yet as alive, vigorous, and inwardly stirred as the older ones.

After further stops in Lethbridge due to illness I finally arrived back among the Dariusleut, where I am always given a quiet single room and find myself surrounded by heartfelt warmth and sympathetic consideration. The lively interest shown by these most warmhearted brothers and sisters is of a still more personal, human, and inward nature and yet goes together with a deep objective understanding.

Johann Wurz, who has learned a great deal from the old Elder Elias Sr., the uncle of our Elias, had very deep talks with me; objectively, he is as close to us as Elias Walter Jr. As regards the impression left by my evening meetings at the Wilson Bruderhof he said that in three evenings I had done more to stimulate and enthuse the brothers and sisters there for total community than preaching had done in three years. I am only telling you that by way of comfort after the trouble I just told you about, which is now all set right. That comment is quite clearly an exaggeration. Johann Wurz not only gave us very fine old writings but would also like to visit us in Germany.

Next I visited the big Felger Farm (5,500 acres, nine grown-ups and about twenty children) of the Walter family, who welcomed me with much love. Old Christian Vetter wants to win their consent that when we have completed our task in Germany, we should all be accepted among them under my leadership. But it is not yet certain whether the Felger folk will have the courage to receive, without serious misgivings, on their big property as many people as we shall be and to join in with our old-Hutterian church orders.

In my next letter I will tell of my trip to the Pincher Bruderhof with its heavy debt burden of $135,000, where everybody was very loving to me, and of my visit to the Doukhobors nearby. I will also tell of the good care I received at Elias Walter's hof during a week of eye illness there and of my present protein shock treatment. This letter is to go by airmail to catch the Europa in New York.

I still have to give a brief report of the main event—the incorporation. Johannes Kleinsasser, Milford, urged by Jerg Vetter, Peter "Old Vetter," and Joseph Wipf Vetter, Rockport II, had written to Elias Walter, Stand Off, and Michel Tschetter of the new Granum Bruderhof that the Lehrerleut could only take part in my incorporation if Elias Vetter and Michel Vetter were reconciled and their disunity came to an end. Thereupon both declared and proved themselves fully united. The reason for their difference had been Elias Walter's understanding of leadership also in money matters and his objection to the new settlement in Granum—unfortunately in vain because of Christian Waldner Vetter's intervention.

The leading elders finally met on December 8 at Elias Walter's Stand Off Bruderhof: from the Dariusleut only old Christian Vetter, Elias Vetter, and Michel Tschetter (now at Granum); but from the Lehrerleut, Johannes Kleinsasser, Milford, Jerg Vetter, Miami, Joseph

Vetter, Rockport, and the faithful Hannes Vetter from Big Bend. They decided unanimously my immediate *acceptance as a brother and my incorporation* into the church of God *through Hutterian baptism*, without, however, declaring the baptisms at Sannerz and our Bruderhof invalid. On the morning of December 9, old Christian Vetter, assisted by our Elias Vetter, performed this act with the laying on of hands. Elias Walter read the teaching on Matthew 28, and Hannes Vetter lined the songs. The other servants of the Word (see above) were present as well as the members of the Stand Off Community. The reason they chose baptism instead of mere incorporation was above all the certainty and indisputability of that act, which signifies acceptance and incorporation into the church of God, into the ranks of the brothers who were called "Hutterian Brethren" in Moravia and Hungary and who since their time in Russia (not before) adopted that name themselves.

So it came about on December 8, 1930 at the Stand Off Bruderhof that I was informed by Christian Waldner, in the presence of Elias Walter, Stand Off; Johannes Kleinsasser, Buck Ranch, Milford; Johannes P. Entz, Big Bend; Jerg Waldner, Miami; Joseph Wipf, Rockport, Alberta; and Michel Tschetter, Granum, that these elders and older brothers had, in consideration of my illness, decided almost unanimously to accept and admit me as a brother at once, that is, without first consulting the others. And they wanted to do it through baptism with laying on of hands. That, they said, would be safer and better for me, for then I would be accepted and acknowledged just like any other brother, and nobody could afterward raise doubts as to whether I had been admitted in the right and proper way. Asked if I was in agreement with that, I replied, "Yes, I shall ask for baptism, because the older brothers have almost unanimously decided it." I added that I wanted to do whatever they considered right for accepting me.

The baptism took place the following morning, December 9, 1930. This time I was not asked what I thought of the baptism I had undergone in Halle. But on previous occasions, especially in talks with Elias Walter, Christian Waldner, Johannes Kleinsasser, and Johann Wurz, I had repeatedly explained at length that I could not deny baptism by immersion as practised in 1907/08 in Halle (nor our other baptisms of that period). I could not do so, I explained, since my baptism at that time, which was performed by the doctor Gotthelf Müller, did not mean entry into some erring sect of false prophets but had the sense of incorporation into the body of Christ—still hidden to us at that time—and of sharing in the death of Jesus.

This is still my position now that I have undergone the baptism of pouring over with laying on of hands for incorporation into the body of Christ, as it has become visible among the brothers called Hutterian. It is being realized and takes visible form and shape in their and our community of goods and work, even as it first came into being when the Word became flesh in the historical Jesus, in whom the whole fulness of the Godhead dwelt in a physical body. I therefore see this baptism by pouring over as supplementary to my earlier baptism by immersion, bearing in mind what Jesus said to Nicodemus in John 3 and, before that, John the Baptist; that is, I see it as an additional, second symbol. It symbolizes a baptism from above by the Holy Spirit—a being poured over, flooded, surrounded, and blown through by the Spirit. As regards those at home that have already undergone the baptism of burial and resurrection by immersion, no decision has been made as to whether I should baptize them now with this supplementary baptism that symbolizes the pouring out of the Spirit.

I found it actually quite hard to submit to the baptism of pouring over. What made it easier for me was my discovery in some old books here—among others in Tertullian—that in early Christian times a threefold baptism by immersion or pouring over was practiced—all as part of one act. By immersing once and pouring water over twice one would come close to that ancient custom, which is in use even today among the Dunkers[1] and other Baptizers. However, when we look at the whole, at what really matters and is essential, the outward usage is not the important thing but alone the inner attitude of faith and obedience. What matters is our dying and rising with Christ, our receiving the Holy Spirit in faith, our confession and covenant, and our becoming part of the church of God. Both times—in Halle and in Stand Off—what I had in mind and sought in all weakness is what Elias Walter put into words when he comforted me, "Let it be so. You have shown complete surrender."

So they were all unanimous to accept and incorporate me as a brother at once on December 9, 1930, about which I will write more fully after December 17 when the confirmation of the service of the Word has taken place, for mission and the establishment of our Bruderhof. All servants of the Word in America will be informed of

---

[1]Now known as Church of the Brethren.

this and invited to attend. Because of the injection I am unable to write more today.

But it is as a Hutterian brother that I can today send you my best wishes for my earliest possible return and for a richly blessed celebration of Christmas. Hopefully my packet of Hutterian Christmas confectionery will arrive in good time. As a loving reminder of our first Bible study together I am enclosing with this letter a Hutterian teaching on the same text, which Else should read to you and copy and then put safely away. May God in his indescribable mercy grant that we meet again soon and with a truly successful result for our Bruderhof!

To the housemother, steward and Brotherhood: Christmas 1930. The support and arrangement is planned as follows:
1) From each debt-free Bruderhof: $1,000 each.
2) From each Bruderhof, partly in debt: $500 each, (completely indebted, about ten: $0 each).
3) Thirty of the best work horses to be shipped overseas for use on our Bruderhof and to be sold.
4) Fifteen of the best milk cows to be shipped overseas for our own cow stall and to be sold. Hans and Adolf should then go to Hamburg as horse and cattle dealers. They should make inquiries about customs and freight charges.

The Diary continues after December 19:

Of greater, still much greater significance than our becoming part of the brothers—an event that makes us very small and humble—is my appointment to, and confirmation in, the service of the Word and the task of mission. That took place on December 18.[1]

---

[1] These historic church actions are documented by the accompanying letter in German, signed by Elias Walter and sent to all Bruderhofs. An English translation follows.

An die Bruderhöfe den Hutterischen Gemeinden zur Nachricht.

1.   Am 9 December 1930 ist Eberhard Arnold von deutschländischen Bruderhof der Gemeinde Gottes, den Brüdern
die man die Hutterischen nennt auf den Stand Off Bruderhof einverleibt worden. mit der Lehr Matth. 28
von Elias Walter, Christian Waldner, Johannes Kleinsasser, Johannes Entz unter Beisein der Stand Off
Gmein und Joseph Wipfs und Jerg Waldners.

2.   Am 19 December 1930 ist Eberhard Arnold für den
Dienst des Wortes Gottes bestätigt worden, mit Hand-
auflegung der Eltesten. Christian Waldner, Elias
Walter, Johannes Kleinsasser und Johannes Entz.
Es geschah im Stand Off Bruderhof mit der Lehr
Titus 1. die Johannes Kleinsasser vom Buck-Ranch
Milford Bruderhof hielt.

Damit ist Eberhard Arnold für Deutschland der Auftrag
der Gmein erteilt worden, dort das Wort Gottes an-
zukündigen, die Eifrigen zu sammeln und den bei
Neuhof (Fulda) in Hessen - Nassen Bruderhof in
bester Ordnung einzurichten.

Elias Walter.

The Hutterian Brethren   March 20, 1931[1]
Stand Off Colony
Macleod, Alta.

To the Bruderhofs of the Hutterian Church
For their Information

1.   On December 9, 1930, Eberhard Arnold from the German
Bruderhof of the Church of God was incorporated into the Brethren
called Hutterian at the Stand Off Bruderhof with the teaching on
Matthew 28 by Elias Walter, Christian Waldner, Johannes Kleinsasser,
and Johannes Entz in the presence of the Stand Off Church and Joseph
Wipf and Jerg Waldner.

2.   On December 19, 1930, Eberhard Arnold was confirmed in the
Service of the Word of God with the laying on of hands by the Elders
Christian Waldner, Elias Walter, Johannes Kleinsasser, and Johannes
Entz. This took place at the Stand Off Bruderhof with the teaching
on Titus 1, held by Johannes Kleinsasser from Buck Ranch Bruderhof,
Milford.

With this Eberhard Arnold is given the task by the Church for
Germany, to proclaim the Word of God there, to gather the zealous,
and to establish the Bruderhof near Neuhof (Fulda) in Hessen-Nassau
in the best order.

[signed] Elias Walter

---

[1]The acts of incorporation and confirmation took place in December 1930. The confirmation
took place probably on December 18.

My *Amselchen*, my dearly beloved bride and wife, mother and companion in life, my best co-fighter and co-worker, I wanted to make you uniquely happy on our wedding anniversary. So on December 19, as a special greeting for that memorable day so dear to us, I sent you a telegram telling you of the following events: on December 9, 1930 my incorporation and on December 18, 1930 my confirmation in the service of the Word through the laying on of hands, entrusting me with the care of our beloved Bruderhof in Hesse and with mission in Germany.

That confirmation, a deeply moving act that you will all find described in the old writings and their copies, is of the very greatest significance. My service has been confirmed on the basis of my insight into the history, faith, and life of God's church during the last four centuries, on the basis of our own history in Sannerz and on the Bruderhof, but above all because our dearly beloved members of Sannerz and the Bruderhof have again and again born witness to faithfulness and unity. My confirmation gives me unlimited authority to establish a genuine Hutterian community life, both temporally and spiritually, to the best of my insight.

It means, too, that the brothers in America will fully and forever support our Bruderhof both in its inner life of faith and in its outward economic life, also when the two of us and all our older fellow fighters are no longer alive. Actually, that unspoken longing was one of the main reasons urging me to make this extremely burdensome journey. Our fellow fighters and fellow workers have shown unprecedented trust and self-forgetfulness. For their sake, in place of the will a rich man would make, I want to establish our community life on as deep, strong, and firm a foundation as possible, to ensure its continuance beyond my death.

That applies, to begin with, to our own five children—our children in the flesh and in spirit, who justify such great hopes. It applies to the dear children of the other parents and mothers in the community and to Olga's and Else's adopted children. It applies equally and no less to the spiritual children of our children's community in Sannerz and at the Bruderhof and to its Sun Troop, now forming anew for the third time. It is truly a miracle of the Holy Spirit how the future of the kingdom pulses in these children, who are truly ours. That is due not only to our education and school, unique and wonderful though it is, but more than anything else to the blowing wind of the Spirit, which stands above all influences and all laws of cause and effect.

I would not find it too hard to sacrifice my eyes and more for the sake of assuring the continuance of our Bruderhof for the next fifty to a hundred years. All the same, I am extremely careful about my health—more than I have ever been at home, for I feel such an unspeakable longing for you, my *Amselchen*, and the beloved communal life of our Bruderhof.

This safeguarding of our Bruderhof's future, which could be cancelled only by our own unfaithfulness, is such a strong one because the American Bruderhofs in spite of their weaknesses, which I have openly brought to light, have kept a spiritual vitality, a strength to work and organize along communal lines that comes from the creative Holy Spirit and is certain to be equal to the cunning and violence of any hostile powers for several generations to come.

It should be seen as a divine confirmation of the task I am given with this journey that we are now the first Bruderhof to belong at the same time to the Dariusleut, Schmiedeleut, and Lehrerleut. Already, important voices among leading Dariusleut declare they want to have no more conferences or annual meetings of their servants of the Word without the Lehrerleut. And some of the most serious-minded Darius hofs would like to join together completely with the Lehrerleut, because they find among these a stronger spiritual energy, a more manly earnestness, a stricter, more unyielding carrying out of the living old church orders, a more inviolable bond of unity, as well as a stronger togetherness in economic matters.

It has not been given me to successfully bring about an immediate union of all three groups under one elder. But it is to be hoped that first the Dariusleut and Lehrerleut and then the Schmiedeleut, too, will talk over and do everything (or at least very much) together, until they are so welded together that they can appoint a common leader with his council of elders.

The Lehrerleut must first feel assured that their earnestness is taken seriously and is finding followers. Only then will their opposition change to a fighting spirit, with the result that in all probability they will have to be acknowledged as the leaders. They already showed that spirit of attack at the meeting for my confirmation. That gathering, for which we were the occasion, was the first time since World War I—that is, in twelve years—that the Dariusleut and Lehrerleut took counsel together. In meetings lasting far into the night, the Lehrerleut used the opportunity to attack the evils that, they said, had made themselves felt among the Dariusleut. Briefly, it all comes down to over-great softness: toward members that have fallen away or are halfhearted, and toward new settlements not made in the order of the

church. Places like Murphy and Felger, for example, because they
are short of people, make use of trucks and take to wearing "English"
working men's overalls—all things that are not permitted; besides,
they have no proper service of the Word. Above all, though, the
Dariusleut are too soft and indulgent in allowing a "carnal" sticking
together of close blood relations, whether called Walter, Tschetter,
or Hofer. You will most likely not understand these insights fully
until the end of my diary, for they go far deeper than Bertha W. Clark's
impressions. But the infinitely precious value of community, which
is strong enough among the Hutterites to last for generations, will
grow on you as you come to see how here, too, it has to be fought
for again and again.

The Lehrerleut declare that they will have to break off all community
with the Dariusleut unless they get satisfaction in at least the main
points they are pressing for—for example that the Dariusleut fight
for the church order wherever it is not fully observed, as in the
uncommunal conduct of the Felger, Murphy, and Pincher (Creek)
hofs. That, of course, means that the Dariusleut must agree fully and
unconditionally to the demands of the Lehrerleut. It was decided, for
example, to do away with "foreign" (that is, American-English)
clothing, to reduce wedding celebrations, no more driving from hof
to hof when there is a wedding (apart from exceptional cases), to fight
more resolutely against the use of cars and trucks, to apply sharper
church discipline where there is a lax attitude to halfhearted relatives,
and so on.

One example: When the unfaithful and deeply hostile David R. Hofer
people had gone so far as to carry off a girl by car from the Granum
Bruderhof, a boy from kindhearted Hannes Vetter's hof (Big Bend)
had taken part in the wedding without permission. The boy had to
show his repentance by kneeling in front during the first hour of the
Lehr and standing in front during the second hour; he also had to ask
the church's forgiveness.

The Dariusleut had no opportunity to lay before the Lehrerleut their
own concerns. What these amount to is that with all their strictness
the Lehrerleut should show more heart and not use rough, sharp
language such as is not possible among the Dariusleut. The Lehrerleut
on the other hand, true (by an inner logic) to their own distinctive
ways, stand more firmly together in that their members speak but very
seldom behind the backs of those concerned or to outsiders about the
weaknesses, mistakes, and punishments that naturally occur among
them too. That particular fault is more likely to crop up among the

Dariusleut, whose actions are mainly governed by their hearts and emotions. To be sure, the Lehrerleut do speak all the more about the faults of those *not* belonging to their own close-knit group.

But enough of such differences, which will serve to sharpen rather than cloud your vision of the magnificence of the Hutterian communal strength. After all, these human frailties bring the victorious struggle going on among the Hutterites far closer home to you than Bertha W. Clark's rosy, feminine description can possibly do. Naturally, these inner struggles, sufferings, victories, and cleansings were not revealed to her, an outsider. These battles, which are here seen in their full depth, are struggles to let truth and love become reality in the flesh. I am putting them on paper for you brothers and sisters in strict confidence and trust.

You will now understand why the question of our material support was not dealt with at my confirmation in the service. The confirmation itself was carried out with the unanimous agreement of the more than twenty servants of the Word present, as well as of the few hofs not represented, whose servants were prevented from attending by sickness, a wedding, the length of the journey, or similar weighty reasons. The *Lehr*, from the Letter to Titus, was held by Johannes Kleinsasser, and the laying on of hands was carried out jointly by Elias Walter, Christian Waldner, Johannes Kleinsasser, and Johannes P. Entz. I was first given the opportunity for a detailed statement and account of our origin, faith, and life, of which I will give a summary later.

Because the very low price of wheat—no more than a quarter or a third of last year's price—as well as the general situation among the Dariusleut has had a depressing effect upon them, Christian Waldner, their elder, did not respond in a very encouraging way to my urgent, fervent plea for a large-scale effort to set our Bruderhof on its feet economically. That is why I had to come to the decision to travel once more from hof to hof, so as to get together from all the various communities as much as possible of the sum needed to put us into a sound economic position.

> Stand Off Bruderhof
> December 25 and 31, 1930,
> January 1, 1931

On Christmas Eve I was quite alone in a small hotel room in Lethbridge; I read the letters from you, Emmy, and from you all and started writing to you. I was taking care of my eye, and in front of me I had Luise's transparency and a little twig that I myself had cut off a pine tree in the Rocky Mountains. Unfortunately I was interrupted in this quietness, which had done me a lot of good, when two automobiles arrived at once. One was sent by Christian Waldner of West Raley, and the other was that of the Mennonite English teacher of Stand Off. They also came to pay my hotel bill. The brothers had heard that my series of seven "lacteal-fever" injections was finished.

And so I had to hold the meetings during the Christmas days and also today, New Year's Day. I was able, besides, to work on the old books. I also went to the new Murphy Bruderhof, which made us a gift of 100 sheep for Christmas; this was a particular proposal by their members, Paul and Darius Walter. Here in this country, according to the business situation, this would mean $500 to $900. Likewise, I got good news in regard to the decisions of the Lehrerleut Bruderhofs in Alberta, Rockport (Joseph Wipf) and Buck Ranch at Milford (Johannes Kleinsasser) about the money provided for us. This news came to me from Rockport's "bone doctor," Johann Entz, who is my very good friend. And in the same way the Stand Off Bruderhof will set a good example.

There is no other course left for me than to travel once more around all the Bruderhofs in Alberta to gather the brothers together everywhere and ask for a really large sum. This is going to be a great strain on me, the more so since Elias Walter will be going with me in order to assure that I really receive help in large quantities. This is very loving of him, but it means that I will not have a moment of quiet from early morning until late evening. And my nervous system and my body— perhaps my inner life as well—simply is not really adjusted to this. I am always exhausted after a few days. Then I realize deep in my heart how fortunate I am when with you, and how considerate and understanding is the love of our Bruderhof members surrounding me at home. I can't expect the same of the Hutterites here. They all have nerves like steel cables, thick as an arm. I, on the other hand, have to collect my entire strength in order to carry out this fund-raising for our building up.

All this is the reason that I wanted to have this seven-fold injection for my eye, which is still very poorly; I wanted to get it in condition to be able to cope with the exertions of a second round of visits to all Bruderhofs in Alberta. At the same time, the brothers and sisters everywhere pour out upon me the greatest love and attention; they bring me handkerchiefs for you too, confectionery, simple candy, nuts, and other things. For Christmas I sent you the kind of little packages the children here receive on Christmas Eve.

I would not write to you about how weak and overstrained I am if I didn't have to; otherwise you just won't be able to understand how much time and effort it all takes. There is only one possibility of storming these fortresses, and that is to besiege them continuously, like the importunate widow who pestered the judge.

You must also consider the fact that the price of wheat is very, very low. Last year a bushel (about 60 lb.) of wheat sold for $1.35, and now it is only about 30 cents. Old Christian Vetter, who presided at the big confirmation meeting of the twenty-one servants, was very unwilling to give more extensive support, especially as his Raley Bruderhof has used up its funds completely through a large purchase of land. So he just sent me $100, and says he is unable to give more. Please thank him really lovingly for the hundred dollars. For the time being I am keeping them so as not to run out of money during this strenuous time.

Mostly I have refrained from writing to you at all whenever I wasn't feeling so well. I waited until my eye and my health got stronger and better. But this time the fever-cure for the eye, the overstrain in the communal work, and the traveling followed so quickly one after the other that I can't let you and all of you wait any longer for news. Certainly my homesickness and terrific longing for all of you is partly to blame for this exhaustion. Mainly, however, it is the unaccustomed style of living, without a stop for a breather. At the same time I have plenty of reason to be joyful. Yet I believe this joy will not fully burst forth until I am at home with you again and can rejoice with you and all our brothers and sisters in the establishment of our community and our Bruderhof, which is after all the best. I have sent you a telegram and a letter telling about the great blessing of the confirmation, the mission task, and the laying on of hands. The telegram was meant as news for December 20, our wedding anniversary, sent off on December 19. In it I asked for a second sending of Friedmann's list of those writings that are missing in Europe, but available in America. I had lost the list.

I also rejoice, with heartfelt thanks to God, in the grateful way many brothers and sisters have responded to my talks and meetings. Most of all, however, I rejoice in the very comforting letters and greetings you and the others have been sending, though some of them haven't reached me yet. They mean infinitely much to me! But now Elias Vetter, dear man, is already standing next to me and asking me to finish writing. In the coming weeks you can only count on very brief news from me, since I must at last come to a stop here.

Calgary, Canada,
January 20, 1931

Now at last I can again send you a letter. It will not be so depressing
as the last one, which I wrote in a condition of unusual exhaustion.
My eyes are also somewhat better. My fund-raising journey is not
without results, and yet so far distant from the goal Hans and I have,
that one can have doubts of reaching it. I hope you will not be too
dissatisfied with me if I only bring back part of the $25,000, the sum
truly needed and set as our goal. At any rate I am trying my utmost,
and force myself to a most unpleasant begging journey to all the
Bruderhofs which are not deeply in debt; I will visit each of them
two or three times. This work is unpleasant to me only in so far as I
do not like this pressing for money; besides every fiber of my being
draws me forcefully to you and all at home. However, it must be,
otherwise only part of my journey will be accomplished, even though
it is the most important part. My longing is that after my return home,
we shall also manage a joyful building up, inwardly and outwardly,
and not have our consciences burdened by the debts which have been
such a hindrance until now.

However, in order not to have to write each time about these painful
money questions, and so that I can have a surprise for you on my
return, I will not describe in detail each sum given to me, nor every
step taken on the way towards our economic goal. In this way I can
keep the uncertain but quietly living hope of being able to surprise
you with substantial help when I return. If you and Hans and the
others are in agreement, I will send sums of money to you from time
to time for your housemother responsibilities, starting today with $20.
This is especially to pay your housemother debts, and I will be sending
2,000 German marks to Hans, as steward, in the next week or two.
I greet Hans very warmly, and ask him to use this money with your
agreement and that of the responsible members, in order to free his
conscience and his burden of worries by paying off the most unpleasant
obligations and if possible all our debts, undertaking as few new
purchases as possible. Apart from the above mentioned sum, my
request is that I do not have to send any more money to you before
my return home, so that we may have a hopefully large sum available
for the financial actions I have planned. I would like to combine
purchases of farm land and houses through new mortgages with paying
off our debts as far as possible. Therefore use the money I am sending
you with careful consideration and as slowly as the creditors will
allow you.

I could report very wonderful things about the powerful religious awakening of hearts on many hofs; it happens here and there that not only women but also some strong men are shedding tears following my proclamation of the truth and are asking to hear more. But I must report about that later. Today I return to the most important matter— the confirmation and laying on of hands by the elders. I sent an account of all this to you on December 19 (see p. 183).

I will report to you in my next letters the progress of my journey and my experiences on hofs that I have not yet described to you. But I must hurry to a finish, since tomorrow I wish to visit for the second time Paul Stahl near Beisecker, who weighs 300 lbs and so finds walking difficult. The length of this letter is to be explained by the sad incident last Sunday when Elias Walter, our faithful companion and friend, collapsed at the end of his teaching in the middle of that solemn meeting, as he couldn't stand up any longer. The servant of the Word of the Montana Bruderhof near Rockyford, Calgary, caught him as he fell and arranged for him to have a Turkish bath in Calgary, letting him go home somewhat strengthened.

Since Michel Tschetter also had to go home, I could again visit two experienced eye doctors here in Calgary. From here I can also write to you and send off for you and Else the gift of a large number of books—a very precious burden—of which I will ship a good portion.

I greet our faithful children and all other faithful ones, especially those who have recently given such joy to me through their Christmas greetings.

Lethbridge, February 1931

Enclosed are letters and newspaper reports. Please save everything carefully.

Just a short greeting about the slow and only partly fulfilled results of my strenuous begging journeys. For this matter I have again been on twelve hofs. Hopefully, I am at last approaching the end with a not too modest result—to be followed by the journey home. Your last letter to me with the very appropriate dream of the Canadian highway; also with the reports about Else's sickness, Hans-Hermann's condition, the difficulties with Gustav, F.K., and F.D., the conflicts with paying our bills, and Frieder's running away, have all moved me deeply. Hans should write to all our friends to try to get from Frieder the book with the names of all our friends. And—take greater care with having anyone who is unsure or halfhearted working in the office!

You, beloved Emmy! It is almost unbearable to be so long away from you and not being able to see you or experience your faithful love and caring motherliness. And our beloved Bruderhof! It is, and remains for us, the best and only possible one. Here also, I am confirmed in this in the deepest way, also that we should remain as long as possible in this European country of Germany, which is once again burdened with suffering and conflict. Else's sickness disturbs me very much. I would be grateful for frequent news. I shall be sending the 2,000 marks to Hans as soon as I have the money in my hand.

Lethbridge, February 1931

It is nearly midnight, and I have some very strenuous days behind me, working with the books and visiting brothers, but my heart will not allow me to send off the shipment of books and covering letter to Else without writing a short letter to you; anyhow the long report could not be finished in one hour. I must of course go to the Lehrerleut at Buck Ranch, Milford near Raymond early tomorrow, since a letter from you is waiting for me there.

How much I feel urged to hurry back to you! But my begging task was interrupted by a visit of the four most important Lehrerleut leaders to David Hofer in South Dakota, so that I turned again to my work with the books, which I have just sent to you. But now I must move on again. It is said that David Hofer of Rockport, South Dakota, who is still the most respected of the elders, is coming here himself. The raising of funds gives such slow results, although some. One could despair of obtaining such a large sum if a higher faith did not guide us, making us independent of circumstances. So I have to still wait patiently no matter how unspeakably heavily it weighs on me. And I ask you all, whom I greet from my heart, and especially you yourself, to wait patiently just a little while longer. The reward will then be so much better! Every moment I am close to you with all my love! I am sending you and all the Brotherhood members who are surely interested, a copy of some of my travel experiences. Herr Schwarz's business letter will interest you less than his impression of the communal life of the Hutterites. You will certainly be glad to work on the pattern of the sunbonnet. Head coverings are on the way. I rejoiced greatly in your letters to dear Elias Walter and others. They are very good. I have some more letters for you from Hutterian women but cannot find them at the moment; they are fine letters. Impressions here confirm my opinion that well-trained people are very necessary in community life. My request then to you is not to grow weary of letter writing but write often, really often and in detail. I myself will also do this again now that I did not succeed in hastening my return as I wished. But one day also this difficult time will be over and then, only then shall we rejoice together really from our hearts, that God has given me the grace to undertake this difficult journey for us all.

Lethbridge, March 1931

With this letter I am sending you thirty-seven pieces of material for head coverings, some enough for more than one. So now you have sufficient to provide for all, including the novices and children. Mölein so much wants to wear the *Tracht*. Each head covering should have the initials and the year clearly embroidered on it. The little bonnets are for the older, sick sisters, to be worn under the head covering. They are a gift for you. The black woolen head covering is meant for winter, but is seldom worn. Hutterian women wear the head covering both outside and in the house according to the order of the church. You should thank especially Gertrud Ziebarth for the copy of the prayers out of the *Early Christians*. It is a great joy for me to receive this as a sign of her growing into the faith. I will write later about all the Christmas presents. I am now in a great hurry as these packets are at last ready for mailing.

Lethbridge, March 1931

God's wonderful spirit has led you through all difficulties under your and Hans's leadership, and I have written shortly to Hans what I have to say in this matter.

I especially greet Trautel, whose teaching Mö writes about and which could not be "forbidden" any more than any other basic training. What we are concerned with here is a question of religious usage or tradition; that is, that no idolatry, including that of feeling, should crowd out the faith in the Spirit. All this I will consider, think over, and clarify with our dear Heini, with all our children, and with the whole household.

All the brothers here are of the opinion that we should develop our garden and potato growing on a large scale. They think this to be the only way out of our food shortage. The products could then be exchanged for bread.

Lethbridge, March 1931

Now at last is really the time for my departure! Here is my worn-out first suit with trousers. Then two Hutterian hats for our museum. Also to be saved for our museum and not to be used is the broom made in the Hutterian workshop of Jakob of Old Elm Spring who is over seventy years old—made and given by him. The work gloves are for the horse drivers, Arno and Richard, and a pair for Roland. Take note of the tags, also on the aprons, called in Hutterian dialect *Fittiche*. There is also material in one packet for children's aprons. The lambskin caps are very good from the standpoint of our clothing; they were given to us by Samuel Kleinsasser, a teacher at Rockport, Alberta, a fine and serious man. Please thank especially the women of Old Elm Spring for the head coverings.

You will learn many more things through my diary which I shall be bringing with me; but I can only write it when I am away from the Bruderhofs because every one, especially from among the leading brothers, wants to read it.

South Dakota, April 10, 1931

Your last dear letters show the same agony of longing that I have been suffering here, especially since Christmas, and have only overcome with the aid of sleeping medicine prescribed by the doctors because of my eyes. But it is no help to complain or weep, although I have so often had to struggle against tears. For this one-time opportunity must be used. I know for certain that I would never again in my life undertake such a journey without having you with me. And although I have added many pounds to the weight of my body, and experienced the most loving care and nursing, yet homesickness and the great distance from the unique freshness of spirit at our Sannerz and the Rhön Bruderhof was so very hard that I feel that I have aged by ten years.

Now I am almost at the end of my return journey through the Bruderhofs, but for the sake of money I must search out the "Amana Inspirationists." Only when I am again back home with you, with our beloved children and with all the beloved Bruderhof members who have become so dear to me, shall I again become truly lively, joyful, and healthy. For there is one good thing about homesickness—it's cured as soon as you come home! Also how wonderfully has the strong, good spirit of God and of Jesus Christ, and the enlivening and purifying spirit of the church community held and bound all together—with the exception of Hugga! What a grace! And how you and Hans and all our members have been filled with the spirit and strength to struggle through in such a responsible situation. The Hutterites often say, "Those who sit at the back listening to the teaching can have no idea how difficult it often is to have to stand at the front." For this reason I am sending in this airmail letter to Hans, apart from a few lines about money, an enclosure from Johannes Kleinsasser of Buck Ranch, Milford, together with the document of my incorporation, confirmation, and commission. Else is already copying this out as a gift from me to you.

Please say to all our dear ones, all our old and young Bruderhof people, that I think daily with great thankfulness of each one of them. It was quite impossible to write to them or even to our own children for their birthdays, if I were at last to bring this difficult journey to a conclusion. It is my nature to be quite unable to write concentratedly what is on my heart if onlookers and questioners do not withdraw. In order to write this letter I have again been in town, which always means the loss of two days.

We must be courageous. You ask for the reasons for the unbearable lengthening of the journey. The reasons are:
1) in me: my eye infection and my infirmities.
2) the indescribable difficulties of asking for money.
3) (but least of all) my work on the handwritten manuscripts, which I always make time for when points 1 and 2 cause me to stay longer. This will all become understandable when I can explain it to you by word of mouth. But it was really the very last moment to undertake this journey. A year earlier would have been far more successful money-wise. (Wheat prices!!)

Radio-telegram, May 1, 1931

Finally at sea! Meet me Bremerhaven, Sunday, May 10.
Joyful, your Eberhard.

The Year of the Journey

Introductory Remarks

During the almost 12 months (May 1930-May 1931) that Eberhard Arnold was away visiting the Bruderhofs across North America, there was a lively exchange of letters with the members of the Rhön Bruderhof. Else von Hollander, his sister-in-law and faithful secretary, wrote frequently about the old Hutterian writings she received from him and her work copying them, but also about events on the Rhön Bruderhof, which for a year was without its Word leader. Eberhard's wife, Emmy Arnold, wrote faithfully back to her Eberhard throughout this long year. Indeed her letters would make a book of their own, and so have not been included.

There are letters from Eberhard Arnold to the different Bruderhofs; letters between the brothers in America telling of Arnold's visits; and also correspondence between Elias Walter and Robert Friedmann and John Horsch.

These should all be read in connection with the description of the "Journey to the Brothers" in Chapter 2.

Else von Hollander
Rhön Bruderhof, June 30, 1930

Dear Ebbo,[1]

At last we now have news from you. We had a great shock when we received the news of the fog and the burning ship. How thankful we are that your ship arrived safely. I am more and more certain that everything, really everything depends on our reaching God's country where God is the Lord of every hour we live.

It is truly an almost unbelievable fact that he will always help us to start quite afresh and belong completely to him. How will your meeting with the Hutterites be? We think about it all the time!

I am now proofreading the *Worms-Prozess*[2] with Gustav. It is truly wonderful, and I am always amazed. It is really the truth that we meet here. All that you struggled through in Oeynhausen[3] already in 1919, and which only a few understood, is to be found there. I become more and more certain Peter Walpot helped write this answer, for I

---

[1]Eberhard Arnold.

[2]The Baptizers' answer to charges in the Proceedings at Worms 1557.

[3]A conference of the German Student Christian Movement in Bad Oeynhausen, August 1919, which Eberhard Arnold attended.

can't help thinking of his passages in the Michel Hasel Book. All that is timeless in the Michel Hasel Book must be lived out in our time. When working on the accounts recently I even wrote by mistake the year 1529!

You know, Ebbo, concerning your eye, I do not believe that it is already chronic, for every time after fourteen days it is nearly healed. A woman we met told us that for many months she had to wear patches over her eye. Herr Förster from the revenue office at Fulda was recently with us and told us that for sixteen weeks he had rainbow inflammation and was completely blind in one eye, and that now he can see well with both eyes again. That is already over ten years ago. Ebbo, I always think God will give your eyesight back to you.

Unfortunately I cannot work so much in the house as I would like. For you know there is so much work copying the old Hutterian writings and proofreading, and so the time flies. Everything must be finished so that you can send more writings from Elias Walter soon, especially the comments on the Revelation. I wonder if they are from Hans Hut? Today I gave Georg the "New beginning of a Hutterian Bruderhof in Germany" for binding. We will read this at the ten years' anniversary. I always think when I look back over these ten years: God shows such love—far beyond what we can imagine. You have certainly heard about the Bertha Clark book. It is so wonderful that this first book about the Hutterites rouses so much interest. Yesterday evening we were a long time outside. There was a wonderfully starry sky. Those are the same stars that shine a few hours later for you. The whole hill behind the Rhön Bruderhof is often alive with glow-worms in the evening. It has never been like that before. Georg is making the quarry nice with the children. You would rejoice to see it. Emmy and I often go through the fields and meadows. We always think then of you and how you would love to see how plentifully everything is growing this year. We have five to six acres garden land, and had fresh vegetables from the garden already for one meal every day this week. The early potatoes are flowering profusely. Today the children went blueberry picking for the first time. You should have seen how happily Mö ran off. Walterle is always very happy. He put his doll's cupboard in your room and said, "This is for Papa." He always says, "Papa is coming tomorrow." If only it would be tomorrow! Till then I think of you and your meeting the Hutterites and the mission task.

In faithfulness, your

Else

P.S. Our anniversary celebration in Sannerz was a joyful one. Only you were very much missed! We noticed how close we felt to the Sannerz people, especially the poor ones, because of the seven years we had lived with them. All rejoiced from their hearts and said that it had never been the same in Sannerz since we left. At that time they used to hear us singing. We had a quiet hour by the spring in the woods. Then I was with young Heini on the sheep pasture. We thought of past times. In the evening we returned home with torches. Many sang with us on the way as far as Vollmerz. Everybody knew "Kein schöner Land"!

Do you know that we now have a night watchman? Every three days another brother takes over. They sing every hour, "Hear good folk!" It sounds very nice and moves my heart deeply when I wake up in the night.

In deep faithfulness I think of you and your task, your

Else

Greet all the Hutterites from us.

Eberhard Arnold described the old books he was copying as he traveled through the Bruderhofs and also wrote personal notes to Else von Hollander on the back of some of the pages. Else was seriously ill with tuberculosis and by April 1931, when the last of these pages were written, she was in a convalescent home in Switzerland where she continued to work on Hutterian writings. The letters EAH and a number identify each manuscript.

Written on the back of a booklist of old writings located at Bon Homme, being the first three pages of manuscript EAH 700a.

I want to always use the blank pages of the manuscripts for you, dear Else, our faithful Tata. You can see that I worked hard, as often and as long as my eye could bear it. Today on July 30 I am sending you three long manuscripts in my own hand. Please look through them carefully and if possible type them yourself rather than giving them out to other typists. I would be glad if you would not let this work out of your own hands. You always save things and store them away so well. I often think of your little room where your and our dear little Walter is, and of your beautifully tidy closet and desk. . . . There you should keep all these manuscripts and copies which I send. Some things will have to be typed more than once. Then it would be best if you would type it on your typewriter and compare it with my handwritten copy, which I made *very exactly*.

I would so much like to send you the original books. Perhaps I still may. But these wonderful books are so extremely valuable to me that

I would rather bring them home by my own hand over land and across the ocean. Yes, home! After this month of July with my bad eye, my time at Rockport—the most difficult Bruderhof—and the birthday I had there, you will believe me when I tell you that I feel as homesick as is possible for such a dry old stick as I often am. I have such a longing for Emmy and the children, for my little room and our work together, yes, for our unique Bruderhof, the only one of its kind. But the enormous task I have here is of value for time and eternity and must be carried through. Unfortunately, neither Rockport, South Dakota, nor my birthday presented me with the possibility of my and our beloved Emmy's coming. Sad to say, it would be a mistake if she came as things are.

This unfinished list of old writings already shows how our brothers here are, and that they themselves do not know what treasures they have. At both Bon Homme and Wolf Creek Bruderhof I found that very few members know that the books I have listed are here. As a result, I too was able to draw only some out of their hiding places. This strange state of things is due partly to the fact that people work very hard. Second, that the teachings written from 1600 to 1700 are the main source of their daily life of faith. Third, and most of all, anyone who has a book, whether quite small or enormously large, protects it with anxious care.

Written at Rockport on the back of manuscripts from Wolf Creek.

The venerable old man, Jakob Hofer, truly demands respect. He was nearly dying but for the time being has recovered. Three of his white and gray-haired children had hurried to him from Canada, but he does not let the famous, original Chronicle or the even more famous Epistle Book out of his room. He claims that in his whole lifetime (seventy-five years) nobody has copied the whole book of epistles because it could only be done in his room. And indeed, dear Tata, you can see from this present large consignment of the First Epistle of Jakob Hutter to the Church in Moravia[1] consisting of less than nine out of the 625 sheets—which means 2,500 columns—how tremendous in every sense are the wonderful contents of this book written in 1566. For every column I need one and a half sides of this paper, since I am writing so big and leave margins. The books are

---

[1]Copied out by Eberhard Arnold at Rockport, SD. See p.99.

written in an incredibly small hand. I am quite worried about how we will manage to make a copy of this Epistle Book!!

Written on the back of a book list from Rockport, South Dakota.

To the amazement of all, David Hofer gave me the Ehrenpreis original and the "Meldung 1633,"[1] which is also unknown to Elias Walter and is an unheard-of find for our work on the Small History Book [*Klein-Geschichtsbuch*]. I am allowed to take it with me until I return to Rockport. He most strictly forbade me to leave it in Elias Walter's hands, and he knows very well how to be emphatic. If, compelled by God's leading, I cannot get back to South Dakota at the end of the year by October or November, whatever happens I may give the book *only* to his sons at Rockport in Alberta, and it must be done personally. It is therefore all the more amazing and wonderful that I got the book, and that David Vetter, who for the first three days rejected me in an *ice-cold* way, was in the end *very, very warm, loving, and trusting* to me. It was your constant thoughts, dear faithful Tata, that did this!

David Hofer Vetter, Rockport, South Dakota, the strict bearer of the office of elder among the brothers was moved firstly, by my eager copying of the old writings from six in the morning (I got up at 4:30!) right through till 8:30 in the evening, until *Gebet* (a very long daily meeting with a teaching), secondly, by the extremely reserved and unassuming manner with which I respond to him, and thirdly, by the energetic intervention of many older brothers and sisters who stormed him with the most pressing, almost enthusiastic recommendations for me. My loyal supporters were in particular Peter Hofer, the second minister; Maria Hofer, widow of one of the two Hutterites martyred in the World War for their great faith, and now remarried to another Hofer; also Jörg Wipf Vetter, retired work distributor [*Weinzedel*]; Johannes Hofer, teacher from Old Elm Spring and a much respected, deeply spiritual, and educated man; Jakob Hofer, now close to death; and "Old Vetter,"—retired steward and son of the founder, Jakob Wipf the teacher—with whom I slept and worked.

See the picture of Rosedale. In his old age he looks after the 1,000 geese. He is helped by two boys, who often run away from him to go swimming.

---

[1]Proclamation, possibly the First Easter Letter, on how to prepare for the Lord's Supper.

It caused quite a sensation among everybody that David Vetter, Jakob Vetter, Jerg Vetter, and Peter Vetter (can you keep these reverend Vetters straight, dear Else?) gave me the old writings to copy. As a result, this work became difficult and strenuous. Every half hour a group of "a few" of the 170 Rockporters who had not gone out to the harvest came to my open window or through my door. They watched over my shoulder for a long time, wanted me to read to them from the "very wonderful epistle," were amazed at my "Latin script," and brought me countless apples, glasses of ice water, iced lemonade, and soft vanilla ice cream because of the murderous heat. It was over 100°F! At Wolf Creek two horses died of heatstroke, and at Rockport three. In general, daily contacts among our brothers and sisters, also among the happy and lively children, are much more natural, confiding, trusting, intimate, and full of fun than we imagined they would be. At the same time deep and godly thoughts are always there through admonitions genuinely in keeping with the Spirit. You, dear Tata, would have great joy in this.

Written on the back of manuscripts sent in the third package from Milltown.

September 15, 1930

I would like to see the amazed look on your face at the wealth of this material, and also perhaps at all my eye has managed on this huge job, my dear Else! This Great Article Book, part two of this volume, is probably by Peter Walpot. The others (three articles, etc.) perhaps the small article books too, are excerpts from it. The first part of the volume, truly thrilling, is *Anschläg und Fürwenden*.[1] It is one of the two writings which Lydia Müller was so upset over because of their courageous, attacking spirit. You, dear Else, should have great joy in working your way deep into my two book lists and EAH manuscripts [Eberhard Arnold Hutterian books, etc.], for even the titles alone offer an amazing amount and have given me a lot of work, and all the time I was thinking about you, my dear, reading it all.

Ebbo

Written on the back of manuscript EAH 746, sent from Beisecker, Alberta.

We still have far too few of the epistles in our EAH collection. We should soon write to Gran, Pressburg, Vienna, Budapest, and Brunn.

---

[1]Hutterian writing of 1561 to refute attacks made against them.

I just heard of the death of Michel Waldner,[1] Bon Homme, South Dakota. This is a great sorrow to me, for I had grown to love him very much. How much I would have liked to see him on my way back! He was going to give me a little epistle book, a very old one. I wonder whether it will still come to me and us. But for the moment let us be happy about what we have. I was so glad about your deep joy in the old writings that tears came into my eyes. I am looking forward immensely to your beautiful copies of Jakob Hutter's letters and Revelation 14 and am deeply moved by all that you have copied with your dear hand. This includes Ulrich Stadler for Christmas and Jörg Rack's heading to the baptism book for my homecoming. I think of your health every day and ask to have reports really often of your progress and very soon, I hope, of your recovery. I have learned how difficult sickness can be in this time of separation so far away from home. But it also leads us deeper to inner quiet and to God himself, as has been your experience with these old writings in your dear, little room in the West Gable.

Written on the back of a book list from Stand Off.

As far as I can do it in America, this book list is finished with this shipment. It was a huge, difficult project which nobody had done before, though our dear old Elias Walter worked toward it. He was often surprised at the discoveries I made. I still have a number of loose pages which I will sort first when I get home, so that I can still return at last in the middle of May, when you, dear Tata, should also come home in good health.

Written on the back of Elias Walter's book list EAH 704, page 39.

My stay in America was lengthened little, if at all, by my work on the book lists. Wherever I went, I had to wait upon the decisions which dawned so unspeakably slowly upon the brothers. My heart could not have borne the pangs of homesickness without such wonderful work. The only reason my letters home and my equally time-consuming work on the EAH lists made my trip longer and more expensive was that it was impossible to do it on the Bruderhof. This was because the brothers and sisters showed so much of their well-known, trusting familiarity and *Neugierde* (meaning something like

---

[1] Son of Schmied-Michel and father of Michael Waldner, servant of the Word at Bon Homme.

"expectant participation and curiosity"). If they had really seen how many old treasures were entrusted to us, they would have stopped giving them. When I was sick, I did this EAH work in the towns while my eye was being treated. The whole time it was absolutely necessary to give my weak nerves some rest from the expectant 2,000 adults and 1,500 children who surrounded me day and night, even if "only" two, three, five, twenty, or forty at a time. No suitcase, no bag, no letter, and no book could be protected from being looked through—without being asked and without asking, in my presence or in my absence—with no uneasiness whatsoever. Difficult questions often arose through this and answering them held me up for weeks. Compared to this absolute, communistic collective-consciousness, we at home are still very individualistic!! But enough of that.

On April 10 I sent you at Fidaz, *dear* Else, a telegram and an airmail letter from South Dakota, in which twenty dollars for you were enclosed. I also sent you a telegram from Winnipeg. If I could only express to you my deep, deep thanks for all the good you have done me through the long years from Cröllwitz to Oberbozen, and from Dölau, Berlin, Thüringen, Schlüchtern, Sannerz to the Rhön Bruderhof! If only I could express to you how much I expect for the Bruderhof, for its health of soul and spirit and for a power-filled life and witness, through your recovery and our work together. I ask you again and again to put the quietly concentrated strength of your soul into your *will* for health and *believe* in health of spirit, soul, *and* body. You know the source of strength and the *way* this power wants to come to us! So let us continue to pray for one another. Let us again and again ask God and believe that just like the big children, Hardy, Heini, Hans-Hermann, and Mö, we can always begin anew! God is so unendingly merciful and can free us completely from all bacteria and bacilli, so that we can breathe his pure air, as you are doing in Georg Blaurock's mountains of Graubünden.

Else von Hollander
Rhön Bruderhof, July 7, 1930

You dear Ebbo,

We have to send off our greetings for your birthday today already, so that they will reach you in time. I have very many wishes for you. You know that these wishes, or rather prayers, concern all of us. Everyone of them expresses a longing for the great mission to the whole world. As long as I have known you, you have been waiting for it—and actually the whole creation waits for it. Your being together with the Hutterian Brothers and the relationship with them is absolutely necessary for this mission. All of us here wait for the Holy Spirit, which we asked for on the last Sunday you were with us. Already then something was kindled in us.

You will be hearing about all our experiences through Emmchen. Sometimes they seem to overwhelm us, but we always receive help and support. How glad you would be to see how God stands by all our faithful ones. We have all reason to be grateful for this. The whole Brotherhood circle stands united behind you. All, really all are with us! How great will be our joy at your return! When will it be? September or October?

When your Paul Tschetter cards arrived there was great rejoicing. Who is Paul Tschetter? You thought of everyone! There was a really festive atmosphere. We are quite curious to know what you are going to write about the Hutterites. Emmy gave Walterle his card just before his afternoon nap. He held it in his little chubby hands while he slept. I took it away from him as I thought he might tear it. When he woke up he cried, "The picture Papa has drawn for me has gone!" Now I show him the card every day. As he is not yet able to write, he is sending you a flower from our garden.

The "Letter to the seven churches" (Revelation 1-3) will be finished today. I will send it to you tomorrow, as Emmy has gone to Fulda today to send off all the letters, so that they reach you in good time for the 26th. But I think my present will arrive in time. What God expects of his church in the letter to the seven churches gripped me very much: "He who overcomes!"

I copied your comments on the History of the Habertshof with amazement. How powerfully you provoked the struggle! It almost frightened me. But that must not be, because there has to be a struggle. And if we think of the struggles and sufferings of the old Hutterites, and what it means to follow Jesus, then we may not be fearful. But then we need a power quite different from our own very limited strength, which only stands in the way.

Last night in the Brotherhood we read the 'comments' [on the Habertshof] with the newly baptized members; everyone listened eagerly till twelve o'clock. When we read about the family tree the reading was interrupted by hearty laughing. Trudi exclaimed, "It's a long time since we heard anything so interesting!" We want to have a longer talk about it some time this week.

It was good Hardy could read everything with us before leaving for Bieberstein.[1] He will go today. He is joyful and courageous, also humble. We will miss him here.

You prepared and led Emmchen and Hans's working together so wonderfully well, and you would be glad to see it.

Much was going on again yesterday, Sunday, with so many guests. We have about fifteen every day.

Now I have to close. Emmchen is going to Fulda. She just read your letter from Bon Homme to me. How I rejoice about everything! I can hardly wait for the list of writings to come. Everything, everything, including now the new founding of the Hutterian Publishing House, shall belong to God and his church.

When I was ten years old a girl said to me, "The Rhön, you know, that is God's little country!" And that it shall be!

Closely standing together, wanting to fight with you the good fight of faith, your always faithful and thankful

Else

Else von Hollander
Rhön Bruderhof, July 9, 1930

Dear Ebbo,

As my birthday letter to you had to end so abruptly, I will send further heartfelt and faithful greetings today with the "Letter to the churches," thinking especially of your meeting with Elias Walter, whose illness makes me quite sad. We want to support Elias especially and the need to publish the old writings. We would be so grateful if God helped us so that it could happen in this new year of your life.

John Horsch sent us the *Ausbund* printed in 1842. He wrote a dedication to the Bruderhof in it. I have not yet been able to go to Stuttgart and to the places of the old Baptizers, because money was lacking. We have asked for estimates and will send them to Stand Off as soon as we have them. We have also asked for samples of their type from thirty-three printers. Best of all would be to have our own printing shop. I wonder when you will come home and tell us about everything? When will the full uniting with the Hutterian Brethren which you write about in such a wonderful way take place? Has perhaps one third of the time of your absence passed?

We think of you with great love and all look forward with great

---

[1]Country boarding school attended by Hardy Arnold.

joy to the moment when you are back with us again united for ever with the Hutterites. Reading your 'comments,' it felt as though you were actually here! It was a great joy to me to copy it out. It was as though we were working together.

Looking forward joyfully to that, I think of you, faithfully, your

Else

July 10, 1930. Today we celebrated Hugga's fiftieth birthday. At a meal we read the letter you wrote to Hugga ten years ago for her birthday. We have many guests here just now. Actually at present we are a household of eighty people and some of them have many questions. So when you come home you will have a lot to do!

Else von Hollander
Rhön Bruderhof, July 28, 1930

Dear Ebbo,

This is the first time since I have known you that your birthday was celebrated without you. We were all with you thinking of you on that day and of the love the Hutterian Brothers show you. We also thought of your eye. Is it getting better or doing well? And where are you just now? Are you still in Wolf Creek or with David Hofer or Joseph Stahl or in Manitoba or already with Elias Walter?

I am sending you today different estimates and samples of paper and type for the Small History Book [*Klein Geschichtbuch*]. But as it will probably become thicker than forty-four signatures, it will be even more expensive. We must now unfortunately copy out about 200 pages of part II of the *Geschichtbuch* for Professor Loserth, for without the text he cannot write a preface for it. That will be a lot of work but we shall do it gladly. I enclose Bender's postcard for you. Just imagine, he has found a Hutterian Bruderhof in Mannheim. What all may yet be discovered in Germany and also in Swabia? Köster wrote today in a very friendly way. He requests that you speak again in Vienna this winter. But we don't know yet when you will be home again, and whether Emmchen is still to travel to America. Everything is so uncertain. Actually how is it with your eye?

We are already looking forward to having Hardy next Sunday for his holidays, and two weeks later our dear Emy-Ma comes home for good, and then Ruthi comes for her holidays. We have so many requests from guests for August that our household numbers could rise to ninety! Then we shall miss you especially with your gift to awaken and arouse. If only you were back home with the blessing of the dear Hutterites! Hans has a really heavy task, but he remains in every situation faithful, firm, and yet humble. When you come home you will find him a great help. If Emmchen were to go to you it would be difficult here, and only by looking up to another strength than ours could we dare it. On the other hand we believe that your both being together there is very important for the uniting with the Hutterites. Emmchen could be a good support for you, too, as you are hindered by your weak eye.

I can hardly wait to hear what writings are still in America and what you will talk over with Elias Walter. Best of all I would like to copy everything by hand, but that is not possible. Concerning the estimates, please note that 2,000 copies are cheaper per copy than 1,000. Would it not be better then to have 2,000 printed? Under the estimates I have always written the cost of one copy including the paper, or without the paper, because we could perhaps get the paper ourselves from a factory. I would have gladly shared all these problems with you personally; writing about them is not so good. I hope dear Elias Walter is well so that you can discuss and read everything with him!

On your birthday we sang outside Emmchen's door, "God is Might and Fire." We had a wonderful hour in which we read together your article "Love to Christ." We realize so clearly that this love is the only thing by which we can live.

Else von Hollander
Rhön Bruderhof, August 1, 1930

Dear Ebbo,

At last mail comes from you again. That was really a test of *Gelassenheit*. We were indeed very worried about you. Now the reports about your eye and about the Hutterites are a very great joy. After all you write about them we love them and can see what the good Holy Spirit can give, and we are amazed. What a pity that they are not with us in Germany. For I, and not only I, have the impression after our efforts this year, that the time is now ripe for the Hutterian message. All is in ferment in politics and economics and people are looking for a solution. It seems as if everything points to mission.

You say the earliest you can return home is shortly before Christmas, but that really is a long time. I had always thought that the end of October would be the latest, but if it must be then we have to wait

patiently. If Emmchen travels to you at the beginning of September
we will have a hard time when we shall need to be given new strength
so that you can find us in a fairly good state when you return home.
Oh, that will be a joy! Emmchen shares everything with me daily and
Emy-Ma will be a great help for the house.

I always said, once Emy-Ma is back from her training we will be
better off for when Emmchen leaves us for a short time.

Emmy and I are sitting today on the Küppel under the beech tree
for the first sunny day after a rainy period, gazing towards the far
west. Behind us, Roland, Manfred, and Heini are just binding Oma
Isedor's rye. Adolf and Georg are making a survey for the drainage
on the "stone meadow" in preparation for the work week. The hay is
being turned on the Kühlmann meadows. This year we have a specially
good hay harvest. Everyone is amazed at our garden. From next week
on, Irmgard will copy out daily, for half a day, the teachings on Acts 2
and Matthew 5-7. Georg binds all the Hutterian books so nicely in
half-leather, so that our Hutterian Archives looks more and more
attractive.

I was very happy about the verses you sent to Mölein. You know,
Ebbo, I'm copying them by hand and making a nice present for each
teacher in the Children's House. Each copy should look different, and
the first one I will send you through Emmchen for you and her. The
thought of it makes me happy. I look forward to what you will have
to write about David Hofer, Rockport. I'm very interested in it.
Concerning your eye, we want to stand firmly together and ask that
it gets and stays completely well.

Always thinking of you faithfully and thankfully, your

Else

Joseph Stahl
Huron, South Dakota, August 7, 1930

Dear Elias Vetter,

I greet you with God's peace and blessing.

After spending four days with us, dear Arnold left on the Great
Northern at six this morning for Winnipeg, Manitoba, and the brothers
there. During the day he worked on our old books, making notes of
them all, and in the evenings he told about their beginning. The whole
community was gathered in front of our house, old and young, big
and small, until twelve every night. So everyone got to know him.
For myself I have to say that I no longer have any doubt but that we

should unite with him and his little group, because we need such a man very much. I cannot express the spirit and joy this man has in our forefathers and their writings. It puts us to shame. He awakens a new zeal and love. Only he should be able to stay longer in every community. He told me several times that he feels so at home here with us.

For the first four days old David Vetter was so cold-hearted, but in the end it went better. Arnold Vetter managed this much: David Vetter will be satisfied with whatever the Dariusleut do with them, if they are also satisfied. He was with him for almost two weeks. It seems to me that Arnold is a second Jakob Hutter in all his efforts, especially against greed and personal money in the church.

You will soon be able to see and test him for yourselves. Warm greetings,

Joseph Stahl

Else von Hollander
Rhön Bruderhof, August 21, 1930

Dear Ebbo,

Yesterday our dear Emy-Ma came back home, and we are very glad to have her among us again. Her radiant disposition makes us all so happy. She had completed her exams, so straight after her arrival we had a wonderful celebration nicely prepared by our dear Emmy. We began with your baptism song and Emmy read your letter about the life of faith of the Hutterites, which moved us all very much. I had written out the verses, games, and songs of the children at Wolf Creek for Emy-Ma in beautiful colored writing, like a picture book, and Georg bound it in red with linen spine and corners. It was such a joyful time; only we missed you very much, and we all thought how wonderful it will be when you come back home.

Many, many thanks for sending the wonderful writings, especially the letter of Jakob Hutter to the church. It has certainly taken me a long time to look through everything carefully and rejoice over it. Now I am beginning to copy out the writings. Here I feel an ever increasing wish and prayer that this great power which drove Jakob Hutter may take complete possession of me also and that it may use us all together for mission. In this sense I am thinking every day and always about your journey and the way you stand together with the Hutterian Brothers. Then I also have great hope that the uniting could perhaps suddenly happen quite quickly as a gift, and then maybe not too long afterwards you could come back home. For in spite of the faithfulness of all Brotherhood members, we really do need you back soon.

Did you receive all the estimates? Which do you find the best? We should come to an understanding about the terms of payment. Please examine everything carefully. I think that in spite of pressure from Loserth it would still be better to have the Small History Book printed after your return, when you will have discussed everything in detail with Elias Walter. The entire printing project must and will turn out well if we want to be there, with all that is given to us, for God's kingdom alone.

[Continued] August 23 in Fulda

Publishing the Hutterian writings is certainly part of all this, so that they are widely available and can challenge many people to the way, the way to which all men are called. Oh, how much I long for this strength for us!

Yesterday evening we had a Brotherhood meeting with Willy and Albert. It really did not come to anything decisive. You know how it is when the brothers working on the farm are so overtired and dull from all the hard work. Especially in these last weeks there has been a tremendous drive in the work because we have had real harvest weather at last, after many weeks of waiting. Apart from the oats and second crops of hay, everything should be brought in this week. We all felt we have so little of the Holy Spirit, that we are so helpless. At such times we miss you so very much, for you are always shown what should be done. Emmy and I spoke yesterday evening about it, that you cannot stay away too much longer.

But we will wait for the hour of our merciful God. Yesterday evening when I returned to my room after this lifeless meeting, little Walla suddenly stood there and said, "Pray," and when we had done this, he said, "Now I want to see whether the stars are shining." We went together to the window and saw a break in the clouds in the western sky with a great star, and we rejoiced about it quietly. Then I put him to bed and told him I would open the window for the night. To this he said, "Yes, then the angels can fly in," and then he fell quietly asleep. I felt how God speaks through children and how, in spite of my age, I want to become more and more like a child. We all enjoyed your description of little Joshua very much. It brought the little lad very near to us. Mölein was so happy about your letter. She said never in her life had she enjoyed a letter so much.

Every day the Sun Troop gathers faithfully together. After they have sung very seriously, "Rise my soul to watch and pray," and read together under the new Sun Troop banner which I sewed for them, they all climb to the very top of the beech tree!

Hardy is now very lively and happy, and on his birthday we could think of his new year of life with great courage. Hermann is really happy with his beautiful gray angora rabbit. Young Heini is working again very joyfully in the garden. His work together with the Tirolean Johann often depressed him. This man was often so dejected and on the other hand so very conceited. Now he has left. He took with him ten marks from Elisabeth Loewenthal and Kurt's jacket. He wrote to us from Würzburg together with Heinrich that he was a communist-Bolshevist spy and that we should still be hearing some good things from him! It is very sad!

Will Emmy be coming to you still? She is packed and ready for the journey and is only waiting to see if she is called. We are always thinking of your eye. May God keep it well and healthy, but please do not strain it. How good it would be if we could have the Great Article Book here for copying. Are you at Elias Walter's now? All the manuscripts you send I copy out myself the first time, then I dictate them for typing and let nothing out of my hands. I keep everything, including the very valuable copies, safe in my own cupboard so that nothing will get lost. I have put it all into the pink folder that closes with a snap, the one we bought together in February in Fulda. Every day Walla wants to see your card of "the big ship" and Paul Tschetter's, and then he is so happy when I put them back in the file and "snap" the file shut.

Emy-Ma feels wretched after her exams and needs plenty of sleep. She must be well looked after. But it is still a great help that she is back home again, especially if Emmy goes away. After you and we had such a hard time on your birthday with you so far away from us all, may God grant us such a wonderful Christmas as never before. May we be visited by the "rising Sun from on High."

Your descriptions and experiences with the Hutterites are so lively. I can imagine it all exactly as you write. Yes, I can distinguish the brothers and sisters very well and love each one with his particular character. Only David Hofer, Rockport, causes me some anxiety, although I admire the decisiveness of his character very much. But together with you, I am very sad about the difficult days that you experienced there, and I have gone through it all with you. Now we are very glad that you are—hopefully—with Elias Walter, whom we have to thank for so much and whose love has given us so much joy in these last years. Ebbo, you have sent us such precious things and have written about so much that still has to be copied that I realize more and more how many tasks there are, how short life is, and that certainly very much will still be left for the long span of eternity.

Here in Fulda, I have just lettered out the first page of Jakob Hutter's letters. I am sending it to you with the copy. Then you must tell me what is wrong, so that when I write out the whole letter I can do it correctly.

Now I must find some things for Mölein, who has been in bed for a few days with a little fever. It is probably a touch of "flu."

I always think of you and of your great task with our Hutterites, and I greet especially Elias Walter and everyone very, very much in thankfulness for everything.

Faithfully, your

Else

Winnipeg
August 25, 1930

Dearly beloved, faithful Elias Walter,

Already for a long time I have wanted to write to you about my journey through the Bruderhofs and about my joy in the faith, love, and community of the brothers. But my health is not good, and I have to gather all my strength when I am with the beloved communities so that I can be attentive and do and say everything that I have been entrusted with. Added to that, I must diligently supply my dear ones at home with letters and writings. Therefore, it is hard for me that my stay here has been prolonged by my illness while all my letters from our German Bruderhof are there with you, and I cannot reach you before September 14.

Today Tekniepe from the Hamburg America Line (who drove me to the Iberville, Maxwell, and Barickman Bruderhofs) told me that my faithful, beloved wife Emmy hopes to arrive in Winnipeg around the 12th, 13th, or 14th of September, and then we will travel immediately to you. We look forward to this very much. So I have to ask you to send me *all* the letters and packages that have come from Germany. Send them to me here at Joseph Kleinsasser's address, Milltown, Benard, Manitoba. Please, please do this right away! I have to check the letters to verify this unexpected news. I know that my dear wife is very concerned about my health and that she wants to support and strengthen me here in my task. But if she doesn't come after all (I cannot recommend it because of the money, whereas our brothers at home have decided on her journey), I will in any case have to remain here in Manitoba until Sunday, September 14.

The dear, *very* dear Schmiedeleut have all agreed and decided to meet with Joseph Kleinsasser Vetter, whom I regard and honor as an especially blessed brother, in order to give me a letter acknowledging and recommending that I be incorporated, appointed, and confirmed by you for my emerging church. They say (words of Joseph Waldner, Huron) that through the very fact of our continued existence and the order of our community, we have already been tested and proved. No further testing is needed therefore, except for the questions and answers according to the proper order which lead to the acceptance and appointment.

I also achieved this much through God and through the help of the brothers and sisters at Rockport that after continued efforts David Hofer said, "When the brothers ask about me, tell them that I am too old, too much burdened in my family with my poor wife and thinking of my death, and too alone in South Dakota to make a decision here on my own. Don't hold it against me that I have not concerned myself more with you. There is too much weighing on me, and the others in Canada are too far away. But you should tell everyone that I am at peace and in agreement with every decision the brothers in Canada make with you and for you." He had said the same to the former teacher Johannes Hofer, son of old, sick Jakob Hofer, as he left for Canada. I then received $10 for my trip from Rockport, and for the need at home where it has already arrived, $200 from Michel Vetter, Bon Homme, and $100 from David Wipf, Wolf Creek. I will tell you all the details myself.

I must say a heartfelt thanks to God our loving Father for his undeserved grace, which until now has given me complete unanimity with all brothers and sisters so that we are of one heart and one soul. Everywhere I went I was given writings and teachings and so forth. But there's still a lot missing before I will be able to take the *Lehr* each Sunday as you do.

Unfortunately, I have not yet received a copy of Beck's Latin History Book. The prospects of getting a copy in Germany are very slim, and I need it very badly almost every day. I have done much copying and note-taking, especially in Rockport where the brothers and sisters, particularly Maria Basel, "Old Vetter," old Jakob Vetter, Jörg Vetter, and the servant, Peter Vetter, were so loving and completely one with me in hoping for our acceptance, material support, and uniting. The blessing of old Jakob Hofer Vetter, the miller, almost on the point of death, especially moved and strengthened me in an unforgettable way. I have found a close friendship in our Lord and in the spirit of his church with Michel Vetter, South Dakota, Joseph Stahl, South Dakota, David Wipf and our whole loving Wolf Creek, David Hofer, James Valley, the two Joseph Waldners, David Glanzer and your daughter Susanna, her Joseph, and Johann D. Hofer, Blumengard, as with many others. It is especially the younger ministers like Joseph Vetter, Bon Homme, Peter Hofer, James Valley, Joseph Kleinsasser Jr., Milltown, and others, who are so thankful for the stimulation and renewal of their faith, which they sense anew through our coming and through our holding strictly to the life and confession of the oldest, earliest forefathers. I myself have experienced deep inspiration and encouragement from Michel Vetter, South Dakota, and Kleinsasser Vetter, Milltown. So please, please send the letters!

Loving you with the love of God, which is poured into our hearts through the Holy Spirit, I send greetings to the community.

Your very lowly

Eberhard

In Elias Walter's handwriting:

I sent a copy of this letter to all communities in Alberta, but only this one to the States. E. W.

Elias Walter
Stand Off Bruderhof, August 31, 1930

Dear brother,

I received some more letters witnessing to Arnold, from which I extract the following:

Joseph from Huron writes on August 13:

Elias Vetter,

I received your letter and understood its contents. I wanted also to see that Arnold Vetter at least gave a talk at the Baptist Churches. For the holy Baptists in Chicago told him completely false things about us or the Hutterian faith, saying we did not believe in rebirth or remorse and repentance. So he asked them whether they had ever read Jakob Hutter's epistles and Peter Riedemann's *Rechenschaft*. They said "No," so he said to them, "Then you don't know anything about the Hutterian faith," and some other things too. But I thought it might be a hindrance to his uniting with us and they would say, "Joseph messed up everything with Arnold." While we were eating, he told the old servant, Johann Tschetter, that Joseph Tschetter in Chicago knows absolutely nothing about the Hutterian faith. He must have spoken very sharply to this old servant, J. Tschetter, because he came and sought him out. He was just working in the school on the old Epistle Book, and after we had eaten supper, he said, "Dear old father, do not take it badly that I spoke to you in that way about community of goods. But as I am just working on the old Hutterian writings, I am so loaded with spiritual gunpowder that if someone appears before me, I start firing off right away." But he said, "That is all right."

David Hofer, Manitoba, wrote to me on August 20:

My dear brother in the Lord,

I want to report to you a little about our dear Arnold Vetter and how he is. He is a true child of God, full of love and Christian virtues. We cannot talk of teaching or instructing him; rather we have a lot to learn from him, for his only longing is for the welfare and unity of our communities, to the glory of God. This will hardly suit the rich communities, and I am afraid that for this reason he will not find much support for his uniting. It would be good for us to see how we stand toward the children of God, and whether we are only wanting to protect our mammon by making various excuses. Could it be that perhaps today, as in the time of Israel, the Lord has to send his prophet Elijah away from Israel in order to preserve him? Therefore, dear Elias Vetter, test it according to the word of God, and see whether you can really pull away from dear Arnold Vetter and his community. See that you yourself drive with him to all servants and communities concerned. As to the rest, what he is and what spirit leads his work he himself will show and prove to everyone. I believe and hope that everyone will say with the Apostle, "Can anyone forbid the water, that these should not be baptized?" (Acts 10:47) As I believe and trust, God will direct and lead hearts according to his will.

I brought Arnold Vetter to Joseph Kleinsasser Vetter on Saturday, and we rejoiced together that he also wants to fulfill Arnold Vetter's longing.

Today Arnold Vetter is with David Glanzer. He plans to be with us again on the 24th and to stay ten or fourteen more days in Manitoba. I wish him good luck and blessing on his trip and his plans. May the Lord's name be magnified through God-fearing men, that true love and noble peace may enter again also into the communities, to his honor and our blessedness. Amen.

To close, heartfelt greetings to you and to all who bear a burden for the good of the church.

David Hofer

Else von Hollander
Rhön Bruderhof, September 3, 1930

Dear Ebbo,

The wonderful shipments of old Hutterian writings were a tremendous joy for me. I can hardly wait till I have transcribed them all. Hans read Jakob Hutter's letter last Sunday. It is so moving and shattering that I just cannot express it in words.

Yesterday midday Emmchen and I sat together on the Küppel for the first time after a long period and looked towards our beautiful Rhön mountains. Hugga sat at home with Mö. Till then neither of us had dared to go so far away from Mö. But since yesterday her fever has practically gone and she has a good appetite. Now we must only watch that she doesn't jump out of bed for joy over her recovery. Since she got better her apathy has gone and she is her former wild, lively self. Now Emmchen and I were together and Emmy read aloud, "Jesus talks to the Soul" and the wonderful Jesus song which is pervaded with a warm love to Jesus. We were both completely filled with it. Then we both sang one of the songs to Hildebrand's tune. It was a lovely and unforgettable hour and you were certainly there with us. Emmchen promised to write it out for my birthday. Now how glad I am to copy the other writings. It is such a gift that I am allowed to do so.

The eight shipments have all arrived safely. I am sending you a typed copy of "E.A. Handschriften" (List of Hutterian manuscripts given to Eberhard Arnold), also a list of the earlier writings which we have here. Georg will first make a folder for the small-sized manuscripts, and then I will write on the front what it contains, so that absolutely nothing is lost. Georg has repaired and bound your torn books in the library beautifully, so you will be delighted when you come home. But the old Hutterian books are even more beautifully bound in half-leather, parchment and so on. He will send you sometime a list of them: two of Wolkan, two of Pilgram Marbeck, and three of

Liefmann, Balthasar Hubmaier, and Lydia Müller, and all are bound. He is now especially looking forward to using the typesetter and will start work with it as soon as you are here. He is so sensitive now and is always one of those who senses most deeply what is given to us through these writings for our life and also especially for mission. Right now there is a wonderful working together; he binds everything so quickly and is deeply interested in it all. You will receive a copy of the Church Register [*Kirchenbuch*] with a copy from part II of the Small History Book in the next days. I will compare exactly the teachings and the Church Register with the Small History Book, and then will write down where the passages in the teaching can be found and which parts in the Chronicle and the Church Register are the same, and which are missing. Soon I will write more about it; but this letter must go off today.

In joy over this wonderful work, I think of you in great thankfulness.

Your Else

John Horsch   Elias Walter
Scottdale, Pa.   Stand Off Bruderhof, September 4, 1930
Old friend,

I hope you are curious to hear something about Arnold. He is still not yet here. David of Manitoba wrote again yesterday that he had received my letter and was very glad about it, but he did not mention anything about his wife coming although without doubt it will be considered. It would, however, be too much to be decided so quickly. He writes further that he, Eberhard, is so loving he feels compelled to travel from one Bruderhof to another. Everybody likes him. In all this he gives a good witness, and he himself seems to be satisfied with the Brothers. Didn't he once write to you that he doesn't expect to find angels? Sympathetic hearts, that's what he needs, and there still are some, and partly many, such among them.

With greetings,

E. Walter

Else von Hollander
Rhön Bruderhof, October 1, 1930
Dear Ebbo,

Today at last I will send all the lists which you need, so that you can find what you want easily. They will go by registered mail, accompanied by this letter. I worked till late in the night so that you would get them before our work camp week. Already tomorrow Mohrs are coming, and on Saturday more than twenty who will work on the drainage with us. In the morning we want to have a short gathering together, and at midday, as always, we plan to read something, and in the evening to have an exchange of seeking. This demands much strength.

I am so thankful and glad that through extracts from the manuscripts I can gain a glimpse of the loving and trustful life together of the earlier and present-day Hutterites. And I am so happy that you are living in such a loving atmosphere; nevertheless we are counting the days till you come home. The other evening, as we were singing, *"Segne und behüte,"* (Lord protect and bless us), it seemed to me that you entered the dining room with a radiantly joyful face. Surely that will soon happen. But now we wish to stand firmly and steadily to the uniting with the Hutterites, hoping that soon, very soon this great gift may be given to us through the great love of Almighty God.

Have you read the Michel Hasel article in the *Mennonitisches Lexicon*? I am sure I crossed out the "Dr." at least once from your name. We read the article yesterday at midday. For all those of us who know the Michel Hasel Book well or very well, it was especially nice to hear.

Hans is at present in Berlin trying to get exemption from customs duties. Emy-Ma is recuperating for two weeks with Mother Zumpe. She is exhausted from her exam and did not feel well, yet she had thrown herself with enthusiasm into the work. Heini has just come in from the potato field and asked me if one could expect a letter from you today. When I said "Yes," he shouted, "Oh, I hope we will not be disappointed." I am thinking all the time that now you must be with Elias Walter, to whom we owe so much, and that the hours of decision for our Bruderhof, our publishing work, and for still much more have come.

I will stop now for today. Emmchen is already waiting for my help for the work camp week. United with you in thankful expectation, thinking of you, your faithful

Else

Emmy Arnold
Rhön Bruderhof
October 2, 1930

Jakob and Rahel Waldner
Huron Colony, Manitoba

Dear brothers and sisters and friends in Canada,

God's grace as greeting to you whom we do not know personally but have come to know through my dear husband, Eberhard Arnold.

How thankful we are for all that our Eberhard could tell us about you loved ones and that the Schmiedeleut in Manitoba want to help us in our need with wheat flour and clothing! Our steward, Hans Zumpe, is now on his way to a government department in Berlin hoping to obtain custom-free entry for the wheat flour. It is very possible that we will get it. The clothes and shoes should have been used a little, so that they are not completely new when they arrive here. As soon as we know, we will write to you.

I can imagine so well how happy Eberhard was among you, for we here in Germany are very much alone. Although there are many churches and religious communities, the only fellowship is in special study and prayer meetings. Otherwise people live with their families in private property. We cannot be thankful enough that we are allowed to go this way. We came on this earth with nothing, and we will leave in the same way. In these few years of pilgrimage on earth why should we accumulate things which we will have to leave behind anyway? We want to live and go the way Jesus lived before us, as written in the Acts of the Apostles, chapters two to four.

We hope you can read this letter that we have typed on the typewriter for you. It is a great joy to us that you take such interest in all we experience here. When Lieschen Zinkhan comes to us again, we will read your letter to her. She has a very hard battle to fight. She is only eighteen years old and her parents do not want her to come to the Bruderhof. Her brother hits her with a horsewhip if she comes up here to us. Recently she wanted to follow her inner calling to come to us. When she packed her belongings to flee to the community in the night, this was noticed, and she was locked up. Now she has lost courage to come until she is twenty-one years old, legally of age, and can make her own decisions.

We also know the song about which you write, "Even if everything is against me, if God is for me, each time I call and pray all troubles leave me." We have very seldom sung it here, but we will sing it in these days and think of you. We ask you to continue praying to God for her and for us.

You write that you would like to have some songs that my husband Eberhard has written. I will send some with this letter. Eberhard rejoices again and again over the books you gave to him. They are a special joy to him. We already have quite a few here and are copying them.

What you write about your work in the kitchen, in the diet kitchen, and with the children interests us very much. I would have loved so much to be with you also. Then I, too, could have learned a lot from you. We are only beginners in community life, but you have had years of experience. My service here is housemother of the Bruderhof and I have to think of everyone, grown-ups and all the little ones. We have over thirty children in our Children's House, including the children of our families. We send all our children to our own school, which is recognized by the government. Our daughter Emy-Margret works in our Children's House after being away for two years' training and taking her examinations for kindergarten teacher. She learned a great deal about health care and activities for children. She is nineteen years old and engaged to our steward. We have another kindergarten teacher here, who has been with us for two and a half years and is now a full member of our community. Her name is Gretel Knott. She is twenty years old and engaged to our storekeeper, Alfred Gneiting. These two sisters share in the care of the children, including dressing, undressing, and bathing, and in their activities.

Apart from these, we have three sisters in the school who teach our children. They also are full members of the community. When not teaching, two of them help in different departments cooking or mending and sewing. Three married Brotherhood sisters work in our kitchen with an old grandmother who lives with us and a sixteen-year-old war orphan who has been with us for nearly seven years. Sophie Schwing is a very lovable girl, who also shares our faith.

Of course we cook very simply, always just what we have on hand. Meat we don't have at all except when we slaughter, which happened four times this last winter. In the summer we have vegetables without meat. For breakfast we have rough oatmeal porridge with a piece of plain bread. At ten a.m. we usually have a hot drink with bread and a spread. At dinner for around eighty people we use about one and a half pounds of coconut shortening in the vegetables, along with our potatoes. Of course this is very little, but it is all we can afford. For a whole week we have three and a half pounds of bread per person, counted out for each one. In the evenings we usually eat potatoes. When your supply of flour arrives, we think our food will improve a great deal. We will then double the bread ration. Everyone is very happy about that because up till now no one has been able to eat their fill of bread, only of potatoes. We have realized in these years that we actually don't need as much as we often think we do, for "man does not live by bread alone."

In the next week we will have a work camp here. Friends of our Bruderhof will help drain a very wet meadow, and later we will use the water for a little swimming pool. Because of all this work, it will be quite unsettled here this week.

Apart from this we are still in the middle of the potato harvest. Then will come cabbages and root crops. In winter most of our men work in the turnery or in the carpentry shop where we make plates, egg cups, candleholders, and other things for sale. Also a lot of maintenance is necessary again on our houses as well as on our farm machinery. The very best would be if you could send us one of your agricultural experts who could advise and help us with all your rich experience.

Eberhard will now be with Elias Walter in Stand Off. We are very eagerly looking forward to his return then, for it has often been very difficult with our many guests. It has not always been easy to find the right way and do the right thing with the problems that come up in the community. But we can really say that we have felt the leading of the Holy Spirit in these months and that our steward, Hans Zumpe, has been very much helped. Still it is very difficult for him to manage practical affairs as well as to lead the inner life of the community.

I would like very much to come to Canada to bring Eberhard home. Then I could experience with him the day of the uniting and of his being sent out for his task. Now we greet you all with very much love in the community of the Holy Spirit.

Your brothers and sisters in Christ
Emmy Arnold

Elias Walter
Stand Off Colony, October 5

Dear friend Horsch,

I have received your letter of September 23; many thanks. In response I would like to ask how many of the little book[1] should be printed and where they can be stored. Because for the most part they are to be given away, they will bring in very little. I can do no other than leave it to you or the publishers. They should keep an exact account of it. I cannot tell you what today's census would be; in 1926 it was 3,018 souls. When I was in Dakota, I took it myself. You may hold on to letters which I have not specially requested back from you.

Frau Arnold has not come here. Arnold has also not asked for her; he himself is at present with the Lehrerleut and will come to me in a

---

[1]Probably Horsch's *Hutterian Brethren*.

few days. Then he will travel to the Bruderhofs around Calgary; they love so much to have him, that he can't get away easily. His time will be all too short; he must board ship again on December 10.

His acceptance as a "Hutterite" cannot be denied him, since he is a Hutterite such as we have no other among us today. Very many such should come to us! The Bruderhofs could really do with them.

He has with him a very fine letter from your son-in-law, Bender, written to him on May 26 from Heidelberg. It is wonderful to read.

The harvest in South Alberta (wheat) was fairly good apart from fodder. In the North it is scantier, but the prices are so poor that there is little profit to be made.

With best wishes, your friend,

E. Walter

Elias Walter
Stand Off Bruderhof, October 13, 1930

My dear Friedmann,

Thank you for your letter, received on September 14.

You write to ask for some more assistance. I am not really able to help you, however, as I am not well acquainted with Hans Denck's writings. I have never copied them out. But I have the following: *Was geredt sei, das die Schrift sagt, Gott tue und mache gutes und böses* (What is said about the Scriptures saying God does and creates both good and evil). We have this as a manuscript. In addition John Horsch, Scottdale, Pennsylvania, USA, has a small book which was published by the Mennonite Printing House. Its title is *Deutsche Theologie*. Perhaps it is still available. There is also *Von der wahren Liebe* (On True Love) with Hans Langenmantel's commentary on "Our Father," printed in Elkhart, Ind., 1888. But I cannot say I have ever seen or heard of the three articles you ask about.

John Horsch has written a book called *Kurzgefasste Geschichte der Mennonitischen Gemeinden* (Brief History of the Mennonite Churches) with a summary of their fundamental teachings and a bibliography of Anabaptist Literature: Johann Horsch, Elkhart, Indiana, 1890. But this may now be out of print. It includes a list of all our writings, printed and in manuscript.

It is a main article of faith for us that we must not swear oaths. But I cannot say whether there is a written statement of this particular article.

I have Loserth's edition of Pilgram Marbeck. Would this be of any use to you?

E. Arnold is visiting the Bruderhofs here. He is being received with heartfelt love so that he is well satisfied. He will certainly be accepted as a brother, and will return home appointed to the service, a zealous Hutterite.

Greetings from

E. Walter

Else von Hollander
Rhön Bruderhof, December 1, 1930

Dear Ebbo,

Your two last letters to Emmchen, the one from today and the one from nine days ago, made us so happy and showed us how much God is with you; they filled us with hope and joy. Only the indication that perhaps you will not be home for Christmas was a bit hard for us to take, but we don't want to push you in any way because you should not overstrain yourself with your weakened eye. Every day we come together to ask for the uniting with the Hutterian Brothers. Hans reads out of the two chapters from *Inner Land* about the Holy Spirit. We sense so clearly that we can live only through this witness, and that this unity with the Hutterian Brothers exists, even if it is very imperfect on our side.

Today I am sending you pages seven and eight from the small baptism book of old Jacob Maendel for the Small History Book. I don't get very far with the transcribing work as there is always so much to do here. Also the library takes longer than I thought, and that has to be finished before you get home. Now we are also preparing in an inner way for Christmas for the villages. On the Saturday of the third of Advent fifty young teachers from Fulda want to come up to us with School Inspector Hammacher to get to know our way of life. I am frequently with Emmchen in Fulda and also work a lot with her together. We discuss daily what is most important to achieve before your return. We still don't know exactly when we can expect you. But we will gladly wait so you can complete your whole task without you and your eye overdoing it. With how much joy we look forward to the day of your arrival!!

You sent such special things again in parcels XVII and XVIII that I would love to start straight away with copying. Yesterday we sent a little Christmas parcel to Stand Off for you. I had also written out something for you, and it really came out nice, but when I wanted to bind it, I pricked my finger, and blood dripped over all the writing. If ever I find time again, I will re-write it. I copied out these words of Ulrich Stadler in the night when I was watching by Walterle, who had bad earache. Emy-Ma has a wonderful influence on the little children in the kindergarten. She has such a special sympathetic love for the children. She works with such untiring enthusiasm that you really have to watch out that she does not overdo it.

You can surely imagine Emmchen preparing for Christmas in her motherly way. How she thinks of each one! Hopefully the transcript of the Christmas article (forty-two printed pages) will get finished as a present from you! In case you are not here for Christmas, we want to prepare between Christmas and New Year for your return and for the great tasks that will be given to us then! I long so much for a strength, which I feel wants to come and yet is so lacking in me!

When we bring the Christmas message to the villagers, I have these very wonderful words to say: "God is love; whoever believes in him and holds to his commandments shall not be cast out. Hope! Have faith, you people of the night! God will take your punishment from you!" "Holy, radiant light! Send your rays into the darkness of men, that they believe and hope!" Isn't that wonderful!!

Today your list of books arrived from Alberta. I am simply amazed at all the wonderful things: the Dröscher book etc., but also all the tremendous amount of work. I cannot imagine when you did it all! Hans now reads every morning out of the *Geist-Buch* (Book of the Spirit) which you sent him. He is very moved by it, and he is glad when he can find an hour to prepare and can read to us. He is also very impressed by the old writings.

There is much I could still tell you, but this letter has to go with Herr Gärtner.

In great thankfulness and joy for everything given by God, I think of you and your task, your faithful

Else

This article appeared in the *Christian Monitor* of January 1931, although Harold Bender had visited the Rhön Bruderhof in May 1930 shortly before Eberhard Arnold's departure.

THE NEW HUTTERITE BRUDERHOF IN GERMANY
By Harold S. Bender

Last summer the writer had the privilege of spending a week-end visiting the new Hutterite "Bruderhof" in Middle Germany, called

"Bruderhof-Neuhof," which is located at the edge of the Rhön Hills, sixty miles north-east of Frankfurt. Having been much impressed by the experience, and believing that this modern revival of old-fashioned Hutterite principles would be of interest to our readers, a brief account of the visit is here presented. This account will probably be of particular interest just now, since the leader of this "Bruderhof," Eberhard Arnold, is at present on a visit to the Hutterites of the United States and Canada, in the course of which he visited Scottdale and several other Mennonite centers.

It was on one Saturday afternoon in early June that I reached the little town of Neuhof, in the district of Fulda. I did not know how to recognize the "brother" from the "Bruderhof" who was to take me to the farm of the Brotherhood, but as soon as I spied a sturdy, friendly looking man in simple, plain clothing, and with a good-sized beard, I judged at once that this must be my expected friend, and so it was. Adolf Braun, the manager of the farm, had come to meet me with team and wagon (an auto is too expensive for the Brotherhood at present), and had already made a number of Saturday purchases. We had a very pleasant drive into the "back country," up into the hills of the Rhön. The long ride gave me much opportunity to learn Adolf Braun's life story, as well as to become partly acquainted with the life on the "Bruderhof." Braun had formerly been a Baptist, but had become dissatisfied with his group after the war, partly because of their attitude on the war question, and for other reasons. He had been with the Brotherhood almost from the beginning. Through him I received a very good impression of the quality of the life on the "Bruderhof," for Adolf Braun was the soul of kindliness and Christian charity, a consistent representative of the simple, plain principles of the Brotherhood.

Eberhard Arnold, the leader of the group, had been absent on business in Frankfurt, but met us as we were almost at the "Bruderhof," so that we drove the last two miles together. At last we reached the "Hof," away back in the midst of fine natural scenery, with splendid views out over the hills, quite a distance from the nearest village and with no close neighbors. The buildings of the "Bruderhof" consist of a group of three modest houses about a central court, and a few scattered smaller buildings, workshops, and a barn. The three buildings about the central court are the living quarters, and contain also the school rooms and the common dining hall, in addition to living quarters for the families and single members of the Brotherhood.

On first sight the buildings seemed to be small for the number of people in the group, and otherwise inadequate, although very neat.

The furniture was also very meager, though in good order and repair. I soon learned from Eberhard Arnold what I had suspected, that the "Bruderhof" was really living in poverty, in need, and that much as they wished they might be able to build better and larger buildings, with better furnishings, they lacked adequate finances. They had bought the small farm with its buildings in a sadly run-down state a few years before, in 1926 I believe, and were working hard to improve the land and the buildings. They were succeeding visibly in their purpose. It was in connection with this fact of the poverty of the Brotherhood that I received one of my strongest impressions, namely the devotion of these people to their faith and their principles. Many of the members of the Brotherhood formerly had good positions in the world, as school teachers, as social workers, as laborers, and otherwise, but they had surrendered everything and were willing to suffer and sacrifice and bear hardship for the sake of their cause, — this in addition to the misunderstanding, criticism and abuse, from society in general. I do not think the friends on the "Bruderhof" will object at all to this mention of their poverty, because it is an honorable poverty, and they, least of all, are concerned with "worldly goods," since they have given up the principle of private property. However, they do have hard times, and, as Eberhard Arnold said, in the winter and spring until the new garden and farm products are available they often have but very little to eat. Yet no one complains.

But to go back to the narrative. When we arrived at the "Bruderhof" I was impressed at once by the spirit of simple brotherhood and evident love which existed. They were as one great family, from young to old. And I felt this spirit the longer I was among them. Forms and formality were done away with, "Sie" had disappeared and been replaced by the familiar "Du," even with visitors. First names were used, titles forgotten (although Eberhard Arnold is a university graduate with a Ph.D.), stiffness and all signs of vanity and pride were gone, and in their place was a simple, hearty, friendly, good cheer and a spirit of true Christian charity and regard for one another. The spirit of fellowship (Gemeinschaft) is very strong in the Brotherhood, as it must be if such a group is to exist at all. Private property is abolished, and a community of goods set up in its place, where all must live and work together for the good of all. I could not help but wonder whether the possession of money and property is not after all a great enemy of Christian love and fellowship, and was reminded of the word of our Lord, "How hardly shall they that have riches enter into the kingdom."

I have already referred to my impression of the simplicity of the people and the life of the Brotherhood. This is also marked in the clothing. As I learned upon inquiry, there is no compulsion in this matter, no required forms of clothing. Nevertheless the members dress much alike, and all in very simple fashion, in plain, modest apparel. The married men wear beards, for the most part, although this is also not required. Jewelry and ornament are not seen. It was a relief to enjoy the simplicity of life, including the clothing, of these good Christian people, and get away from the fashions and pride of display of the world in general. Here again I was made to wonder how much we have become slaves of fashions and customs of clothing, to the detriment of simplicity and sincerity, and even comfort. I refer here not only to the vanity of prevailing fashions, but also to the foolish customs into which we of this age, both men and women, have fallen, and of which we ourselves are perhaps not conscious. I was also made to wonder why we prefer to wear only the dark and somber colors, or why we prefer heavy and fine fabrics, instead of the coarser, natural fabrics.

I mention some of these points partly to indicate the strong impression made by the life of these people. Here in the "Bruderhof" they really live an unworldly life, separate from the world, a separation in comparison to which we Mennonites who emphasize unworldliness are still quite worldly. The life here was and is so different from the ordinary life, even of Mennonites, that I was forced to reconsider the life which we live, and the spirit which animates our Brotherhood. The power of the testimony of the life in the "Bruderhof" was so strong that I could not help but think along these lines, even though there was no attempt made in any way to "work" on me, or to "convert" me to the principles of the Brotherhood. Again and again the thought came to me, how many of our modern Mennonites would be willing to sacrifice as these people sacrificed, and do it with joy and unwavering faith in the truth and right of their principles?

Several meetings were held during my stay in the "Bruderhof" on Saturday and Sunday, one of which took the place of our regular Sunday morning service. Great emphasis is placed on singing, and the group has a hymn book of its own. Eberhard Arnold, as the leader, is the spokesman, the preacher of the group, the "Diener am Wort." After his talk in the morning service, at my request, the meeting was turned into a sort of testimony service, in which the adult members told how they came to accept the principles of the group, and what experiences had brought them to where they were. This meeting was very valuable to me as it gave me an insight into the inner forces at work in the group. The background of the different members was quite varied. All had been shaken loose from their previous life through the upheaval of the World War and the years following. Many had gone through the youth movement, seeking something better, tired of the shams and artificiality of the world, and unsatisfied with the deadness of much of the evangelical church life. One or two had for a time been in the Marxistic Communist group in Germany, one or two had been members of other religious groups outside the state church. All had come into the new movement as the result of sincere seeking after a better way of life, and all were members of the new group by deep conviction.

I was also impressed with the depth and strength of the religious life in the Brotherhood. Their whole life is a seeking to do the will of God, and to be His servants and messengers among men. Because of the reaction against the forms of the ordinary church life, they have perhaps gone too far in the abandoning of religious forms, but that does not seem to have hindered their spiritual life, and no doubt they will in time develop their own forms. The Bible as the Word of God is their only authority for faith and life. They practise adult baptism on confession of faith, and celebrate the Lord's Supper.

Lest the movement be misunderstood, I should like to emphasize the Christian and Biblical character of the group, as over against the idealistic. The Brotherhood is a Christian Communism not on the basis of philosophical principles, nor because of their belief that Communism is the ideal world order, or because of their belief in this system as the climax of evolutionary social development, or confidence in it as a workable political system. On the contrary they do not believe in the evolution of human society and of man in general; they do not believe that communism is possible on any other basis than among Christians thoroughly obedient to the will of God. They do not believe that any great number of people in the world will ever be able to meet these conditions, and do not look for world betterment. On the contrary, they look toward the coming of the new world in the return of the Lord Jesus Christ. Their view of the world and the world system is therefore eschatological and not idealistic and evolutionary, if I may be permitted these technical terms, although it is not millenarian.

But lest this account become too long, I must go on to a description of their organization and a brief account of their history. There are many more details which I should like to relate, and other impressions of my visit which would be worthwhile recording, but space will not permit. It should be mentioned that drinking and smoking are of course unknown, that swearing and harsh language are absent, and that labor and industry are expected of every one. Hospitality is also strongly emphasized and freely practiced in spite of the poverty under which the group is struggling.

First, a very brief account of the origin of the group. Eberhard Arnold, who is the founder and moving force in the group, was the son of a University Professor of Theology. He had secured his own doctor's degree and was offered a professorship, and a pastorship, but preferred rather to work and preach free from obligation to the state church even as a young man. A man of gifts of leadership, he soon became known, and was for a time prominent as one of the secretaries of the German Student Y.M.C.A. and a director of the publishing activities of this organization. After the war, he was unable to continue with this organization because of his radical pacifism and his insistence on the application of the Sermon on the Mount. Refusing to compromise in any way, he and his family finally made a complete break with the organized religious forces of their day, and sought to find the will of God, and to be led to the way which was right for them in full obedience to God and His Word. For a time they were active with many others in a strongly pacifistic and semicommunistic Christian movement associated with the Youth Movement, with its center at Schlüchtern, near Frankfort, and with the Press known as the "Neu Werk Verlag." Soon, however, they were forced to separate from this group and establish a group of their own which was more radical in its application of the principles of the Sermon on the Mount. At first this group was located at Sannerz not far from Schlüchtern, where a farm had been rented. Gradually the group became more communistically inclined until finally a definite step was taken to establish a Christian Communistic Brotherhood, which ultimately found its expression in 1926 in the definite organization of the "Bruderschaft" with the purchase of the "Bruderhof Neuhof," where they are at present located, not far from Sannerz and Schlüchtern.

At first the group knew nothing at all about the Hutterite Brotherhood in the United States and Canada. Accidentally hearing of them, they began to investigate, and found themselves drawn very much to these people. As they received the writings of the Hutterites and came into personal touch with them through correspondence, especially with Elias Walter of Macleod, Alberta, the fellowship became more and more intimate, and they adapted themselves more and more to the old Hutterite principles and organization. Finally in August, 1928, they made application for acceptance by the Hutterites of Canada as a Hutterite Brotherhood, and in August, 1929, they drew up and adopted a constitution and regulations altogether in the style and spirit of the Hutterite Brotherhood. The story of this acquaintance between the two groups is certainly very remarkable. The leader, Eberhard Arnold, is now on a tour of Hutterite Colonies in the United States and Canada in order to make the union of the two groups complete.

At present there are about seventy persons, adults and children, on the "Bruderhof." Of this number about thirty are members, twenty-five children, and the remainder children or others placed there temporarily for care. This group is strictly organized on the following basis of a fourfold division.

(1) Full, baptized, communicant, life members.

(2) Novices, or applicants for membership, who must undergo a one-year period of testing before being admitted.

(3) Helpers, who come for a longer or shorter period of time to live on the "Bruderhof," and take part in the life and work of the group, but not as members.

(4) Guests.

At the head of the Brotherhood is the "Diener am Wort," or elder. Under him is the steward, who is directly responsible for the material side of the Brotherhood, and who was in older times called by the Hutterites, "Diener am Notdurft." As assistant to the steward (Haushalter) is the matron (Hausmutter). Subject to the steward are two foremen or directors (Arbeitsteiler und Arbeitsordner) who are directly in charge of the work on the "Bruderhof." Every member of the Brotherhood has regularly assigned tasks. At present the following forms of work are conducted in the "Bruderhof": Writing, publication and lecturing; child-training and school; farming and gardening; carpentry and other crafts such as pottery, smithery, saddlery, sewing and housework, etc. Since the number of members is yet small, a number of the crafts are not yet in operation. The only persons who have to do with money are the five higher officials, and here primarily only the steward, who is in charge of all the business of the "Bruderhof," and makes all sales and purchases. When one joins the group he surrenders all his property and becomes a member of the group for life, subject to the discipline of the organization.

Finally, it should be said that the Brotherhood has a strong mission spirit and has a definite program of evangelization. First of all, evangelization is to be accomplished through testimony to the many guests who come to the "Bruderhof." In the course of a year the number of guests reaches a thousand or more. Further, all contacts of members of the Brotherhood with the outside world are viewed as evangelistic, not so much through direct propaganda as through the influence of the life. Another mode of evangelization is through literature. Finally there is the mode of direct teaching and preaching by the "Diener am Wort" in special meetings, lectures and addresses, as the occasion presents itself. This "Aussendung" is conceived quite in the spirit of the older Hutterite Brotherhood.

The history of the old Hutterite Brotherhood is a remarkable one, going all the way back to Switzerland and Tirol, to the time of the Reformation. The Hutterites claim with right a common origin with our own Swiss Mennonite Church in Zurich. In spite of severe persecution, particularly in the time of the Counter Reformation, and after the Thirty Years War, 1630-1700, as well as later in the time of Maria Theresa in Austria, they have been able to continue down to the present time with the maintenance of their historic principles, including a Biblical Christian communism. Almost as remarkable is the story of the rise of the new Hutterite Brotherhood in Germany, without the least connection with the ancient Hutterites. It will be of great interest to watch the future career of this new colony, "Bruderhof-Neuhof."

                                                              Goshen, Ind.

                                                              Emmy Arnold
Jakob and Rahel Waldner   Rhön Bruderhof
Huron Bruderhof, Manitoba   January 14, 1931

Dear brothers and sisters in the Huron *Gemein*,
in particular Jakob and Rahel Waldner,

Your letter of December 2 arrived here. We are all in good health. We were heartily glad to know you were thinking about us so faithfully. We are so glad at heart that we have been shown the way of true community and are allowed to live it, and we want to do this better and better. When Eberhard returns, which we expect in a short time, he will tell us much about how it is among you over there, and there will surely be a number of changes still to be made among us.

Starting a Hutterian Bruderhof has not been easy for us! Wanting to live such a different life in this world! Through the Sermon on the Mount (Matthew 5-7) and Acts 2-4 we were led to live not in private property and self-will, but in real community. It cost us many struggles in the beginning years of our life because it was often not easy to recognize the way we should go. We have also experienced a lot of hostility, which is to be expected when one tries to live a God-fearing life. Through the leading of the Holy Spirit, who has especially chosen Eberhard as his tool, we have been led as far as we are today.

We have been very stimulated by the writings of your and our forefathers, which we received from you: Wolkan's book about the Hutterites, the *Chronicle of the Hutterian Brethren*, Peter Riedemann, and Ehrenpreis. Eberhard has also sent us many of your old writings. A special joy was a small book by Michael Sattler, a letter he wrote to his wife on the day before he was executed. Around Christmas we read a lot from the big Christmas book on Micah 5, Luke 2, and John 1, which Eberhard also sent us. Lately we have also read a great deal from Ulrich Stadler, which made us feel very much at one with our whole origin and history. Now we are again reading a lot in the Chronicle about our and your forefathers suffering and dying for their faith.

By now you probably all know that Eberhard was taken into the Hutterian Church on December 9 and that on December 17 and 18 he was confirmed as a servant of the Word. It will have been a great joy for him to be united with you at last; it had been his wish for such a long time. How glad we would all have been to have been there and have experienced this important day!

On the whole it goes quite well here. In spirit we all stand very much together and await Eberhard's return with great joy. With regard to our temporal well-being, we still have to struggle with very many economic worries. This comes because our hof was never properly set up. We are nearly eighty people but have only four cows and two young cattle and therefore very little milk. We have not yet slaughtered this winter. In the spring we had no money to buy little piglets and could do this only in the fall. But we have enough vegetables and potatoes to last until the next harvest. Unfortunately, the grain for the bread is already used up, in spite of weighing out the bread weekly for each person from the first day on. Each person received three pounds per week—that is not much. We especially lack fat because we have not slaughtered and also have little milk. So we still have to buy margarine and coconut fat, which is very expensive. It is too bad it did not work out for you to send a boxcar load of wheat flour. We were already rejoicing at the thought of it, for then the need of our bread shortage would have been met. But the customs authorities at the border would have charged such a high duty that it unfortunately would not work out.

Our people are working again full swing after a week between Christmas and New Year when we concentrated more on spiritual things. Now lots of repairs are being done, which we cannot do in summer because of lack of time. They are very hard at work in the school and office.

What you write about yourselves interests us very much. We wish your daughter-in-law Katrin a good recovery from her rheumatism. Our nurse, Monika, will write to you about her nursing experience, and perhaps there is a remedy that would help.

In connection with your little babies, Monika, who takes care of our little ones, will write. Our little babies also are taken care of by the community.

We greet you all in the love of Christ. Even though we do not know you face to face, we feel inwardly bound together in spirit.

Your Hutterian Brothers in Germany
Emmy Arnold

Elias Walter
Macleod, Alberta
Jan. 19, 1931

First of all, greetings, dear friend Horsch.

I have your letter of Jan. 8th, for which I thank you. Arnold is still here and you can still hope to see him, since he intends to visit you and Goshen. The acceptance into the Church has taken place and he preaches without fail nearly every Sunday and is listened to gladly.[1] But he is troubled very much with his eye and often goes to the doctor, which takes time. Since January 3 he is visiting the last Bruderhofs around Calgary. I was with him but did not wish to stay so long and left him to inquire into everything and take enough time. I hope he will come in these days. Then he will visit the Bruderhofs here once more and then go to Manitoba and back.

My feeling is that he will travel home more sadly than he came here, because he cannot get the help he needs. The times are so uncertain, and the people on the Bruderhofs in Alberta and also on mine are aware that we cannot keep up with our taxes and commitments, and so there is nothing left for helping him. If only he doesn't get into more difficulties through staying here so long. He should have planned his visit for a whole year.

This, not to keep you waiting. With best greetings,

E. Walter

---

[1] See Appendix D.

Elias Walter
Macleod, Alberta, March 5, 1931

John Horsch,

I have received your letter. I'm sending you a "report" on the two prisoners. I do not know if this is the one you wanted. I don't know of any other.

Concerning what you write about the author's preface for the book, I don't know if I understand it sufficiently. I don't know if I can improve it somewhat for you. You yourself surely know that the church comes into being through the free working of the Holy Spirit without compulsion and without pressure, and faith must bring it about. In contrast, in Russia everything is done with force and without mercy and above all, they don't want faith.

Arnold has been with the Lehrerleut brothers for several weeks already. It seems as though he has really won their trust and their love. More will be moving. Old David Hofer Vetter from Rockport is to come up here himself to remain here so that new ministers can be elected in various places, and for that Arnold wants to be present too. If only he doesn't run into unpleasantness or difficulties through remaining here so long! I also think that the world (or better said, the wolves) should not be fearful of a sheep, that it might cause harm. You see it with our brothers—the borders are firmly closed. Yet the Hutterites go to and fro, up and down. That is a great credit and a great grace of God.

Greetings,

E. Walter

Joseph Kleinsasser
Milltown, Manitoba
May 10, 1931[1]

John Horsch
Scottdale, Pa, USA

Worthy Friend,

About a year ago you promised me the book you have put together and written about the Hutterites from 1528-1928 and which I have not yet received. Hasn't the book been printed yet? Or what is the situation? I would be very glad to get it.

Did Eberhard Arnold come to you and stay with you on his return journey or not? I would like to know. He spent quite a long time in

---

[1]Although this letter belongs at the end of Chapter 3 by date, it has been placed together with other letters to John Horsch.

Alberta, Canada, and without doubt met several unexpected things among the Hutterites; certainly some bad and some good, some to be criticized and some to be praised.

Did he also stop in at Goshen, Indiana? I hope to hear from you soon. With friendly greetings, respectfully,

Joseph Kleinsasser

South Dakota, April 1931

Dearly beloved Hans, with your, my, and our dear Emy-Ma,

The same wishes for your birthday on April 19 as for Emy-Ma's new year of life, begun on March 10!

I was so glad to hear through Mama about Emy-Margret's birthday celebration. Her new year of life—twenty years old, no, young— should bring your uniting in marriage, in which you should make her happy in body, soul, and spirit and give her joy and strength!

Today I am sending you news (which you must surely have heard already) about the $800 + $400 + $400 from the three Lehrerleut communities in Alberta. Through Elias Walter you will receive in addition $100 from Paul Stahl, Beiseker, Alberta (Dariusleut). Guard this money carefully and use it only for the most necessary things— food, housemother expenses for the most basic needs, orders for spring cultivation, the purchase of a horse, and for payment of the most urgent debts. Do this according to the advice of the wider committee and with the agreement of the whole Brotherhood.

I am also enclosing for you the very important document of my incorporation, laying on of hands, and commission.[1] See that you keep it safe and, if possible, get it certified with the stamp and signature of a notary and duplicated. It is the most valuable result of my journey.

To close, I stretch out my hand to you in great thankfulness that during this long time the almighty spirit of God protected, led, and used you in the tremendous responsibility transferred to you before I left. You will soon be relieved of a small part of this, although we want to carry everything together.

Your father and Eberhard
soon to return home!

---

[1] See p.184.

Else von Hollander
from Switzerland, Spring 1931

To Eberhard Arnold.

. . . I left the last shipment from February, which you packed up so nicely, just as it was. It made me so happy. Lene and I recently numbered all the books in your library and entered them in a card index and two nice catalog volumes. I think you will be very happy about it when you come home. How I would like to show you everything! But I am not permitted to come home before May. Georg has bound all your much-read books, which were worn out from your working through them, so nicely that you will not recognise them at all!

I have also copied out for you Jakob Hutter's letter to the prisoners in Hohenwart Castle. Emmchen will give it to you when you are back on the Bruderhof, or when she finds out where she should send it to make sure you will receive it.

Here I am reading *Inner Land*, the Gospel of John, the Chronicle, and other Hutterian writings. It is my ardent longing that I become inwardly so new that only Christ—and he alone—reigns in me, and that my life belongs to him completely and is used by him at every moment. I wish to become someone who is really waiting for the day when all struggle will come to an end. So I always think of you, praying that you can take up the work of mission for which you have yearned your whole life long, with a healthy eye. Mission was always your greatest and deepest joy. Your heart longed for it in burning love to all men. How grateful I would be if I could help a little with this! For the whole world waits to be helped out of its need. How thankful we can be for our Bruderhof and for what God has done there. The last evening when we interceded in faith for you and Hardy and for my departure, is unforgettable for me.

Dear Emmchen has nursed me so touchingly and is so wonderfully courageous. She stands wonderfully together with Hans in leading us. And dear Emy-Ma who leads the little ones to inner life, and all, all stand so firmly together. My room here also faces west.

Spirit fills, breaks through;
He scales the walls of mountains high.
Brings the farthest near;
He brings refreshing wind to all.

Bound closely with you in this Spirit with endless thanks.

Your faithful Else
who, after the quiet, wants so much to work again

Else von Hollander
Fidaz, May 7, 1931

Dear Ebbo,

I send you the most heartfelt greetings of joy that you are home at last on the Bruderhof. I write from distant Switzerland where the Hutterian movement began. My heart is full of thanks to God that he has protected you and helped you complete the work of uniting with the Hutterian brothers, and that the confirmation and mission for which all are waiting could now happen. I was deeply moved and full of thankfulness. I have written for you and Emmy on parchment the document[1] of the uniting and confirmation, which I will send you for your welcome, as well as some gentians I picked on the mountains of Georg Blaurock as a reminder of the Tirol.

To you, dear Ebbo, I want to express again today my heartfelt thanks for the difficult journey which you undertook for us. In this way you have shown your great love, for which we will always thank you!

What a wonderful homecoming that will be, and how much you will have to tell! I have only one wish, that in these days of deep and joyful experience, I will have the deepest inner community with you through the spirit which leaps over the mountain walls of the Alps. For in spite of the joy at your homecoming, you can imagine my other feelings after the long separation. Of these I do not want to speak at such an hour. Maybe my faith was not strong enough, otherwise I would surely have already been better as you wrote so lovingly.

My thoughts and prayers have accompanied you hourly on the sea, and will continue to be with you when you are finally together with Emmy and the children and also celebrate on the Bruderhof. In a few days I will write you about my work and homecoming.

Always with you in great thankfulness, your faithful

Else

---

[1]See p.184.

A song for Eberhard's return

HOMECOMING

O mighty God, our Father,
We thank Thee from our hearts!
Protection hast Thou given
O'er land and sea afar

To him who was Thy envoy
In foreign lands unknown.
Thou gavest him fulfillment
In all his tasks for Thee.

In love the Spirit binds us
In Jakob Hutter's Church.
The Spirit binds forever
All those who witness true.

This mission Thou hast given
To gather all Thy band,
That they, united living,
Share all things from Thy hand.

Our lamps are kindled, ready;
For holy oil we plead
That when Thou, Lord, appearest,
We haste to follow Thee!

Else von Hollander
Written for Eberhard's return
from America, May 1931

To the tune of *"Mein Gott, ich tu Dich bitten"* ("My God, I ask and pray Thee").

Standing Together

Introductory Remarks

On his return to the Rhön Bruderhof in May 1931 Eberhard Arnold told of his experiences with the Brothers in North America and what concerned him for the future of the Hutterian Church there and in Europe. After a year away, he also wanted a report of events at the Rhön Bruderhof. All of this was written about to Else, who was still away in the Alps on account of her poor health.

He also wrote back to the Brothers in America, sharing his concerns, and pointing out the dangers he saw within the Hutterian Church. His letter of June 15, 1931 to Elias Walter is especially important.

In July 1931 and again in June 1932 a printed Sendbrief was sent from the whole Brotherhood in Germany to every family on every Bruderhof in North America. These—and other—letters described the mission work and the gathering of new members especially from Switzerland. They tell of the need of buildings to house and land to feed the growing community and beg the Brothers to send help so that "the zealous" can be gathered.

With the coming to power of Hitler a time of persecution broke in upon the church in Germany. By early 1934 a second Bruderhof had to be established, the Alm Bruderhof high up in the mountains of Liechtenstein, where the children could be educated free from the hateful spirit of Nazi teaching and the young men of military age could continue to serve a life of brotherhood.

The economic need intensified, as can be seen in the later letters. Eberhard Vetter traveled between the two hofs, his broken leg in a cast, trying to protect the church from the worst need. He had no time to write. His wife Emmy shared the bitter need in letters to America. Her husband's untimely death in November 1935 left the two communities without a Word leader to guide them through these troubled times.

But God was faithful. In spite of human weakness and unfaithfulness, the Brotherhood was protected. Through the God-given presence of Michael Waldner Vetter, Bon Homme, SD, and David Hofer from James Valley, Manitoba, at the moment of dissolution of the Rhön Bruderhof in 1937, all members were able to leave Germany and reunite on the Cotswold—and later Oaksey—Bruderhofs in England.

The unity with the entire Hutterian Church was upheld and reaffirmed in a letter from Joseph Kleinsasser, elder of the Schmiedeleut, in June 1939. It was confirmed anew in 1974, and stands to this day.

243

Irmgard Keiderling
Rhön Bruderhof
May 15, 1931

Dear Tata,[1]

Today I want to try again to share with you something about the events of the last days; whatever I have taken down in shorthand I have put in quotes, and all the rest I tell according to my memory and with the help of my notes. But my report will always need to be supplemented and improved, especially since I have hardly taken any shorthand notes for about a year, and am pretty well out of practice.

On Tuesday evening we saw the play of the Ten Virgins on the meadow of the burial ground. Its deep meaning in this serious hour was especially impressive. At the end of the play Eberhard Vetter set all the torches in the ground in a ring, and we made a big circle around them. Eberhard then spoke about unity in voluntary freedom and freedom in unity, against all legalism and halfheartedness. He said that just as he and Emmy formed a new unity of two, and just as the Hutterians in America made a bond with us, uniting our two groups, so Christ and the Church are bound together in true unity and freedom without any rules. His words were so living and powerful, always in symbolic unison with the torches.

At first all twelve torches were burning, and he spoke of the pouring out of the Holy Spirit over the twelve disciples. Suddenly two torches went out and five burned very faintly. Then he spoke of the five wise and the five foolish virgins and again affirmed that our way is truly a way of complete freedom that allows no halfheartedness; anyone who is halfhearted and unwilling should leave immediately, to be given over to the judgment of God.

He spoke about the temptation of the false prophets in today's Christianity, who always want to tempt God with the words, "Did God really say that?" They believe that true unity in community is only possible through the strictness of the law, and therefore they mix the spirit of the world with the spirit of God. He pointed to the significance of faith. He told of the great love and voluntary dedication of the Hutterites, their great sense of responsibility, and mentioned that Hutterianism had nothing to do with legalism and its restrictions. At times he spoke enthusiastically and loudly of the freedom given to us, and emphasized even more loudly that each one who does not go this way wholeheartedly should remain outside and keep his hands

---

[1]Else von Hollander, still in the Alps on account of her health.

off, saying that the doors are open for anyone to come in and to go out again. He said all this so loudly that even the nightwatchman on the Bruderhof could hear.

I believe everyone was deeply moved. When only two torches were still burning brightly, Eberhard went inside the circle, placed them together so that they flared up still more brightly, and spoke of our uniting with Hutterianism, whereby both groups with their different characteristics should complement each other and yet be completely one, as is the case in a true marriage.

We then sang *"Gott ist Geist und Kraft"* ("God is Might and Fire") and went home in a procession with torches. Back on the hof, we stood in a circle and sang the evening blessing, "Lord, protect and bless us."

The confirmation of Eberhard's task given him by the Hutterian Brothers should actually have been on Wednesday evening. Eberhard was to resume his accustomed place in the Brotherhood, and Hans was to be released from representing him. But since Mama was very tired, and Emy-Margret also was not so well and had been sent to bed by Mama, this important meeting took place only on the following day, Ascension Day. Wednesday's Brotherhood meeting was, as it were, a transition to the subsequent meeting, in which Eberhard wanted to get his bearings.

We began with considering the novices: Joseph, since coming back for the second time, has found his way very well into the life in his own way; he takes a more active part, and is remarkably steady and reliable in the work; he is quite uncomplicated, talks in a childlike way, and loves to sing childlike songs. Also he has freed himself from the influence of the Catholic Church. Joseph was called in, and Eberhard asked him a few questions. Everyone rejoices that Joseph will be taken into the novitiate, and also Friedel, who, we must admit, has a good will for what is necessary for our life, and who certainly also has some faith. Gertrud Ziebarth was also taken into the novitiate, for, in spite of many weaknesses, she means it very seriously. Leo-Fritz, Trautel, Martha Sekunda, and Fritz Kleiner have asked to be taken into the Brotherhood. It was considered and decided to take Leo and Trautel into the Brotherhood on Sunday.

We have not talked in the Brotherhood yet about Gustav and Sigrid. With reference to them I'm writing to you only the main things that Eberhard said. What has happened with any of us before the Bruderhof time is blotted out by the very act and deed of repentance when we come out of the turmoil of sin and of our own will. If that is difficult for someone, he can go to the Word leader and make a confession, but that is not necessary. "Once it has been cleared up, the past is buried, done away with, forgiven and forgotten.

"That is why we come to baptism, where everything is in fact washed away, buried, and forgotten. That is why community is given us. . . . I will only say further: we don't want to dig up old matters, for it would be the absolute ruin of a community. But what we do want is that if in the life of an individual and in the life of the church, the demonic powers of the past spring up again, and through these powers from the past, some deception takes place against the common life, then and only then must we intervene in earnest. How far are they dragging old things around with them and in among us? Please not the past! We regard the past itself as fully finished with through the forgiving power of Christ, for he said, 'Accept the Holy Spirit; whosoever's sins you forgive, they will be forgiven.' Only when old sins surface, when they rear their serpent's head once more and snap and bite—then we can err again. That is the main thing that can be said about the matter.

"For us, the novitiate means that whoever takes that step has the obligation to live in Brotherhood with his whole will and love; and on the other hand it means that the Brotherhood takes this pledge quite seriously, but does not exaggerate its importance, so that it says, 'We believe that you are completely in earnest, but yet we advise you—agree to a testing time of a year; for it could happen that you go through a character crisis, in which you see things differently.'"

Gertrud Ziebarth said in the Brotherhood meeting that she has a very strong self-will, and that because of it she comes again and again into difficulties. Eberhard answered her more or less as follows, "What actually does this self-will want? Is it, after all, a will? If God is truly more important to us than anything else, then that doesn't mean a changed insight or an altered discernment, but it means that our self-willed striving flows into the striving of God's will, so that we will what God wills. Therein lies the salvation which Christ brought, that our sick will becomes healthy, since now our will desires the will of God. Thus we shall become sound, sensitive, stable people, instruments of the will of God—not in the sense of having no will but meaning that our members are the instruments of our brain cells, our hearts, and our nerves; that we become willing, with all the strength of our will. What we call self-will is in actuality no will at all. To strive for what *we* want in a certain situation is not important, since it is clearly a distortion of the will. There is no value in wishing for it. But when God's holy will comes over us, then we become willing people in another way, so that now the great and mighty goal, namely the precious substance of the kingdom of God, overpowers us. Now we know what we want. We will become willing people. . . . And Christ is ready to give us this will."

Early yesterday morning, Ascension Day, we came together in the Brotherhood. Firstly, Eberhard asked Hans about the inner situation of our Bruderhof; secondly, whether we are in agreement with the results of his journey; and thirdly, he asked for an account of our practical situation.

Hans began, and reported about the past year. The experience of the baptism was most decisive for the first period when we were alone, as it was done completely in the context of Eberhard's journey and his task in America. In spite of all the struggles which soon followed, we were able to find a foundation quite quickly. We met together very often, and came forward well.

Just a year ago today, on Ascension Day, we had the encounter with the representatives of New Russia—Dr. Kellner and others—and afterwards we had the impression that our witness had been rather poorly represented.

There followed struggles, personal failures, especially in a decisive moment.

We had to fight, especially with Pharisaism and flirting which don't go together with Hutterian humility and *Gelassenheit*. Of course the incidents were cleared up and done away with. The Michel Hasel Book was a help to us. This book expresses especially what is most important: mission. We also had struggles with the so-called "tail of guests"—people who actually were not seeking much, and yet stayed. There was little left of the high tide of guests in July, and few of the visiting relatives remained. One of the more important visitors during the guest period was Richard Träger. Erich and Ernestine Mohr came for the second time during the work week, and Karl Falkner came for the third time about a fortnight ago.

Hans also told about reading Hutterian teachings, standing behind the American journey, and also the decision to send Emmy.

In August and September some exams took place: Emy-Margret, Liesel, and Sophie—later Hardy, Ruth, Hansemann.

At Pentecost we read a great deal from Matthias Müller on John 3. There was a meeting with Erich Mohr.

On the third day of Pentecost the horse Freya died.

Little Ula was born.

In these eventful days Erich Mohr laid his proposals before us, but we could not deal with them properly. That was our mistake.

We shared together about the uniting of September 14.

At this time we read the *Worms-Prozess*. About the leaving of Hannah Paulmann: Eberhard did not take this very tragically, and said, one could see her as a guest, who mistakenly called herself a novice.

Then we spoke at some length about the work week. On October 27, as a consequence of the work week, we experienced a crisis in the Brotherhood. The following time was somewhat better.

In the meetings in the morning we read Acts 2, and the Wisdom of Solomon.

We started with copying work. Eberhard drew attention to your beautiful handwriting and said, "We must learn to write as the forefathers have written."

At the end of the past year we concerned ourselves often with the questions of pictures and musical instruments. In this connection the question of law and freedom came up. Eberhard expressed that it was in no way a matter of forbidding pictures. The question simply is: Does the spirit of brotherliness and love, does this spirit urge us to lay these things aside as much as possible in order to understand Hutterianism? . . . In this we can remain frank and open. We want to strive courageously for a simple and pure style, but continue seeking our direction in regard to pictures. With music it is more complicated. It is not forbidden. It only amounts to this: no music is tolerated which produces religious ecstasy. The Hutterites cannot say that instrumental music is evil in itself; the main point is that living the truth should be free from any musical suggestion. All this is especially understandable because the Hutterites originate from the sixteenth century. The Catholic Church used three senses as a sort of religious intoxication: smell (in the use of incense), hearing (through the playing of instruments), and sight (in the viewing of idolatrous pictures of the saints); yes, even in the sense of taste (kissing some wooden statue of a saint). All the five senses are involved in this continuous intoxication. This explains the attitude of the Hutterites. In contrast they say, "What is important is the recognition of the truth, doing the will of God, leaving everything to do the will of God, in possessionless communism. We want to count the cost beforehand. He who does not want to do this, should leave it alone. We do not want to overwhelm people through religious intoxication. We want no frenzy, no sentimentality. We want the total purity of the spirit." One could call it soberness and objectivity. This and even more Eberhard expressed in a wonderfully clear and understandable way.

So it is not music, also not pictures which the Hutterites reject, but idolatry in every form; the intrusion of music into worship; art should not lead us into an illusion which displaces our clear recognition and decisiveness.

In response to a question whether the simple Hutterian folk were clear about this, Eberhard gave the following example: He once met two young Hutterites in a coffee house. When Eberhard remarked, "If only this awful music would stop," one of them said, quite astonished, "Don't you like it? We like it very much. That is why I always sit here so long." This shows that they are not against any one particular kind of music (e.g. coffee house music). Their only concern is that music does not get smuggled in and thus cloud their clear recognition of the truth. The Hutterites often asked Eberhard, "Do you also sing our tunes as we sing them?"

Here the following words of Eberhard are of great importance for us: "I am of the opinion that our turning to Hutterianism means that we should become like the early Hutterites. We don't want to become Hutterites in the sense of 1692; we don't want to become Hutterites in the sense of 1780; we also don't want to become Hutterites in the sense of 1930-1931; but we do want to become Hutterian in the sense of 1529-1589, in the sense of these first fifty years. With this the Hutterites are in agreement. They also listened when I told them, 'You don't act like them! You are not like them! You are missing a lot! You must go forward more on the offensive, more aggressively!' Then they said, 'Yes, we would be glad if you could do it better, only come over here!' They are also very thankful and say, 'We cannot contradict you. We can in no way contradict Arnold Vetter.' "

Hans went on with his report: Our impression of Ulrich Stadler; Eberhard's Sendbrief; the turn of the year; time of human weaknesses. Tata's illness weighed heavily on us. In January we had to fight the lying spirit again in all circles of our household, including the young people and children.

Political and natural events were of decisive importance. Eberhard drew attention to Russia's five-year-plan which everyone is talking about. A consequence was that our means of support had also lost its value, since Russia had flooded the market with wheat so that the price declined by one third. We spoke of the wave of National Socialism, about the mission task through books, journeys, talks. Eberhard thinks that all these things find an answer in brotherly community. The kingdom of God is the answer.

After this the second part of the meeting began. The results of Eberhard's journey. We read the documents of the appointment and confirmation and the letter of September 14.

Eberhard: First of all you must take me again into the Brotherhood through your agreement with the Hutterites' support of my appointment as Word leader. . . .

In short, the overall impression of my journey is as follows: the community life of three thousand five hundred souls in America is something overpoweringly great. That means that the spirit of community on these thirty-three Bruderhofs is genuine, pure, clear, true, and deep. Their teachings also are so unadulterated that I must assert: there is nothing in the whole world, neither in the available books and writings handed down, nor anything in present-day life-communities, which can be compared to the essence, character, and spirit of the Brotherhoods men know as Hutterian; nothing else could bring us forward or deepen us more strongly.

So, in full recognition of our origins inspired by the Youth Movement, of our experience of communal living, and of the Sermon on the Mount, I want to work for our growing fully into Hutterianism.

I am given the authority by the Hutterites to commence a great mission task for this life throughout the whole of Europe, so that even the money we accept from the Hutterites is untainted. Our entry into Hutterianism is quite independent of the need for money. Even if we had met completely impoverished communities, we would not have hesitated for one moment to unite with them. The question of financial support is of a secondary nature, but it follows the first step of becoming incorporated. We accept gladly every assistance from the Brothers, knowing that the fact of accepting this money does not influence our attitude to money or trouble our conscience. That in short is the outcome of my journey.

Hans: We cannot thank you enough that in spite of great difficulties you remained for so long over there until this goal was achieved. We surely cannot yet foresee all the consequences of this confirmation and incorporation. The direction we took for our beginning has been confirmed in a unique way, the only way it could have happened. We ask you now to take over the leadership of the Church as you find right after studying and getting to know the Hutterites through many months.

Eberhard: Early-Sannerz, early-Christianity, early-Hutterianism, true-humanity!

For my part, I would like also to relieve our dear Hans Zumpe of his burden, in the name of the Hutterian Brethren in America, who are united through God's Spirit, live accordingly, and have the faith which is active in love. In the name of all those communities I want to relieve Hans, and also all the others who have held any kind of service. We have proof that the power of the Spirit and of love has not grown dim, that grace has not forsaken us, and that the witness of the life has been strong. In spite of little help, Hans has succeeded in coming through the economic needs again and again, and reaching the shore with the little ship, which held more debts than treasures.

Eberhard greeted Hans in this way, and suggested him as assistant to the Word leader, to which the whole circle answered with complete, joyful agreement, and all were united that the best confirmation of his service had been given during the past year. Eberhard suggested that the full confirmation should come about only after Hans's wedding. The assistance to the Word leader should not be understood in the sense that now two people would lead the church; the Word leader alone would do that. But every Word leader should have a helper by his side to read the Word of God, and represent him when he is not present. He also stands staunchly at his side in caring for the people.

Hans's main task shall at present be the steward service. Eberhard also mentioned the possibility of sudden death. In this case the gift of laying on of hands which Eberhard had brought with him from the Brothers, would not be confined to him alone.

(Irmgard adds greetings in her own hand—her typewriter has given out!)

Irmgard Keiderling
Rhön Bruderhof, May 27, 1931

Dear Tata,

In today's letter I will tell you about the first day of Pentecost. We met in a big circle with all the guests to give an opportunity for questions and to speak about our main concern on this special Sunday.

Our main concern is which spirit can be called the spirit of Pentecost and what this spirit does. A further question concerns our guests: "What is the spirit of the Bruderhof, and is it the same or another spirit?"

The guests included Heinz Bolck, Ulrike, and father and mother Schultheiss. The question came up, "What brings the community to live in such a heart to heart relationship, and what is its basis?"

Eberhard: I would like straightaway to pass the ball to the ten or twelve old members from Sannerz and this Bruderhof to answer this question; but first I will tell you about the impression I received on returning from nearly a year's absence. It is very difficult—almost impossible—to express in words what I feel when I watch the life and activity on the hof from the verandah, or go anywhere else where I can see all this life and activity. A deep, powerful feeling moves my heart when I am among you—not only in the wonderful meetings; not only in our most holy times of quiet together; not only when I see in my room and about me the copies of writings and the presents you have made me in love. I have the deep impression that God has protected you through his Holy Spirit in a wonderful way. After more than ten years' experience I am not surprised when I see a weakness here and there, in the work or some other place. That is not hidden from me. I have the feeling that these weaknesses have not in any way increased, or kept you from being true to the right way. I have the strong impression that the Whitsun spirit of true church community has worked a powerful miracle here, not only in holding you together, but in doing something far greater. I believe this spirit has upheld you on the right way. There is no standing still on this way, only going forward, and so I must acknowledge that the church community on our Bruderhof has clearly gone forward. It is hard to say what shows me this. It has nothing to do with individual people, either Hans or anyone else. Nor is it that the sum of persons collectively makes for more strength than the individual. But, especially in these days, I have the very strong impression that it is the question of a spirit which is far above me or any one of us. It is the question of a spirit that does not come from us or from the fact of our living together, or from our confession of faith. Already in Sannerz and now here on the Bruderhof, I have received the strong impression that something wonderful and unique is at work.

Over there I was with brotherhoods that also live in full community of goods. The wonderful thing is that the same love rules there too; love from the Spirit, that bears fruit through faith, leading to work.

There is a very clear difference. These communities are characterized by a thoroughly clear steadiness, endurance, and firmness, and that is something quite powerful. I must testify again and again that the spirit over there is the same as here, and that we cannot in any way stand apart from them. We must be together with them and they with us. And yet our Bruderhof community has a character completely of its own. How can that be explained? The gifts of the Spirit are many-sided and different. In spite of our beards, our Bruderhof has not yet been given that quiet steadfastness that is found over in America on the old Bruderhofs with a four hundred-year-old history. One could say that the Brothers over there are given the particular spiritual gift of ruling the church, the firmness of character of mature manhood and a fatherly and grandfatherly manliness. As John writes: "I am writing to you, fathers, because you know him who is from the beginning. I am writing to you, young men, because you have overcome the evil one. I write to you, children, because you know the Father and the word of God remains in you." That is my impression of the Bruderhofs over there. This constancy, steadfastness, and unshakeability of manly brotherhood is a gift of their fatherly and grandfatherly nature. "You know the very foundation of faith and have matured in the depths of faith." That is why the old fathers are of such decisive importance, for even the young men there have this unshakeable firmness of character which belongs to true manhood and is a gift of the Spirit. How is it with us? Are we still at the stage of childhood, unaware and innocent, putting ourselves trustingly in the Father's hands? Do we find ourselves still at the stage of the unconscious and subconscious where we have not yet learned to walk . . . and where problems have not yet arisen for us? . . . But the budding strength is obviously there and the feeling of being sheltered in the family community of the Father, of the coming kingdom. . . . Perhaps we are at this childish stage of the new birth. Is this our situation? Perhaps we are already at the stage of youthfulness, of developing maidenhood and of young manhood which storms and presses forward. But I think that in this youthful development we have actually reached a deeper insight so that the word of God will remain with us. At this stage our awareness of God's presence is no longer instinctive or subconscious; instead, we are living in a state of war with the prince of this world. That is the young person's breakthrough from the subconscious to a conscious fight. After this breakthrough, he is further equipped for struggle, because the word of God is constantly with him. This is the maturity I would wish for us, that the true reality of the word of God is constantly with us and in us; that truth leads us, and no longer the exuberant feeling that we could throw the devil out of this world. For if the word of God remains in us and among us; if it is held deep in our hearts after it has been written on our hands and on our brow; if the word of God, the complete revelation of the truth is constantly with us, then we have reached the time of youth and of manly courage.

God wants to free us, so that no one remains caught in the surging emotions of puberty. He wants to lead us forward toward manhood, so that we develop into young people in whom the objective truth grows strong in manliness. I have the feeling that during the past year a little progress has been made in this direction and something of it has become firmly anchored in your hearts. It is an infinite joy to me that after passing through the unconscious and subconscious stage and that of exuberant confidence that we can overcome Satan, we are gradually breaking through and merging ever more deeply into the reality of God's kingdom and his revelation. I rejoice that in our youthfulness we have become a little more manly, although of course none of us are fathers like the old Brothers with whom we are now joined in community.

That is why I ask you to tell me and our friends how you explain the deep bond between us and the deepest roots of our common life.

As we sat together on the terrace a little while back and came into conversation with one another, I could not help thinking how easily and intimately we can talk in our big circle of forty to fifty people in a way that elsewhere in the world is possible only between two or three. There, as soon as many are together they are no longer able to do this.

It is still more the case with community of work, where, too, I have the feeling that the spirit of mutual sharing has taken hold of us more strongly, and that practical sharing and cooperation in our work are growing among us. I still feel the overwhelming joy of coming home and seeing you again, and I am inexpressibly happy to be in your midst, yes, in our midst. I feel blowing among us the spirit which is the only source and explanation of this community.

Irmgard continues:

For the first time we could do what had been expressed in the previous days as the wish and longing from our midst: as a united circle we could lift our hands to God and kneel before him together.

The fact that we could do this will show you how intensively we experience our communal life at the moment, especially through what Eberhard has brought to us from America. A special example of this was when we went up to the fire on the third day of Pentecost, and other meetings at which Eberhard portrayed the difference so clearly. I hope to report more about this later.

At the moment we are having glorious summer weather here—in fact, it's very hot. Because of all the work outside, we have decided to have our midday meal at noon, followed by two and a half or three hours for Brotherhood meetings and not have supper till eight o'clock. Then we will have a short meeting for worship, which includes everyone, and go early to bed so that we can get up early next day, fresh and full of energy for the work. This means that during the great heat at midday we will sit in the cool Brotherhood room—not to sleep, but to do work with the mind and spirit. It will be like this from tomorrow on.

Now I must close. Heartfelt greetings from your

Irmgard

Katharina Waldner
Bon Homme Bruderhof, SD, 1931

A letter to Arnold Vetter and family and to all brothers and sisters.

I will also answer you.
Because we got to know you,
We will not forget you so easily.
Dear brother Eberhard Arnold!
    Praise God that we have seen
    One another united in love.
    Also that we have been strengthened in God
    With song and prayer in supplication
    Like the brotherhood
    Of the early Christians
    Was united in God
    As one heart and soul.
    But now we are saddened.
    It brings pain to our heart
    That we, here on earth,
    Have to part from one another.
    But this separation
    Will last for only a short time.
    Soon we will see one another again
    With Jesus in great rejoicing.

Dear brother Arnold Vetter, we rejoice greatly in the spirit that you are such a loving, gifted brother. May God bless you and help you to keep your dear community upright. Without God's help we cannot do and accomplish anything. He must send us his Holy Spirit from above, and we must ask God for the good spirit. Without him we cannot endure in community because it was through the Holy Spirit that community was established. And God the Father, Son, and Holy Spirit are one. We have promised on our knees with God's help to surrender ourselves completely to God and the church, to sacrifice ourselves, even at the cost of our lives.

A song says:
Fight to the blood and your last breath.
Press on into God's kingdom.
If Satan wants to oppose you,
Do not grow faint or weak.

May God be with you on your long journey home to your beloved *Gemein* and to your dear ones who are already waiting for you, dear Arnold Vetter, with great longing. May God send his angels to protect you from all misfortune on your long journey home. May he lead you home in good health just as Raphael led young Tobias back happy and in good health to his parents. That is our hope.

Dear brother Arnold Vetter, God has led you home in good health, where they all came to meet you. Their joy will have been very great. We would have liked so much to have you still among us, but that cannot be since you have been away from home for so long.

Oh, the evening was so short when you read to us and told in the school about your starting in the community.

Oh, that poor, dear girl who would have loved to be in the community to serve God and wanted to be set free from the world—and her parents did not allow it. I have so much pity on her. It nearly broke my heart as you told about her. When you get home, write to us about that dear girl—where she is.

But I would also love to read your letters if you write to Michel Vetter or to the whole community. Maybe Michel Vetter will read them to us.

When you spoke to us in the school, it was much too short for us women folk. It seemed to us just only a few minutes. We would have loved to listen for a longer time.

Now you, dear Arnold Vetter, you are out of sight, but not out of our hearts. We will not forget you so quickly, and we will not forget your loving teachings or talks, the way you expressed what community is, and how you imprint it into people's hearts. My husband, my dear Joseph, sometimes said to those who asked for baptism and came to him to be admonished and taught, "Oh," he would say, "if only I could, I would write it with my finger into your hearts, so that you could grasp it better." He devoted himself very much to the children. He was schoolteacher for twenty years and for some of that time servant too. He was a servant for thirty-four years. He was born on March 4, 1856, and passed away on May 5, 1915, with a heart attack. We were still talking together—then he began to die. You can imagine what pain of heart that brought to me and my children and the community too.

And now it was hard for me to be left behind with poor Zacharias. He always helped me to carry him at night, and I did not have to get up for him. Now I am old and have to do it by myself. I thank God that I can still do it. Dear Arnold Vetter, think of us in your prayer. The prayer of the righteous can achieve much when done in earnest. Now dear Arnold Vetter, we thank you for your visit, also for visiting me. Unfortunately, it was always too short for me.

Now I must close, so that it is not too long for you to read.

Farewell! It is most likely that we will not meet again on this earth. But with God's help we hope to meet in heaven. Grace and peace be with you from God our Father and Jesus Christ.

You dear sisters in the Lord, out of love to you I greet the whole community and with great joy that God let a light be kindled, so that a community was built up again. Though you are poor in temporal goods, God has never forsaken anyone who goes his way.

I am still pretty healthy considering my age, though I have also difficult times. It will only be on this earth; that is a comfort. The heavier the cross, the closer is heaven. A song even says that he who has no cross has not God. Therefore, I must persistently beg God for patience.

Now I wish that dear Arnold Vetter finds you all in the best of health in soul and body. That is the greatest treasure we have and blessed peace as well—for God has called us in peace. Our dear Savior said, "My peace I give to you; my peace I leave with you, not as the world gives."

Well, dear sisters, our dear brother will have lots to tell you about all the communities, and you will be as curious to hear about us as we were to hear about you. I wish I could be with you for a month and talk over everything with you. We are so curious about your dress and everything.

Two of our women folk do the cooking and yet another is the head cook. We have twelve-week periods—they cook on the twelfth week, two for the week. The girls start to cook when they are seventeen years old. But field work and other work they start at fifteen, milking too. They milk every third week, eight women each week. Dish washing is also done by us women every third week. Also eight are in the garden and fields for a week. The gathering of the wheat sheaves is done by women and girls up to the age of forty-five. Also the older brothers help there. The picking of corn is done by men and boys, women and girls. That takes about two weeks, then this work is done. Threshing is done earlier on, only by men with the threshing machine. In August and September we are very busy with drying apples for the community. The apples, shared out to families, we dry ourselves. We can also send them to Canada, since they have no apples there. Even after the age of forty-five, women still often help in the kitchen in the summer. In winter all women help with potato peeling. If everyone comes, it does not take long.

When we are fifty-five, we sit at the old people's table. We get better coffee and better milk. On January 29 I was seventy-two years old. I still help in the kitchen. If I am well, I still do my week's dishwashing. It is best to do some work.

In summer—June—is the time for spinning. We get one and a half pounds of wool per head from fifteen years up to the old people. The children in the big school get one and a fourth pounds, the Kleinschule get one pound, also the little ones. There is lots to spin in families of ten or thirteen; their girls from twelve years up help to spin. We do not put the spinning wheels away till all the women have finished. We help with knitting. We like to do it when we sit down to rest from gathering sheaves; there are many of us together. In summer they do their washing one week—four families in one day. The next week they do garden work and weeding. It does not take them all week. Each has her own sewing machine and does her own sewing, and anyone who needs help gets help.

Community is a wonderful work for one to help the other. On July 18 I will have been living in community for fifty-four years. I was eighteen years old when I came. I had such a longing for community. God knew what was in my heart, and therefore he helped me. I thank his wonderful name again and again for all his goodness. Widows and orphans are cared for so well. I can never complain about anything. Only it is hard for me to be separated from my beloved children. Eight of them moved to Canada. One son, Michel Waldner, a minister in Scharp Community, died there. Also my daughter Margretha Hofer, daughter-in-law of Rebeka Basel who walks with crutches, left behind six orphans. She was in her thirties. My Joseph W. is servant of the Word in Huron Community. My Jakob Waldner, steward at Bon Homme. Kath. Waldner, Michel Jos. Waldner, servant in Bon Homme. Daughter Maria and Paul Kleinsasser, Bon Homme. Daughter Elisabeth Waldner, Servant Mich Waldner, Jr., Bon

Homme. My son David J. Waldner, Bon Homme — all in Canada and all married. My son Johanes Waldner is work distributor *Weinzedel* and his wife is Sahra. My daughter Anna, her husband Danil Wipf, and poor Zacharias are with me. I have often hard times. I am not walking on a bed of roses. I hope through mercy and grace for something better in the world beyond. We poor folk have always to struggle. We must always be watchful so that we do not lose our salvation and blessedness.

I have seventy grandchildren. All live in community, which is a real joy; if only they were all God-fearing — that's what one would wish. Only one of the seventy got to love the world. He promises to come back. I hope the prayers and tears of his parents will have come before God. I also pray for him. His parents write heartrending letters to him. They would even melt a stone.

Now, dear brothers and sisters, all of you together, I have to come to an end with my poor writing. From all my heart I greet you each and all, young and old, no one left out, with the kiss of love, and our dear brother Eberhard Arnold Vetter once more with his dear wife and children and all brothers and sisters.

It will be hard for us to see dear Arnold Vetter leave.

Badly written but faithfully meant. My glasses do not fit; therefore it is so bad.

Write a letter back to me. It would be such a joy, also one from Arnold Vetter.

> This is a letter as a memory from Katharina J. Waldner
> *Brudergemein*, Bon Homme, Tabor, South Dakota
> to all brothers and sisters in Germany *Gemein*

Rhön Bruderhof, June 15, 1931

My beloved Elias Vetter,

Unfortunately, I did not manage to write to you on the ship as I had planned. I was not seasick, as I am not inclined to be so, but my other ailments were very troublesome. Now at home both my eyes are bad again, even the better one, and this is very unpleasant. Then on the ship many people came to me even when I was in bed, sharing their needs, confessing their sins, and asking me about true faith and true community. In Germany I have been accustomed to this ready inner contact with people who are deeply disturbed, though not yet Christian. But I did not encounter it in American cities. Now I met it again the moment I stepped on board a German ship, though I was not yet on German soil.

When I reached home, I had the great joy of being greeted and welcomed by the whole Bruderhof in deep gratitude to God and in the strength of complete unity of heart and mind in the spirit of Jesus Christ. To our great joy, the well-packed sacks that you and yours took so much trouble over have now arrived in Fulda. The contents of the first packing case, which came with me on the ship, had been shared earlier among the brothers and sisters, among jubilant thanks. You will learn of outward events in our common life from our steward's report and from the enclosed copies of my letters to other brothers. I ask you to read Hans Zumpe's letter with particular care. If you do not have enough copies of any of these, let us know and we will forward more to you.

Once again I was surprised by the inner life of our Bruderhof with its glowing first love and its burning enthusiasm for total dedication, self-surrender, unity, and community. On the other hand, after a whole year's absence and a deep insight into the dignified, serene, and peaceful atmosphere among you, our Bruderhof strikes me as rather passionate, youthful, and impetuous, and in need of your maturity and long experience.

Since I need to rest so much because of my eye, I have thought a lot about how I can best repay the great love you showed me during my journey. I am thinking of the general situation of your communities and of all brothers and sisters. Later maybe, if and when a request comes from someone over there, I would like to share in detail with all the elders what I see as your strength and as your weakness, and how the great strength given you by God can overcome the great danger presented by your weaknesses. To you, my beloved and deeply respected Elias Vetter, I can already touch upon these things briefly in this letter and tell you a little of my thinking. But I want to do this quite confidentially, that is, in the deepest trust between you and me only.

First, leadership through the Word should be represented more strongly and firmly in the service of the Word, particularly by the older brothers.

Second, those who serve through leadership should act in all things in full accord and innermost unity with all brothers.

Third, this is possible only if the gifts of bringing to belief, of warm encouragement, of speaking from heart to heart through the

Spirit in great love are living among the servants of the Word in the strongest possible way.

Fourth, every trace of personal property and private money ought to be completely done away with.

Fifth, the grave disorder of having small communities made up of a few related families must be completely stopped. In any case, family ties must never be placed above the spiritual community.

Sixth, then all evil gossip can be sharply fought and abolished. (Such evil gossip helped lead to the ending of the first great period of the church after the death of Andreas Ehrenpreis and Hans Friedrich Küntsche.) Furthermore, the differences between the three groups (Schmiedeleut, Dariusleut, and Lehrerleut) with their friendships among closely related families would not cause separation.

Seventh, instead, the uniting of all Bruderhofs in faithful obedience and innermost unanimity under one elder would be possible. This can happen only if the easily influenced brothers always submit to the firmer ones.

Eighth, I firmly believe that these seven goals, which seem almost unreachable, are in fact one goal and can be reached. For I have seen among you, in particular with you, dear Elias Vetter, that there is a great love coming from all brothers in all these closely knit groups. This love, rooted in pure and genuine faith, is coupled with the sharp teaching of truth and, in some places, with discipline still kept in its original force. Only when love keeps its salt and when salt keeps its love can true community be preserved. Then we will have the strength to show and maintain this love which never loses its salt, even towards the weakest brothers and those not always moved by the spirit, yet without taking sides.

Ninth, then the most serious danger to your present-day communities will be overcome in the following way: in the future a Bruderhof made up of closely knit families, an individual Hutterian community, will no longer consider itself the legal owner of its property, goods, fields, income, and harvests. Instead, in the obedience of faith and total surrender, the community will see itself as the steward of its goods and possessions, its livestock and fixtures, in the name of the whole church of God under the authority of the main elder. Only when the church is integrated and united in this clear way will we be able to withstand all the dangers with which the devil threatens us.

Tenth, therefore, I wish for all our church communities an Andreas Ehrenpreis for the present year 1931, who will bear a different name today but will reestablish the unity and the harmonious working together within the church with the same love, the same inner clarity, and the same well-defined order and strict discipline that he used. Without Andreas Ehrenpreis and such clear, firm co-servants as Hans Friedrich Küntsche in Kesselsdorf, the community would have collapsed long before 1699. That collapse would have occurred around 1650 or 1660 in the wake of all the terrible weakening and brutalizing effects of immorality brought about by the Thirty Years War and the Turkish invasions.

I do not believe that the habit of communal living can prevent the collapse of the community. Only the fact of daily asking for the Holy Spirit and the reality of the daily strength of this Holy Spirit in the proclamation of the Word and in the communal work can keep us in truly full community. Therefore, we are with you daily in our prayers, especially when, united with you in the Spirit, we bend our knees before God and raise our hands to him.

In the future we must find a way to send simpler greetings from time to time, so that you do not have to wait as long as you did this time for our detailed explanations and letters. It is very difficult that our best secretary, the one whose lettering you have so often admired, is now seriously ill with tuberculosis. Like my terribly thin daughter, Emy-Margret, whose marriage is planned for July 26, Else has spent several months with friends in the mountains of Switzerland. Otherwise she would certainly have lost her life.

The troubles facing me here were and are such a heavy burden, and the main facts are so well known to you, that I would rather not go into other details. Since your laying on of hands, I feel much more acutely the weight of responsibility for the right life for our seventy people, and this care and anxiety are agonizing.

We must provide rooms with bare necessities, yet fitting, for our six newly-married couples and receive the earnest and believing people who request to visit us. This is absolutely impossible, but we must nevertheless prove it possible through faith. For instance, there is the question of inviting a fifty-year-old tailor from Frankfurt. At the same time you, too, have many worries, which weigh on me also.

I should not actually have come home without the means needed for our sound building up. In spite of all your loving care, the journey through South Dakota, Manitoba, and especially through Alberta has been such a strain on me, both in body and in soul, that I have come home exhausted and will hardly be able to undertake such a long journey again.

All the more, we hope for a visit from our brothers and particularly from you, beloved Elias Vetter. We, your brothers and sisters who love you with all our hearts, plead for this once again. And especially I, your brother who loves you from the bottom of his heart and embraces you in trust and respect,

Eberhard Arnold

Emmy Arnold
Rhön Bruderhof, June 24, 1931

Dear Elias Vetter,

I greet you in God's grace! I do not know if you have heard that our Eberhard arrived safely in Bremen on May 10. You can well imagine our joy and thankfulness, for we have really missed him very much during this whole long year. But now we are so glad and thankful, especially when he tells us about you dear ones. We become more and more aware of how much ahead of us you are, and how we are only beginners on the way of community and faith. And yet we must confess that God has led us wonderfully, so that we are able to recognize the way of community and faith and to live it.

Eberhard very often reads to us from your old writings. Last Sunday we had the double wedding of two very beloved couples who have been among us for several years. Our hearts were deeply stirred by the Hutterian wedding ceremony and its power. On July 26 our eldest daughter Emy-Margret will marry our steward Hans Zumpe. Whenever we are able to prepare rooms for them, three other couples will follow.

For the last few weeks Eberhard has been writing to you dear ones about his journey, what he found in our Bruderhof, about the printing of the Small History Book [*Klein-Geschichtsbuch*] and so on. Although Eberhard's eye trouble is a great hindrance to him, his letter will surely be ready to send in a few days. His eyes do not look good; even his healthy eye is thought to be endangered. Recently he went to a very competent eye doctor in Bad Liebenstein, who wants to give him special treatment this fall at the latest. At that time the costs are lower than in summer, when so many people go there. Without this treatment the doctor considers the healthy eye also in danger. So we have a special request to you, dear brothers and sisters of Stand Off. Could you send us one hundred dollars so that Eberhard's eye can be cured? We would be so grateful if he could gain strength this fall, as he will surely go out this winter to speak at meetings and will need all his strength. I am writing the same request to David Hofer, James

Valley Bruderhof, asking him also for one hundred dollars, which will surely be needed. Eberhard will write to you himself about our economic situation and everything else.

Many of us want to thank you for the presents you sent us with Eberhard. They bring us great joy! The pillows, clothing, head scarves, aprons, yarn, soap, and so on, will be very useful to us. We also received very lovely presents from your Stand Off Bruderhof. There was a head scarf with the name Maria Tschetter, which our youngest daughter, thirteen-year-old Monika Elisabeth, is now wearing. Altogether, the Hutterian clothes are being worn with great joy and real reverence. When we wear them, we feel very much in harmony with you dear brothers and sisters so far away. We thank you from our hearts for all the love you have shown our Eberhard. We only wish and pray that you may also visit us some day.

Letters from other brothers and sisters of our community will follow soon.

With heartfelt love, in the community of Jesus Christ and in faith in him, we greet you in great thankfulness,

> Your Hutterian brothers and sisters in Germany
> Emmy Arnold

Peter Hofer Vetter   Rhön Bruderhof
James Valley Bruderhof   May/June 1931
Manitoba, Canada

Beloved Peter Hofer Vetter,

To you I want to send a very special greeting of love in the bond of friendship, although it will be very short, for I have taken a most lively interest in all your inner questions and spiritual tasks. I wish very much that you could once come to us for half a year, for I believe that just because of your calling and vocation the encounter with the mission church would be of greatest importance. But since it is even more important and urgent that our much beloved David Vetter be sent to us really soon from your Bruderhof, we will surely have to wait a few years for your loving visit. Till then, I would very much like to enter into a really deep and detailed correspondence with you. There is so much that we need to discuss and consider together, especially about the old writings and how we can best bring them home to the people of today.

Please greet your beloved, suffering wife and your children, also your father who is so dear to me, with very much love, from your

Eberhard Arnold
who thinks of you very much
in faithful, constant thankfulness

Andreas Gross   Rhön Bruderhof
Old Elm Spring   1931

My dearly beloved Andreas Vetter,

The peace of God, the love of Jesus Christ, and the fellowship of the Holy Spirit be with you and all!

Please give my heartfelt greetings to your dear wife and your dear co-worker, Peter Kleinsasser, also to your steward, Jakob Wipf, and all brothers and sisters. Please convey my warmest thanks to all of them for your loving hospitality and for the gift you dear ones put together for our Bruderhof. I want to tell you also how deeply thankful I am for the faithful care you took of my eyes, and for the gift of the wonderful teachings to take with me.

My long delay in writing has been due in part to the poor condition of my eyes. It has also been due to the strain of the great amount of difficult work awaiting me here, which would have taxed the strength of the healthiest man.

Please tell all your brothers and sisters that we plan to send our printed letter to your address, a copy for each of your twenty-three families and the nine single, baptized people. This letter is being set up in type and printed, but printing it on the hand press in our own printing shop means quite a lot of work still. But we want to send it to you as soon as possible.

In this printed letter you will find everything important about our work and what is happening to us. And you will certainly be glad to hear of the grace given to us, the enthusiasm of the Holy Spirit, the earnestness of love, dedication, and self-surrender that hold sway in our faithful brothers and sisters. You will also be glad to hear of the many zealous newcomers. During recent weeks some twelve to twenty of them have been among us every day. Again and again we are moved to bring close to them the full gospel of complete community and the grace of Jesus Christ, which results in complete obedience in faith to the church. The printed letter will tell you in more detail about these guests. They come not only from Sweden, Austria, Holland,

and Czechoslovakia (which now includes the district known to the old Hutterites as Moravia), but especially from all parts of Germany. A large group wants to come also from Switzerland to seek and find the will of God in actual community and true discipleship of Christ. You will see at once that this faces us with very hard tasks we are unable to master in our own strength.

We also know how difficult it is for you in America, since the dry summer brought poor prices for wheat and only a slight improvement in prices for rye. We know well how hard this will make it for you to care for your big communities in the way they are used to, with their more-than-good standard of living. You will find it especially hard when with your 139 souls, Elm Spring 178, Joseph Vetter of Rockport 164, Big Bend 141, Jamesville[1] 139, Wolf Creek 143, and David Vetter of Rockport 170, the question comes up of starting a new Bruderhof. Added to this is the fact that the two well-loved Bruderhofs in South Dakota cannot move across the border, and you may have to take over the Wolf Creek Bruderhof for your families.

But how much worse it is for our beloved brothers and sisters in the dear Manitoba communities where the number in each community has greatly increased! For instance, Zack Vetter's Rosedale Bruderhof has 154 souls, and Joseph J. Waldner of Huron has 143. Then there is our dear Michael Waldner's Bon Homme, and most difficult of all, the Maxwell Bruderhof of Joseph Hofer with 179 souls. These dear Manitoba brothers will have a hard time starting a new settlement. But faithful Michael Waldner Vetter in Bon Homme, South Dakota, with his 178 souls, will probably reach his goal sooner and more easily, since his corn did not turn out as badly as his wheat. Nevertheless, I am convinced that if their servants of the Word are faithful and watchful, these very big hofs are far better off, both in temporal and spiritual matters, than some too-small hofs in Alberta. Some of them number even less than we do. There are seven of your Bruderhofs which have seventy-five souls or less, like us. And there are two with even less than sixty. It seems to me very regrettable that the smallest Bruderhof of all, Murphy, numbers only forty souls. When there are so few people the great, holy cause too easily takes a back seat to personal family concerns. So, dear Andreas Vetter, I really cannot wish that you divide your community very soon.

We here feel strongly that the expected growth of our small Bruderhof of seventy-five souls will lead us forward inwardly and

---

[1]Spring Valley near Rockyford.

help us not only in temporal things but especially in our spiritual life.

My deepest and most heartfelt thanks go to God for his great grace in showing me so much through all of you, for all I was able to learn with you, and for the teachings, truth, and experience I could bring back with me. A far stronger and more definite power than we had experienced before has come to us through the three weddings which I have held here; through the election of our steward, Hans Zumpe, as my helper in the service of the Word; through the great gratitude and deep enthusiasm with which the teachings are accepted in our meetings for prayer; through the old books and writings that have become so tremendously precious to our brothers and sisters; and most of all through the whole picture of your life and faith—indeed, through the blessing of my appointment and confirmation through you. So all our brothers and sisters thank you from their hearts for your help in temporal and spiritual matters and ask that God's grace may richly and gloriously replace and repay what you have given.

I thank you for your great love and embrace you with the arms of my heart. Bound to you in faith and in the love of God and of Jesus Christ, your loving

Eberhard Arnold

Jerg Waldner   Rhön Bruderhof
Miama, New Drayton   1931
Alberta

Dearly beloved Jerg Vetter,

The peace of God, the love of Jesus Christ, and the community of the Holy Spirit be with you and all of you!

You will certainly have wondered why I have not thanked you for the gift of four hundred dollars your Bruderhof decided on and sent to us. We received it with heartfelt gratitude, and I ask you to express our thanks again to your dear brothers and sisters. In the hard times that now have the whole world in their grip, I ask you also to pray to God that his kindness may repay your love in a special way.

My health is not too good. My eyes are still very weak and often very bad. Besides this, the work is so pressing and the poverty here is so great that I have to ask you to excuse me in love when I cannot write as often and as punctually as I long to with all my heart.

There is a great longing here for the word of God and his glorious

truth as contained in the old writings and books I brought with me
from you beloved brothers and sisters.

Warmest thanks to you and Peter P. Hofer for the teachings you
have given me. He is very dear to me, and I ask you to give him my
greetings. You would be astonished at the glowing participation and
innermost enthusiasm with which our brothers and sisters receive the
service of the Word at the *Lehr* and *Gebet*, and all the readings from
the word of God and from the old books. We have now chosen our
steward, Hans Zumpe, to be my helper in this service.

You will see how things are here from his report as steward. I hope
you will read this report with dear Peter Vetter, your dear wife, your
dear father-in-law, and your dear steward. Please greet them all from
me. While you do this, old Peter Vetter, whom I have grown to love
so much, will certainly be sitting by the cradle and rocking the baby
to sleep. I have gained very much from his words and from the deep
insights and the rays of hope God has revealed to him through the
holy Word and the history of the church. To all eternity I shall thank
God for the gracious guidance that brought me several times to you
all. I simply cannot describe how very much I learned with all of
you. Through you I have gained depth and clarity and have recognized
truth more deeply. I firmly believe that the years to come will gradually
show how the blessing you sent to Germany in confirming me in the
service of the Word will have its effects on the work of our Bruderhof.
Through this I was able to join three couples in Christian marriage.
For this wedding we read the oldest orders of the Brothers and the
oldest teachings and prefaces on I Corinthians 7 and Ephesians 5,
which made a powerful impression on our circle and also on our guests.

You will find all this, and all that I want to tell you besides, in the
printed letter that is almost ready in our printing shop for every family
on every Bruderhof among you.

Today's letter is only a heartfelt greeting of thanks to you all and
has to be short. Every day for several weeks we have had sometimes
twelve and sometimes more than twenty guests, eager to hear the
word of God. They confide in me, confess their former lives, and
long for the right foundation of faith and for full community. In
addition, there is the regular work of printing the Small History Book,
the farming, the workshops, and the household, so I must ask you to
let me close now.

All that remains is to send greetings to your dear work distributor,
your dear bone doctor, your dear teacher, and all your brothers and
sisters in advance of our printed letter.

I greet you once more in the love of God, which is poured into our hearts through the Holy Spirit.

From your ever grateful, most humble brother,

Eberhard Arnold

From a Sendbrief written by Eberhard Arnold and signed by the whole Brotherhood, printed on the printing press of the brothers called Hutterians on the Bruderhof near Neuhof, Kreis Fulda, Hessen-Nassau, Germany.

July 1931

To the church of God on the Bruderhofs in America
to the Brothers called Hutterians
in South Dakota, Manitoba, and Alberta

O brothers, what a tremendous struggle has come over the church of God! How we have had to wrestle with wild beasts! How much we needed to be armed with the spiritual weapons the Holy Spirit speaks of in the Scriptures! And if God had not stood by us with his great power, we would certainly all have been driven apart, scattered, and destroyed. But God has been our victory and captain; he has held us together like a strong wall and powerful fortress. (From Jakob Hutter's letter to the church in Tirol in the year 1533, sent with brother Peter Voit from Auspitz in Moravia to the Adige Valley)

Dear brothers, whom we love with all our hearts, and all beloved brothers and sisters in South Dakota, Manitoba, and Alberta,

We greet you, each one, with these words of our brother and forerunner, Jakob Hutter, a witness through martyrdom. These few words most aptly and concisely express the hope of our faith and our whole situation in the present world epoch. In this Holy Spirit of God, this spirit of Jesus Christ, we wish for you as for ourselves full unity in God's peace, full joy in the love of Jesus Christ, and full strength in the community of the Holy Spirit.

Certainly neither we nor you have yet come into such tremendous struggle and conflict as our early brothers in the bloody persecution of that beginning time. We have not yet been expelled from house and home into bitter poverty and starvation. But without doubt these things will come over us in our time.

Brothers, the last hour is near! We all perceive this in the countless antichrists and false prophets, in war and danger of war, uprisings and massacres, earthquakes, damage to crops in the fields, rising prices here in Germany and insufficient farming returns there in America, lack of money, and bankruptcy everywhere. The injustice of mammon, impurity, and immorality are on the increase. Should the love of most of those who have been called to faith now grow cold? You are oppressed by drought, floods, and possible loss of harvest, embarrassment through debts and the stubbornness or financial straits of those who owe you money, unfortunate or untimely purchase of land, and last but not least, the long-standing restriction on sales across the border, affecting two of your more favorably purchased and well-equipped new colonies. All this is the uplifted hand of the almighty God, who speaks to us as to you and to you as to us, "Repent, for the kingdom of God is at hand!"

So we all sit on *one* bench. God calls us all together. He should not call in vain. With us as with you, with you as with us, yes, with all of us brothers in America and in Germany, no injustice should gain the upper hand, no heart should grow cold, and no deed of love be left undone or postponed. No community or close-bound group should seek its own advantage at the expense of other communities. Instead we want to let the true community order of surrender and discipline, the true fruits of love and unity, grow and materialize in work and deed and mutual help.

The approaching judgment of God is his love. As his discipline, this love wants to judge and direct us aright, to prepare and hearten us. May God's hour at long last be recognized and held fast to! This means that all the brothers who are by nature soft or lenient follow the sharper and firmer ones, obeying the spirit of the united church. Likewise those brothers who are harder, slower to respond, more anxious and less easily moved, follow the compassionate heart of God in Jesus Christ, take on the task of carrying the weaker ones, and put an end to all grievances and abuses through firm, loving counsel. Thus they give spiritual as well as temporal help wherever needed for the honor of God and of the church. This way of the holy spirit of love will reveal God's hour. It will also be a sign of his hour when we, over here and over there, plainly show to all the world that we are one united church of God in all spiritual and temporal matters: united under one elder with the main spiritual authority; united in dress and modesty; united in order and purity; united in poverty and possessionlessness; united in the management of property and work; united in caring for the poor; united in oneness of heart in the service of the Word; also united in mission and in seeking and accepting new and zealous hearts into the church as into the ark in the last days.

Then if the main elder, with the advice of his co-elders, has to take in hand the removal of wrongs and weaknesses in the services of the Word or of temporal need, all of us, especially those affected, should be thankful from our hearts for this spirit of grace and discipline.

The printing of the Small History Book [*Klein-Geschichtsbuch*] is a reminder of the early power-filled elders of the church from Jakob Hutter until Andreas Ehrenpreis. Here these thoughts of God for his church become so clear and living for us that we cannot doubt that God's unchangeable will wants to be revealed. Surely it will be revealed today in his church in America and in his church in Germany, as in the church of Moravia and Hungary long ago. How much we thank you from the depths of our hearts for entrusting us with this history book, also *Das Grosse Gemeinde-Geschichtbuch* (Chronicle, Volume I), as well as smaller chronicles, stories about the martyrs, the splendid, extremely precious orders, epistles, confessions of faith, songs, article books, prayers, and teachings of the old church to look after and use for the benefit and blessing of the entire church today! For us they are a great comfort, strength, and encouragement on the holy way, also in hours of deepest distress and threatening, pressing trouble. Through this we perceive daily the faith and trust of your loving hearts. You have so lovingly received our servant of the Word, not only confirming him and sending him back to us but also supplying him most generously with spiritual help. For this our thanks to you in all eternity is even much greater, stronger, and deeper than for your temporal help, which practically seen has kept us from being reduced to complete destitution, yes, from actual ruin. We can never thank you or love you enough for what you have done.

From a Brotherhood meeting August 22, 1931, at the Rhön Bruderhof on the occasion of Hans and Emy-Margret Zumpe's return home from their *Hochzeitsreise* (wedding trip). Eberhard is reporting:

There was a distinct connection to be felt between the double wedding of Alfred to Gretel, and Leo to Trautel on the one hand, and the later wedding of Hans to Emy-Margret on the other. Some time before, Fritz-Leo and Trautel had told us about proposed visits from Switzerland, and the visitors all happened to come at the same time, so all met here at the wedding of the third couple. Some of these visitors we really learned to love, while others, like the Dutchman, seemed rather difficult. Hans and Else Boller's visit was certainly extremely important. Our encounter with them reminded us of our

own new beginning when we left Berlin and went to Sannerz. I can't
help comparing these two events—if it is at all possible to compare
such things. How wonderful it was that Hans and Else Boller's decision
was not one of yesterday or the day before! Instead, their way to full
community had been long prepared for them through their innermost
calling, rooted in the very depth of their being. They had already
decided quite a while ago, somehow in touch with the Rüschlikon
Werkhof,[1] to pluck up courage and make the break to actually live
in community. But the agreement was of a general nature rather than
definitely spelled out. It soon became clear that what was involved
was not a mutually-binding promise, but rather an agreement very
clearly setting forth the communal direction, but leaving it open to
question whether this way is possible on the Rüschlikon Werkhof.
Especially with Else Boller there was a strong reserve and hesitation
to be felt, whereas with Hans it seemed that a uniting with the
Rüschlikon Werkhof was close at hand.

When they were both with us here, they met with something
unexpected. They had already realized that the Bruderhof was calling
them, and both Fritz and Trautel had told them they should come and
get a complete picture. So they came. They came into the middle of
a wedding. That certainly is quite significant. Just this question of
marriage and its relationship to religion and society, of responsibility
to the nation and to the community, has been a burning one for them
for quite some time. For a long while they had wrestled with the
question: how is it possible to live a true life in marriage and the
family in a community that demands absolutely everything? Else
especially had strong reservations. And now they were plunged into
the experience of our wedding. And the strongest and greatest
impression they received was that marriage is the symbol of full unity
between Christ and his church, between God and his people; marriage
is the symbol of the unity of God's kingdom and a symbol of the
church; marriage is a small reality of the unity between God the
creator, the Son, and the Holy Spirit who is the spirit of the church
and of the future. Actually they were won on that wedding day. And
yet a few questions remained that needed to be solved. Therefore it
was good that they still had a little time to search with us in the old
teachings on Acts 2 about the pouring out of the Holy Spirit, and to
seek in other important teachings. They could also ask us questions
and work with us. Above all, they had the chance to get to know our

---

[1]A community in Switzerland, not to be confused with Werkhof, part of the Rhön Bruderhof.

whole circle and have one or more conversations with almost all our Brotherhood members.

Among all these experiences, what impressed them deeply and took them firmly by the hand were the Hutterian articles of faith on marriage, the statements on complete community and on the questions of arms and the government, the forgiveness of sins through the authority of the church, and brotherly admonition. They were gripped by the truth. One felt it clearly. The question was not whether one human conviction was grappling with another human conviction, or whether one speaker or a whole circle of people was exercising a suggestive, hypnotic influence. All that totally disappeared just as little candle flames vanish from sight when the sun shines. Instead, the influence of the Spirit was there. They were met by the Holy Spirit. They were impressed by these articles of faith because each person became part of the one whole through the reality of the Holy Spirit, in the radiance of the Holy Spirit. That was the only thing that mattered for Hans and Else and for all of us who were gathered then and are gathered now—the reality and working of the Holy Spirit. That is something one cannot tell or lecture about. It is something that has to come over us again and again, so that through ever new events and experiences, all that has happened in our past is brought back vividly to us and we see it in a clear light.

Soon both of them were shaken to the core about their past, and longed to be forgiven and gathered into the one body of the united church. And it happened. It was the childlike spirit and simplicity of it all that expressed it most clearly and made such an impression on us. In connection with something so powerful it seems almost impossible to speak also of financial things. But the Spirit who takes possession of everything material and wants to control it also wants a clear settlement about material things. In all our meetings we hardly touched on money matters except on the last evening. It is true Hans and Else Boller began talking about it, but we only referred to it very briefly. The one decisive thing was that the Holy Spirit should grip us to the very depths and take possession of Hans and Else and all of us, for only in this way can all financial questions be settled.

Here I felt that I carried an especially heavy responsibility, almost unbearable for a human being, because of the authority given to my service when the brothers confirmed my task with the laying on of hands. From day to day I felt more strongly and oppressively that an hour of decision had come in our house, an hour that was much more significant and much more dangerous than the threat of a compulsory auction. I tried to protect the whole household from being poisoned by the spirit of mammon. The whole purpose of my service (and I hope soon of Hans's service) is the task of the church and its mission. I am convinced it is the real and deepest reason for a uniting with Hans and Else Boller and thereby the solution to the financial question also.

I had to think of what dear old David Vetter[1] had said, and what at that moment I had not found very pleasant to hear, "If you have the right foundation of faith and true *Gelassenheit*, God will surely help you to do mission but perhaps not through us. It may be that many will join who have nothing, ninety-nine who don't bring anything, but perhaps the hundredth one will bring so much money that you can take in all the hundred." Even if what he says is bitterly hard to accept, yet, as so often before, old David Vetter has proved to be a prophetic figure among the Brothers. At any rate his task as elder is very strongly confirmed. I also believe in this prophecy. Our blessings have come to us because the Brothers have kept us above water the whole time, have sent us the old books and writings, and above all have given us the authority to build up the church. Blessings come because, through the laying on of hands and the confirmation of the service of the Word, we have the authority to build up the true church, to forgive sins, and to conclude marriages. It is important to me that the source of our blessings is with the Brothers and with the very great witness of the apostolic mission throughout the centuries. Our blessings come in this way only and in no other.

Thus it was my inmost endeavor that we should meet Hans and Else Boller with the same love and care, with the same readiness, decisiveness, firmness, and resoluteness as we would any other poor person whom we have recognized as brother through our common humanity, and whom we want to help become a brother in Christ. It does not matter whether he is the old shepherd, Heinrich, or Karl Gail, or the pastor with plenty of money, or any other person. No one should be favored and no one discriminated against. We have always accepted the very poorest with jubilating hearts and loving readiness. Therefore we have endeavored, in the authority of the church, to tell Hans and Else the truth and to keep nothing back.

On the basis of their inner readiness we could even go a step further than we generally do, and on the last evening, when Ruth was taken into the Brotherhood, we put to them directly the questions that normally are asked only at baptism. We let them stand up and we put

---

[1]Of Rockport, SD.

to them in the most solemn way these fundamental questions of the Brothers. They were the questions from the confession of faith and the twelve points asked before baptism, as well as the questions about purification of the former life, about readinesss to be admonished and disciplined and to admonish and discipline others, about readiness for the prayer of the church for forgiveness of sin, and readiness to give to the church without reservation their entire property and all their working strength and abilities. We put before them these and all other questions about the decisive surrender that leads us to give ourselves not only to God with our whole soul, but also to give ourselves to the church with all our bodily powers and material property, now and for always.

In this connection the question of surrendering all our property became clear, and thus it also came to the point that we could explain the difference between giving in goods and valuables when accepted into the novitiate and giving them in when accepted into the Brotherhood. In the first case, goods and valuables are given back and laid before the novices at the end of the novitiate. On entry into the Brotherhood they are given in once and for all to God and the church and will not be given back. In this connection we asked if they wanted to give in all their property in the sense of the novitiate or the sense of the Brotherhood, whereupon they answered with all firmness, "in the sense of the Brotherhood."

Still more important was that all these discussions were held in connection with mission, and all questions and objections which were still occupying them were talked over in a most thorough way. Questions were gone into which would still come to them from people outside about the church and sects, about children and their education in the church, all culminating in the question of mission. They said afterwards, "What thorough consideration you gave to all the questions we are going to meet!"

Regarding their children, Hans and Else were quite ready and decided to surrender them to the education of the church. They were very thankful to be able to continue looking after them at night. They showed the deepest childlike trust, wanting to surrender their children completely. They said that they would not do that everywhere, "but we will do it here."

Mission was of such decisive importance because, naturally, we could foresee that when they returned to Switzerland, they would certainly hear, "How can you give up your wide sphere of influence and all the good a pastor can do to withdraw to the solitude and narrow limits of the remote Rhön? Your life will be nothing but a flight from

public life." Mission was also of decisive importance in making clear
the difference between the church and a sect. We have to say with
Wesley, "The world is my parish." We spoke about just this point
with the Bollers, showing them that our communal life has meaning
in the history, in the experiences of the kingdom of God, only because
our actual living in community is of decisive consequence for mission.
We do not believe that a private person can or should carry out
evangelization on his own initiative. We also do not believe that
anybody can be sent on mission by a group, a church or sect, if they
themselves do not have complete community; but we believe it is
decisive to be sent out on mission as an apostle. Apostolic mission
began in Jerusalem. Without Jerusalem there is no mission. We tried
to show that when the servant of the Word is sent out and speaks in
various places, it is not actually he who bears the task of mission.
The church alone carries on mission through the unity which is brought
to all hearts by the Holy Spirit and affects all material matters. The
servant on mission is the instrument for the task given through unity.
He is the representative of this unity. He puts this unity to work. He
is the voice calling aloud across the lands, cupping both hands around
his mouth. The church is the body and he is only the voice. So we
became clear that it does not depend on Eberhard Arnold or Hans
Boller or anybody else who is sent out, but on these and all others
living in such a way that mission can and must take place. It is an
unavoidable must, a holy must, which urges us to immediate mission
through the reality of the unity of the church.

So far everything was clear to Hans and Else Boller. They declared
their withdrawal from the established church of Zurich, resigned their
pastorate, and broke off all other connections. We also hope that they
will become free of the last fine silken threads which bind them in
gratitude to other men, that warmth and thankfulness which produce
a feeling of moral obligation. We wrote to them that it does not matter
to us if there should be monetary losses, but that everything connected
with money is to be brought to an absolutely clear settlement.
Everything is to be quite clearly handed over to the Bruderhof and
the church of God. That is what Hans and Else Boller want, and we
hope that they will carry it through in every respect, even down to
the smallest details.

The intercession of the church was granted, the forgiveness of
sins—more fundamental than I can say here—for entering into the
Brotherhood and being united with the Bruderhof in the faith of the
church. The communal prayer, in the manner of the Brothers whom

men call Hutterians, was perhaps the most powerful experience we had with our newest novices. We felt the power of forgiveness and purification working directly among us. Hans and Else Boller then received their first leave of absence with permission to go home to put all their affairs in order in accordance with their vows. At the same time they were given a letter for the people of the Werkhof challenging them to start on their way and come to us. Hans and Else faithfully delivered this letter. Up to now that challenge has had no positive results. However, we firmly hope that the members of the Werkhof, who are in a tremendous tension between their willingness on the one hand, and their disunity on the other, may finally encounter the thunder and lightning which can give them a healthy shock and lead them to true community.

Above all we must go into the cities hand in hand and take up the task of mission. This winter must not pass without two or three going out to speak to hundreds of people, so that some of these, perhaps a few, perhaps many, are brought to us on the Bruderhof.

Robert Friedmann,   Elias Walter
Vienna   Stand Off Bruderhof
                                                              November 3, 1931

My dear Friedmann,

I have received your card and also the special printing which I read. Indeed, it is very interesting for me and probably also for others; order me a half-dozen of them.

Concerning our situation, it is not the best; also I myself do not feel well. Moreover, we have had a dry summer and a poor harvest; for the last two years everything pays so poorly that we can hardly make a go of it. Arnold has been a good friend to us, and has also been accepted as a brother and taken into the service of the Word, and has served us also with the Word. Everyone has joy in him; he was also to some extent given gifts of love, but certainly not enough to set up his Bruderhof materially in proper shape. And now poverty is getting the upper hand in our country also. There is a great scarcity already on many Bruderhofs. The one must help the other, but there is nothing to spare. I am concerned how Arnold will get through. Many greetings, your

E. Walter.

Milltown Hutterian Mutual Corporation,

P. O. Benard _____ Dez 31 _____ 1931.

An den Brüdern u Brüderhöfen der Hutterischen Gemeinden
zur Nachricht.

Hiermit bezüge ich, daß den Sept. 14. 1930 Eberhard Arnold
von den deutschländischen Bruderhof der Gemeinde Gottes, bei der
Rosedale Hutterischen Gemeinde, in Manitoba, Canada, von den
Dienern des Worts der Manit ober Gemeinden ist befragt worden
Glaubenssachen halben, u befunden daß er (Eb. Arnold) völlig über=
einstimmt mit den Artikeln unsers Glaubens in allen Dingen.
Und darum sehen wir dieser Bruderhof seine Vereinigung
mit den Hutterischen Gemeinden die er suchte u begehrte. Und geben
völlig unsern einfältiges Zeugniß dazu, u wünschen ihn Gnad
u brüderlichen Beistand von unsern himmlischen Vater dazu. Amen.

Unterzeichnet von mir in Namen aller Diener des
Worts der Gemeinden in Manitoba

Joseph Kleinsasser.
(Der ältere)

Josef Kleinsasser   Rhön Bruderhof, Post Neuhof
Milltown Bruderhof, Manitoba   December 1, 1931

Dear Josef Kleinsasser,

Herewith we are sending you the confirmation of our Eberhard
Arnold[1] with our deepest request that you also write your confirmation
of September 14 on the back of this page and return it to Eberhard
Arnold.

With heartfelt greetings from all our brothers and sisters to the
whole Milltown Community, your

Else von Hollander

On the back of the above letter:

Milltown Hutterian Corporation
P.O. Benard

December 31, 1931

To the Brothers and Bruderhofs of the Hutterian Church
For your Information

I bear witness herewith that on September 14, 1930, Eberhard
Arnold from the German Bruderhof of the Church of God was asked
questions of faith by the Servants of the Word of the Manitoba
Communities at the Rosedale Hutterian Church in Manitoba, Canada.
He, Eberhard Arnold, was found to be in complete agreement with
the points of our faith in all things. Therefore, we saw no hindrance
to his uniting with the Hutterian Church, which he sought and desired.
We willingly gave him our unanimous testimony, wishing him grace
and the help of our heavenly Father for this. Amen.

Signed by me in the name of all Servants of the Word of the
Churches in Manitoba,

Joseph Kleinsasser (Sr.)

---

[1]See p.184.

Rhön Bruderhof, April 12, 1932

Dearly beloved Elias Vetter,

Thank you very warmly for encouraging me to send you at long last a full report and the writings connected with it. Please do not think it was carelessness or indifference that have made the long delay. The special situation of our Bruderhof and my poor health kept me from writing and sending these things at the right time.

In order to let you know something about this situation, which has already been reported to you repeatedly by my dear Emmy, I send you today the material that will give you an impression of the faith and work and final days of our Else von Hollander. These accounts that we want to leave for our descendants still have to be shortened and summarized to avoid repetition.

Our Else's faith and final days remain a great comfort and strong encouragement to us. Up to her last evening she worked on the Hutterian writings. You must bear in mind that this death was the first in our small church circle, apart from the death of a very dear little child in 1927, which also brought to us great powers of eternity. Thus it has a special significance for the history of our Bruderhof.

Else was our best secretary. Her illness, which has been weighing on us for a long time, and especially her death, have brought a heavy loss to my work on the Small History Book and on other books and writings of the Brothers. This explains many delays in our correspondence and in our copying work. From our accounts of the dying of our beloved Else you will see that she thought of you, too, while she lay resting. She said, "Do write loving letters to Elias Walter, for he is a man with a great heart." So I hope that reading the loving words of this dying sister will bring you the peace of God, the joy of Jesus Christ, and the power of the Holy Spirit.

If God gives me time, I hope to publish many books that will carry the witness of the Brothers out into the world. It seems doubtful, though, whether I will be able to carry out the larger part of this task, for my health is rather poor and this has greatly reduced my working strength. This will explain to you the long intervals between my letters. However, if I am not to do it myself, then I hope to teach and guide our beloved brothers and sisters, so that they can continue this task as well as, if not better, than I would have been able to do.

In the near future we will print a letter for you. In it I will report to you about the growth of our community. Increasing tasks and declining health do not allow me to write separate letters to individual brothers very often. If God gives me the strength, I will write a few brief lines to Rockport, South Dakota, and to Hutterville, Alberta, because of the passing of our beloved David Hofer Vetter. I will send these to you also. Otherwise, I have not written to anyone in a long time, so another printed letter will be needed.

In dear David Vetter I saw a deep earnestness worthy of the cause and an anxious concern for the renewal of the church that I will never forget. The deeper I thought about it in these past months, the more I came to recognize that our old David Vetter, who has now been taken from us, had deeply foreseen and often correctly named the dangers and troubles that threaten the church. It is true that heavy sorrow for his poor, beloved wife may have contributed to his gloomy views. It may even be that a man of his temperament is inclined to a spirit of anxiety. And yet I must say that the whole impact of this man, who tried in all earnestness to bring back a readiness for God's word and for the church, was given us by God in order that we might learn from it.

Ever since I returned home I have made great efforts to bring alive for our beloved brothers and sisters all I have seen, experienced, and learned among you, and to help our Bruderhof in every respect grow into the true Hutterian orders. It is difficult to explain to you how much hard work and distress such a new founding of a Bruderhof brings with it, how much time, and still more how much grace, is needed until the members in all their loyalty, diligence, and dedication come to grips with these things and accept them fully, so that full community in all its earnestness and all its joy can be revealed in all areas of life. Then the spirit of unity will work among us and unite our hearts, so that each work department will be planned and carried out after the pattern of God's kingdom. This is how it should be: the light of God's kingdom and his justice are to shine out from the form of life visible in God's church, the city on the hill, into all lands and to all peoples. True community living in full harmony of spirit, which penetrates all work, is the only basis of true mission. By this we can recognize the true nature of God's kingdom.

I wish you and all the others great joy in the peace of the church and in the power of the witness to truth, and also in all your work and in all you accomplish.

I understand that your beloved Stand Off Bruderhof, like most of the others, has to suffer from the need of the times, even though your needs and worries do not in any way approach the great need of our church community life. Again and again it is a miracle to us that we got through the year 1931. It is a great miracle of God that, thanks to his love and that of his beloved children, we were allowed to remain together and to turn toward the new year 1932 with courage and with gathered strength.

So I wish for you in all your struggles, difficulties, and troubles that same comfort of the Holy Spirit, that same power of Jesus Christ's love, and that same faithful care of our heavenly Father.

With love and respect, your humble and forever deeply grateful,

Eberhard

To the church of God on the Bruderhofs in America
to the Brothers called Hutterians
in South Dakota, Manitoba, and Alberta

(Written by Eberhard Arnold and signed by the whole brotherhood)

Rhön Bruderhof, June 1932

Beloved Brothers and Sisters on all Bruderhofs in America!

Today our letter begins with what Peter Riedemann expressed in his first confession of faith, written in Gmunden in the Tirol around the year 1530:

Christ has been given to us and was born as Savior for all. He set aside the law, making *one* new man out of the two (Jew and Gentile, Ephesians 2:15) and preparing a sure way to the Father. "To become children of God" means to be born of God through the living Word given into our hearts. Christ led the way, and we should follow in his footsteps. He has given us an example of the lofty submitting to the lowly. Through his death we have received life and true spiritual food. Through the bond of love, we are being made into one body, whose head is Christ, and we become of *one* heart, mind, and spirit. We have the mind of Christ, and just as he has loved us, so should we love one another. No one should love himself. He should love his fellow members, the whole body, and serve them with the gifts he has received. It is the Holy Spirit, who as power from God on high, brings about all the good in everyone and renews the new man, searching out and recognizing all things. In revealing and imparting his gift, he gathers and unites the church and the house of God where men receive forgiveness of sins. The uniting spirit joins us together into *one* body with him through the bond of love.

We wish for you and for us what is expressed in these words of Peter Riedemann:

How One Should Build the House of God
and What the House of God Is

Since Jesus Christ is the cornerstone, let us begin to build with joy on the foundation of all the apostles. Therefore, as living stones you, too, should build yourselves into a living temple of God, that God may dwell in you and establish his work in you. Yes, this is surely the time when the whole world lives in its wantonness and seeks only to fill its money bags, not caring about the poor and showing them love. But we should be different from the world. Christ is the mountain on which we should build the house of God, the wood with which we should build is the gift of the Holy Spirit, and the house is the church of God.

We wish for you and for us the pillars of this house, which Peter Riedemann describes:

The seven pillars are the pure fear of God as opposed to the fear of men, God's wisdom opposed to human wisdom, the understanding of God opposed to human understanding, the counsel of God opposed to human counsel, the power of God opposed to human power, the spiritual knowledge of God opposed to worldly knowledge, and the gracious kindness and friendship of God opposed to human friendship and favor, love of possessions and show, and the like.

If with us and with you these seven pillars stand firm in the spirit of God and of Christ, we will always be completely one. No storm or wind of these evil times can overthrow the house because it is founded on hearing and doing the words of Jesus Christ.

From our hearts we thank all of you for your loving letters written since August of last year. Your remembering us proves to us this unity and stability of the church of God. We thank you also for your great love in sending gifts and presents and all your help in spite of bad times. How gladly I would have responded immediately to your love that has helped us forward so very much! How I would have liked to send a greeting to each one of you personally! But it is not possible. I must ask you to read and understand this second printed letter, like the first one, as a greeting and report from our hearts to yours, because it tells you as deeply and openly as possible how things are with us, and how much we love you in Christ and as his church. There has been a much longer pause than I had planned between these first and second printed letters.

Unfortunately, I did not receive as many answers from you as I had hoped for, and I did not hear from all colonies. The death of the cofounder of our common life (our sister Else von Hollander, who helped me with my writing), my eye trouble as well as other illnesses and needs on the Bruderhof, our hard work situation, and most of all the demands made by the Small History Book claimed so much of my time that I could not write this second letter any earlier, nor could I answer personally your many individual letters and thank you for your gifts. After many months I am now able to express to you again my wishes for the peace of God as the unity of the church, the love of Jesus as great joy in the kingdom of God and in all members of the community, and the power of the Holy Spirit as the inward stirring and readiness we need every day.

Meanwhile, our brothers and sisters here have exchanged many a letter with you dear ones in America. Please continue in this. Every letter of yours is of greatest significance for us because we want to share heart and soul with you in all you experience, and we are constantly with you in our thoughts and feelings.

For this reason, the death of our venerable and beloved David Vetter on your dear Rockport Bruderhof has moved us very deeply. Recently in the Brotherhood we read once more all the words he had spoken to me on my repeated visits to Rockport. It was the unanimous impression of our brothers and sisters that David Hofer Vetter was given by God to the church as a watchman to warn and admonish. Again and again in deep, almost bitter, earnest he had to make us aware of the dangers in which we all stand in this extremely corrupt time. We will always think of him with deep thankfulness and with reverence for the hand of God over his church.

We hope to hear soon how the question of an elder has been settled among you beloved ones who came from Old Elm Spring. You know our longing, born of faith and based on the true understanding of the New Testament and of all the old writings, especially the brothers' history books: our thirty-five Bruderhofs should have one common elder as were Jakob Hutter, Hans Amon, Peter Walpot, Andreas Ehrenpreis, and all the others. Or perhaps two elders, in complete unity and with the counsel of other older brothers, should share this service for all churches as did Leonhard Seiler (Leonhard Lanzenstiel) and Peter Riedemann. We cannot refrain from pleading with you again and again to be more obedient and to give the spirit of the church more freedom to act, so that this important point of complete unity in leadership and order may be established again among us. With faith in this unity, we wish that true peace, the deepest unity and harmony, may rule in each individual church and that among us the strength of faith and valiant courage of our forefathers may never die. We long that the faithfulness of the servants of the Word toward the church may increase and that the obedience of all brothers and sisters toward all servants, born of faith and love, may grow both here in Germany and there in America. Then without doubt at God's own hour the full unity of all churches under the united care of one elder will be given.

No mountain or tree can be too big or too mighty for faith to remove. Your economic needs are well known to us. We follow with sympathy the present trend in wheat prices and know the exceptional difficulties the United States, and even more the Canadian Provinces, undergo to sell their enormous supplies of wheat. Haven't we ourselves experienced the refusal of the German authorities to permit the great gift of duty-free wheat flour which you dear brothers in Manitoba had thought of sending to us? We sent you in Manitoba their official answer. So even a gift of wheat involving no money is not allowed. Although at times you sigh under a good deal of oppression, you can be very thankful that you have enough food, housing, and clothing. Millions of men do not have as much and cannot find any work. The best and greatest of all temporal goods is work. How good it is that with you as with us there is plenty of work for all, enabling us to provide for the poor, the sick, the weak, and the children of the whole church. In addition, we have the wonderful task of mission, finding and gathering from year to year more and more of the zealous.

We ask you to consider again that, in spite of your own plight, your situation is easier and better than ours. In our Bruderhof we must provide for many people, more than some of your churches have to care for. To many who know us it seems impossible that we are able to manage this in spite of poverty and need. We ourselves feel it is a wonder that we have been able to live through another year since my return from you. During this year we have lost only one of our members through death. We are allowed to grow even though the need increases within our circle and around us. . . .

Our Bruderhof is then a church with a mission. In spite of poverty, yes, just in this poverty, eyes, heart, and doors must be open wide in order for her to be an ark for all awakened and zealous people in their deepest need. She must let something of the saving community of God's kingdom shine out above the waves of today's flood. In spite of your own need, you, our dear brothers in America, are without doubt appointed by God to help in this task.

You know that you are called to send out the message of Jesus Christ into all the world, just as you are called to live in full community. You know that your and our early forefathers practiced mission year after year for over a century, making the greatest sacrifices of life and property. You know that for centuries they took upon themselves severe privation and poverty in food and housing in order to share their poor dwellings with zealous newcomers. Their cramped living conditions caused their opponents to abuse and slander their life together. In the letter begun by Jakob Hutter, finished by Peter Riedemann and Leonhard Seiler, and sent in 1545 to the reigning princes, we read:

> We are said to be a great number of people living together, a multitude—some talk of thousands. We want to let you know that there are about two thousand of us, not counting children, living in about twenty different places. At some places there are many people, at others less, depending on the work available at each one. At Schäkowitz, where such an outcry was raised, there are quite a few people, but many of them are children, and many are old or sick and cannot work much. We are not writing this because we are ashamed of them and would rather ignore them. On the contrary, we wish there were many thousands more seeking nothing but to serve God alone.

Our brother and teacher Peter Riedemann also writes in 1540 that we should accept and live with as many as the Lord gathers together:

> For it is the Lord's will that as many of us as the Lord in heaven leads together shall house together, be it many or few. The authorities have ordered that no more than seven community members live together, but they cannot give us orders nor can we agree to act differently. We ourselves will not make any rules about how many should live together in each community or household but will accept whoever God sends. Do not let yourselves be swayed, dear brothers, for you stand in the true grace of God. (From the seventh epistle of Peter Riedemann, sent to the brothers imprisoned in Falkenstein and preserved in the book of epistles, in Rockport, South Dakota)

Further, on page 136 of our Article Book we have this epistle from the year 1561, written by our brother Leonhard Dax. This is from an important writing, unfortunately too long unknown:

Thorough Refutation of Slanders by the Godless
Against the Church of Christ
Making Many Suspicious of the Truth
Written for the Comfort of All the Good-hearted

Through the grace of God and through the daily preaching and power of the Gospel, we are no longer a small number, so that we cannot give each one a separate room. In addition, we are having to bear fierce hostility because of our building, having been forced by the need of our many people to put up dwellings. Our beds have had to be close to one another because of lack of room, and we have borne this in the fear of God with modesty and chastity. If it were pleasing to God to give us enough room, we would prefer to give a separate room to each of those we so thankfully receive. But in this as in everything else the word of God must be fulfilled as Christ said, "The foxes have holes and the birds of the air have nests, but the Son of man has nowhere to lay his head." As members of Christ and as his disciples we rejoice with all our hearts and thank, honor, and praise the Lord in heaven for the space we do have. With this we hope to have briefly but adequately answered your slander.

As you well know and I also found during my visit of almost a whole year with you, among modern Americans no such zeal for the kingdom of God and for a true, loving, communal life in the spirit of Jesus Christ has awakened. For North America evidently the hour of extensive, fruitful mission has not yet come. During the last three years God's judgment has fallen on the mammon worship of present-day American business—a sign that his hour is drawing near. While you await its coming, you should know that over here in the old German homelands the time to proclaim the gospel to all creation has already arrived. In the old books of the martyrs for the years 1525 and 1526, Jakob Hutter's time, stand these words:

God's word and the gospel of Jesus Christ have broken in again in the whole of Germany. God the Lord wants to let the light of his grace shine anew alongside his judgment, so that the long-oppressed church of Jesus Christ may raise her head again and proclaim Christ in truth!

Today while the last hour of the day of judgment begins to strike over all the world, the words on pages 21 and 30 of Elias Vetter's Book of the Martyrs about the witness our forerunners gave through death and "the visitation of the German lands in these times" should and must be fulfilled anew. Although our strength is small, this has slowly begun:

We stand in the world's last age. God has again brought forth faith and his divine truth in all parts of the German-speaking lands. The dove of his Holy Spirit has been heard in our country, and he has visited these nations with his Word. Through the Word the church, our mother in Christ, has gathered her children to herself!

One of the martyrs has expressed:

They told of Christ and of brotherly love to all throughout the land. They proclaimed that his followers must take up his cross, and if someone has nothing, his neighbor should share with him. (Small History Book)

You know that our brother Jakob Hutter "always had true zeal to take the divine word to those eagerly seeking for God, and courage to be active in the Lord's work." Therefore, he could say that he was God's helper, an "apostle of Jesus Christ," a "servant of all his children in the mountains of Tirol and Moravia," and that this came "from God's great grace and mercy" through no worth of his own but only through God's "boundless faithfulness and overflowing goodness." (Beginning of his last epistle from Tirol in November 1535, sent by Hieronymus, and now at the Rockport Bruderhof, Alexandria, South Dakota.) Should it be different today with those called Hutterians, who claim to have the same grace?

Surely the words of Jakob Hutter are as true today as they were when he spoke about full community and mission:

The city built on the holy mountain of Zion cannot be hidden. The light shines out and is not covered up but burns brightly like a lamp lighting up the darkness. The children of God are the light, for God kindled his flame in them. (Epistle sent from the Tirol to the church of God in Moravia in 1535 through brother Wölflin Zimmermann and now with the brothers at the Rockport Bruderhof, Alexandria, South Dakota.)

This light is the flame of love in the lamps of faith, fed by the Holy Spirit's stream of fire. With these burning lamps, we are to go to meet the day of the Beloved One. This day will come from heaven, from the Jerusalem above in God's kingdom. We wait for it as citizens of the city on the hill, to which we are allowed to belong as God's church. The lights of this city of God will shine far and wide for all who are ready heart and soul to abandon their friendships, their property, and their own way of life to go into the land that God's light will show them. From this church burning with love, light bearers will be sent out to show the way to the people who dwell in darkness, the way leading to the light that has dawned in Jesus Christ, the way to his church and to his kingdom.

I have told you about the gathering of such surrendered people[1] from all parts of the country, from all kinds of work in today's world, and from all present-day movements. We long that all this brings close to your hearts the small, bright light God has kindled, the small but firmly-grounded city on the hill he has established and wants to continue building for the salvation of the many who are still to come.

And you, beloved brothers and Bruderhofs in South Dakota, Manitoba, and Alberta in distant America, who are called to the church of God and all her loving services, you have come close to us with your gifts of love. Through God's grace you have helped build this small city on the foundations of the most holy faith. You have helped to build up the walls of her daily service, to provide something for the table, and to support her work. This could happen only through the love of God poured into your hearts through the Holy Spirit. Your love has already borne much fruit. But we cannot hide from you that we must go on pleading that your love continue, for your works of love are needed even more urgently today than at the time I was allowed to tell your church about us. Again barns and roofs must be built so as to keep the harvest from harm. Again ten to sixteen of our people often have to spend the night a mile from the hof among unfamiliar people, alien to the spirit of the church. Again six more of our young men often have to sleep under the roof above the pigsty, without a window or a proper floor. Further, we have not the necessary land and cattle to feed our many people. As I finish this letter, our numbers for the last few weeks have mostly reached 110. Again our neighbors are offering to sell us their small farms next to our land and work places at reasonable prices.

In spite of your own need, God's loving, holy spirit without doubt wants to move your hearts again to do all the good you can for the members of your church in the old German lands, whose need is even greater. Do this without any long delay by sending your help across the wide ocean for the sake of our mission, confirmed by God's almighty hand. With one's own eyes as well as with the eyes of faith, one can foresee that this help will return to you in God's own time.

Some of you, dear brothers and sisters, may wonder why we are

---

[1]The Boller, Meier, and Mathis families from Switzerland, and others, are referred to elsewhere in these letters.

using so much precious paper and weeks of work time for writing and printing this letter, since we are so poor that we cannot even provide our household with shelter and food. We came very near to wondering this ourselves, so at the close of this letter I want to answer this question by recalling the history of the brothers.

Toward the very end of a period of decay a small, new beginning was given in the church through your beloved forefathers who came from Carinthia to Kreuz in Transylvania. At that time, when the love of most had grown completely cold, the communities at Vélke Leváre and Sabatisch had not heard from the church at Alwinz for ten long years, from 1750 to 1760. (The church at Alwinz in Transylvania was a small one then with only six families, sixty souls in all.) In the midst of new persecution that threatened to destroy everything, they would certainly have been able to stand more firmly in spite of their weak faith, if they had only sent each other letters and news. The churches in Sabatisch and Leváre, which were becoming very weak, would then have received new strength through the new beginning of full community at Kreuz about the year 1756. This was certainly the case for the church at Alwinz. A third of that community, also very weak, took part in the dangerous flight to Wallachia and in the building up and renewal of the community there.

So it would be a sin against love to you and against community with you if we did not send a letter like this to you, our brothers and sisters, at least once a year. (In the future we hope it is twice a year.) These letters would let you know about our temporal and spiritual condition as thoroughly and understandably as we are able to tell you with our limited gifts. Just as we remember you daily in our prayers, so you would be stimulated by and moved through the Holy Spirit to raise holy hands to God. You would plead to the beloved heavenly Father for us all, that his good and Holy Spirit might keep us on the way. You would plead that our newly-won and gathered brothers and sisters, often in a hard struggle with friends and relatives, be protected and remain true to the end to the honor of the Father, in the name of Jesus Christ, and in the strength of his Holy Spirit.

For this reason we are sending this letter to every family on each Bruderhof, so that the father of the family, if he feels a divine urge to do so, may read it aloud to his family circle after the day's hard work. He could then send back an answer, even a short one, from his family. To our joy we heard that something similar to this happened on some Bruderhofs after you received our first letter. We pray that our merciful and loving Father in heaven may, through Jesus Christ and the Holy Spirit, give you the eyes of understanding so that you may grasp and accept in your believing, loving hearts our often very awkward words, different from your own language which has become so dear to us.

All our brothers and sisters greet with heartfelt love each one of your Bruderhofs, so intimately familiar to me. We greet each one of you with the prayer from our deepest heart that every large and every small Bruderhof may let the light of Jesus Christ burn ever more brightly and purely. Thus you will be freed or entirely shielded from every temptation to mix with the evil spirit of this time and of the world. This we ask of you all as we conclude this letter with its description of the conditions of our life up to the middle of July, 1932. We began writing it by hand at the end of May, finished on July 17, and printed it in our printing shop from June 20 to July 23.

We wish you the peace of God the Father as the full unity and community of his church, the love of our beloved Savior Jesus Christ as full redemption, forgiveness, and discipleship, and the power of the Holy Spirit as true prompting and steadfastness for his holy work! This is the daily prayer for you from your brothers and sisters in our church, who love you from the bottom of their hearts. We are writing to you in the name of all, with special greetings from our Hans Vetter, my beloved Emmy, sister in marriage, our witness brothers, and our servants of temporal affairs.

In the service of the church of God, your very humble brother who completely belongs to you

Eberhard Arnold

Johannes Kleinsasser   Rhön Bruderhof
Elder and Vorsteher   October/November 1932
in the Service of the Word
Buck Ranch Bruderhof, Alberta

Very beloved Johannes Kleinsasser Vetter,

Your loving letter moved us deeply and spoke to us of many things that are on our hearts too. For your appointment as elder and *Vorsteher* in the service of the Word for the Bruderhofs that originated from Old Elm Spring, we wish you the strength of the peace of God, of the love of Jesus Christ, and of the clarity of the Holy Spirit.

I rejoice with my whole heart that God has led the beloved brothers to a united decision to lay this great responsibility upon you. Among

brothers I have come to love very much, I have always had a special
and deep trust to you. I felt very much at home at your Buck Ranch
Bruderhof.

It is my most burning desire that your eldership may be used in
such a way that we servants of the Word, who are responsible for all
Bruderhofs, may work toward an undivided church, a church that is
led in all matters, both spiritual and temporal, from a united leadership.

It is clear to me that, under the present difficult circumstances and
conditions, this cannot be achieved from one day to the next by all
the servants of the Word meeting to make a decision. Therefore it is
my suggestion that you, beloved Johannes Kleinsasser Vetter, meet
as often as possible with your beloved friend Joseph Kleinsasser Vetter
(Milltown Bruderhof), who has also become very dear to my heart,
and with our old, venerable Christian Waldner Vetter of West Raley
Bruderhof. The three of you should be so fearless in faith, so
courageous in love, that you can tackle all problems. You should
meet every two or three months for several days in an openhearted
way in the childlike spirit of truth and love to clarify, improve, and
set everything in order. I believe you three elders should meet three
or four times a year, and it should be possible to use the words of
Jesus about these meetings: "Where two or three are gathered in my
name, I will be among them." Then your directions would be followed
by us all in greatest trust and deepest gratitude.

We at our German Bruderhof rejoice in saying that we will be
obedient to you in all things; we submit to you in the spirit of which
Paul speaks, a spirit showing the patient and courageous self-surrender
of Jesus Christ and the obedience born of faith. This, my very beloved
and respected Johannes Kleinsasser Vetter, is what I have most on
my heart to share with you and the other two deeply respected elders,
Christian Waldner Vetter and Joseph Kleinsasser Vetter.

You have now received our second printed letter and will certainly
have become more and more concerned with its contents. One thing
I am sorry about is that our language in present-day Germany is
different from your old language which I grew to love so much, so
that the letters of those who haven't visited you, as I did, will be
difficult in some things for you to understand. But I am certain that
with some effort it will be possible for even the simplest sister to feel
the spirit of every page in her heart and sense what God and his church
has done anew in our land. I do not need to tell you in detail about
it; I only ask you to read the first and second Sendbriefs thoroughly
and compare them, so that you are well prepared for the third Sendbrief,
which will be necessary before too long.

You will find in the first printed Sendbrief that a "Werkhof" has come into being near Zurich in Switzerland. For two years the members have tried to make it something similar to what our Bruderhof here near Fulda is more and more allowed through God's grace to be. They are now over twenty people including children, and we have the great joy that one family, Peter and Anni Mathis and their little Johann Christoph, have moved to us because they could no longer live without the full unity of the church of God and the true basis of faith. Furthermore, three others were also sent to us from there in response to our call, which is God's call, and to find a common foundation of faith for uniting completely. Up to now we cannot say that this has happened. What the church is, what faith in the Father, the Son, and the Holy Spirit means, and what purity and discipline in the church of Jesus Christ demand is unfortunately not yet clear to these friends, who like to be called "Swiss Brethren" without ever having been in contact with the Mennonites. As a result they lack the complete reverence and humility and childlikeness which has been given, like a miracle of God, to our new members, Peter and Anni.

We have sent our second servant of the Word, Hans Zumpe Vetter, to them. My dear wife Emmy Basel, our housemother and steward's helper, went along too, because the women there are nearer to the spirit of the church of Jesus Christ and of God's kingdom than the men, and they need to talk over some difficult questions with a motherly woman. So far twelve from the Zurich community in Switzerland have declared that, without making any conditions and without slackening in their dedication, they want to unite with us at our Bruderhof.

Quite apart from them, we have been more than a hundred people for many months, usually 105. Some of our brothers still have to live a quarter of an hour away from the hof. The house is full right up to the roof, as it was in the households in Moravia. We, too, have little attic rooms and very, very small windows like those I saw in Sabatisch and Leváre. Thus we have been forced to build. We can no longer postpone buying land, or it will be impossible to feed so many people.

So we find ourselves in an extremely difficult situation. On the one hand, the holy spirit of love and gathering is urging us forward, and we cannot shrink back in a cowardly way. We must take upon ourselves what love and mission demand, even under danger of death. So we have no choice but to ask you again, most urgently, to send us a larger sum of money, in spite of your own poverty.

I have been careful to wait quite a while before asking your dearly beloved communities for money, but I urgently have to do it now. I know well how difficult it is for you to collect anything in the present time of need. I know well the inner spiritual need that is a greater hindrance than the serious lack of money under which you suffer. But we have reached a point here that does not allow me to wait any longer. I feel urged by the wonderful confirmation of the little mission we have carried out, which God himself has stamped with his blessing, to say to you and all communities, "You must not forget mission!" If we, with our very little strength, accept this heavy burden for the beloved and ardent new people continually coming to us, we must ask you to help us with this load. Then the work of God can be carried on as it was in the time of the apostles and later in the time of Jakob Hutter, Peter Riedemann, Peter Walpot, and many others.

I have the heartfelt request that you in your communities talk about my plea for help and send help without delay in spite of your own great need. From the second printed Sendbrief you can learn everything in detail and get a clear picture of our economic situation, so I don't need to write about it again. As much as my very full time allows, I will write also to several other brothers one after another. For today I will come to a close.

Beloved Johannes Kleinsasser Vetter, at the time of my visit you had already been in the service of the Word for a quarter of a century, and now you have to take on your heart a great and glorious but also extremely heavy responsibility. We want to think of you daily and also of your dear helper, your son Joseph Kleinsasser Vetter, whom I greet from the depths of my heart as my dear friend and brother. Please greet dear Paul Wipf Vetter too. I often see his face before me when I think of you. Do not forget to greet our dear Samuel Kleinsasser and Jakob Kleinsasser, your dear sons, and also your nephew Josef, the work distributor, also Elias Wipf, the servant and teacher who once accompanied me to the train station. In particular I ask you to greet our Johannes Hofer and our Jakob Hofer, the two witness brothers. The little book from Johannes Hofer has already been copied out and will be bound and returned to him. Please be patient for a while because, as a result of the conditions I tell of in this letter, we have much work, especially now. Please greet your very dear wife and all your children. From the depths of our hearts all our brothers and sisters greet you and all the members of your community. It would be wonderful if many of you would write to us in answer to our printed letter.

In faithful and heartfelt unity, your lowly and loving

Eberhard Arnold

Brotherhood of the Rhön Bruderhof
October 24, 1932

Warmly beloved Max and Eva, Hans and Margrit (Meier),
and Robert,[1]

Your letters filled us with great joy. We reach out the hands of our joy-filled hearts to you all and Peter and Anni (Mathis), and with you experience all that is happening among you. The history of the kingdom of God is the issue. You with us, and we with you are ready to follow unity, wherever it may be.

In the communal prayer for the divine answer, we hear the call to the task for the dying world entrusted to us. Mission includes all people, especially the wider circle of your household. They also are called. They also have the freedom to surrender their will to the call. Mission goes out to our neighborhood, both near and farther away. It goes into the countries of Europe. It embraces all parts of the earth. It strikes at the present moment in which economic need, social injustice, and the approaching danger of new wars between the peoples have come to a climax.

First we must gather together in one place to gain the communal strength of spirit and economic resources in order to make inroads into the great need of the people. Everywhere there is evidence of men waiting for the message of unity. But only from the reality of unity can unity be preached and offered.

Unless through you we are shown a place where more than 110 souls can live and work, we will for the present moment unite on our Bruderhof until we get a new call to us all. A sign from God that at any time a call can come to another country and urge us to action, came to us in a number of very significant letters from the Brothers in North America. We received and read them out on the same day as your welcome letters came, which moved our hearts deeply. In two of these letters the Lake Byron Bruderhof near Huron, South Dakota, USA, shared with us through its Word leader, Josef Stahl, that we could immediately occupy that hof, which offers enough room and work for us. "Perhaps now would be the best time for you to come to our hof, as we want to go to Canada. For my part I would be all for handing over our Bruderhof to you, while we rent a place in Canada. We must first discuss it with our other Bruderhofs. It is my will to hand over our Lake Byron Bruderhof to you, while we rent in Canada, and I would gladly do it. How would it be with your

---

[1]Members of the Werkhof Community in Switzerland.

coming here? Could you get permission to emigrate to the States, or should the light of holy truth be lit up more clearly in Germany first? Please let me know what you think."

We are tremendously thankful that this light which was lit by God in Europe, will also flare up again through you. Therefore it seems to us that the task in our German-speaking countries, in Switzerland, Holland, and Sweden, and now also in Italy, is extremely urgent and still far from being accomplished. This is so much the case that we could not see how to answer the very loving and faithful offer from this Bruderhof across the sea in any other way than as expressed in the last-but-one sentence: to continue here at present so that a light may still shine in our lands. So we accept this invitation for the future which God alone knows, and understand it as a powerful sign of God's leading, that all in united community, be "on call" as soon as the hour of departure comes. We do not know the hour. Only God can show us the country. We need only to be ready and free. First we must become united, and we must not put off this uniting even for one moment. So we will now build three rooms for married couples for you as our beloved members, for Peter and Anni, for Max and Eva, for Hans and Margrit and children, and a suitable place for Robert. This sudden decision for further building up should not cause anyone anxiety, as we are used to being surprised by new tasks from God, and are thankful not to fall too soon into a comfortable tempo of life. But certainly there are economic worries, which we trustfully share with you, so that you can carry them with us, as we carry yours with you. The setting up of suitable rooms with the part we undertook several weeks ago to repair and renovate, will cost about 2,200 Reichmarks. Together with you we pray for this sum from the One over all, who has a controlling hand over funds we know nothing about. In this active expectation we here, and in the same way you there, want to do our utmost for it.

We need to consider together what is to happen about the special tasks entrusted to you in Switzerland through God's leading; the life of each one who has lived with you until now in the wider household circle; the necessity perhaps of dissolving the contract with the diaconate union, even if some others might stay behind; also all the other things indicated here. In view of all this, we ask you if at all possible to come at once to the Bruderhof with Peter and Anni, in order for all five to come to a united decision, even if some of you, after a short stay, have to be given leave to return for the settling of the affairs in Rüschlikon and Nidelbad. We can, however, imagine that the economic and farming responsibilities resting on your shoulders until today do not allow all of you to leave together. Such a journey of all at once may appear impossible especially because of caring for your children while we are still building here, and because you want to talk everything over with all your household.

If that is so, which we would be very sorry about, then we ask that at least one from each family—Max and Eva, and Hans and Margrit—would come to us with Peter and Anni and their Johann Christoph for this unanimous decision-making, especially as Robert was only a short time ago with us in warm-hearted harmony. For it will not be possible and also not practicable to consider all the questions and tasks which occupy us now just in letters to and fro. Rather, everything will depend upon our being given directly, in the experience of undisturbed communal unity, that which we human beings can never achieve through mutual explanations, even if there is a united willingness from heart to heart.

So with great joy we expect you in our midst in the next days, and enclose a few lines to Peter and Anni, the faithful ones. We wish Mother and Father Fischli the clear leading in the light of the Spirit, the same leading of the good spirit for their whole future, and to all the other dear household members without exception. We greet from the depths of our hearts you who belong to us just as we are yours for ever.

> The Brotherhood of the Bruderhof at Neuhof, Fulda,
> Germany, as your Brothers whom men call Hutterian

> Rhön Bruderhof
> October 24, 1932

Beloved Peter, and very dear Anni,

It was a great, very great joy and we were deeply moved when we received the letters from Max and Eva, Hans and Margrit, and Robert, which were so clear in the good spirit that they stirred our hearts very deeply. We could not be satisfied only with reading them out both at the beginning and end of our Sunday inner meeting, but had to give them round from hand to hand so that each one could grasp them.

We are tremendously happy, and have given praise to the overwhelmingly powerful spirit of the Father and of Jesus Christ as the spirit of the church and her mission, that carried, led, and authorized you so wonderfully.

This impression was deepened in the most remarkable way by quite a number of brotherly letters from America, in which all the points of our task for the present-day world, given by God to us weak people, were stated in the utmost clarity of the Spirit.

The greatest was a vision granted a short time ago to two brothers of the Rockport Bruderhof, South Dakota, while ploughing at night. For several hours on two consecutive nights they both saw a shining animal with imposing antlers, out of which came three warriors facing each other. If you remember the Revelation of John, you will sense with us something of the significance this vision has in thinking of the battle of light in the coming day of judgment over the world powers, and the blazing up of the kingdom of God. In the same way some brothers looked in our direction and saw the dawn of the future and were, in the spirit, living among us in such a way that they could recognize and name some whom they had never seen.

So we also in the living spirit placed ourselves in your midst in the days of your coming to your much loved old Werkhof, and were among you and with you in the faith of love. And as, at the time of your decisive visit, the difficult and worrying birth of little Hannah Martin led to such healthy and joyful life for the mother Ruth and the beloved child, so now on the same day as the letters came from Max, Eva, Hans, Margrit and Robert, a little daughter, Susanna, was born to our faithful Brotherhood members, Fritz and Martha Sekunda Kleiner. This was on the birthday of our witness brother Georg Barth, and again through God's goodness mother and child are well.

We would still have had so much to tell you dear ones and still would have so much liked to hear more about you and your experience in these meaningful days. But it is much better that you are in our midst very, very soon with your beloved Johann Christoph. Please write at once which day we may expect you and what beds and things you are bringing with you, so that we can prepare everything well for the arrival of you dear ones. Now from you three have grown ten beloved people. Will it become thirty? We do not need to know that yet. The numbers are not important in themselves, but only the spirit and the power which comes through them, so that the gathering of the spirit is revealed to the whole world and shines out into the division of the whole of mankind, and that the call of truth and unity reaches and moves many hearts before the heaviest and greatest hour of world history breaks in! We are very happy that this spirit and this power are with you, and we look forward indescribably to you both and your dear Johann Christoph, and to your and our beloved ones, Max, Eva,

Hans and Margrit with their children, and Robert and to all, all who will still come. Greetings from our deepest hearts,

Your ever-loving brothers and sisters of the large family of the spirit which is both motherly and childlike.

Eberhard Arnold

Christian Waldner Rhön Bruderhof
Elder and Servant of the Word November 1932
West Raley Bruderhof, Alberta

Respected and dearly beloved Christian Waldner Vetter,

I thank you from my whole heart for your letter of April 25, written with so much love and respect. I return your wishes from the bottom of my heart, that the peace of God and the love of Christ and the power of the Holy Spirit may be and remain with you in your advanced age, with your whole church community, and with all the Bruderhofs entrusted to you. With this greeting I also send my love and thanks to your dear wife, your dear son and daughter-in-law, and to all belonging to you.

I am so glad that you received and distributed our Sendbriefs, and I hope that you will still find time to let me know exactly what you think about the individual reports in this letter. Perhaps your son Christian, whom I grew to love especially, can support you with that. Your dear Christian already wrote a little about it, and that comforted and encouraged us. We hope to hear still more.

I hear from all sides that things are not going so well for you in Alberta. It is through God's great grace that you have enough food and drink for body and soul and that your spirits are daily strengthened with the power-giving nourishment of the Word. I am deeply sorry that a hailstorm hit you twice! How wonderful it is that the Bruderhofs of Rockport and Old Elm Spring helped you, and that you helped in the meeting for the burial of our dear Hannes Vetter's beloved wife. It was a joy for me to hear this.

What interests me most is how our dear Darius hofs are doing in spiritual matters. I am often heavily grieved and very worried because my fear that here and there secret private property has already gained ground is apparently not completely without reason. Here and there the real, true unity and unanimity of the spirit is breaking up, as if the bond of peace were torn. My most deeply beloved, respected Christian Vetter, I wish that, with the great power and clarity which only God himself can give, you intervene on all Bruderhofs to help all those who want to become a true church, so that they truly seek the kingdom of God and his righteousness, surrendering everything else to God.

Our friends at Felger Farm have asked me to send them a teacher, either man or woman, perhaps because they think we have an overabundance of intellectual strength. Unfortunately, this is not at all the case; we know we are extremely poor in all things and again and again we need the gifts of the spirit of grace for everything. We need to stand deeply and firmly together with all our strength, and God in his great grace continually grants us this unity anew.

Please tell the Walter family that we thank them at Felger Farm for everything, that we hope they find true submission to the leadership of the whole church of God, that they surrender everything they are and have to God and then to *you* in complete *Gelassenheit*, so that you can give them the right help in the name of all servants of the gospel and all communities. Please tell them, respected Christian Vetter, that we wait for direction from you as to whether you give us this task from the church, which we would then follow as a service to Felger Farm. If we are not given this task, it is impossible for us to fulfill such a private request, because we belong to God and the unity of his church with everything we are and have.

There is much that I could lay on your heart concerning several Bruderhofs, but I am certain that you know everything much better than I do. I can only ask God that at your great age of seventy-eight years you receive strength upon strength and grace upon grace so that, like our forerunner and brother Andreas Ehrenpreis, you can abolish many wrongs which here and there seem to be getting the upper hand. If I could give advice in the humility of the childlike spirit, it would be this: that you, beloved and respected Christian Vetter, meet three or four times a year for a few days with Joseph Kleinsasser Vetter, Milltown (Schmiedeleut Elder) and Johannes Kleinsasser Vetter, Milford (Lehrerleut Elder), over whose eldership I rejoice from the bottom of my heart. Then all the communities should stand behind you with their prayers that Jesus Christ himself, to whom all power and authority is given, may be in your midst as he has promised. Then in full unanimity and clarity of spirit you should do away with all wrongs on all Bruderhofs. If we can act according to this suggestion, we will have taken a significant step in the necessary direction toward appointing one common elder once again, as it was in the first church in Jerusalem in the time of Peter, and later in the time of Ignatius, and as it was in the time of our forerunners for almost two hundred years.

We at the German Bruderhof are wholeheartedly ready to obey you brothers, who carry the elders' service for all servants of the Word and for the spiritual and temporal matters on all communities, in the fullness and completeness of love in faith. Through our unity the world should recognize that God sent Christ and that Jesus Christ sent us into the world just as he was sent by the Father. You will surely understand completely that, in this trust in the leading and guidance committed to you, I must also lay our poverty on your heart. You already wrote to us on April 25 in great love that before the new year you would help us with a small sum, and your dear son added that we should not take it badly if you cannot send much.

Yes, dear and worthy Christian Vetter, if you have a little, you should wholeheartedly send that little, but I have to lay it on your heart and the hearts of all Darius communities that our need has increased considerably since we sent the printed Sendbrief. As a rule we had a hundred souls to care for in the last months. Recently this number rose again, first through the birth of two children to families of our community, which made us very happy, then through the fact that the Swiss Werkhof, about which we wrote to you fully in the printed Sendbrief, is now so moved that almost all twenty are thinking about coming to us. But, unfortunately, they are not yet fully clear about the basis of faith in the Father, the Son, and the Spirit, and about submission to the kingdom of God and to the church of Jesus Christ. Therefore, they cannot yet comprehend the Holy Scripture of the prophets and apostles nor our church's confession of faith. We have sent Hans Zumpe, our second servant of the Word, to them. Following the visit of two of them to us, my dear wife Emmy, our housemother, also went, because the women there need her motherly advice.

One thing I have to say for them: our friends of the Swiss Werkhof proved themselves in refusing military service and in giving a public witness. One of them accepted a month in prison and gave a good witness to Jesus Christ. But they are still lacking in true humility and childlikeness, without which we cannot live peacefully in community. On the other hand, one of their families has already joined us—Peter and Anni Mathis with one child, Johann Christoph. These two are completely united with us on the basis of faith and have fully submitted first to God and then to us. So we have to reckon that by winter we will have to supply more than 112 adults and children with housing, food, and clothing. In addition to this, we constantly receive letters from those who long to be accepted into our Brotherhood. We answer them with written and printed letters, so that by corresponding we can sift out many whose basis is not deep or clear enough. Again and again there are some among them who truly want to reach complete *Gelassenheit* and full submission. It will be impossible for us to support so many without buying land, and it would also be against the character of Jesus Christ and his love if we did not provide our friends with sufficient housing. For about $1,000 we have had to build additions to some of our houses and acquire fields and meadows, a house and stables, set in the middle of our land. We shall need $6,600 for food, heating for all the apartments, and necessary work. We shall have to do something about this. Therefore, I ask you seriously to read our second printed Sendbrief once more very carefully. Then you will understand why we plead and urge all communities, in spite of their own need, to help us with a contribution of $15,000.

Perhaps through the grace of God's spirit it will be given to you when you meet with other brothers and servants of the Word to suggest such a gift of love and to send part of it to us as soon as possible.

Dearly beloved and worthy Christian Vetter, you know that we lowly beginners on the holy way do not want to tell anyone what to do. In no way do we want to make demands on any Bruderhof; not even the weakest member of our church would think of such a thing. The one and only thing we mean is to ask you in the name of Jesus Christ, for the sake of God's pity, to think deeply in your prayers that this is a question of mission, not only of one Bruderhof but of the whole church of God, as John the Baptist, Tobit, and Paul the apostle have said about alms, about fellow believers, and about contributions to the church community in Jerusalem.

So we ask for one thing only, that you let yourselves be led in this fully and completely by the spirit of God and Jesus Christ. We are certain and convinced that the blessing of such surrender and dedication will return to you.

To close, I wish that God's good spirit of perfect love and unity may fill you completely in all that you do.

I ask you to greet from us all your dear steward and the witness brothers, the Walter brothers, and the dear families of those members who have just died, the whole community, but most of all your beloved son Christian and his dear wife Katharina. I remain true and bound forever to you. I love you very much, and all the brothers and sisters of the German mission think of you before God's countenance.

                                                          Eberhard Arnold

Joseph Kleinsasser Vetter   Rhön Bruderhof
Milltown Bruderhof, Manitoba   November 1932

My very beloved and deeply respected Joseph Kleinsasser Vetter,

We were just about to write to you when to our great joy a letter came from you, beloved Joseph Vetter, and letters from your dear wife Elisabeth, from Jakob and Christina Waldner, and from Josef and Sarah Wollman. I also received an especially fine letter from the dear widow who lost her husband this year. Was he perhaps the brother of David Hofer of James Valley, the Michael Hofer whom I came to love very much?

In response to your very loving letters I send every good wish and greet you in the peace of God, the love of Jesus Christ, and the fellowship of the Holy Spirit. I follow your inner and outer situation with great interest and with my whole heart. Above all, the spiritual weakness in a number of Bruderhofs gives me cause for much concern and anxiety. I would like very much to hear from you in more detail how it went with Barickman and Maxwell Bruderhofs and their daughter communities; or perhaps your dear son, or David Hofer Vetter of James Valley Bruderhof, could write about this. I would very much like to know the names of the daughter communities, their precise addresses and the number of souls, number of families, servant of the Word, teacher, steward, and so on. Above all I would like to hear whether it came to a good understanding in the unity of the Spirit between you and them.

I well know your great burdens, although I do not like to write about them. But much more alarming is that I often have the impression that among the Darius communities things are going downhill more rapidly than complete community and *Gelassenheit* is among your communities. I feel deeply that although there are quite a few weaknesses, much love and a sense of full community has been preserved in your Bruderhofs in Manitoba. Since love is that power from God which never ends, I have faith for you that your church communities will stand the test in these hard times better than it sometimes appears.

Be courageous, my very beloved and respected Joseph Kleinsasser Vetter, and do not lose heart. Faith is courage and love is valiant. Out of faith love dares again and again to take everything firmly in hand. If we tackle something too softly or too weakly, it's not much help. We have to jump right in if we want to rescue someone who is sinking.

I rejoiced with all my heart that the service of elder for all servants of the Word of the Lehrer Bruderhofs has been laid on our beloved

Johannes Kleinsasser Vetter, who is a dear friend of yours too. May God grant him great strength, clarity, and wholehearted love by giving him the power of the Holy Spirit always anew. I have written to him and to Christian Waldner Vetter at West Raley Bruderhof my suggestion for the elder service for the whole Hutterian Brotherhood. I want to lay on your heart also this counsel which I offer you respectfully. I can certainly see that it appears almost impossible to appoint one elder for all the communities, one who could direct all spiritual and temporal needs. He would have to so represent the witness of the gospel and truth in love for all the church communities, that mission would be practiced with the same power that once sent brothers out from Moravia and Hungary for over a hundred years. But my advice to Christian and Johannes Vetter and to you, beloved and revered Joseph Vetter, is to meet three or four times a year for two or three days. Thus you could consider and decide before God, in the love of Jesus Christ and under the leading of the Holy Spirit, what should be done away with in the churches, which Bruderhofs need immediate help, and how the service of the gospel can be newly established. Through such meetings of the three elders three or four times a year, a significant step could be taken toward complete uniting. Without doubt, our exalted Lord and Master Jesus Christ would rejoice with all his heart in this, for that would bring us nearer to fulfilling his will expressed in his high-priestly prayer in the Gospel of John, chapter 17.

Now I know well that this idea would mean a very great effort for you because of the long distances, and you also do not have the money for such frequent long journeys. I would very much hope that the other two elders would help pay for this. Just on this point, I can see clearly what a difficult situation you are all in, and what a great burden of responsibility you have to carry on your heart. I can well imagine that your hair and your beard have grown much whiter since the time when I was able to be with you and your dear Elisabeth Basel and listen to your words. For me it is an unforgettable memory and constant source of strength.

It will also be difficult for you if I now make a very urgent request to all Bruderhofs to help us with a large sum, because our mission task is beginning to grow and flower more and more through the testimony of the Holy Spirit. Because of our weakness, which certainly still holds back many people, there is far less visible fruit than was the case through Jakob Hutter's apostolic mission and through Peter Riedemann's and Peter Walpot's mission work and that of many other forerunners at the beginning of the newly established church. The thirst and hunger of seeking and questioning people in this land is very great, but our meager strength is not enough to help them all as we should. Only a few of them gather with us for the sake of the word of truth and at the table of full community.

In spite of this, we have grown to be 110 people now in November, the beginning of winter. It is the time of year when our numbers are usually low compared to the count of our community including the summer guests. Certainly, among these 110 are a few with whom it is not clear if they will follow God's call for always with complete faith and a surrendered heart. We have with us a conscientious objector and teacher named Seifert from Bohemia and Moravia. From Switzerland we have a married couple, Peter and Anni Mathis with their child, Johann Christoph, who have grown very dear to us. We can only say that we have become completely one with them in faith and love in the spirit of Jesus Christ. They came from the Werkhof near Zurich.

The other members of the Werkhof near Zurich are also seriously considering whether they should break away and come to us. They have even written two letters in which they declared themselves ready to unite with us without any conditions or claims. My dear wife Emmy already wrote to our beloved David Hofer at James Valley Bruderhof about this. But when their two Word leaders were sent to us, Hans Meier and Max Lezzie, we had to point out to them that the basis of their faith did not give sufficient reason for them to join us. Rather we had to advise them not to come until they, in the humility of the childlike spirit, had accepted into their hearts the true faith in the Father, the Son, and the Spirit, in God's kingdom, and in the church of Jesus Christ. For this purpose we read to them out of Peter Riedemann's *Confession of Faith* and other old writings. Certainly, these two stand firm in refusing to take up bloody weapons—Hans Meier has already been in prison for several months and has given a good testimony for Jesus Christ. Unfortunately they have not yet recognized what the Church of Jesus Christ is—God's lantern kindled for the whole world—and how the unity of the spirit shines forth from this lamp.

Therefore we have sent our dear Hans Z. Vetter, our second servant of the Word, to them in Switzerland, and with him my beloved wife Emmy, our housemother, because several women there need her motherly help. In the letters from our brothers and sisters whom we have sent there, we hear that the women are actually further along than the men, so we can perhaps hope that all on the Werkhof will break through to full clarity and unite with us completely. Robert Häberli, one of the members of the Werkhof who was with us for some weeks already, pleads for this strongly and clearly.

Meanwhile we have celebrated here the wedding of our young Swedish couple, Nils and Dora. They returned to Sweden to put their money affairs in order, as we were in great need of money for building dwellings and expanding our fields, meadows, and garden land. In the meantime, we have had various reports that our young brother and sister, who are journeying through Sweden in the old Hutterian *Tracht*, are giving a strong witness to divine truth in a childlike and humble spirit. We rejoice to receive this good news of them.

From this short report, dearly beloved Joseph Kleinsasser Vetter, you will no doubt see how great our task is, and how indescribably weak and poor is our economic foundation. I could add more details, such as our joy that the typist of these lines, Hella Römer, has decided to join God's church. The printed Sendbrief, for which you thanked us so lovingly, makes all this still clearer.

I am very sorry that our language is difficult for your beloved brothers and sisters to understand. It is not easy for us to write differently from the way we speak and express ourselves to each other. It is especially so with the Sendbrief because I wanted to give you a glimpse into the thoughts of our new members from what they themselves wrote. In the future I will make an effort to avoid all difficult sentences; for, more than the speech of today, I treasure the old dialects of Tirol, Moravia, Transylvania, Carinthia, Swabia, and Switzerland as they were spoken in the sixteenth century. Unfortunately I am not able to express myself in these old dialects as clearly as I have tried to in the German of today.

We thank you from our hearts for your words of love about our sister Else von Hollander, who was called from us; about the gathering of our small flock, the protection of our steward and his driver, and about our poverty and need. As you can well imagine, this temporal need has meanwhile increased still more so that we cannot neglect making an urgent plea to you, our beloved brothers across the sea, to send us help as quickly and generously as possible. We cannot possibly continue like this, while from all sides come urgent and passionate requests to be taken into the church of God. I realize that it does not come into question for your Bruderhofs to give a large part of what we need when you cannot pay your own taxes and interest.

However, I must not let you be an exception. It seems to me that I would be looking down on your poverty if I wrote only to the more well-to-do Bruderhofs about our needy situation and remained silent toward you. We do know from the Holy Scripture of the apostles and prophets that even the very smallest gift, if given from the heart, means as much as a great sum. Our King and Master, who has shown us the right way in everything, tells us of the widow who gave her very last and only coin. It is a matter of true love and surrender that we give everything to God and his church, whether it is much or little. That is why I urge you to do the utmost possible as far as is demanded from you by your conscience and before God. My trust in you and yours is unlimited and absolute.

I shall be in complete agreement with whatever you decide. How gladly I would write more at length, and how gladly I would send an immediate answer to the dear brothers and sisters who gave us such joy with their loving letters; unfortunately our very intense work does not allow it at the moment.

So allow me now to close and send heartfelt greetings to all beloved servants of the church communities in Manitoba, and especially to your beloved son and his dear wife, to your dear wife Elisabeth Basel, also to your dear daughter Susanna and to the whole church and all the Bruderhofs in Manitoba. May God still give you in your old age great joy in the growth and faithfulness of the church! We think of you and yours before God in the name of Jesus Christ and the power of the Holy Spirit.

Your lowly brother who loves you greatly,

Eberhard Arnold

Joseph I. Waldner   November 1932
Huron Bruderhof, Manitoba

My very beloved Joseph Vetter,

Just now you have written me such a very loving letter. We thank you and all the beloved brothers and sisters of your Bruderhof most heartily and sincerely. We wish all of you the peace of God, the love of Jesus Christ, and the strength of complete community that is given to us through the Holy Spirit.

I understand your situation and conditions very well. Times have become considerably more difficult since I was with you and, if we see things as they really are, we cannot say that they will get better very soon. On the contrary, there are many signs that our times are close to the last hour. The day of judgment, which is the day of wrath, is closing in on the injustice of the world of today. Now it all depends on the church of God keeping its distance from the increasing injustice of mammon and on pure, holy love not growing cold but increasing. We do know it is hard for you to take part in the mission work entrusted to us by giving your financial help. But, beloved Joseph Vetter, since you always had such a joyful and trusting faith, I do want very much to lay it on your heart that it is very necessary now for the communities to stand by us in the work of mission. In the midst of the darkness of this sinking world, the light of truth must dawn anew. The little city on the hill must show to all the justice and peace and the spirit of unity which the coming kingdom of God will bring. With God this kingdom is already in effect as the kingdom of heaven. Erring mankind must be made aware of what this means, and of what God wants to say with it. For this purpose we must set the light of true community in the midst of this dark world, and from this church of light we must send out torchbearers to carry the light to all. We must go to the ends of the world. That is what Jesus has commanded. That is why we ask that all the communities do their utmost to help make this mission possible.

Our beloved Joseph Kleinsasser Vetter, whose inner image I always carry in my heart and whose good spirit often speaks to me, will surely tell you the contents of the letter I have written to him, since you are often over there with him. Then you will see that since our second printed Sendbrief there have again been some small indications which move our work forward, especially from Switzerland— although actually it isn't our work but the working of the Holy Spirit. But for this work also we shall need a lot of help from the church of God in things of the spirit as well as in economic matters. I wish for you also that you are given the help that makes it possible for you to remain firmly together and carry on the work of community to the end.

I send heartfelt wishes to all the dear brothers and sisters who wrote to us, especially to your dear co-worker and helper in the service of the Word, Joseph Glanzer Vetter, to your dear wife, and to the two old Basels on your hof who have become so dear to me, as well as Jakob Waldner and his wife. I greet you from my heart.

Your very loving, lowly,

Eberhard Arnold

Johannes Hofer Vetter   Rhön Bruderhof
Rockport Bruderhof, South Dakota.   November 1932

My beloved Johannes Vetter,

Unfortunately, I have not heard from you for a long time, and still I think with such joy of how you looked through my window as I read in the old books and copied them, also of the very loving ways in which you gave me your help. If I understood everything aright, you now have the great responsibility and load on your shoulders of caring for the Rockport Bruderhof in South Dakota alone in the service of the Word and of guiding all the work of your Bruderhof, together with the other brothers. So I wish you God's great and powerful strength in his peace, in the love of Jesus Christ and the leading of the Holy Spirit.

Unfortunately, our Hans Zumpe Vetter did not quite understand how it has turned out with your Rockport Bruderhof and your Hutterville Bruderhof, as to whether Peter Hofer Vetter is really in the service on the Hutterville Bruderhof and you in the Rockport Bruderhof in South Dakota. For that reason he never knew how to write to you. You must please take the trouble to write a letter to us. I well know that you feel like some of the prophets who were fetched away from the cattle they were herding in order to become henceforth voices for God; but please believe it of us with all your heart that we love the simplicity of the childlike spirit more than learning and an artificial manner of speaking and writing. We cannot deny that we have learned these things, but just for that reason we can honestly say we do not think much of them. An upright heart with a childlike, humble, and loving spirit is a thousand times better than all the learned writers and speakers put together, since there are always very few among them who take upon themselves the humility of Jesus Christ.

I hope, beloved Johannes Vetter, that you and your whole community received our printed letter and also understood something of it. There you will have seen that things go forward slowly with us. It is much too slow, but at least it is something. The spirit of God wanted to bring mission much faster into all lands. However, there are still far too few among the many millions ready to receive it, and the church of God living in community is still too weak to represent this great, universal task in full power to the ends of the earth, as Jesus Christ has commanded. Again and again we receive letters and visits, especially from Switzerland. From these letters we notice how many people have a very difficult struggle within themselves to find if and how they can go the true way of love and unity.

We are usually between 105 and 110 people here now, who all want to seek true community and put it into action. There may be a few who will leave before they have gone through the time of testing for their acceptance into the church and before they are baptized. Many others still want to come. Our second servant of the Word, Hans Zumpe Vetter, is at present with my dear wife, his mother-in-law, in Switzerland to proclaim there on the Werkhof the gospel of complete community, since many questions arose to which they hadn't found the right answer. Only one couple, Peter and Anni Mathis, have moved to us with their little boy Johann Christoph and feel completely united with us in the spirit of the church community and the kingdom of God.

You can imagine that with this steady, slow growth our means of providing food and living quarters are not adequate. It is more and more obvious that it is impossible to nourish this small flock with the land we have. We have had to start building again and adding more land as our little group grows. It was absolutely unavoidable. If you have correctly understood our situation from the second printed letter, you can see that we are trying to feed one hundred people on one hundred acres, while as a rule you have 3,000 to 5,000 acres for one hundred people. Now surely our circumstances are a bit different because we do more garden work; but even so it is impossible to nourish so many with so little land, also under the conditions in Germany. So for the present we had to add at least seventy-five acres and doubtless will have to buy more agricultural land.

Also in other areas we have to go forward if the mission is not to come to a standstill. We therefore call on you, beloved brothers, to take upon yourselves, together with us, the mission work in the German-speaking countries, as our forefathers and forerunners did. At the end of last year you, beloved Johannes Vetter, sent us some faithful help. I thank you again from my heart for this! Our Hans Zumpe Vetter has also thanked you in January. Now I ask you and your whole church community, in spite of bad times and even though you yourselves are preparing a second move to Alberta, to decide again for a large gift, so that the work here can continue. Unfortunately, I do not know which brothers and sisters moved with Peter Hofer Vetter to the Hutterville Bruderhof and who stayed with you, so I cannot pass on any greetings. To my pain I heard that recently you had to see a young twenty-two-year-old man die under sad circumstances. Our beloved Michel Waldner Vetter gave the funeral sermon.

Please greet dear old Wurz Vetter and his poor girl. May God be a real comfort to him and to you all. All our brothers and sisters greet you from their hearts, and we all think of you always in great faithfulness and love.

Eberhard Arnold

Elias Walter   Rhön Bruderhof, December 23, 1932
Stand Off Bruderhof

My most beloved, deeply respected Elias Walter,

I am sending you a letter to read at Gebet to your dear Stand Off Bruderhof and to consider with the brothers. In addition, I am sending this personal greeting, a statement of accounts, and the request for your support with the Small History Book.

I wish you and your dear Elisabeth strength of body, soul, and spirit through unity in God, love in Christ, and grace from the Holy Spirit. I pray that you may have joy in all your children.

Unfortunately, my efforts on behalf of your son, who is living outside the community or perhaps not living any more, have been in vain. He could not be found anywhere. But God may grant that he decides to come home of his own free will, just as both sons of Michel Waldner Vetter of Bon Homme, Manitoba, have done to my joy. My heart is full of pain and sorrow that I have not been able to help you, for I well know that your heart is oppressed by cares for your relatives, more than you wish to express.

Having met young Hofer from Raley,[1] I found it impossible to seek contact with his father and with a spirit so destructive to community. After this experience I would have been very happy to help your and our friends on the Felger Farm. Concerning their request for a teacher from our Bruderhof, however, I feel we cannot do this without being unfaithful to the spirit of loyalty and order, even if we had a surplus of suitable teachers, which is certainly not the case. I would gladly send our printed letter and a personal letter to Felger Farm, but my repeated impression has been that they do not respect my advice as much as would be good, considering that it comes from the spirit of the church, which is the spirit of Jesus. The best way would be for the families of Felger Farm to offer their obedience to our Christian Waldner Vetter and allow themselves to be relocated in three well-

---

[1] See p.18.

proven communities living in the best of order, harmony, and peace. A completely new Bruderhof would then be established on the Felger Farm, drawn from spiritually strong and united communities, without any of the Felger Farm families taking part. Such a way through would give an example of the surrender, love, and humility of Jesus Christ, an example which could be an encouragement to many Bruderhofs. All the self-seeking at Bruderhofs which care first and last for their own interests only could be better fought against and overcome. This would be a help to all. Christ and his kingdom would be honored, and the past would be blotted out through the forgiveness of God's church.

The greatest evil that can befall a church of God is disunity, for the mystery of God is the *unity* of the Father, the Son, and the Spirit. Therefore, the mystery of his will is the *unity* of the kingdom of God and the unity of the church of Jesus Christ through the power of the Holy Spirit. May this be fulfilled and preserved. From our hearts we pray for it for each Bruderhof and for the whole church of God, which is to draw all Bruderhofs together in unity. May those in the elder service, our beloved Johannes Kleinsasser Vetter with the help of Christian Vetter and Joseph Kleinsasser Vetter, take decisive *action*. For without any doubt the spirit of wisdom and counsel desires to bring about such action. Our Christmas teaching on Isaiah 11 clearly testifies to this.

May the whole church of God assist you and me in spreading the witness to truth, also in printing the Small History Book. It would be good if you sought counsel and help from other older brothers and their Bruderhofs for the economic support of this great work. It is doubtless evident and known to all that our Bruderhof in Germany is too poor to provide any of the heavy costs of this book.

May God show his children the way in which we can work for his honor and live as a witness to his truth.

So, beloved and deeply respected Elias Vetter, heartfelt greetings in trust and love to you, from your fellow worker and brother,

Eberhard Arnold

Michel Waldner   Rhön Bruderhof, 1932
Bon Homme Bruderhof, South Dakota

Beloved Michel Vetter,

Your loving letter of November 9 was such a joy to me! I like to think of you and your dear family and your beloved Bon Homme

Bruderhof, so I hasten to send you my special greetings. May the peace of God and the strength of the Holy Spirit in the love of Jesus Christ be with you. I thank you very much for all the kind words through which you have reported about our Sendbrief, your journey, and all your experiences.

Yes, I do know very well how difficult things already are in some of the communities. It is clear that the long period since the re-establishment of full community in Russia, now already about eighty years, brings with it the great weariness that accompanies growing old. I must say that I am very worried about the Darius communities particularly. Certainly there is great danger in the Manitoba communities that the spirit of the world and of present-day life may creep in here and there. But there seems to me a still greater danger among the Darius communities of love growing cold, injustice increasing, and unity being extinguished. It may still last several years if things go on like this, but one day a decision will have to be faced, right will have to be separated from wrong, and a new beginning will have to be made. That is why I asked your Joseph Kleinsasser Vetter, Johannes Kleinsasser Vetter from Buck Ranch, whom I have come to love very much, and also Christian Waldner Vetter from West Raley Bruderhof to stand really firmly and strongly together, also to meet very frequently. In this way, through the joint decisions of these three elders, gradually a unity of our whole Brotherhood and church of God will be revealed under a united leading, so that all evil conditions, whether spiritual or temporal, will be done away with.

Something of significance also has to happen for the mission that God has asked of us here, through a united, common effort of the Brothers. I know very well what poverty and need have come to the Manitoba Bruderhofs, and I also know how difficult it is in South Dakota to pay taxes and rent nowadays and to care for so many people. But I don't want to leave you out, my dear beloved and respected Michel Vetter, as I turn now with heartfelt urgency to all the communities and lay it personally and deeply on their hearts that we very urgently need effective help right now for our establishment and mission in Germany. This could be brought about by raising a general contribution from all communities.

The work goes slowly forward. One Swiss family . . . [In shorthand it says here "very detailed." This probably means that the detailed report in the letter to Joseph Kleinsasser Vetter, Milltown, Manitoba, (p.305) should be inserted here.] So you will understand that we urgently need money for building houses and for buying land and buildings. It is otherwise impossible to get ahead. If it wasn't high time, I would not be writing to you so urgently. Whoever has much, should give much; whoever has little, little—and give it from their hearts.

However that may be, my love and thankfulness toward you will always remain. I wish you all, you and your dear family and dear Joseph Waldner Vetter, the richest blessings of God in inner and outer things and real, courageous boldness to find and do the right thing in this difficult time.

With heartfelt and faithful greetings from all of us to all in your very dear community. In constant, faithful love,

Eberhard Arnold

Jerg J. Waldner   Rhön Bruderhof
Word Leader at the Maxwell Bruderhof   Feb. 14, 1933
Manitoba

My dearly beloved Jerg Vetter!

We received your loving letter of January 2, 1933, with great thankfulness and deep joy. We had been looking forward to it for a long time. May there be with all of you the peace of God as the perfect unity of his kingdom and his church, the love of Jesus Christ as the greatest joy of his grace, and the power of the Holy Spirit with the full community it brings!

You must never think that letters written simply and from the heart are not every bit as valuable to us as those written by educated or even very learned people. The opposite is true. The simplest and most trusting are the best. Someone with the gift of learning is like a rich man who comes to the community and has to give up all his possessions and take the lowest place. We have every reason to be ashamed that we have read and learned so much. For the more we have and know, the more will be asked of us. And in the end, the best we can say will be, "We are useless servants. We have done only what we ought to have done."

Now I am at home again in the midst of all the rich experiences of the Holy Spirit, whose stimulation and movement work in our weak little community as a continuously purifying and fully uniting power. But the longer I am here, the sadder my heart becomes when I think of all the threatening signs of disunity, unclarity, uncertainty, permissiveness, and indecision which has sapped the vitality of the old orders and the strength of some Bruderhofs in America. In some, the inner authority of the servants of the Word, which can be given only out of the unanimity of the believing and loving church, has suffered serious harm. In some, obedience toward those responsible, which is born of faith and love and can come only from the holy spirit of childlike and trusting humility, has grown less. The boundary stones so firmly erected against everything of one's own—against every bit of private ownership, against every bit of uncalled for independence and self-glorification, also against any collective selfishness of larger or smaller or even very small family clans—seem in some places to be getting dislodged. The holy demands of a rightly-ordered service in the services of the Word and of temporal affairs, in the school, and in the kindergarten are not taken seriously everywhere and are even despised in some places. The evil fruit of these conditions shows itself in wicked and slanderous talk. Still worse, in some places obedience to the leading of the elders lacks true respect and acceptance. This causes mistrust and disunity, so that the unity and cohesion between Bruderhofs threatens to break up and almost disintegrate. When the unity gets less and less in work and dress and in the use of money, including money for mutual help, the time may come as it did in Raditschewa when one or the other may say, "It is too late. We cannot keep a community going that has collapsed inwardly and is only hypocrisy at heart. We would rather have private property and no hypocrisy than community with hypocrisy and untruthfulness."

Oh, what a horrifying end that would be! It has not gone that far yet. God still holds his hand over the thirty-seven Bruderhofs now in America. But in some places need and misery in inner and outer things is increasing. It is as if the hour of temptation has come over the earth. It is as if the time has come for judgment to begin over the house of God. Will the love of many grow cold and injustice gain the upper hand more and more? What must we do? Some action must be taken.

Love knows what to do. I have advised the three main elders, Christian Vetter, Kleinsasser Vetter, and Johannes Vetter, to meet several times a year and, with a firm hand, unitedly get rid of all abuses and establish the unity and the harmony of all Bruderhofs in *one* church. This can be given to them only through the grace of the Holy Spirit. But I too, however weak, will be prepared to offer my services, just as you will no doubt offer yours, dear Jerg Vetter. This service can mean only one thing to us: that we work along the whole front, work for the whole, perfect *truth* in perfect, glowing love. We must work in the most devoted love, prepared for any sacrifice in unwavering, genuine, and unalloyed *truth*! A new and purer bond must be established between the Bruderhofs, a renewal and confirmation as sharp and clear as the covenant of baptism was of old. Whoever does not want to join in must leave the Bruderhof. However, those who are prepared even in weakness to repent again and again and accept any and every discipline will be helped through, whatever the cost. If we ask the Holy Spirit to help us do this, it must succeed. Our Father will not give us stones when we ask for bread. Ask for the Holy Spirit.

How much there is that I would still like to write! But I must close and comfort myself with the thought that you have our long printed letter. There you can see how it is with us in temporal and spiritual things and what we ask and hope for from you.

So through the community of God's truth, the love of Christ, and the community of the Holy Spirit we remain your faithful brothers and sisters in Germany.

Your humble brother and helper in the service of the gospel,

Eberhard Arnold

Joseph Hofer   Emmy Arnold
Maxwell Bruderhof   Rhön Bruderhof, July 27, 1933
Manitoba

You dear and very respected Josef Hofer Vetter,

Heartfelt greetings to you and the much respected Jerg Waldner Vetter, father of Jerg M. Waldner Vetter and Johann and Susanne Hofer, and to the whole community.

Your letters of December 11, 23, 30, and January 2, lie in front of me, and we have the heartfelt desire to visit you beloved ones again through a little letter. I have just written a letter to your daughter community, the Sundale Bruderhof, and I would so like to send you a sign of life also. We can well imagine how much work you have now that harvest time has come. May it also be in eternal things as Christ says, "The fields are already white for harvest; pray therefore the Lord of the harvest to send out laborers into his harvest." So the Father in heaven and his son Jesus Christ have called us out of this wicked and godless world to enter into his ark, that is, the church.

It is so wonderful and fine, dear Jerg M. Waldner Vetter, what you wrote to us about Michel Waldner and Jakob Hofer and about how united and in the spirit everything went. May we also carry on our hearts, morning and evening, the awareness that the Lord is with us! The story you told us about the servant, Jakob Waldner, gripped us deeply—how he was not gifted in speaking but nevertheless spoke in such power of the Spirit to those who live in private property that everybody who heard him thought him a very gifted speaker. When he was asked how this happened, he answered, "I only opened my mouth and the Spirit spoke through it." Yes, one can surely imagine it has often happened like that. It is also good that way. When we can do and achieve nothing ourselves, then the strength of God can best work through men.

Now, my beloved brothers and sisters, may God help us to be ready, as were the five wise virgins who had enough oil in their lamps, to go all together to the wedding feast when the bridegroom comes. May we make the best use of this time, so that God's spirit can work and light a fire on earth that will burn and shine and be seen by many people.

How are we making out? You will have received a letter from our son, Eberhard, from Zurich after Easter, in which he tells you about our situation. In spite of the present need, new, zealous, and seeking people keep coming to us to live in community, leaving good jobs behind. Poor people also come to us, who have grown weary through the need of the times and having no job, and now seek help and salvation with God and his church.

We are now 140 people at our Bruderhof, and new guests, who want to stay for a shorter or longer time, arrive almost daily. In the evening after the work is done we talk with them about those things which concern the kingdom of God and his church. There are quite a number of new people who have entered a time of testing. Some of these have to fight through hard struggles and conflicts with their relatives. Some have had to cut ties with their relatives, which is not easy because they had a real family life. The parents reproach them for breaking family ties and going to strange people instead of earning money to feed their mothers or helping their brothers and sisters find jobs in this difficult time. But what are they to do if they are called to a life of discipleship to Christ in the community of faith? So they have left everything and followed Christ, as the disciples did when they left their boats and everything.

It is a great strengthening to all of us when new ones come, but can you dear ones imagine what a great burden it is when so many come and there is not even enough to carry our own tested brothers and sisters through! We have only 175 acres of land, including all fields, meadows, commons, and woods. If everything turns out well, we might have enough potatoes and vegetables for 130 people until spring. But the bread will last only two, at the most three, months, although from the first day on we have been issuing strict war-time rations. You can imagine that it is not very easy when so many new and zealous guests come and the larders are empty. But still we have to say that our dear Father in heaven has put us to shame again and again by far exceeding our small faith. Each midday and evening we have been able to put a meal on the table in spite of "Mother Hubbard often being head cook," as we would say. (There was little to eat.)

We know, dear brothers and sisters, that you don't have it easy either in this time when the value of the dollar has dropped and the price of wheat is so low. But put yourselves once into the shoes of our little community in the midst of the roaring breakers of the present time. Above all, think of us in your prayers and don't forget to send us help, so that we do not have to send anybody away in winter, can buy wood and coal, and can equip rooms, even if quite scantily, for the eager new ones. If we want to do all this, it has to be done soon, or it will be too late. It would also be helpful to us if once again you would send us a box of clothing—especially men's suits, dresses for women, head coverings, and aprons. The best would be if some of your brothers would come over to talk about all the things which have to be done.

We remember you so far away with heartfelt love, and united with you in faith, we greet you.

Your Hutterian brothers and sisters in Germany,
Emmy Arnold

My husband Eberhard, whom you know, greets you all from his heart. He has so much work with the books now, also with the many dedicated new people, and has to go off very often to talk with the authorities. It's good then that the two Hanses can represent him.

This letter was drafted by Eberhard Arnold on December 28, 1933 and then copied and mailed to Zacharias Waldner Vetter, James Valley, as well as to the following, by Hardy and Edith Arnold in January of 1934 from Holland (as it was unsafe to send such a letter from within Nazi Germany).

1) David Hofer . . . . James Valley, Manitoba
2) Josef Kleinsasser . . . . Milltown, Manitoba
3) Michel Waldner . . . . Bon Homme, South Dakota
4) Johannes Kleinsasser . . . . Milford, Alberta
5) Johann P. Hannes Entz . . . . Big Bend, Alberta
6) Josef Wipf . . . . Rockport, Magrath, Alberta
7) Peter Hofer . . . . Rockport, Alexandria, South Dakota
8) Christian Waldner . . . . West Raley, Alberta

 9) Elias Walter . . . . Stand Off, Alberta
10) Johannes Wurz . . . . Richards, Wilson, Alberta
11) Jakob Wurz . . . . Spring Valley, Rockyford, Alberta

Rhön Bruderhof, GERMANY
December 28, 1933

Dearly beloved Zacharias Vetter,

May the peace of God, the love of Jesus Christ, and the community of the Holy Spirit be with you and all your dear brothers and sisters. Your letters have refreshed us again and again and given us deep joy. I have been confined to bed since the beginning of November, because I broke my leg and have it in plaster, and my letters have been hindered by the troubles of the times as was the case with Jakob Hutter in 1535. But the letters written to you by my son Eberhard, by my helper in the service of the Word, Hannes Boller Vetter, and by our witness brother Hans Meier were all written at my request and confirmed by me, also those from my beloved and faithful wife Emmy Basel.

We have been notified in writing that the Bruderhof "can no longer be maintained to the same extent as before, since no guarantee is given that education will be in the national interest or according to a recognized church form." We suffer this tribulation on account of the articles of faith, as set down in Peter Riedemann's *Confession of Faith* of the year 1540 under the following headings: Concerning governmental authority, Why governmental authority hath been ordained, Whether rulers can also be Christians, Concerning warfare, and Concerning the making of swords. These are also to be found in the fourth article of our sixteenth-century article books. We suffer also on account of the articles in Peter Riedemann's Confession: Community of goods, Community of saints, What the Church is, How one is led thereto, Concerning the baptism of Christ and of His Church, all of which can also be found in the first and third articles of the sixteenth-century article books. Finally there is the article Concerning the education of children in Peter Riedemann's Confession (of 1540), also in the Chronicle and in the old epistle books by Hieronymus Käls and Peter Walpot in the same period, and by Andreas Ehrenpreis later.

We cannot depart from these articles of the apostolic and New Testament faith of our forefathers. It is as though beloved, respected David Hofer Vetter was saying to me again, long after his death, what he said repeatedly during my visits in 1930-1931 to the Rockport Bruderhof in South Dakota, "Remain in Germany as long as you are able to maintain the school and the education of the children according to our faith."

Our schoolchildren and their teacher have been invited to
Switzerland by a group similar to the Rappists, who live in community
of goods and await Christ and his future. They would probably be
ready to accept part of our community, as many as thirty-five souls
immediately. These would be the schoolchildren with their parents,
and would form our daughter community. But the Swiss government
is making difficulties with the immigration, since they do not want
to admit so many foreigners. We would much rather be all together
on one new Bruderhof. In spite of some increases we are only 110
people, because some unbaptized novices have broken their word and
become unfaithful in the face of tribulation, and children whom we
loved and cared for over a long period have been taken away. We
would only divide such a small Bruderhof reluctantly. If we emigrated
quickly with the whole community, we would have to sell at such
low prices that we would lose almost all the little money and goods
we have and could not even pay our passage to Canada. The German
Mennonites help us with their advice. Their Professor Unruh, who
arranged the emigration of the Russian Mennonites to America, is
prepared to travel to the government in Canada for us, if we will pay
the fare! There he would arrange our journey and entry into Canada
with the help of the Canadian Pacific Company. You will learn of the
persecution we are meeting and the need it brings us from my
memorandum, sent for the time being only to the three elders, and
also from the helpful statement of Karl Heim, a university professor
in Tübingen.

We plead for your counsel and help in all these questions. When
you write to the Foreign Minister and the Minister of the Interior of
the German government, make it clear that our Bruderhof does not
belong to us but to the Hutterian Church in America and to all its
communities, as expressed in our statutes. Could you try to get
permission for our immigration into Canada? Could you send us
money? We have to make many journeys to the government and need
to have money on hand in order to undertake the emigration from
Germany, which we do not wish for but which will probably soon
prove necessary. We want to do this with the friendly agreement of
the German authorities. But we would rather see our almost seventy
baptized members without house and home, without bed or shelter,
than do anything against our faith. We want to do everything we can
to preserve for the church of Jesus Christ the little property we have
obtained with loving help from you and our Swiss brothers. We often

have not a cent in hand, for all the community's assets are tied up in our houses, while our own harvest provides our food as long as we can remain here. We beseech you, in spite of your own poverty, to send us sufficient to help us do what is necessary for our children and prepare for emigration.

We know of no way to help ourselves without a large gift of money. However, God gives our hearts courage and joy in spite of many tears. He can also change everything, providing for us so that we can continue with a clear conscience in the service of the church in full community, proclaiming the gospel and educating our children.

May God's Holy Spirit lead both you and us and keep us all in the discipleship and poverty of the love of Jesus Christ, that we may be found faithful to the end in all things. These are great and serious times, and just such periods of severe affliction are given to the church as a blessing. Our faith grows all the more deeply and we find it all the truer that "Joy in the Lord is your strength." At the beginning of the Sermon on the Mount in Matthew 5, which I ask you to read again, Jesus said, "Rejoice and be glad!"

We greet you in this joy of the suffering and cross of Jesus Christ and with the kiss of fellowship in the Holy Spirit of God.

From your brothers and sisters in Germany and their lowly Servant, who loves you with all his heart as his brothers and sisters. your faithful

Eberhard Arnold

Postscript:
Utrecht, Holland
January 8, 1934

If you are able to send money to us, please do not send it to Frau Meier in Zurich, who is still living in private property. Send it to "The Swiss Bank," Frauenfeld, Switzerland, addressed to the account of the "Hutterian Church in America." The authorized business manager and servant of the Word for Europe is Eberhard Arnold, Bruderhof Neuhof, Kreis Fulda, Hessen-Nassau, Germany. The bank account in Frauenfeld belongs to the whole church of the Hutterian Brethren and can be used only for the tasks of the Christian church and brotherhood of America. This is important! This letter was completed and sent on instructions from my dear father.

(Signed) Eberhard C. H. Arnold (Hardy)

Our school has now been closed. For their safety the children are being taken to Switzerland.

Alm Bruderhof, Liechtenstein
April 7, 1934

My very beloved Elias Vetter,

May the peace of God, which is the complete unity of his heart and of his people, the love of Jesus Christ, which is complete joy in the powers of his future world, and the strength of the Holy Spirit, which builds and protects his church and community, be with you, you dear one, and with all your beloved brothers and sisters. Beloved Elias Vetter, whom I will never forget, you will have felt puzzled and pained that I have not myself written to you for so long. But I have been very worried about the needs of our Bruderhof community, and have been traveling for nearly five weeks to find a means of livelihood for us.

Meanwhile your letter with all your love reached us all right. The Frauenfeld address has proved to be completely reliable. We have already used it for several years. So in the name of all our brothers and sisters, especially their children, I thank you with all my heart. We are thinking of you every day, especially in the work on the Small History Book, for in spite of our pressing need and distress, we hold to our commitment to print it. We are now looking through it again, and because of the great expense, we shall omit my huge work and publish the book in the short form proposed by you and J. Loserth.

Today I can only send this short greeting of love and thanks to you in advance of a longer letter.

Here we are working on a handwritten letter of about twelve large pages to all the Bruderhofs in America, in which we pour out our needs to you and tell you also how God has powerfully helped us through and of the joy we have in the midst of distress. Please do not be shocked that we have to ask for help once again. In the meantime much has happened. We now have a second Bruderhof, a Hutterian community up in the mountains—the Alm Bruderhof, Silum, Triesenberg, Principality of Liechtenstein. The new community will begin with forty-five souls, while seventy-five remain at the old community, our Rhön Bruderhof, in Germany.

Since January 1934, our children and young people have been fleeing from that violation of their consciences which is threatening all school children and young people of military age in Germany today with an evil, compelling force to make them hate and take part in civil war and in war between nations. At first some of our children and young people were kept hidden at different places in Germany with friends or relatives so that after a few weeks they could be taken across the border without risk. We have now gathered nearly all of them at the new little community. Many new people, zealous for the truth, will certainly come to us there after a time, for it will become ever clearer to people "outside" that all who want to be serious Christians in Germany will be subjected to harsh oppression. In this trial some will quite certainly long for life in total community, so that in it they can be genuine disciples of Christ and live out his pure love and unity. In a few days our detailed, handwritten letter to all communities will give you a fuller account of all this and much more.

So for today I can close this brief letter. Today I will send only this short greeting in advance and ask you to greet your family and the whole Stand Off Bruderhof in heartfelt thankfulness. May complete peace and unity protect you all! Our community is indestructible as long as it is and remains in complete communion and fellowship with the Father, the Son, and the Holy Spirit. In this faith I remain faithfully and firmly united with you and yours and am your very loving

Eberhard Arnold

Emmy Arnold
Alm Bruderhof
Principality of Liechtenstein
August 1, 1934

Very beloved and respected Jörg G. Waldner Vetter,

First of all, I greet you and your community with the greeting of peace and unity. My husband Eberhard Vetter, who is well known to you, and I have been at our second Bruderhof here in the Alps for nearly four weeks. We want to stay here for about four more weeks to celebrate the wedding of our oldest son, Eberhard, who wrote you a detailed letter from Holland at the beginning of January in the name of his father, our Word leader. Our son wants to become a teacher for our school. It is unfortunate that he cannot study in Germany since, as a student there, he would have to do certain things against his conscience and ours, which are bound to Christ. Therefore, he studied in Switzerland and also in England for a year. God used him as a witness to some who came to recognize life in community as lived by the early Christian church in Jerusalem as the right way. These people have or will be coming to the community. That is also how his bride, Edith Böcker, came to us two years ago. She has since proved herself a true member of our Brotherhood and was baptized last year with twenty-one other brothers and sisters. Edith waged a very hard struggle with her parents and relatives, who thought her no longer right in the head because she wanted to live such a completely different life. So they locked her in her room. Since all her begging to let her come to the community did not help, Edith left home secretly. In the night she lowered herself out the window on a rope, and that is how she came to the community. Edith also wants to become a schoolteacher, so they will finish their studies together in Zurich, Switzerland. Their wedding will take place on August 25 and 26 on this new hof. Since God our Father in heaven, through the grace of Christ, has often used the service of our son, Eberhard, he is to become a witness brother for our new hof.

Your loving letter of July 8 has reached us, and we thank you from our hearts. Also we thank you that you want to help us in our truly great need by sending us twenty-five dollars and that later on you want to give us a little help again. We thank you for this, especially as you write that you yourselves are having a hard time because last year the locusts destroyed your feed crops.

We heard with great joy that you decided to appoint Kleinsasser Vetter as the elder of your communities. We believe that it will bring great blessing. We wish Joseph Wipf much strength and wisdom from above for his task as work distributor. We wish God's support for Johann Hofer, the former work distributor, so that he can still do many a task for the church.

That you, beloved Jörg Vetter, have not yet been given a helper should unite us in prayer, so that the right brother is shown who can share with you the service of the Word. It was a special joy to us that you started *Kleinschule* again, like you had years ago. We also think it is better when from an early age the children are educated and led by those appointed by the community.

We are very sad to hear that it is not going so well with material needs at the Sundale Bruderhof. May our heavenly Father bless your prospects for a good harvest this year so that everything comes in at the right time.

Now you would like to know how it has continued with us. We can't praise God enough that up to now he has kept his little flock together here at the Alm Bruderhof, as in Germany. One could say he has nourished us as Elijah was fed by the ravens. We are now about forty-five souls on this new place that we have rented. In Germany we are still eighty-five. We don't know how long, or even if, our community can stay there; the clouds get darker and darker. The prospects for the harvest on our hof in Germany are not bad, but the harvest in the whole country is expected to be scanty. We have one-fifth less feed than last year. Here in Liechtenstein we have little agriculture so far—only two cows and two goats, which give us milk for our twenty children and sick people. We are also producing wooden plates, bowls, and candleholders. Each week three or four brothers go out to the cities with our books, writings, and wood products to speak of Christ's message and way and also to offer our goods for sale. This is how we can often buy something for our needs. But we cannot yet afford to buy shoes, clothing, or wood for the winter. The meals are often very skimpy, but we manage to serve something at each mealtime. For this in a foreign land, without an agricultural foundation, we cannot be thankful enough! We have planted some potatoes and some vegetables, but apart from the milk we have to buy everything. Up here on the high mountain where we fled in the wintertime, one could get quite fearful looking into the future. Often there is so much snow in winter that we cannot get down into the valley. And yet we are happy that this little country has taken us in and given us permission for our school. You would like to know how far this Bruderhof is from our other hof. If you leave here at three o'clock in the morning, you arrive about eight in the evening on the other hof.

We thank you again for all your love and help and ask you to think of us in your prayer of the church. Ask that we may stay firm and steadfast in spite of the dangerous times and that we not let our mouths be closed but proclaim God's word abroad.

We greet you all without exception in the love of Jesus Christ.

Your Hutterian brothers and sisters
Emmy Arnold

My husband greets you all, especially you, beloved Jörg Vetter. He has a lot of work and is now writing an account of our faith for those who ask about our beliefs and life.

Othmar Müllner was a pastor in Rossbach, Czechoslovakia, who had an important influence on Adolf Hundhammer in his search for a life active in love.

However, when Adolf asked that he and his family might visit the Alm Bruderhof for a time, and was then invited by Eberhard Arnold, Othmar Müllner charged that "Adolf was being won over by human persuasion."

Eberhard Vetter made every effort to clarify the situation, even visiting Pastor Müllner in Rossbach and inviting him to the Bruderhof to "come and see." This he never did and the matter was never completely resolved.

Extracts from Eberhard's letter follow:

Alm Bruderhof, September 1934

Beloved Othmar F. Müllner,

Accept my warm thanks for the openness of your February 24 letter. In the meantime I have had to prepare and establish our second Bruderhof here, so that only today I managed to read your letter. I will answer it today, because I had planned to visit you around this time.

I prefer to tell you by word of mouth how far your wish has been fulfilled that we would be thrown into the glowing fire of great affliction, and how it became necessary to establish this Alm Bruderhof for conscience' sake and for the protection of our young people and children.

We Hutterian Brothers have always loved the open, sharp admonishment if it is done with the love that does not rejoice in unrighteousness, but in truth. When it comes from God, it is combined with clarifying of the facts and is unjust to no one. In admonishing, a conscientious Christian makes no false accusations.

The main positive element of your letter has our full agreement. What you write about the Carinthians, awakened by Luther and Johann Arndt around 1760, has often moved us. Above all, we feel the same as you about the free spirit of God that blows everywhere and about faith for completely unknown people who, according to Kierkegaard, can be Christians in a deeper sense than those in world-famous churches and communities.

All the more it surprises me how unfairly you speak against us Brothers called Hutterian. A thorough examination of the true facts, under the Spirit, will show you how false is everything you think and write against our life and mission. Those who call themselves brothers ought not to sin against one another. The love of Jesus Christ requires both you and me to clear away, in heart-to-heart sharing, whatever misunderstanding has piled up between us. The name of Jesus Christ and his truth urges us to meet one another in his holy presence.

Spare me from speaking about myself, for it is best when we can forget ourselves completely and speak only of the cause we serve. For the sake of love to Christ and his name, carried in our hearts, I will tell you briefly our answer to your unfounded accusations. This will embrace the true witness, which also represents my personal attitude. The Brothers are no sectarians and do not make converts. Least of all are they wolves who want to break into the flock of Christ to snatch people away from their teachers who have helped them toward inner security. Even to attempt it would be as shameful to our Brothers as using human tricks of their own.

My dear Othmar, not a single member of the Bruderhofs known to me has come into the Gemeinde through human persuasion. That would be absolutely impossible as long as the church community is truly pleading for and receiving the Holy Spirit through the wonderful working of God. You ought to experience this first, before allowing yourself to say anything about this question. This is the one and only reason for the time of testing before baptism and acceptance into the Brotherhood! In the furnace of *Gelassenheit*, in self-examination before the Holy Spirit, and in the reality of communal life, it becomes revealed whether God and *only* God, Christ and *only* Christ, the Holy Spirit and *only* the Holy Spirit, are and remain the moving power behind the awakening, the change, and the gathering. Human influences and manipulation *do not exist* in the church community called down and brought into being by the Holy Spirit. Words and outward arrangements mean nothing to us unless they witness to and are born out of the innermost working of the Spirit, free from outward show.

I would wish from my heart that you could read the old Pentecost teachings of the Brothers or take part in our Whitsun meetings. Then you would experience a reverence for the infinite working of God's spirit everywhere. In my limited experience I have never met this in other churches and communities. Any religious overestimation of self is very remote from the Brothers, under the influence of truth as they are. One cannot describe in words this grace given them by the Spirit. They believe in the absolutely different One. They, as well as we, have never wanted to be a sect claiming to be the only saved ones. We are no sectarians and do not want to become such. If only you knew how far the Brothers are from sectarianism and converting by persuasion. The foundation of the God-given essence of our life is the opposite: human activity stops, takes a Sabbath of trusting surrender, so that through faith God's working can take place. Here no human law or power has value, but only the love which comes from faith in the spirit of Jesus Christ. No man, but only the Spirit, can bring about true community. Certainly he wants to do it everywhere. Wherever man's own work is laid down, there uniting will take place.

How can you describe this faith as "absolute halfheartedness"? That is not truly spoken and is directly against Christ, who through the Holy Spirit has poured the wholeness of his love into our hearts. No brother has ever believed that this Spirit and his peace can be passed down from father to son or be transplanted through human education. Each brother acknowledges Eckhart's word that outer works do not get us anywhere, but that from first to last the spirit of Jesus Christ leads to the surrender of self.

Jesus did not point us toward Bruderhofs. But Bruderhofs arise from what he points to. The outward form arises from within, through the same spirit of creativity and order which Meister Eckhart also knew well and confessed. It does not mean the loss of true surrender if, in following it, we live from the innermost strength of Christ, so that Christ shapes the whole of life according to his kingdom. If we take seriously the creative acts of God, as affirmed in the first article of the Apostles' Creed, then there is no division between earth and heaven, spirit and flesh.

The New Testament and the history of monasticism, especially of the fifteenth and sixteenth centuries, answer your question about why the Brothers marry. Let us now as ever love true Hutterianism as a renewal by God of New Testament Christianity (Acts 2 and 4).

Please do not forget for a moment that the name, Hutterian Brothers, was given in narrow-mindedness and lovelessness from outside by those who opposed them. Today, as always, they call themselves simply "the Brothers." For this reason their correct name today is "the Brothers whom men call Hutterian." They do not call the church after any name or place. Your circle also will not escape being named as far as it will enter into history and be described by speakers and writers.

I admit that this writing of history is a bad business. Lydia Müller's booklet is full of misrepresentations and also bad blunders. The renewal of the little church community through the Carinthians of the eighteenth century has also never yet been presented correctly. The relationship with the old communities was strong and just as decisive as the new movement.

The renewed church in Vishenka did not consist only of the old Hutterian members from Alwinz, Sabatisch, and Vélke Leváre. These were exactly one half, but those at Kreuz, who were newly gripped by the spirit of the church, were led to baptism by the old Hutterian elders. They requested and received the confirmation for their service of the Word through the laying on of hands by the elders. The old writings as well, were saved and handed down through both the old and the new brothers. It is astonishing to learn from these old handwritten teachings that the word of faith, the truth of Christ, was proclaimed and proved to be effective even in times of declining faith. Some lived the truth with the constant prayer for a renewed outpouring of the Holy Spirit. So you would particularly appreciate the fact that, during these weaker times, the outward form of the church was left for a time until the Spirit gave new strength for life in God. Without this strength of God, baptism, Lord's Supper, community of goods, and everything else are meaningless.

That is how it was before 1763 and before 1853. One undervalues these outwardly and inwardly troubled times if one does not know or forgets what a patient and humble pleading there was for a revival and re-establishment of true community. The fact that this longing was not present in the majority of the descendants is not at all important. The physical descendants have to be awakened and newly born in the same way as those coming from the Bernese uplands and lowlands. For them, too, the message of the living gospel is never without promise. Believe! Salvation will come to your household! But it comes only through Christ as the life-bringing spirit!

What you write about the decline of the old communities in the eighteenth century is true to a great extent. It does not, however, quite fit the situation of that time, something you can learn only from the writings of that period. Their fall into ruin was indeed dreadful, very similar to that of the early church at Jerusalem in the third century. But as you know from your own experience, God never forgets the prayers of parents and forefathers.

Please do not think for one moment that I want to belittle the truth and love given to you by the grace of God. Rather, my heart is drawn to you, and I want to listen and recognize whatever light God has kindled in you and whatever work he wants to achieve through your witness.

I feel a burning love for you and for all that God has put into your heart. Therefore I thank you from my heart that you do not want to be aggrieved but want to love me with the deepest love. And do have a little joy in my coming visit with my dear Emmy. We come out of love to you and to all that God is working. Seeking the best in you, I greet you in faith.

Eberhard Arnold

Emmy Arnold
Alm Bruderhof, July 20, 1935

Beloved Elias Vetter with your Elisabeth Basel,

For a long time Eberhard and I have wanted to give you a thorough report, and Eberhard had intended to write to you and to the elders of your and our Bruderhofs. But he could not come to this because,

unfortunately, our Bruderhofs here have come into great need. Now
Eberhard asks me to send you and all your Stand Off Bruderhof a
heartfelt greeting to let you know that we are still united with all our
hearts in God's love and in the community of his Holy Spirit.

On March 16 Germany introduced compulsory military service,
about which I will report later. In spite of our heavy problems, new
people are finding their way all the time into the life on both hofs.
Altogether on both Bruderhofs, the Alm here in Liechtenstein and the
Rhön in Germany, we were able to take twelve novices into full
membership of the church. Here on the Alm there were four brothers
and two sisters: Werner Friedemann, a baker, aged twenty-one, Willi
Fischer, businessman, also twenty-one, Herbert Welz, a plumber,
twenty-four, and Gerhard Wegner, a bookbinder, who came to us
already as a child and is now twenty. On June 3 of this year he arrived
here from the Rhön, fleeing on foot over the border. All these had to
leave their homeland to avoid military service. The two sisters were
Kathleen Hamilton, an English teacher who was accepted among us
last year for a time of testing, and Erna Steenken, seventeen years old.

In Germany three brothers and three sisters were also taken in for
a time of testing last year. They were an English couple, Arnold and
Gladys Mason, Kathleen Hamilton, and Freda Bridgwater. All these
left their home country for the sake of community. Then there are the
thirty-five-year-old brother, Johann Arno (Schill), Kaspar Keller,
about thirty, and a twenty-four-year-old sister, Waltraut von Dziengel.
All were accepted into the church through baptism and the celebration
of the Lord's Supper. Each of them preferred to share the poverty of
the church rather than continue living in private property outside. This
accepting of new members is always a great encouragement to us.

This year, too, some have been taken in for a time of testing.
Recently on the Rhön Bruderhof there were Wilhelm Tisch, a Swiss
teacher named Balthasar Trümpi, and Martin Laackmann, a gardener
and son of a Lutheran pastor. Here on the Alm Bruderhof, Hermann
Arnold, the son of my Eberhard's brother, was taken in on trial at
Easter. He is twenty and also had to leave his country because of the
military service question. At first it caused great pain to his mother,
but now she feels that he has been called to life in community and
does not want to hinder him.

On both hofs we have many guests who want to experience life in
community. They often come with difficult questions. The outer need
on both our places is very great. There is enough food on the German
hof, which has been so suddenly reduced in numbers, but they have
no money to pay the rent and little money for clothing.

The recent development in Germany has brought much hardship, especially for those who had to leave their homeland. On the Alm Bruderhof we are now ninety altogether. Thirty-six are children, the rest grown-ups. Most are fathers of young families, who are liable for military service, or young brothers.

We have rented some land at a high price and were able to plant some vegetables and potatoes. We also have three cows in the stable, and we bought three small piglets, which we hope to raise on scraps. Now we try to make a living by producing wooden plates and other articles. Our brothers go out to the towns and villages to sell them, and when it is possible or they are asked, they witness to the way of community. Soon you will receive a wooden bowl like the ones we sell here. Sometimes we are able to sell a lot, and then the sales drop again and no money comes in. Then it gets difficult with food supplies. We hope to be able to harvest vegetables and potatoes soon, but at the moment it is very difficult to provide a livelihood for all.

Our living conditions are especially poor. Our families live in summer huts up here in the mountains. It is hardly possible to heat them, and already in summer the wind blows through. Think what will happen in winter when the snow is sometimes twelve to twenty feet high and we are lacking in footwear! It is hardly possible to buy clothing, and one item after the other wears out. We are hit with great and severe poverty. Many people fall sick and we have to bring the doctor; he thinks the sickness is caused by bad living conditions and insufficient food.

The principality of Liechtenstein is friendly toward us, but of course we do not know how long we can stay here, especially if war breaks out. It is a small country and we do not know what is going to happen.

We often wonder if it is God's will for us to come to you, but we want to hold out until God shows us the way. What joy it would be to see one another face to face, we who are so closely bound in faith!

From the bottom of my heart we ask you to think of our need, so that each evening you can bring us, your brothers and sisters who live far away, in prayer before God.

We greet all you brothers and sisters, big and small, especially you, beloved Elias Walter and your Elisabeth Basel.

United in heartfelt love,

> Your Hutterian brothers and sisters
> and Emmy Arnold

P.S. As soon as we can leave here, Eberhard and I will travel back to the Rhön Bruderhof.

Samuel Hofer   Emmy Arnold
Barickman Community   Rhön Bruderhof, Germany
Headingley, Manitoba   October 28, 1935

Dearly beloved brothers and sisters of Barickman Bruderhof,
especially our deeply respected and beloved Samuel Hofer Vetter,
together with your helper, David Decker Vetter,

We greet you all, brothers and sisters and everyone old and young
on your Bruderhof, with the greeting of unity and of peace. It would
be a great joy to us if you would visit us once again with a letter, for
we have heard nothing from you for a very long time. We would so
much like to know how things are going in matters spiritual and
temporal: how many souls you are, whether you were able to baptize
some, whether children have been born, whether any marriages could
be celebrated, or new people have come to you, and whether there
are any in your neighborhood who seek and are zealous, set on fire
by the Holy Spirit himself and wanting to hear about the life of the
church community. We would also like to know how things are going
now in temporal matters, whether you had a good harvest, whether
you will have enough to get through this winter. Our beloved David
Hofer Vetter from James Valley wrote us that they had a very poor
harvest there and will hardly have enough to live on this winter. Surely
your communities will help the James Valley Bruderhof as far as you
are able, for it is written, "Break your bread for the hungry and if
you see somebody naked, then clothe him." Christ himself told us
how it would be at the last day when he would say to those on his
right hand, "I was hungry and you fed me. I was thirsty and you gave
me to drink; I was a guest and you gave me shelter, I was naked and
you clothed me, I was sick and you visited me, I was in prison and
you came to me." And what will he have to say to those on his left hand?

Now I would still like to tell you a little about how things are going
with us in these hard times. You will have read that there is much
unrest in Europe. War has begun to flare up again down by the
Mediterranean. And what may happen in the future? No man can
know that. Our communities stand firm and faithful, believing and
trusting in the help of God. Our message is still being heard, even if
it is only individuals here and there who are eager and listening—so
new people continue to be accepted for a time of trial and testing
among us. At Pentecost we were able to take twelve brothers and
sisters into the church through the bond of baptism. And as long as
our task is still here, we also think that we must stay in Europe and
especially serve the people of our homeland. But it often seems to us

as if we should unite with you over there, for the material side of our life is going so badly on both our Bruderhofs that we have no possibility of providing for ourselves. If things continue like this we do not know if it will be possible for us to stay here. We had a real failure in the harvest on the home Bruderhof, especially with the garden produce and potatoes. Up to now these have always been our main source of food and we could always eat our fill of them. This year there will only be enough till Christmas, and we can hardly imagine how it will be in the spring. The failure of the harvest was due to the summer drought and pests that ate off the young plants. We have never had enough bread to eat, and this year too we can only give out three pounds a week per person. Now our mortgages have been called in so that we have to raise a big sum all at once. On top of this there are taxes and interest to pay. If we do not come up with the money, we do not know whether we can stay here. We have not yet been able to provide wood and coal for the winter, and as a result we have quite a lot of sickness from the cold, especially among the children.

The Bruderhof in Liechtenstein faces great difficulties too. They have nice garden produce on the rented fields and meadows and have harvested some potatoes, so they will be able to have one good meal every day through the winter. But they have no bread at all, and at times have been unable to buy any. They have only three cows which provide just enough milk for the smallest children. The housing is especially bad. The families with little children have to live in quite wretched huts of wooden planks, which the farmers built only for the summer time, when they drive their cattle up to the mountain pastures. It is almost impossible to heat them. The walls are in no way weatherproof and it rains and snows in. We can scarcely imagine how that is going to be in the winter. The interest rate in this small country is very high, and we dare not owe anything. So you see, beloved brothers and sisters, that we are really in great need and do not know what we should do. Would it be possible for you to help us with a gift of money so that your brothers in the faith may get through this winter? Our servants of the Word are so occupied trying to avert the severest need from the community every day that my Eberhard hasn't time for the detailed letter to you which he would so very much like to write. He greets you from all his heart and asks you to be content with my little letter. He is here on the old home Bruderhof in Germany, and Hans Zumpe Vetter has taken on the Bruderhof in Liechtenstein.

Every evening we gather for the prayer of the church and then we think also of you, beloved brothers and sisters across the wide ocean, asking that God may let his lamp still shine in our communities so that many may still come to the church as long as there is a time of grace. In this sense I greet you all, bound with you in the love of Jesus Christ,

Your brothers and sisters in Germany,
Emmy Eberhard Arnold

Please send this letter to your daughter Bruderhof, the Gracevale Community.

Four years later the Bruderhof was in England after being driven out of Nazi Germany in 1937. As war threatened in Europe, the possibility of emigration being forced on it a second time had to be faced. Preparations were made for this eventuality, and the brothers in Canada prepared the following document in June 1939. It reaffirmed the incorporation in 1930 of the European Bruderhof into the Hutterian Church. This uniting of Eberhard Arnold and the Rhön Bruderhof with the Hutterian Church was confirmed anew in 1974.

Milltown Hutterian Church
Benard, Manitoba, Canada
June 2, 1939

We certify that the members of the Cotswold Bruderhof Community at Ashton Keynes, and the Oaksey Bruderhof Community at Oaksey, both in Wiltshire, England, are members of the Hutterian Church of America and Europe, whose founder and chief organizer Jakob Hutter was burned at the stake in Innsbruck in 1536.

The uniting of the group originally founded by Dr. Eberhard Arnold in Sannerz, and later resident at the Rhön Bruderhof, Kreis Fulda, Post Neuhof, with the Hutterian Church took place on December 14,[1] 1930 at the Stand Off Bruderhof in Alberta, Canada. After the death of Dr. Eberhard Arnold on November 22, 1935 two elders of the Hutterian Church of Manitoba and South Dakota, the Reverend David Hofer from James Valley Bruderhof, Elie, Manitoba, Canada, and the Reverend Michael Waldner from Bon Homme Bruderhof, Tabor, South Dakota, USA, visited the members of the Hutterian Church in England, Germany, and Liechtenstein, and also witnessed the dissolution of the German Bruderhof by the Secret State Police on 14th April, 1937.

Before they left again for America they confirmed and ordained the two members of the Hutterian Church in Europe, Georg Barth, now residing at the Oaksey Bruderhof Community, and Eberhard Carl Heinrich Arnold, now residing at the Cotswold Bruderhof Community, in the ministry of the Hutterian Church. Their ordination took place at the Cotswold Bruderhof on September 13, 1937.

With their ordination by the laying on of hands they have been given the task of preaching the Word of God both within and without the Church, and of leading the European Branch of the Hutterian Church in close contact with their elders in America, in every respect spiritually and temporally.

[Signed]:

Joseph Kleinsasser

David Hofer,

Elders of the Hutterian Church in Manitoba

---

[1]December 18, 1930.

Illustrations

Rhön Bruderhof, Germany, Winter 1930-31

Bon Homme Bruderhof, South Dakota. First North American Bruderhof visited by Eberhard Arnold, June 1930.

Velké Leváre, old Habaner[1] school-house. Eberhard Arnold visited the sites of the old Bruderhofs and brought these pictures back. (p.46)

Grinding mill at Leváre

Habaner smithy at Leváre

Habaner hof, Sabatisch

Sabatisch, Habaner bell tower

[1]Habaner: name given to descendants of Hutterites still living in central Europe.

SOUTH DAKOTA, 1930

Bon Homme (Schmiedeleut)

Wolf Creek (Dariusleut)

Rockport (Home of David Hofer, Lehrerleut Elder)

MANITOBA, 1930 (as referred to on pp. 119-121)

1) "Brothers and sisters everywhere gather around"

2 & 3) "Show the 'fancy clothes'" 4) Watching the *Luftschiff*

5) Group of children—the Hamburg America man is taking photos again

6) Side view of a typical Bruderhof

8) L to R: Hamburg America Line agent, Peter Gross, Eberhard Arnold at Iberville. Typical school house, left background

9) House on a Bruderhof near the big city

10) Dining Room at Iberville. Kitchen behind

11) Stable at Barickman

13) Loading sheaves

14 & 15) One of the many tractors and its wheel

16) Threshing time

17) Threshing time

ALBERTA, 1930

Stand Off Bruderhof, where Eberhard Vetter was baptized into the Hutterian Church and confirmed as servant of the Word.

Milford (Buck Ranch), home of Johannes Kleinsasser, became Lehrerleut Elder 1932

Appendixes

Appendix A

Eberhard Arnold's Journey to North America 1930/31

May 30, 1930	Left Bremen on Karlsruhe.
June 11	Arrived New York.
	Scottdale with John Horsch.
June 18	Chicago.
June 20	Tabor, S.Dakota, and to Bon Homme Bruderhof.
June 26	Rockport Bruderhof.
June 28	Wolf Creek Bruderhof, 3½ weeks, due to eye trouble.
July 21	Rockport Bruderhof.
July 30	Mitchell, SD.
by Aug. 5	Lake Byron Bruderhof.
Aug. 8-9	to CANADA, Manitoba.
Aug. 9	Plum Coulee.
	Blumengard, James Valley, Milltown Bruderhofs.
	Winnipeg.
	Visited all 10 Manitoba hofs before Sept. 13.
Aug. 25	Winnipeg.
	Manitoba hofs.
Sept. 3-4	Winnipeg.
	Manitoba hofs.
Sept. 13-14	Milltown Bruderhof. Important meeting, presided over by Elder Joseph Kleinsasser, when Schmiedeleut supported union.
Sept. 19	Regina, Saskatchewan.
Sept. 23	Medicine Hat, Alberta.
Sept. 24	Stand Off Bruderhof (Elias Walter).
	West Raley Bruderhof (Christian Waldner).
Oct. 2	Cardston, Alberta.
	East Cardston Bruderhof (David Hofer).
by Oct. 8	Big Bend Bruderhof.
	Old Elm Spring (Magrath) Bruderhof.
Oct. 8	Lethbridge.
	Agreed to make a trip through all the Alberta Bruderhofs (20 in all).
Oct. 23	Lethbridge.
Oct. 23	Richards (Wilson) Bruderhof.
Nov. 12	Lethbridge.
Nov. 26	Crows Nest in Rocky Mts.
	(Still 5 more Bruderhofs to visit).
Dec. 9	Stand Off Bruderhof.
	Eberhard Arnold's baptism and incorporation.

Dec. 18-19	Stand Off Bruderhof
	Confirmation of Eberhard Arnold's service.
	Then traveled round all the Alberta hofs
	a second time.
Dec. 25	Stand Off Bruderhof.
	Eberhard Arnold took the Lehr.
Jan. 1, 1931	Stand Off Bruderhof.
	Eberhard Arnold again took the Lehr.
	Continued visiting the Alberta Bruderhofs with stops in:
Jan. 20	Calgary.
February	Lethbridge.
March	Lethbridge.
March 15	Stand Off Bruderhof.
	Manitoba hofs.
April 10	S. Dakota. Almost at end of return journey
	through the Bruderhofs.
	Visited Amana Inspirationists and Goshen College.
May 1	Finally at sea.
May 10	Arrived Bremerhaven, Germany!

APPENDIX B

Hutterian Bruderhofs and their Servants of the Word in 1930-31

SOUTH DAKOTA, USA

Bon Homme (Schmiedeleut)	Michael Waldner, Joseph Waldner
Wolf Creek (Dariusleut)	Joshua Hofer, Peter Hofer
Lake Byron (Dariusleut)	Joseph Stahl
Rockport (Lehrerleut)	David Hofer, Elder
	Peter Hofer, moving to Alberta

MANITOBA, CANADA
(All Schmiedeleut)

Milltown	Joseph Kleinsasser Sr., Elder
	Joseph Kleinsasser Jr.
Huron	Joseph J. Waldner, Joseph Glanzer
Bon Homme	Joseph M. Waldner, Michael Waldner
James Valley	David Hofer, "second Elder"
	Peter Hofer
Rosedale	Zacharias Hofer, Andreas Hofer
Iberville	Peter Gross
Maxwell	Joseph J. Hofer, Jerg J. Waldner
Barickman	Samuel Hofer, David Decker
Blumengard	Johann D. Hofer
Roseisle	David B. Glanzer, Fritz Waldner

ALBERTA, CANADA
(Dariusleut)

East Cardston	David Hofer
West Raley	Christian Waldner Sr., Elder
	Christian Waldner Jr.
Stand Off	Elias Walter
Wilson Siding [Richards]	Johann M. Wurz
Stahlville [Hinds]	Johannes Stahl
Spring Valley	Jakob Wurz, Paul Hofer
Rosebud	Jerg Hofer
Pincher [Creek]	Jakob Hofer
Beiseker	Paul Stahl
Granum	Michael Tschetter
Murphy [Ewelme]	Joseph Hofer

(Lehrerleut)

Elm Spring [Warner]	Michael J. Entz, Jakob Hofer
Old Elm Spring [Magrath] . .	Andreas Gross, Peter Kleinsasser
Big Bend	Johann P. Entz, Jakob Wipf
Milford [Buck Ranch]	Johannes J. Kleinsasser, "second Elder"
	Joseph Kleinsasser
Miami	Jerg Waldner, Peter P. Hofer
New Elm Spring	John J. Entz
Crystal Spring	Peter Entz
Rockport [II]	Joseph Wipf, Peter Hofer
Hutterville	
[Rockport III being built up] .	Johannes Waldner

GERMANY

Rhön Bruderhof . . . . . . Eberhard Arnold

349

Maps

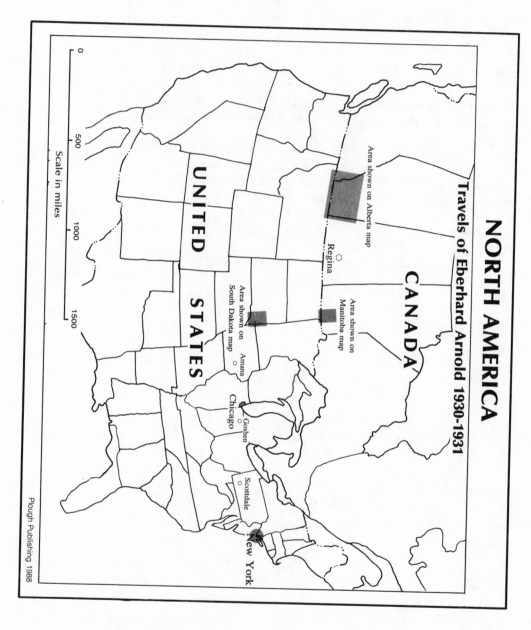

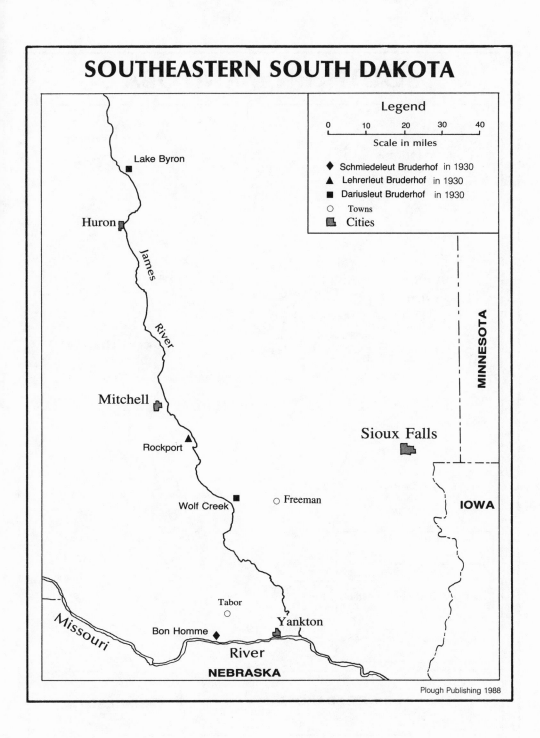

SOUTHEASTERN SOUTH DAKOTA

Legend

0   10   20   30   40

Scale in miles

♦ Schmiedeleut Bruderhof in 1930
▲ Lehrerleut Bruderhof in 1930
■ Dariusleut Bruderhof in 1930
○   Towns
▦ Cities

Lake Byron

Huron

James River

MINNESOTA

Mitchell

Sioux Falls

Rockport
▲

IOWA

Wolf Creek
■

○ Freeman

Missouri

Tabor
○

Yankton

Bon Homme ♦

River

NEBRASKA

Plough Publishing 1988

351

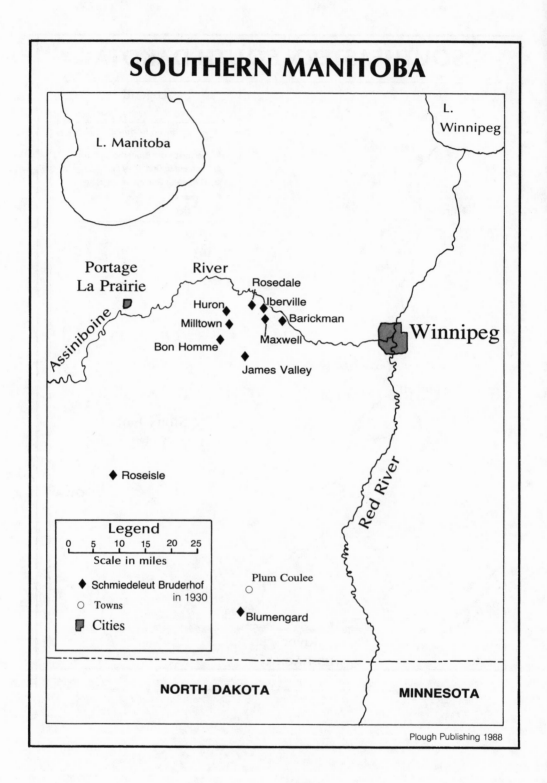

SOUTHERN MANITOBA

L. Winnipeg

L. Manitoba

Portage La Prairie

River

Rosedale

Iberville

Huron

Barickman

Milltown

Maxwell

Bon Homme

James Valley

Assiniboine

Winnipeg

Roseisle

Red River

Legend

0 5 10 15 20 25
Scale in miles

◆ Schmiedeleut Bruderhof in 1930
○ Towns
▨ Cities

Plum Coulee
○

◆ Blumengard

NORTH DAKOTA

MINNESOTA

Plough Publishing 1988

352

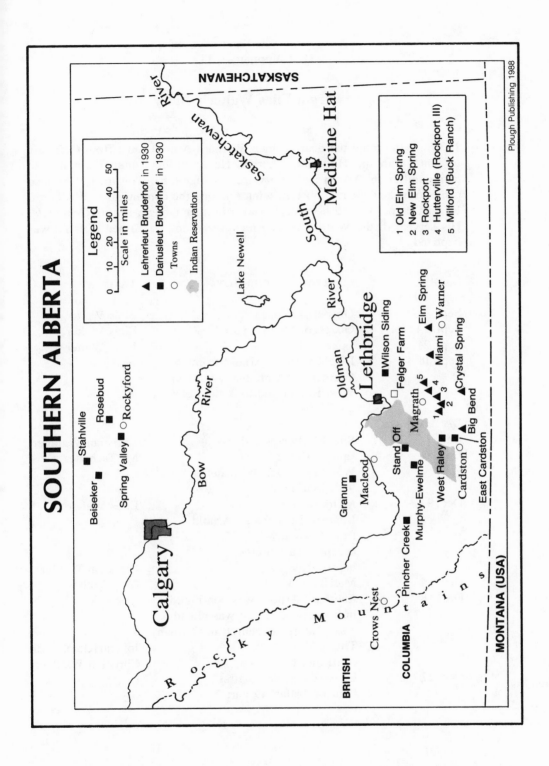

SOUTHERN ALBERTA

Legend

▲ Lehrerleut Bruderhof in 1930
■ Dariusleut Bruderhof in 1930
○ Towns
░ Indian Reservation

Scale in miles
0 10 20 30 40 50

1 Old Elm Spring
2 New Elm Spring
3 Rockport
4 Hutterville (Rockport III)
5 Milford (Buck Ranch)

SASKATCHEWAN

South Saskatchewan River

Medicine Hat

Lake Newell

Oldman River

Lethbridge

Wilson Siding
■ Felger Farm
□ Magrath
Stand Off
Murphy-Ewelme ■
West Raley ■
Cardston ○
East Cardston

Elm Spring ▲
○ Warner
Miami ▲
Crystal Spring ▲
5
4 ▲ 3
1 ▲▲▲ 2
Big Bend ▲

Bow River

Granum
○ Macleod

Beiseker ■ ■ Stahlville
Rosebud ■
Spring Valley ■ ○ Rockyford

Calgary

BRITISH COLUMBIA

Pincher Creek
Crows Nest ○

R o c k y   M o u n t a i n s

MONTANA (USA)

Plough Publishing 1988

353

APPENDIX D

From Elias Walter's Diary

1930   In spring the dear brother Eberhard Arnold came from Germany to unite with the Hutterian Church. He spent the summer among the communities in Dakota and afterwards in Manitoba. Toward fall he also came to us and spent almost all winter among the communities in Alberta. He had come here to be accepted as a brother along with his *Gemeinde*. His service of the Word was also recognized and confirmed after he was baptized.

DATE	LEHR WITH TEACHING ON:	TAKEN BY:
Sept. 1930		
Sept. 7	Gospel of John 11	Elias Walter
Sept. 14	Gospel of John 11, part 2	Elias Walter
Sept. 21	Luke 21:1-24	Elias Walter
Sept. 28	I went with E. Arnold from Germany to Christian [Waldner, West Raley] and took the Lehr on Tobias 4	
Dec. 1930		
Dec. 7	Sirach 7 [Ecclesiasticus]	Christian Waldner
Dec. 8	Ephesians 5:22	M. Tschetter
	Wedding of Jacob Tschetter with Maria Gross	
Dec. 9	Matthew 28	Elias Walter
	Baptism Lehr for E. Arnold from Germany	
	accepted as a brother	
	baptized by	Christian Waldner
Dec. 14	Micah 6:6-8	Elias Walter
Dec. 18	Eberhard Arnold was confirmed in his service, as he was already a servant of his church in Germany	
	Titus 3	Johann Kleinsasser
	confirmed by	Christian Waldner
Dec. 27	E. Arnold took his first Lehr on Isaiah 49 part 2	

354

DATE	LEHR WITH TEACHING ON:	TAKEN BY:
1931		
Jan. 1	At New Year's Eberhard Arnold took his second Lehr on Luke 2	
Jan. 3	I drove with E. Arnold to Granum	
Jan. 5	We went to Calgary Beisecker to Paul Stahl.	
Jan. 6	E. Arnold took the Lehr on Matthew 2. Arnold stayed up there for a while	
Jan. 7	I went alone to the brothers at Rockyford	
Jan. 11	At Johann Stahl's, I took the Lehr on Matthew 2	
Jan. 18	Matthew 2	Elias Walter
Jan. 20	Matthew 2,3	Elias Walter
March		
Mar. 1	Gospel of John	Elias Walter
Mar. 8	John 7	Elias Walter
Mar. 15	E. Arnold was back with us and again took the Lehr on Isaiah 58	
Mar. 20	E. Arnold started on his trip home	
Mar. 22	Matthew 24	Elias Walter
Mar. 27	First baptism Lehr	Elias Walter
Mar. 28	Second baptism Lehr	Elias Walter

APPENDIX E

A song on Eberhard Arnold when he came to America in the year
1930 to visit our communities in U.S.A.
Written in English by M. J. Waldner on a western colony after reading
Eberhard Arnold's Diary. August 1987
(Melody: "Ein Lobgesang, das sing ich nun.")

> Once there a man from Germany came.
> Eberhard Arnold was his name.
> He was clothed like a Tyrolean,
> But he was a goodhearted man.
>
> He came to Bon Homme Colony first,
> With a great hunger and with thirst
> To find his brothers and sisters fine,
> From whom he had heard a long time.
>
> When he then came to this old place
> He had a wonderful friendly face,
> As he first saw the old Hutterian style
> And how they greeted him with a smile.
>
> Many years he had waited for that
> Which he at last so friendly met.
> He was so happy and jumped around
> As he at last his brothers had found.
>
> It was in 1930 then
> That he had the first Hutterians seen,
> The descendants from Moravians
> And also those from the Carinthians.

He was so delighted in their books,
The wonderful writing and the looks,
With their history over 400 years,
That made him great delight and cheer.

And then about the epistles from them,
He had such a delight to read them
That he could hardly quit to read,
Took little time for him to sleep.

But when he looked at the machinery,
He hardly could with that agree,
The big farm and operations there.
He thought there is too much earthly care.

The farm machines like giants too.
The thresh machine had such a flue--
Almost like a steamship do.
The farm tractors were enormous too.

What would he have said to his Woodcrest?
I think he would nearly outpass.
They are so modern as the Western too--
But I think they apply it more true.

What did he say to the big grain fields?
The crops hauled in with so many wheels.
Cornfields as far as one can see.
How much will then the bushels be?

And then the sheep and cattle herds!
Who can explain then that with words?
Almost as the rich man then did--
Broke down his barns and built them big.

But as he then to Wolf Creek came
To treat his eyes and stay with them,
He was there treated so wonderful,
That hardly he could say it all.

He fell in love with the people there,
For their good hospitality and care.
The children were so good to him,
They sang to him again and again.

But when he later to Rockport came,
Dave Vetter was not so kind to him,
Said he should stay in Germany there
And get along without us here.

Was concerned about the English school,
As with Christians they had nothing to do.
He was against typewriting too.
What should we then with the Bible do?

It is almost all in type today.
How could we put all that away?
How ignorant some get anyway.
It looks he liked something to say.

He said he should stay in Austria
And should get along without him.
But Arnold like to unite with them
As it belongs with good Christians.

Finally he said his meaning then too.
What the old preachers in Canada will do
He will agree to that then too.
He were too old anymore to do.

But when he came to Bon Homme again,
He was comforted in most everything.
Only if dear Emma were here
To help him on his eyes, so dear.

As all here wished Emma to see,
It's not good that it should not be.
It would have been great help to him
In writing and in many things.

When he then came to Joseph Stahl,
To the Beadle Colony after that all,
He was so very welcome to him,
And his good wife the Katharin.

He came to Manitoba by train
To Joseph Kleinsasser and David Vetter then.
They enjoyed him with more books again,
Were glad to get acquainted with him.

He came to Huron Colony after that,
Where I was living with Brother Fred.
We were so very interested then,
Took every chance to go to hear him.

My mother exchanged letters with Emma then
In Sannerz and after that in Rhön.
She made him a nice suit then too,
As she was very skilled to do.

He visited all the colonies around.
I don't know how much good he found.
He urged that we get more united
And not in 3 parts be divided.

He said we should under one Elder be,
As it always was in the old community,
And as it was when we came here
When my grandfather was Elder dear.

But it is very sad to say
He could not bring that on the way.
But if mammon had not such a hold,
He might have brought us in one fold!

After that he went then to the West.
Even on the train he had no rest.
He was there met by slanderers rough.
They thought they were not honored enough.

360

When he then came to Elias Vetter,
To Stand Off where it was much better,
He was then much encouraged again,
With such books where he delighted in.

But when he came to Christian Vetter,
There was again much cloudy weather.
He was questioned so much in all
That he was tired to climb that wall.

And even the school was questioned here,
So that Elias Walter said with cheer,
"They have better schools than we all together.
Oh, Christian Vetter, what is the matter?"

After that he visited the Lehrer Leut then.
In John Entz he found a good friend.
Their hearts were bound in love together.
He agreed with him in any matter.

John Entz took him to Joseph Vetter
In Rockport, who taught us a little better.
He was treated as they used to do.
There Arnold preached to the threshing crew.

Right in the caboose in the wheatfield,
That there so bountiful did yield,
They listened attentive to him there.
Might have listened better on bodily care.

When they then went away from there,
Then Arnold said to John Vetter dear,
"You need not worry for bodily care.
Just see the wonderful crop that's here."

John Vetter said, "You are far wrong,
Don't you know to whom this crop belong?
It belongs to Joe Vetter and to his alone.
So on this all our hopes are gone."

Then Arnold Vetter expressed on this,
"Such things belong to the Bolsheviks
And not to the good Lord Jesus fine,
By whom there is no *yours* and *mine*."

Arnold's eyes did much bother him
That he had to see the doctor again.
He went to Lethbridge in the hotel there,
Where he could then take better care.

But one day when he treated his eye,
There came to his door Alberta Leut.
They asked him to open quick
And did not mind that he was sick.

He told them to wait a little while.
The doctor forbid him otherwise,
When he was treating his eyes not to rise.
So they out there went away like mice.

They went and made a stink of it
And said this man doesn't care a bit.
He does not even open the door
If someone comes to visit him more.

They slandered him for that so bad
It made poor Eberhard Vetter so sad
That some old preacher on that said
That such should be punished very bad.

The final meeting came then at last,
Where the ministers held it for the best
To baptize Arnold and confirm him too
And to incorporate him then also.

When Arnold Vetter came back again
To Elias Vetter, where he had begun,
And knew he needed alms at home
Because they were at breaking point,

At last I think on this meeting there
They agreed that it were only fair
That all the colonies that were debt-free
Should give Arnold $1000 dollars each.

And others that were halfway out
$500 to the poor Arnold Leut.
But I think they had a happier day,
When poor Lazarus (Arnold) was carried away.

So he had to make the rounds again
With Elias Vetter, he that began.
But with a closed car they then did,
Because his eyes did not otherwise permit.

If that was worth the time to go,
Those that tried it themselves will know.
I suppose he got many promises there
As it usually happens to the poor.

Some people go the roundabout way,
When they see the wounded before them lay,
Have no time to bring him to the inn,
As did the good fine Samaritan.

When he then came to Manitoba again
He preached with full authority then,
In Huron Colony by us there too,
And made himself ready home to go.

For that he longed so much to come.
His people there were too much alone,
Because he was a full year here,
And longed for his beloved ones there.

We wished him good luck on his way.
He was very happy to see that day.
Oh, how welcome will he have been
When he again his beloved had seen.

Now Eberhard Arnold and Emma both,
Let us never forget how hard they fought
For righteousness here all their time
With Heini Vetter and Annemarie fine.

And what about Else von Hollander?
She was Arnold's faithful bookkeeper.
She had so wonderful visions too,
We can surely say that they came true.

And what about our poor Hardy Vetter?
He went through all that stormy weather.
If he and I would get healthy again
He could be my guide to Austria.

We would visit Eberhard and Else's graves
With Sannerz and the Alpine Bruderhof.
In Innsbruck and Klausen we might
To see where our Jakob Hutter died.

We would first go to Switzerland,
To Zurich that there is close at hand,
Where our dear forefathers made the start
And where they fought for the truth so hard.

We might have gone to Moravia
If it were not in Bolshevik hand,
But that was once our fatherland.
We could then go to Transylvania,

To Bucharest a little way from there,
Where our forefathers two years did fare,
Not far from where Georg Waldner died,
My ancestor on the mother side.

Let us not forget the faithful here
That have followed their Master dear
And lived here in God's righteousness.
Let us follow them in faithfulness.

Oh, let us follow them to the best,
Them that now under the altar rest.
Let us walk here in their footsteps fine
That we with Jesus there may reign.

                    Amen

It still reminds me of the time
When I tramped bags of clothing fine
Which were shipped to Cotswold, England,
Where they were persecuted from Rhön.

"Gemeindschaftliche Eigentümer"
Eberhard explained our name a bit.
He called it a communal self-ownership.
And I think he was quite right on it
Because in Jesus it does not fit.

BOOKS ON ANABAPTISM

Confession of Faith
> by Peter Rideman in 1540-1541.   304 pp. cloth.

The Golden Years of the Hutterites, 1565-1578
> by Leonard Gross. Published by Herald Press.   264 pp. cloth.

Hutterian Brethren 1528-1931
> by John Horsch.   264 pp. cloth.

The Early Anabaptists
> by Eberhard Arnold.   64 pp. paper.

Brotherly Community, the Highest Command of Love
> by Andreas Ehrenpreis and Claus Felbinger.   150 pp. paper.

Brotherly Faithfulness, Epistles from a Time of Persecution
> by Jakob Hutter.   256 pp. paper.

The Chronicle of the Hutterian Brethren,
> Volume I.   968 pp. cloth.

Das große Geschichtbuch der Hutterischen Brüder
> (Wolkan).   740 pp. cloth.

All of the above titles are available from:
> Plough Publishing House
> Hutterian Brethren
> Ulster Park, NY 12487, USA

Complete listing of Plough Books sent on request.